"I deeply admire Ellen Burstyn's scrupulous honesty and the urgency with which she pursues enlightenment. An extremely moving story of a fully lived life."　　　　　　　　　　　　　—Toni Morrison, author of *Beloved*

"A life of probing, seeking spiritual paths, forming friendships with Buckminster Fuller and Carlos Castaneda and, finally, reflecting the ambiguities of human behavior in her acting. *Lessons in Becoming Myself* doesn't stint on movie chatter . . . but its essence is an author's search for inner truth. Gracefully written, the book avoids the soft-focus clichés of a New Age quest. Burstyn spent six years writing it, working between movies and stage work . . . Every word is her own."　　　　—*San Francisco Chronicle*

"With the honesty of a diary, the world-creation of a novel, and the suspense of a mystery, Ellen Burstyn takes us with her on the deepest adventure: the voyage toward one's authentic self. You will hear her voice long after you've put down *Lessons in Becoming Myself,* and it may lead you toward your own Becoming."　　　　　　　　—Gloria Steinem, founder of
Ms. magazine and author of
Outrageous Acts and Everyday Rebellions

"Ellen Burstyn's memoir, *Lessons in Becoming Myself,* is a moving, haunting account of her lifelong search for her true identity, and I found myself completely absorbed in each phase of her remarkable and enlightening journey."　　　　　　　　　　　　—Horton Foote, author of
A Trip to Bountiful and *Tender Mercies*

"*Lessons in Becoming Myself* is a beautiful, unforgettable journey into integrity and authentic power. A very special book of the heart."
　　　　　　　　　　　　　　　　　　—Gary Zukav, author of
The Seat of the Soul and *The Dancing Wu Li Masters*

"Candid and unassuming . . . a balanced mix of insider theatrical anecdotes and inspired philosophical revelations."　　　　　　　—*Booklist*

"Beautiful, inspired."　　　　　　　　　　　　　　—*New York Post*

LESSONS

in

BECOMING

MYSELF

Ellen Burstyn

RIVERHEAD BOOKS

New York

RIVERHEAD BOOKS
Published by the Penguin Group
Penguin Group (USA) Inc.
375 Hudson Street, New York, New York 10014, USA
Penguin Group (Canada), 90 Eglinton Avenue East, Suite 700, Toronto, Ontario M4P 2Y3, Canada
(a division of Pearson Penguin Canada Inc.)
Penguin Books Ltd., 80 Strand, London WC2R 0RL, England
Penguin Group Ireland, 25 St. Stephen's Green, Dublin 2, Ireland (a division of Penguin Books Ltd.)
Penguin Group (Australia), 250 Camberwell Road, Camberwell, Victoria 3124, Australia (a division
of Pearson Australia Group Pty. Ltd.)
Penguin Books India Pvt. Ltd., 11 Community Centre, Panchsheel Park, New Delhi–110 017, India
Penguin Group (NZ), 67 Apollo Drive, Rosedale, North Shore 0745, Auckland, New Zealand (a di-
vision of Pearson New Zealand Ltd.)
Penguin Books (South Africa) (Pty.) Ltd., 24 Sturdee Avenue, Rosebank, Johannesburg 2196, South
Africa

Penguin Books Ltd., Registered Offices: 80 Strand, London WC2R 0RL, England

The publisher does not have any control over and does not assume any responsibility for author or
third-party websites or their content.

Copyright © 2006 by Matrix Movies, Inc. (f/s/o Ellen Burstyn)
Pages 449–453 constitute an extension of this page.
Cover photograph © Herb Ritts/Lime Foto
Book design by Amanda Dewey

First Riverhead hardcover edition: October 2006
First Riverhead trade paperback edition: October 2007
Riverhead trade paperback ISBN: 978-1-59448-268-7

The Library of Congress has catalogued the Riverhead hardcover edition as follows:

  Burstyn, Ellen, date.
Lessons in becoming myself / by Ellen Burstyn.
  p. cm.
  ISBN 1-59448-929-7
  1. Burstyn, Ellen. 2. Actors–United States–Biography. I. Title.
PN2287.B884A3   2006   2006044633
792.02'8092–dc22
  [B]

PRINTED IN THE UNITED STATES OF AMERICA

10 9 8 7 6 5 4

To all my teachers

Invocation

I can remember where I was, but not how I came to be there. It was a large undeveloped field on the corner of a busy thoroughfare. I must have been ten or eleven, maybe twelve at the most. It was a field I passed on the way to the A&P. I had no groceries with me, so perhaps I stopped on the way to the store, always one to be on the lookout for stolen moments of unsupervised solitude. What I remember is lying on my side in the tall weeds, cars and trucks going by, but me hidden from view, being quiet, my head on my left upper arm staring at nothing really, and then my eyes wandering down to the earth only inches from my nose. There, to my surprise, was a teeming busy other world. An ant labored under the weight of a dried orange peel ten times its size. A larger black ant climbed a stalk of wild grass. A fly was devouring a tiny mass of putrefied something. The whole area was alive with activity, purpose, industry. These creatures were consumed with the concerns of their lives. None of them seemed to be aware of me, although I was probably mashing to death whole neighboring villages with my body at that very moment. Should I happen to shift my weight, I could leisurely crush them to death. And suddenly I felt like God. This must be how God occasionally regards us, just as fascinated by our determined comings and goings and then just as indifferent as I would soon be to these creatures. The thought that I was about to turn from their earnest living made me love them and, in fact, remember them well enough to write about them sixty-odd years later. They are long since dead, but they are alive in me because I remember them. It is remembering that feeds consciousness. A mental photograph of that moment is part of me now, and it gives me a Godlike point of view. Had that ant prayed to me to help him with his orange peel, it's possible that I might have heard, felt, sensed some rustle in my awareness that might have prompted me to pick up a stick and urge him along. Or not. But it certainly would have helped him to think he lived in a world where divine intervention was possible. It would have given him courage, as it gives me courage to pray. I can feel God's divine indifference to my supplications for love, fame, money, or spiritual enlightenment. I can feel God not care whether I am successful in getting my orange peel to my chosen destination. But from the point of view of a laborer in the fields of God, I thank Him/Her for not rolling over onto me this day and for allowing me the opportunity to look up as I carry the burden of my ignorance and say thank you. Thank you for the remarkable gift of life, remembrance, and prayer.

In my uniform, St. Mary's Academy.
I was six or seven.

PART I

Beginning

*Life is a succession of lessons
which must be lived to be understood.*

HELEN KELLER

D own in the basement of my house, there is a room where I store my archives: every script I've ever worked on, photos taken of me and photos I've taken, diaries, journals, appointment books, calendars, and notebooks from all the way back to my beginnings.

But that is only the outer room. There is an inner room where I store my feelings. I was blessed with a good memory. John Gielgud once said to me, "Memory is like any muscle. It must be exercised." I have trained my memory and I exercise it often. When I need to access a particular emotion for a role, I imagine taking an elevator down to my inner archive, where I quietly flip through the files until some memory rises up and offers itself. Then I move into that event and it comes alive in me.

In ancient Greece, the goddess of memory was called Mnemosyne. She was a Titaness who married Zeus and then gave birth to the nine Muses. So memory is the mother of inspiration. I call on her every day in my work, then ride her titanic force down into the past, where sleeps my whole life waiting to be called forth.

My earliest memory:

Detroit, 1935. I'm two and a half years old. My brother Jack is five. We live with my mother and her second husband, Don Francimore, whom I call Daddy. My name is Edna Rae Gillooly. I don't know my real father, John Austin Gillooly, very well. We are in our apartment. Something is wrong. My brother got sick and is in the hospital. My grandmother takes care of me during the day while my mother is at the hospital with Jack. My mother is very sad. My aunts and uncles have come over to see her. I'm in the bathroom. I can hear my mother telling everyone that Jack has scarlet fever. I want my mother to stop crying. I want to make her laugh. I'm naked. I take a white washcloth and put it between my legs like a sanitary napkin, holding it in place with one hand in front and one in back. I prance out of the bathroom and into the living room as though riding a hobbyhorse, chanting, "I'm Mommy, I'm Mommy." Nobody thinks it's funny. I get ushered back into the bathroom and into my pajamas. Everyone leaves. I'm put to bed on the couch. My grandma is in the bed I usually share with Jack. My mother sits in her rocking chair sadly knitting. I watch her for a while, but the creak of her chair and the click-click of her knitting needles lulls me to sleep. In the morning I'm in the kitchen eating my cereal. My mother comes in and tells my grandma that a bird got trapped between the walls. She could hear it flapping its wings all night.

My brother's been in the hospital for two weeks. He has double pneumonia and a mastoid infection. My mother is crying a lot; she can't sleep and rocks and knits all night. Every once in a while she murmurs, "That poor little bird is still trapped in the wall. I can hear it flapping." One night she says, "The bird is getting weaker," and she rocks faster, her knitting needles clicking and her face looking tight and strained.

The next night she comes home and tells my grandma that Jackie isn't going to last the night. She says, "The doctor said there is a new drug that has been successful in the laboratory, but they haven't tried it yet on people. He asked for my permission to try it out on Jackie. I said, 'Well, if he's not going to last the night, go ahead and try it.' "

My grandma tucks me in on the couch. All the lights are out except the lamp near my mother's rocking chair. I drift off. Suddenly the chair stops creaking. I open my eyes and see my mother leaning forward, the lamp and a soft smile lighting up her face. She says in a hushed voice to the silent room, "The flapping has stopped. The bird got out. Jackie is going to be all right."

I don't know what kind of magic was at work there, but it was a kind my mother clearly understood. It made a deep impression on me. That drug was pretty impressive, too. It was sulfa. It cured Jack's scarlet fever and the double pneumonia, but when it came to the mastoids, its power fell on deaf ears. My brother was hearing-impaired for life.

Writing this earliest of memories makes me wonder if it wasn't right here that I became intrigued with the third world of our existence. The first world is the world of light, where we see, hear, taste, touch with our senses, and understand with our rational minds. Its opposite is the dark world of death, where we are without even our very breath. But between these two realms there seems to be a third world—a mysterious dimension where a little bird can get caught and flap a fevered message with its scarlet-colored wings to a worried rocking mother knitting her son's return to the land of life.

My mother was very proud of me. She took me to ballet, tap dancing, and acrobatic lessons. When family or friends came over, the rug was rolled back and I was urged to show off my latest steps. My mother made my clothes and dressed me up like a doll. People would say one of two things: "She looks like a doll" or "She looks just like you, Coriene." Either remark would make my mother expand with pride.

But I wasn't a doll at all. I had feelings dolls weren't supposed to have. Not even little girls were supposed to have them. I liked boys, a lot, and they liked me, too.

One day I stayed with my grandfather while my mother went shopping with my grandmother. He was a gruff man, but of his five children my mother, the beauty, was his favorite and her little doll child was the apple of his eye. He let me go outside to play, but cautioned me not to stray from the house. There was a neighborhood boy my age who came over to play. I can't recall his name or his face, only that I felt attracted to him. On the front porch was a metal glider painted green. This boy and I turned the heavy glider around so that its back faced the street and we could squinch down on the cushions and play our dangerous game. The game entailed me slowly lifting my skirt until a patch of white underpanties showed at the top of my legs and then quickly covering them again as the two of us giggled conspiratorially. He seemed absolutely fascinated by this flash of white cotton beneath my skirt and I was excited by his interest. The space between us was alive with desire and curiosity.

I don't know how long we could have gone on, but suddenly we were interrupted by my grandfather.

By turning the glider's back to the street to give ourselves the necessary privacy, we failed to observe that we were performing our clandestine explorations before the living-room windows, in full view of my grandfather's disapproving eyes. The boy was sent off, the glider turned properly around, and I was kept inside until my mother's return, when all hell broke loose. Shouts, slaps, brandishments. I was bad! Very, very bad! She was ashamed of me! I got the impression that the worst part of what I'd done was to be bad in front of my grandfather. I had shamed her in her father's eyes. I had disappointed her. She didn't know I was "like that." I don't think she ever forgave me. Even after she forgot about the incident, she never forgave me for it. I wasn't her perfect little doll anymore. I was bad and needed to be punished. "Spare the rod and spoil the child." I promise you, I may have been bad, but I was never spoiled.

ANOTHER MEMORY FROM AROUND AGE SIX:

We've moved to a house on Ward Avenue. My mother, Jack, Daddy, Grandma, Grandpa, and me. Jack is down the street at Freddy Harris's house. I'm there, too, but they send me away. They're going to play airplanes. No girls allowed. I go home. My mother is shouting into the phone. Her beautiful face looks ugly with rage. I stand very still in the living room. She is in the dining room. I've never seen her this mad. I can tell it's my daddy she's yelling at. I'm afraid to move. Then she screams, "I want a divorce." I turn and run as fast as I can back to Freddy's house. I open the front door of the screened-in porch. Jack says, "What?" I answer, terrified, "Mommy and Daddy are getting a divorce." We go home quickly. My mother tells us it's true. I ask, "Does this mean I won't have a daddy anymore?"

It did mean that. We never saw him again.

SEPTEMBER 1938. I'M SIX YEARS OLD:

I'm being sent away to boarding school! My mother always said, "If you kids don't mind me, I swear to God I'm going to put you in the juvenile detention home!" She says Jack and I are going to boarding school, not the juvenile detention home, but it's still "away." She's packing my clothes. Taking my things out of my drawers, folding them, and packing them in a suitcase. I'm crying harder than I've ever cried. My nose is running, my tears run down into my mouth mixing with my mucus and spit, making bubbles when I sob, the words catching my breath. "Please, Mommy, don't send me away. I promise I'll be good. I promise I won't be bad anymore. Don't send me away!" But she does. She sends us both away to St. Mary's Academy in Windsor, Ontario.

Jack and I are in the backseat of our car. My mother is driving because she doesn't have a husband anymore. We enter the tunnel that goes under the Detroit River. The tunnel is lined with white tiles. Halfway there on the wall are two flags: the Stars and Stripes crossed with the red maple leaf of Canada. Now we are in a different country. We're not home anymore.

We enter the walled grounds of St. Mary's Academy through a massive stone gateway. In the distance is a large brick building. There are no leaves on the trees. They bend and snap in the wind. We get out of the car. It is very cold. I am scared.

Now my mother is gone. My brother is on the boys' side of the building. I'm on the girls' side in Chorus Room #1. All our free time will be spent in this room with Sister Louise. We wear uniforms: black wool with detachable white collar and cuffs, which get washed and ironed every week, but the uniform doesn't. Underneath we wear a white pantywaist with garters that attach to our long black stockings, and we wear black bloomers under our skirt. On Sundays we are given medals suspended from red ribbons to wear around our necks all day to show that we have been good. If you don't earn your red ribbon, you can't leave the grounds with your mother when she comes to visit on Sunday. If you get ten demerits during the week, you don't earn your medal and you have to go to mass without it hanging from its red ribbon, a sign of shame for being bad. The first Sunday at mass, I had to walk into church with no red ribbon. All the girls in Chorus #1 lined up by twos, walking down the aisles in black uniforms with white collars and cuffs and red ribbons, then—a break in the pattern. No red ribbon. That's me. I got ten demerits the first week. Mostly for not knowing the rules. For instance, when we went into the lavatory that had about eight stalls with closed doors, I bent down to see if any feet were under the door like my mother taught me, so I'd know if that stall was empty. Two demerits right there for peeking!

I learned to get up in the dark, put on my black uniform, and stand in line. We ate, prayed, and studied together; all individuality discouraged by our black-robed nuns. Once a day we had free time in our chorus room. From my locker I got my personal items. They were some Shirley Temple paper dolls, a coloring book, and an assortment of crayons. These were kept in a Nabisco Shredded Wheat box with a picture of Niagara Falls on the side. Each time I lifted my treasures from the dark of my locker, I felt comfort and pleasure to be touching something that was mine, all mine.

A MEMORY FROM THAT TIME:

I'm standing in line waiting to talk to Sister Louise. She sits at her desk in our chorus room, wearing her Holy Redeemer habit. There are five girls in front of me. Each one holds in her hands whatever problem they are bringing to Sister Louise to answer or fix. My hands are empty. The room is noisy with the voices of the other thirty-five girls playing. As each problem is solved, I move one step closer to the nun's large oak desk. I wait patiently. Now it is my turn. I step up to the desk, but say nothing. Sister Louise looks at me questioningly. Then tears erupt and I bawl loudly, "I want my motherrrrr." Sister Louise stands, takes me by the shoulders, and leads me crying and sobbing a few steps over to the wall where hangs a picture of the Virgin Mary. As we walk she says in a kind voice, "Oh Edna, you've been one of our bravest little girls. Any time you feel like this, you just come over here and pray to the Blessed Virgin, who is the Mother of us all." She returns to her desk, leaving me standing looking at a five-by-seven picture on the wall of Mary holding Jesus. The room has gotten quiet. I feel embarrassed and wonder how long I have to stand there. I try to stop crying and catch my breath. I didn't know this was going to happen when I stood in line. I wonder what I was standing in line for.

Sunday is visiting day. My mother will come and take Jack and me out for the day. After mass we go to our chorus room and wait until our name is called, which means our visitor is here. An older girl escorts us down the long dark hallway to the top of the stairs, overlooking the two-story reception hall, which is flooded with light from the tall windows on the front wall. Right away I spot my mother across the room. She is the most beautiful mother there. She wears a stylish hat of her own design, tilted over her left eye at just the right angle. Her black coat is trimmed with silver fox fur. She wears high heels. Her legs are slender. There are jewels on her ears and bright red lipstick on her full lips. I'm not allowed to run, but I walk as fast as I can down the stairs and across the huge room and bury my face in her perfumed coat and dazzling beauty. She oozes an aura of glamour that no other mother has, and I am so proud she is *my* mother. Jack arrives and we go to the Radio Restaurant in Windsor. I get a butterscotch sundae and I am so happy.

My mother didn't come every Sunday. My father, my real one, Jack Gillooly, had visitation rights, and legally he could visit every other Sunday, but I only remember him coming once. He had a new wife named Adair. She was seventeen years old. I spent the day playing with her. My father read the newspaper. I called him Jack. So did my brother, Jack, call him

Jack. I don't remember him speaking to me. He may have, but I have no memory of it. I liked Adair, though.

MEMORY:

My brother Jack and I have a secret meeting place. There is a fence separating the boys' side of the school from the girls' side. We hatch a plot to meet secretly at the fence during outdoor time. I sneak away, run to the fence, crawl under some bushes, and wait with a pounding heart. Jack appears. I call to him in a loud whisper and he crawls under the bushes on his side. The fence separates us, but I can still stick my fingers through it and touch his woolen sleeve. We whisper and the vapor of our breaths mixes together in the cold winter air. We are both afraid of being caught. You could probably get ten demerits for this alone. Maybe even be put in isolation like Francine, who was so bad Sister Louise said she was "the devil's football—he could just kick her anywhere he wanted to." But even if we are caught, it would be worth it just to have these few stolen moments together. Then we say good-bye and crawl out of the bushes and separate. I run back to the girls' field and mix with the others. When I see Sister Louise I can't look her in the eye.

Sister Louise is short and heavy. She can't walk very fast. When we take a walk with her outdoors to visit the Grotto of Our Lady, we have to walk so slowly that we end up jumping up and down to keep warm. We like Sister Louise. She's pretty nice, not like some of the other nuns, who are really mean. We are with her most of the time when we are not in school. She sleeps in our dormitory, too. The dorm has forty beds lined up in a row against both walls and another row of beds in front of that row. Beside each bed is a locker in which we keep our toothpaste, toothbrush, a box of tissues, a washcloth, a towel, and our extra pair of bloomers and a pantywaist. At the end of the center aisle of the room there is a statue of the Blessed Virgin where we all kneel every night and say our Hail Marys before we go to bed. Sister Louise has four poles around her area with curtains on them that she pulls closed at night for privacy. But the curtains don't quite come together, so at night after she's gone somewhere (I don't know where) and removed her Holy Redeemer habit, she returns to her cubicle in a long white flannel nightgown and pulls her curtains closed, but from my bed I can see through the slit in the curtains and watch Sister Louise take down her long gray hair. She is sitting on her bed as she picks up her brush and leans to one side so that her hair falls down almost to the floor and she brushes her hair, now silver in the lamplight, with long, slow, sensuous strokes. Then she leans to the other side and pulls her hair over to that side. Her eyes are closed as she strokes her river of hair. I hold my breath. I shouldn't be watching this. I know it must be against the rules, but I can't help it. Even if I've fallen asleep, when I hear the wooden rings pull the curtains closed, I wake up to watch this nightly ritual. Lying in the darkened room with forty sleeping girls and only this slit of light from between Sister's closed curtains, it's breathtakingly forbidden and exciting. It's probably a sin.

In catechism class, Sister Ignatius teaches us about sin and confession. She tells us this story. One day God said to St. Michael the Archangel, "Michael, I want you to go down to earth and bring back the most beautiful thing you can find." So Michael went down and searched the whole earth until he came upon a large field of wild daffodils growing in the sunshine. He scooped up the whole field in his wings and brought it up to heaven and laid it at the feet of God. God said, "That's very beautiful, Michael, but that's not the most beautiful thing in the whole world." So Michael went back to earth (presumably returning that field of daffodils to its rightful place) and brought back his second choice. Of course God rejects that, too, because in a story like this it's always number three that is the magic number. Then Michael returns to earth, and after searching the whole earth, he finally found the most beautiful thing on earth and returned to heaven and knelt at God's feet. God asked, "Well, Michael, have you brought me the most beautiful thing on earth?" Michael extended his clenched hand to God and, slowly opening his fingers, he revealed in the palm of his hand the tear of a child after confession. Then God said, "Yes, Michael, that is truly the most beautiful thing in the world."

Sister Ignatius says to be sorry for your sins and to confess them and promise never to do them again. To never do them again is what pleases

God most. But I hadn't made my first communion yet, so we didn't go to confession and I didn't have to tell the priest that I watched Sister Louise brush her hair.

I did other things that were sins, too. Four of us got together in our chorus room and planned a secret adventure. We would sneak away from our beds after lights out and meet in the lavatory. We wrote down what we would have to do in code: TI. KI. TI. F&B. These meant, touch it, kiss it, taste it, front and back. We plotted this for days under cover in our chorus room while the other girls played nearby. On the big night two girls didn't show up, so it was just me and Bernadette squeezed into a lavatory stall. Now was the test. Are we actually going to do it or will we chicken out? Bernadette hoists her flannel nightgown, tucks it under her chin and pulls down her bloomers. It's freezing. She says, "Hurry up, I'm cold." I bravely touch her body front and back with one finger, pucker my lips so that as little of their surface as possible touches her skin front and back and then, last and scariest of all, with the tip of my tongue I dot her skin front and back. Her skin smells different from mine. She pulls up her bloomers. I'm on my knees. I quickly stand, pull down my bloomers. She does the routine. It's over. We sneak quietly out of the lavatory. Bernadette's bed is next to the wall near the lavatory. I have to cross the center aisle without Sister Louise seeing me. She's sitting in her chair, curtains open, reading her Bible. I dash across the center aisle under the glass-eyed gaze of the Virgin Mary and into my bed, feet freezing, heart racing. What did I do? That was scary. Was that it? We got away with it. But what was it? Maybe we didn't do it right.

DECEMBER 7, 1939. MY SEVENTH BIRTHDAY:

My mother takes Jack and me to the Radio Restaurant. As we walk in the door, I look down the passageway past the counter to where the tables are and see my cousin Carmen, my uncle Chuck, and my aunt Vi. As I approach the table they shout, "Surprise!" and everyone in the restaurant turns and looks at me. I am mortified. They have brought me nice presents. Someone gives me a coloring book with a picture of the Chicago

World's Fair on it. When I see the cake being brought in with lit candles, I beg my mother not to have everyone sing "Happy Birthday." She just laughs and they all start singing. I begin to cry in embarrassment and crawl under the table so people won't look at me.

It felt humiliating to be looked at by strangers in a restaurant, but just two weeks later I faced my first audience and that felt very different. I played Little Miss Muffet in our Christmas program. As I stood onstage looking out into the breathing darkness that would become my future, I recited my lines toward my mother, who was sitting to my left. I heard a woman say, "Isn't she cute?" and another one answer, "Adorable." I hoped my mother heard them, and that she thought so, too. Maybe she might even think I was good enough to live with her again. But she didn't.

Spring comes. The snow melts. It's all muddy on the playing field. We can't go down the toboggan slide anymore. It's May. The month of Our Lady. In my locker next to my bed I make a May altar out of my tissue box and put a holy picture of the Virgin Mary on it. I pick wildflowers in the field and lay them on the altar. In June the tissue box converts to an altar to Jesus because June is the month of Our Lord. I have a holy picture of Jesus, too, and I pray to Him every night to make me a good girl so I can go home. And it works! At the end of June my mother takes Jack and me home to meet her new husband. We're all going to live together. Good! I've got a new daddy! My third. I'm seven years old.

1940, DETROIT, SUMMERTIME:

We are in our new apartment, where we are going to live with my mother's new husband, Lou Schwartz. I don't know him. He doesn't feel like Daddy yet, but I'd like him to. I'm not sure how that is going to happen. He hasn't really spoken to me or Jack. He is in the living room reading his newspaper, sitting in a big chair with his feet on the ottoman. My mother is sitting on the couch knitting baby clothes. She is going to have a baby. I'm in the bedroom I'm going to share with Jack. In my hands is a square fat book, one of the Big Little Book series. In the upper right-hand corner of each page is a little cartoon figure in a square. When you flip the pages fast, the little figure seems to be running. It's like an animated cartoon. To me it seems like magic. I walk into the quiet living room, cross to my mother and say, "Look, Mom." I flip the pages and make the little man run. My mother watches for a moment, says, "Oh, how about that," and goes back to her knitting. I turn to go back to my room. I'll have to walk right past Lou. I feel a little scared, but decide to take the chance. I cautiously approach his chair and hold out my Big Little Book to him. "Do you want to see, Lou?" I ask. He turns a page of his newspaper and thumps out a crease. Without looking in my direction, he says, "I'm not interested."

I hurry into my room and stand there stunned. My face feels red and hot. He is my mother's husband, but he is not my daddy. He doesn't even want to be my friend. And that is how we lived for the next eleven years. When my brother Steve was born, *they* were a family. Then there was Jack and me, a sorry appendage to the happy family. We never spoke to Lou except when it was required; we had to say hello when he came home from work and good night when we went to bed. Otherwise the only contact we ever had was when he was punishing us, which he did frequently. I always wondered why he resented us so, right from the beginning. He wasn't a mean man. He had lots of friends and was quite a convivial fellow. He was a loving father to his own son, my brother Steve, and was reasonably generous with us, paying for tap dancing and piano lessons as well as our food and shelter. Our own father was remiss in his child support. Over the years I often wondered how my mother could have married a man who hated her children. Did she know beforehand that he felt that way and married him anyway? Or was she as surprised as we were when he treated us with such contempt?

As I asked myself those questions, I was startled by three memories from three different periods of my life that rose up and answered me.

MEMORY NUMBER ONE:

When I was about ten, we lived in an upstairs flat in a two-family house on a street in Detroit called Hazelwood. My mother found two wingback flowered chairs at the J. L. Hudson Co. that she very much wanted. Lou was always complaining about how much money she spent, so she bought them on the installment plan and put them in the attic. There they sat wrapped in brown paper for two years while she paid them off with money she saved from her grocery budget. Jack and I knew the chairs were up there, and kept her secret all that time. We piled stuff in front of the chairs and were instructed under no circumstances to let Lou see them. How we would have stopped him from going up to the attic had he wanted to, we had no idea, although Jack and I had much fun plotting what we would do to divert him should he ever attempt to go there. Fortunately he never did. After two years the chairs were paid off and Jack and my mother pulled off the extremely dusty brown paper and lugged the chairs down to the living room and placed them where my mother wanted them. Lou came home from work, took one look and said, "Where did they come from?" My mother, with the feathers of the canary still clinging to her red lips, said demurely, "I bought them." Lou, ire rising, demanded, "How in the hell am I going to pay—?" He got no further. My mother waved her hand dismissively. "Never mind. Never mind. They're all paid for." Lou didn't say another word. My mother knew how to get what she wanted.

A LATER MEMORY:

In 1954 I'd already left home and was living in New York. Lou died in 1953. My mother was living alone in Royal Oak, a suburb of Detroit where she and Lou had moved. I went to her house for a few days' visit. By then I had learned never to spend more than three days at my mother's house or there would be an explosion of some kind. On the second day of my visit, she told me she had a date that night with a man named Elliot and that he didn't know about me. Steve was only fourteen and still living with her, but she hadn't mentioned her other two kids to Elliot. She always had trouble telling the truth about her age, I was used to that, so I just said, "Fine, I'll go out for the evening. What time should I come back?" She said, "Oh, I'm sure he'll be gone by eleven." I visited friends who dropped me off at the house around 11:15. My mother met me at the front door and said in a low voice, "He's still here." What did she want me to do? Wait outside until he left? She said, "No, come in, but just pretend you're a neighbor." Steve came in the living room and she whispered to him quickly, "Just pretend she's a neighbor." Then I was brought to the den and introduced to Elliot as "my neighbor down the street." Now, the flaw in this ruse is that I look like a clone of my mother. We sat and chatted nervously for a few minutes. The room was tight with tension. Elliot was peering at us silently. I blurted, "Have you got any coffee, Coriene?" Her name felt strange on my lips. My mother's face lit up. She wanted me out of there, too. "Yeah, go make some coffee." As I made a quick exit from that painful situation, I heard Elliot say wryly, "Is that how you talk to your 'neighbor'?" I could hear the quotation marks around the word. Obviously he knew. Steve joined me in the kitchen as the coffee perked. When it was finished, I brought it to the den and incongruously served it to them, then said I had to go home. I got out of there fast. Steve followed me out to the street. It was close to midnight and most of the houses were dark. However, there were lights on about five houses down. Steve said, "The Poiers are up. Let's go see them." We watched TV with the Poiers' teenage daughter. After about ten minutes we heard Elliot's car start. He pulled away, going right past us. We said good-bye to the Poier girl and went back to my mother's house. We were all three laughing uncomfortably about it, but it really didn't feel all that funny. I felt sad and strangely ashamed.

In the morning my mother came to my room and woke me up. She stood in the doorway for a few minutes talking about the night before. She was laughing. I wasn't. I was hardly awake, but still felt shame and sadness from the night before. There was a pause. She looked at me for a moment, no longer smiling, and said, "Honey, you know I love you and I'd do anything in the world for you. The only thing I couldn't do was tell him my real age." That brought hot tears to my eyes. I turned my face to the wall. She hurried away and I understood that what I was feeling was shame for her—shame that my mother would deny her own child for some guy she hardly knew. I vowed right then and there never to lie about my age. And I never have. In 1974 I was on the cover of *McCall's* magazine and the blurb under my picture read NEW STAR AT 42. Another magazine devoted an issue to the fifty most powerful women in America. There was a picture of me and under it the caption: "Ellen Burstyn has singlehandedly made it unnecessary for women to ever lie about their age again." I don't know that I really accomplished that, but it was deeply gratifying to read it in print.

THIRD MEMORY:

In 1957 my mother took Steve, then seventeen, and moved to California. Soon after, she met Winsor Meals, who, after ten years of courtship, was to become her fourth husband. At first Winsor was led to believe Steve was her only child. After a few years she revealed she also had a daughter. But she would not tell Winsor about Jack, his wife, and their four daughters— not while she was single, anyway. She was not ready to admit to being a grandmother. Of course Steve and I had to keep her secret.

After ten years together, they finally set the wedding day. The ceremony was to be held at Steve's house; by now he was married and had children, so she was already a grandmother. She decided it was time to tell Winsor about Jack and his family. She invited them all to the ceremony. Jack came from his home in Atlanta and stayed at Steve's. When all the guests were assembled, my mother and Winsor arrived. Whereupon, my mother said to Winsor, "I'd like you to meet my son, his wife, and daughters." Of course Winsor was stunned. "Your son? I didn't know you had another son!" he said. To which my mother replied, "Why sure! Didn't I ever mention Jack to you?" Then to the assembled guests she said, "Come on, everyone. Let's get started." Winsor didn't have a moment to react, and the ceremony was under way.

As I look at these three memories, finally I understand why Lou resented us so. When she divorced her second husband, Don Francimore, his name was never again mentioned. We were instructed to never tell anyone about him. It was 1939 and women just weren't twice divorced. Jack and I were sent to St. Mary's Academy to be kept out of sight, like the two chairs wrapped in brown paper in the attic. She denied our existence as she later would to Elliot and Winsor, until she got what she wanted: husband number three. Then we were brought out of hiding and presented as a fait accompli, most likely after the wedding ceremony, when it was too late for him to protest. Maybe even after she was pregnant with his child. No wonder he resented us! I feel certain now that he never agreed to be a stepfather. He probably wasn't ever given the choice. I called Steve and told him what I just figured out and asked him what he thought. He answered, "That sure sounds like her."

My mother had many wonderful qualities. She was beautiful, vivacious, a talented cook, an immaculate housekeeper, and an expert seamstress. She was a world-class bridge player, an accomplished fisherwoman, and could wallpaper a whole house, which she did frequently. She loved to laugh and have fun. She had many devoted friends and was a popular hostess. She was independent, strong, knew what she wanted and how to get it, and always made sure her children were well fed and nicely clothed. But she wasn't honest.

She demanded we never lie to her and we were severely punished if we ever did and were caught. But she taught us to lie *for* her, to conceal her past, her marriages, her age, the chairs in the attic, and the other many secrets she felt were too dangerous to disclose. The truth to her was an enemy, something to keep hidden until she was sure of her position and she felt secure it could do her no harm. But she was wrong. Her deceit did so much harm. It created a negative atmosphere of anger, resentment, and hostility that pervaded our home and had abiding repercussions for all of us. I can't help wondering if all this didn't somehow influence my choice of Sufism as a spiritual path. A Sufi is defined as a seeker of truth.

When Steve was born in 1940 and I was nearly eight, we moved to the two-family house on Hazelwood. I went to St. Theresa's School, and Jack and I walked together to St. Theresa's Church on Sundays. My mother never went to church. She wasn't Catholic. My "real" father was, and when she married him, my mother promised to raise us Catholic. She kept her promise even though she had no interest in religion herself. I think she thought it would be good for us, rather like outsourcing our moral instruction.

Although I tend to regard that flat on Hazelwood as a crime scene, I have very fond memories of the street itself. It was lined on either side with tall, stately elm trees. For the eleven years I lived on that street, I loved those trees. In the winter, when the branches were bare, they were like two rows of silent sentinels standing at attention on each side of the street with the blue sky between them. As the weather began to warm in late March, I would walk home from school watching the gray branches for the first tinge of green. Every day the green intensified, the branches filling in with chartreuse-colored lace reaching reaching reaching across the street until their tips touched and, intertwining, they created a high arched canopy over Hazelwood and dropped sparkling coins of dappled light in the shadows of the green cave they created down the center of our spring-drenched street.

We lived upstairs at 3271 Hazelwood. Our flat had a living room, dining room, and kitchen, from the front to the back. Off to the side of the dining room was a hallway leading to a bathroom and two bedrooms. Jack was in one room and my mother and Lou in the other bedroom. Through their room was a sunroom; it had five windows and was heated only by the light of the sun. This was my room and I loved it. Out the three windows of the back wall I could see the garage, where we later put on a play and charged two cents per ticket. Between the garage and the fence there was a space not much more than a foot wide where we buried the various dogs, cats, birds, and other animals we found dead. There was a sumac tree in our backyard and a maple tree next door. These two trees pushed their branches up against my windows, begging to come in. When I opened my window they would hurry into my room like hungry pets and I'd sit on the floor and study the complex structure of the veins in their leaves. It was a small room, all mine, and I loved it. That is, in the summer.

When winter came to Detroit, the temperature was below freezing for months on end and often below zero. With no heat in the sunroom and five unsealed windows, it was freezing cold inside as well. The windows rattled in the wind and during blizzards snow would blow through the edges of the windows and pile up inside on my windowsill, which in a way was good because the piled-up snow would seal the cracks and the wind would stop blowing my many blankets. My room was so cold my mother closed the connecting door to their room because leaving it open made their room too cold. In the morning, when it was time to get up, my breath would vaporize and I'd slide out of bed, taking all the covers with me, grabbing my clothes and running to the dining room. (Years later, when director William Friedkin refrigerated *The Exorcist* set so that our breath would vaporize, I felt right at home.) Standing at the wall vent under a tent I created with my blanket, I'd pull on my clothes as my eyes stung from the coal dust rising from the furnace below. I could hear the scrape of the shovel on the cement floor of the coal bin as Jack shoveled coal into the furnace.

We lived in this house for about seven years and when we bought the house next door, my mother insisted I have the master bedroom to make up for "all those years in that darn cold room." I never understood why she felt she had to make up for it. I always loved that room. But many years later I was talking to her about all the sicknesses I had as a child: bronchitis, whooping cough, and innumerable sore throats. I told her a doctor told me that I'd had tuberculosis as a child, though no one diagnosed it properly and I got over it. She once again voiced her guilt about making me sleep "in that darn cold room." That was the first time I made the connection between that room and my many respiratory illnesses.

I had a game I used to play in that room. As I was falling asleep, I had to catch myself in the moment between wakefulness and sleep, when my eyes and ears were turned off and I was already breathing deeply. Then if I could remember to stay just conscious enough, I'd open my eyes and for a split second the room would be far away. Just for a second it was like I could see the room from a distance of about eight or ten feet above the bed.

One time I was very sick, with a wrenching cough and a high fever. I played the game, but when I opened my eyes, the effect of the room being so far away lasted more than a second. I couldn't make it go back to normal again. I got scared and started to cry. My mother appeared at the foot of my bed and asked, "What's the matter, honey?" I said through my sobs, "They put me way up here and they won't let me down." Then I caught myself. I knew she wouldn't be able to understand what I meant. My mother said soothingly, "It's all right, honey. Go back to sleep. You're just delirious from the fever." I was glad she thought that. I didn't want to tell her about "the game."

In 1970 when I climbed the Alps to the Sufi camp above Chamonix facing Mont Blanc, I met Pir Vilayat Khan, the head of the Sufi Order in the West. At our first meeting, he said, "You did a good deal of astral traveling as a child, didn't you?"

"No," I said, mystified.

He peered in my eyes and said, "Well, you did. You just don't remember it." It was months before I realized with a start what he was referring to. Oh! That's what it was—astral travel! I was separating my consciousness from my body. I always thought it was a trick I could do with my eyes.

I'd been skipped a grade, so I was always the youngest in my class. My mother transferred us to public school when I was in the fourth grade and then I discovered how advanced Catholic schools were over public schools. In the fourth grade they were learning what I had learned two years earlier at St. Theresa's. I was already a year younger than the rest of my classmates, so it was decided not to advance me again. There were no special or accelerated classes then, so I hung out in the fourth grade sitting through lessons I already knew and soon I stopped listening. I lost interest in school and never regained it. I went from getting the best marks in class in my first three years to getting the worst. I never did any homework. Never. Seldom passed a test, and skipped school often.

All of this was complicated by the unpleasantness at home. I hated my stepfather. Jack and I were frequently scolded, punished, chastised, and beaten by both of them. My mother called it getting spanked. I think that's too cute a word for the blows we received. I dreaded going home from school. When I was there I spent as much time as possible in my bedroom, so school became the place where I had fun. I was rebellious, popular, a cutup, a trendsetter, a clown, attractive to boys, headstrong, and desperately unhappy. Today a good social worker would recognize the symptoms—such as cutting gym class to hide the many bruises on my body—and order my home monitored and investigated.

I longed to run away from home, and I wrote about it in my diary. My mother would find my diary no matter where I hid it and then punish me for what I'd written. "You are under my jurisdiction until you are eighteen years old," she'd say. "And if you try to run away before that, I swear to God I'll hunt you down and when I find you, I'll have you put in the juvenile detention home." Again with the juvenile detention home! But I believed her and didn't run away. Not until the day I turned eighteen.

Of the many beatings she administered, one stands out clearly in my memory. It started in the dining room. This wasn't a planned punishment, with a switch cut from a tree, or a yardstick, or a belt. This was a spontaneous outburst of rage, so hands were the weapon. As the blows landed indiscriminately on my face, head, body, wherever she could land them, I ran from the dining room to what I felt was the safety of my bed, which was absurd because she was in hot pursuit, knocked me on my bed, got on top of me, pinned my hands down with her knees, and proceeded to slap me in the face as she screamed at me. I looked up into her contorted, furious face. She looked so ugly and mad with foam dripping from her mouth like a mad dog. Suddenly I stopped struggling against her, just observed her, didn't feel the blows as they landed, and a solemn thought walked quietly across my mind: *She's mad. She's crazy. Oh my God. I understand. My mother is crazy.* I didn't feel the blows because I had dissociated. I separated from my body. It was too painful to be in it. This was the first time I experienced this, but unhappily for me it would not be my last. It was a trick I consciously had to unlearn after I discovered how destructive it was.

There weren't only dark times. There were many family picnics and parties with cousins and aunts and uncles. There were sparkling Christmas trees with many presents. My mother made me beautiful clothes.

Jack and I played like fools every Saturday when my mother rode the bus downtown to go shopping. We had a lot of housework to do. I did all the dusting, vacuuming, and ironing. Jack had to scrub the floors and the stairways up to the attic and down to the basement. We never got right to it. Instead, we played all day and then, when it came close to the time my mother was due home, we'd furiously try to do everything at once. As it got down to the wire, we kept checking from the front porch for her to appear on the corner, walking home from the bus stop. As soon as she was spotted, one of us would yell, "Here she comes!" Then with our hearts pounding and in utter terror, we would manically try to finish before she came through the door. We usually got it done, except for the ironing. It's hard to iron fast, especially Lou's shirts, which he was very particular about. They had to be perfect, not one crease anywhere. By the time we started our work, we had torn up the house beyond recognition and often managed some disaster, like taking a flying leap, landing on the coffee table, and breaking off a leg. We knew we were in for it then, and expertly glued it back together. Eventually it would be discovered, and then we would get it. Often when my mother walked through the door, the house would be clean, but I'd still be ironing, which made her very angry. "Lou will be home soon. Put that thing away. You're going to have to do it after dinner. And you can't go to the movies this week."

I continued to attend mass at St. Theresa's. I loved the smell of the incense and the clanging of the chain when the altar boy swung the censer. When the priests walked down the aisle and sprinkled the congregation with holy water, I loved the splat as it landed on me, like an abrupt tap from God saying "Wake up!" I loved the decorations at Christmastime, when the altars were massed with red poinsettias. And during Lent, when the statues were covered with purple cloth while Jesus was in the desert, I fasted with Him and gave up candy for those forty days.

There was no television in those days, but Jack and I used to lie on the floor in the living room and listen to our favorite radio shows: *The Lone Ranger, The Green Hornet, Hermit's Cave,* and on Saturdays while I ironed, *Let's Pretend* and *Grand Central Station.* Often in the evening, we would hear from down the street, "Extra, extra, read all about it" and my mother would give one of us a dime to buy the paper, which would have news of Hitler's latest invasion.

On the first day of August 1941, Jack burst into my room while I lay sleeping and said, "Toots!"—my nickname—"Toots! Wake up! Grandma died last night." This was such an inconceivable idea to me that I asked the brilliant question "Grandma who?" Jack was dumbfounded. "Grandma, Grandma, our Grandma!" he insisted. We only had one grandma—who else could it be? But this was the first person in my life to die and it just hadn't occurred to me before that people I actually knew would ever die. We went to the funeral parlor and saw my big hearty grandma transformed into a powdered, still corpse. My mother cried and cried and took her mother's lifeless hand and tried to warm it. I felt so sorry for her. I never saw her like that any other time. Soon after that my stern grandpa moved in with us and slept in bed with Jack. My baby brother's crib was in my room as soon as the weather permitted. My mother was not well after his birth and had to be confined to her bed for many months. I took care of Butch, as we called him, and it was like having a living doll. I fed him and changed him and we bonded like mother and child. He felt like my baby. We became very close and are to this day.

After my grandfather was living with us for a few months, Lou told my mother that my grandfather had to move out. My mother later told me she never forgave Lou for that. Grandpa moved into a rented room nearby and got a new girlfriend, whom my mother and her three sisters hated. In November 1941, I was out somewhere with my mother, Lou, and baby Butch. We came home and my mother and I walked into Jack's bedroom, where my grandfather had slept, to see if Jack was home. He wasn't. The room was empty, but there was an intense odor of flowers just like at my grandma's funeral parlor. I said, "What's that smell?" My mother said, "It smells like flowers." I said, "It smells like a funeral parlor!" At that moment the phone rang. My mother answered it in the dining room and received the news that her father had just died.

I can't remember whether or not I heard along with my mother that bird flapping between the walls when my brother was sick, but I most certainly smelled those flowers that announced her father's death. At age nine, the supernatural had made itself known to me.

In the car on our way to my aunt Mildred's for my ninth birthday party, we heard on the radio that the Japanese had bombed Pearl Harbor. America was at war.

"And on my birthday, too," I murmured.

Everything changed then. America mobilized. No more butter. White margarine with a little orange button of dye that you squeezed into it and beat until it was yellow, so that when you spread it on your bread, it looked like butter instead of lard. My Girl Scout troop collected scrap metal for the war effort. We had to save bacon drippings in coffee cans and turn them in. I dutifully brought the cans of fat in my wagon to the collection site. Nothing went to waste. Everything was saved, collected, and delivered for the war effort. My mother went to work in a factory that made bomb sights. All the popular music changed to war songs. Patriotism was in the air. We were the good guys. We were fighting evil and God was certainly on our side.

Detroit became known as the Arsenal of Democracy. The automobile plants were converted to factories producing tanks and guns. They were gobbling up the workforce and needed more manpower. The factories reached out to the blacks of the South, who began migrating to the North for jobs and higher wages. Trouble was, everyone welcomed the black laborers into the factories, but nobody wanted them and their families to live in the all-white neighborhoods. The new workforce of 200,000 was corralled into sixty square blocks on the east side of the city.

Detroit had become a stronghold of the Ku Klux Klan in the 1920s, and when tensions finally erupted, an angry mob of thousands of whites began pulling blacks off streetcars and beating them to death in full view of the white police.

Riots broke out and the police killed seventeen people, all black. I was to enter Hutchins Intermediate School, but the school's opening in September was delayed a week. I was told the reason was: "The colored are rioting."

Throughout the war, my mother often came home from work after Lou did and just before dinnertime. Supper had to be on the table at exactly six P.M. or Lou "lost his appetite" and refused to eat. Somehow his not eating was my mother's punishment for serving dinner late. So I became the cook around age ten. At first it was just peel the potatoes, prepare the salad, set the table. When my mother came home, she would fry the chops or whatever. Lou was a big beef eater. In time, I learned how to cook the whole meal. One evening I was in the kitchen chopping cabbage for coleslaw. Lou came home from work and, entering the kitchen, he began chastising me for something I did or did not do. Soon he slapped me in the face for being fresh and that quickly escalated to his grabbing my hair and repeatedly banging my head against the wall. I was in pain with each smash of my head, but more important, I felt I was in mortal danger. As my head bent forward in preparation to be bounced back again, my eyes fell on the butcher knife with which I'd been chopping cabbage. I saw my hand go forward and I knew he was so involved with my head, his body was wide open for stabbing. In that moment, not only did I want to kill him, I knew that I could. I could plunge that knife into his stomach. Then came another of those moments of dissociation. Part of me was screaming in pain, trying to pry his hands off my hair, trying to strain against him so my head didn't bang so hard, trying to get away from him. But another part detached from this chaos and, seemingly in slow motion, observed the knife, its availability, his vulnerability, my desire to do it, and then calmly considered the ramifications. Not only would I surely land in "the juvenile detention home" for good, my life would be ruined. I'd be a killer and even though I could claim self-defense, I would have killed my brother's father. It would have broken Steve's heart. That I did not want to do. I decided not to kill him. I just wanted him to get the hell off of me. My hand flailed out trying to push him away and in the melee I scratched his face. When we parted he was a mess. Scratches on his face, blood on his shirt, and his hair ruffled and standing on end. I straightened myself out and continued making dinner. He sat down in his easy chair to read his newspaper just as he was, purposefully, so that when my mother walked in the door she took one look at him and asked in an incredulous voice, "Well, what happened to you?"

"Your darling little daughter," Lou answered. Of course my privileges were taken away for a month.

My privileges consisted mainly of a movie once a week, usually on Saturday afternoons, sometimes Sunday. Jack and I were each given a quarter, and at the Riviera Theatre or the Annex, we escaped into a wider world of happy families and beautiful people. I loved *The Dolly Sisters*. A life lived in satin dresses trimmed with sequins and feathers was my highest ambition at that time.

I collected movie star pictures torn from movie magazines, and traded them with my friends when we got together. There were some I'd never trade for anything—Betty Grable, June Haver, Rita Hayworth, Linda Darnell, and Hedy Lamarr—and of course Judy Garland, Shirley Temple, Gloria Jean, and Deanna Durbin. My actors were Gary Cooper, Mickey Rooney, and Tyrone Power.

Whenever I was home alone, I dressed up in my mother's clothes, put on her jewelry and as much makeup as I could get on my face. I pulled my hair up high on my head and stood in front of her mirror posing, singing, making faces, and then I would approach the mirror so that my nose was practically touching it and look at my parted moist lipsticked lips in extreme close-up. With my eyes on my gorgeous sensual lips, remembering the way Betty Grable did it, I would make contact with the hard cold mirror and kiss myself.

Snow often came to Detroit shortly after Thanksgiving, before my birthday in early December. It would stay on the ground all winter, turning into big dirty piles that were periodically covered over with fresh clean snow. With the spring thaw, the streets turned into rushing rivers. In fine weather I walked to and from school. When it was really cold, my mother would give us twenty cents to take the streetcar. The streetcar stop was about five blocks away and didn't run on schedule, so by the time I got on, my knees were bright red. I refused to wear leggings; that was for babies, I was now a teenager. I was thirteen years old. The walk home from the streetcar after school was treacherous, and the icy streets threatened to upend me at any moment of inattention.

One day I turned onto Hazelwood, bending into the freezing wind, and as I was about halfway to my house, I heard beneath the wind's howl a frantic, plaintive cry. Following the sound, I discovered in my neighbor's hedge a scrawny frightened kitten. I picked up the tiny furry baby and dropped its shivering body into my coat and tried to warm it by breathing my warm breath down into its terrified face. It cried piteously. I carried it home. In our kitchen I gave it a saucer of milk that she lapped up hungrily. I brought her into my bedroom, where she curled up on my bed and took a nap under the woolen scarf I placed carefully over her because, of course, my room was none too warm. Her fur was gray with stripes like a tiger and her nose was pink, so I named her Pinky Tiger Lily. We often had dogs but never a kitten, and I was very happy that I now had my very own pet. My mother didn't seem too thrilled about it, but she didn't exactly say no when I begged to keep her. However, Lou was a different story. "You don't know where that cat's been. It could have all kinds of diseases!" he bellowed. I kept her in my room out of sight and pleaded her case. I promised to take care of her and swore she would be no trouble. My mother seemed fairly silent on the subject, but Lou continued to rail. I think I managed to keep her for the weekend. She slept in bed with me, curled up at my neck under my hair. I don't know how they got her away from me without waking me up, but on Monday morning she was gone. I searched the house for her calling her name. No one said anything when I asked if anyone had seen her. I couldn't imagine where she was hiding. Soon it was time to go to school. I put a saucer of milk under the sink in the kitchen in case she came out of hiding while I was at school. My mother must have been working the night shift that week because she was home making herself breakfast when I left for school.

I bundled up and walked down the stairs worried, wondering where my kitten could be. As I opened the door to the outside, I got my answer. Pinky Tiger Lily's frozen-stiff body fell in and landed on the floor with a quiet thud. "Oh no, oh no," I cried, and picked her up. Her eyes were frozen open and so was her mouth, showing her tiny needlelike teeth. Her face had an expression of fear and disbelief. Her body was flat, as though she was pressed tight against the door all night as she called and called to me until she was dead. I thought I had rescued her, but I had only delivered her into the jaws of death. I carried her cold corpse upstairs. Her soft fur felt dry and lifeless. Crying, I walked into the kitchen, where my mother stood at the stove. She glanced at me, but said nothing. I found a shoebox and laid her stiff body in it and covered it. All I said to my mother was, "Please don't throw her away. I want to bury her when the ground is soft." I carried the box out to the garage, where it would wait until spring.

After that, at night I pulled the covers over my head and yearned for the day when I would leave home. Five more years. I would leave on my eighteenth birthday. From my bed I could hear the mournful cry of a train going somewhere in the night. Somewhere far from here. I would picture the lights of the train traveling through the dark night and see the passengers inside. I could see the waiter in the dining car serving a man dining with a woman who was wearing a smart hat and I'd make up stories about who they were and where they were going. *I must have money,* I thought, *to be able to buy a ticket.* Maybe I'd take that train and find my real father. All I had was one picture of him that I kept in a box in my bedroom with all my favorite treasures. He looked handsome in the picture. His hand was lightly touching a collie and he was looking at her tenderly, as I wished he'd look at me someday. I must go to work and start saving money. I must be independent. But how? I was only thirteen and too young to get a working permit. You had to be fourteen for that. Shivering under the covers, I plotted and planned my escape.

FEBRUARY 1946—DETROIT:

The snow had been falling furiously all day. Now, in the darkening evening, the blizzard abated and the wild wind weakened to an occasional gust.

Parting the lace curtains that covered our front window, I could see the flakes gently drifting down in the shaft of light from the streetlamp. I asked my mother for permission to go out and deliver my newspapers. She looked out the window and agreed to let me go. My stepfather, nearby in his easy chair, smoking a cigarette and reading his newspaper, said nothing. I hurried past him out the door and struggled into my snowsuit.

This *Shopping News* route was actually illegal employment, but I was eager to work and earn my own money. My mother didn't believe in allowances. I cut a deal with my brother Jack. This had been his route. One paper thrown on each porch in our neighborhood, twice a week, netted him a cool three dollars. When Jack moved up to a regular evening *Detroit Free Press* route, I convinced him to keep the *Shopping News* in his name and let me deliver it. All he had to do was pick up the three bucks and hand it over to me.

Snowsuit buttoned, galoshes buckled, I pulled on my knit cap and clomped down the stairs to the hall outside Mrs. Kuber's door, where my papers were stacked in bundles. I sat on the bottom step and folded each paper tight for tossing, then fitted them snugly in the big canvas bag. When the bag was full, I opened the heavy door to the outside and backed out, dragging the loaded bag to the edge of the porch, then bumped it down the snow-covered stairs and hoisted it into my waiting wagon. Panting, I pulled on my woolen gloves, picked up the handle, turned my wagon toward the street, and stopped dead in my tracks.

The snow had magically transfigured the world around me. Everything everywhere was covered in radiant white with shadows of purplish blue. Nothing moved. The cars parked on the street buried in snow looked like frozen mastodons. The trees were encased in gleaming ice. A gust of wind blew and the trees moaned in their frosted sheaths. The limbs clicked like crystal and the tiny twigs tinkled. All along the empty tree-lined street the wintry instruments sang the song of the wind.

There was no one outside but me. In the quiet between the wind gusts I heard only the crunch of the snow beneath my feet, the chink of my galoshes' buckles, the muted clatter of my wagon wheels, and my own in-and-out breathing. At the end of our walk I turned up the street and there, in front of me, hanging low in a deep blue sky, was a magnificent round full moon reflecting the light of the sun into this shimmering night. The snow was glittering like trillions of tiny mirrors. The distant stars in the newly cleared sky were flashing their diamond brilliance. The tree trunks were gleaming. Everywhere I looked there was light—reflecting, radiant, and beaming.

I walked and pulled my heavy wagon through the enchanting night. Tossing my papers, which landed on each porch with a soft thud, I wasn't thinking about the three dollars at all. I was doing my work with deep pleasure in a luminous world. And then something like a soft miracle happened, a subtle shift, an alteration of the atmosphere—something strange, like a presence—and as I looked and saw the light, the light looked back and saw me. I was alive and knew I was alive in a world of living light.

This was my first experience of conscious awareness.

At Hutchins Intermediate School for the seventh, eighth, and ninth grades, I continued to be the most popular girl but did no better academically. I had little interest in my classes except for music, art, and modern dance, in which I always excelled. I barely passed any of the mathematics classes (I had to take geometry twice) and I flunked biology and other science courses. I did fairly well in English; I loved memorizing poetry, although I never did any homework and didn't show up for tests. Latin was a total disaster. Our teacher was named Miss Adamo. She had gray hair and black eyes. On the first day, she wrote her name on the blackboard: AD AMO = TO LOVE. She wrote it large and underlined it with such force that the chalk snapped with a start and fell to the floor. She usually wore a gray suit, black high-heeled shoes that resounded with each firm step. She had a low-pitched voice like a man's that was loud and strong. Her teeth were large and showed often as she curled back her lip and enunciated.

My seat was in the third row, next to the windows. The classroom was on the third floor of the school, level with the treetops, and it was spring. Miss Adamo's droning lecture couldn't keep me in the room. My ability to dissociate, which was such an effective tool at home, now came and wafted me out the window, where my imagination danced among the spring green leaves. I could smell the yellow daffodils from the gardens below, and the heartbreakingly blue sky was meringued with white clouds.

Suddenly I heard my name and popped back into my body and saw Miss Adamo looking at me. I could feel that a question had been asked and was hanging over my head with my name on it. "I beg your pardon," I murmured, still slightly in my trancey state. Miss Adamo growled at me and demanded I answer the question, which she may have even repeated, but I was so surprised to find myself here in this classroom that I could not hear the question, and again in a bewildered voice I repeated, "I beg your pardon." When I said it a second time, Miss Adamo gasped and her large jaw dropped. Her black eyebrows pulled toward each other forming a straight rigid line with a tuft in the center. "What?" she exploded. "Are you deaf?" What she could not know is that her rage was making me retreat further. I could not stay there. My conditioning by now was to separate myself from the scene when confronted by uncontrolled anger. Dissociation is an escape hatch and you just vacate the premises. I was gone—only my body was there, and it was paralyzed.

Perhaps at this point she repeated the question, or else she may have repeated her demand for an answer. Whatever it was that she demanded, my response was the dreaded "I beg your pardon" for a third time. As soon as the words were out of my mouth, I knew I'd made an unpardonable mistake. My hand darted up and waved the air in front of my lips as though to erase those awful words before they traveled to Miss Adamo's flaming ears. As I did this, I shook my head and a strangled chuckle fell from my throat as I said, "No, I mean . . ." But the words hung there pathetically, then trailed away. At this point, Miss Adamo was in full fury.

"Stand up, Miss Gillooly!" she commanded through clenched teeth.

It was right after she commanded me to stand that the shift occurred. I stepped into the aisle next to my desk and the trance state came to an abrupt end. My consciousness descended into my body and landed in my legs as I rose to face her. I could feel the attention of the class focused in breathless anticipation at the drama about to be enacted. I was one of the most popular girls in school, the star of the class, and I was about to be pilloried in public. I could hear the ticking of the wall clock. Miss Adamo tilted her chin up and her black eyes glinted with power.

"Gillooly," she said slowly. "Gilloooooly, that's a good name for you. Do you know who the Gillooly was in Ireland?" I didn't know the answer to her question. I knew no Gilloolys except my brother Jack. I had never been to Ireland, barely knew my father, had never met his family, and knew nothing of my ancestors. But I sensed it was those unknown ancestors who were about to be maligned and whose honor I was going to be called on to defend. Miss Adamo lowered her chin. "The Gillooly," she said, pausing for effect, "the Gillooly in Ireland was the idler of the village; the shirker of work; the lazy good-for-nothing."

Forty pairs of eyes shifted from her to me. Not a breath anywhere. The spring leaves trembled, then froze in place. Stillness and silence everywhere. I said evenly, "Well, at least I live up to my name, Miss Adamo." That was it! The battle raged. Miss Adamo's high heels pounded to her desk. She grabbed her mighty pen and, enunciating each word for the class to hear, she lashed out a note to the principal and, signing it with a flourish, she sent me forth to his office.

I crossed the front of the classroom calmly, opened the door, and, aware that the scene called for an exit line or my audience would be sorely disappointed, I turned to Miss Adamo and politely said, "I want to thank you for all your kindness."

"What?" she shouted. "What did you say? Come back here! Give me that note!" She snatched it from my hand and tried to add to my indictment, but of course I had created a problem for her. She could hardly write that I had thanked her for her kindness. That wouldn't read well. She stroked the air with her pen impotently a few times, until she finally found the words to e-nun-ci-ate for the class. "She left here in a huff with impudence written all over her face." I was pleased I had forced her to lie.

When the principal read the note, he peered over his glasses and asked, "What does that last line mean? What did you do?"

"I thanked her for all her kindness."

"Oh, Edna," he sighed, seemingly impatient with me. But I could tell he thought it was pretty funny. I suspected he didn't think much of Miss Adamo, either.

I can't remember the outcome. I think I was expelled from her class, which would have been a blessing. I didn't like being around Miss Adamo. And I had walked away intact. She had not taken that thing I felt she wanted to strip from me. To put it in a word now, I think I'd have to choose the word "dignity," from the Latin *dignitas,* which means worthiness of bearing, conduct, or speech indicative of self-respect.

During my thirteenth summer I had a series of different jobs for only two weeks. That was how long I was allowed to work before I had to produce my working papers. I lied about my age (saying I was fourteen) and worked behind the soda fountain at a nearby drugstore. Then I got a job at the grocery store close to my house, bagging and weighing and marking vegetables in the produce department. The butcher in that store was a handsome dark-haired man with bright eyes and gleaming teeth when he smiled, which he often did at me. He looked like the picture I had of my father. Whenever he spoke to me, I felt shy and found myself stroking the bridge of my nose with my middle finger. How utterly exposed I felt in my early teens when a man looked at me with desire in his eyes, as that handsome butcher did. I eventually had to confess that I couldn't produce my working papers and my bagging, weighing, and marking days were over in that store. But whenever my mother sent me to the handsome butcher with a shopping list, I could feel myself lower my chin, stroke my nose, and hide behind the curtain of my hand as I ordered a pound of ground round.

My sexuality was coming alive and a great mystery was unfolding inside me. I had no understanding of it or anyone to talk to about it. Consequently I was unconsciously absorbing whatever misinformation came my way. My brother had a friend, Jerry Gerger, who had a great sense of humor and always made me laugh. I found myself hiding behind my hand more and more when he spoke to me. When I turned fourteen, Jerry asked me to go out with him. I pleaded with my mother, who was reluctant, but because Jerry was at our house so often, and Jack vouched for him, I was allowed to go on my first date. It was in the summer and we decided to take the ferryboat to the island of Bob-Lo, which had an amusement park and was a favorite picnic place. We often went there on family gatherings, dancing to a live orchestra on the way over and back. It was a popular outing for dates, too. My mother instructed me to be home by ten o'clock. Jerry and I had a wonderful time together, going on all the rides, laughing, eating hot dogs and cotton candy. We got to the ferry slip a few minutes late and saw the ferry pulling away from the shore. The next ferry was called "the moonlight cruise" and didn't dock until after eleven, getting me home close to midnight. I knew I'd be in trouble and be punished, but it was worth it. I'd had such a good time with Jerry on my first date, and as we entered my house and climbed the stairs up to my family's flat, I was hoping Jerry would kiss me good night at the front door. I hoped I could do it right, like Lana Turner in *The Postman Always Rings Twice*, where she parted her lips slightly as she reached for John Garfield's mouth. When we played spin the bottle, Jack and I were always considered the best kissers because we pressed our lips tight and never got any spit on anyone. But when we saw *Postman* and saw that Lana Turner and John Garfield kissed with their lips parted, I quickly looked at Jack to see what he thought of their strange approach to kissing. He didn't say anything or even look at me, but a few days later when we were alone, he said, "Toots, I've been thinking. I think you are supposed to open your mouth just a little bit as you kiss." I said nothing. Jack was the authority. Whatever he said was law.

Now, as I climbed the stairs preparing for my first kiss, I swallowed several times trying to get rid of all my spit so I could part my lips without getting Jerry all sloppy. But I didn't have to worry. At the top of the stairs I turned to him to thank him for the good time, the door opened, and my mother's enraged face appeared. She grabbed me by the hair with one hand and pulled me inside, slapping my face with the other hand, screaming, "I told you to be home at ten o'clock. When are you going to learn to mind me!" She slammed the door in Jerry's shocked face and continued slapping me all the way to my bedroom. I was mortified. The next day I approached my mother and said in a calm voice, "Mom, you really shouldn't do things like that to me. These are my formative years and what you do to me now will be with me for the rest of my life."

She looked annoyed and said, "Go on and get out of here, ya damn kid." Years later, when I confronted my mother about the damage done by the violence in our home, she said, "Well, did you ever stop to think of what it was like for me to be the mother of Ellen Burstyn!"

"I wasn't Ellen Burstyn then," I said.

"Oh, yes you were!" she said, her voice rising. She was right. It probably wasn't easy for her to be the mother of Ellen Burstyn. I often wonder who I would be if I had had a loving, supportive mother. Who knows? I'm sure she provided the necessary friction to propel me out of there and onto my path.

I led two lives. At home I was withdrawn and miserable; at school I was outgoing, sociable, and creative. When it was time to go to high school, I told my mother that I wanted to go to Cass Tech like my brother Jack, who was majoring in aeronautical engineering. To my knowledge, Cass Tech was the only high school in America where students could major in specific fields, and the school had the best art department in the country. My mother thought I should go to our local high school, Northwestern, and learn typing.

"But that will just be a waste of time," I said. "I'm going to be an actress." My mother looked at me peevishly and said, "You've got pipe dreams in your head. Go to Northwestern and take a commercial course so you've got something to fall back on when you fall on your ass." She walked away in disgust.

"You'll never amount to anything but a goddamn whore," Lou would say to me around this time. I knew they were both wrong, but I had to wonder what would make them say something so damning to a young girl. By then I had steeled myself against their blows, but those harsh words landed somewhere and would have to be dealt with sooner or later.

Despite my mother's initial opposition, I prevailed and entered Cass Tech majoring in fashion illustration. I didn't know much, but I knew I'd never make it in an office. I was going to be a model or an actress. If not that, then a lawyer. I thought that being good at making speeches was the main qualification for the law. One visit to the Detroit Public Library's Law Department, and a perusal of a few law books I selected at random, cured me of that ambition. I also considered being a veterinarian because I loved animals, but I wasn't sure I'd ever be able to stick a needle in an animal, so that probably wasn't a good choice, either. I was still attending mass every Sunday and was very devout. Sometimes I thought a cloistered life dedicated to Jesus and doing "good works" had an appeal—and it still does in some ways, but I had a calling. The world out there was calling to me. Faraway places that I'd seen in books, where people looked different. They had other ways of living, on mountains, in caves, huts, pagodas, or hogans, where people drank goat's milk from a bowl like Heidi, and dark-eyed women had rings on their toes and flowers in their hair. The world, the huge, wide world. I wanted to see it all. But in the meantime, there was high school.

Soon after I turned fourteen, my mother and Lou bought the house next door at 3277 Hazelwood. It was the first house my mother ever owned. She was very proud of it and decorated the living room so beautifully that we couldn't use it except for company. We used the den. Same with the dining room. She bought a black lacquered Chinese dining set with yellow trim. Very fancy, but not to be used except when "people were over." We ate all our meals in the breakfast nook.

I was supposed to be home from school every day promptly at four o'clock to take care of Steve, whom we still called Butch. I had chores to do, too, including the ironing. One day I got home long before four and went down to the basement to iron. When the phone rang at four, I knew it was Lou calling to check on me as he did every day. I ran as fast as I could up the stairs, through the kitchen, dining room, and living room to the only telephone, but I was too late. As I picked up the phone I heard the click of the disconnect. I immediately called the Fisher Wallpaper Company and when Lou got on the phone, I said, still out of breath from the run, "Lou, it's me, I'm here. I was in the basement ironing and couldn't get to the phone in time." "Too bad," he answered. "You're gonna get a licking anyway. You know the rules." He hung up. I was outraged. The rule was that I be home at four P.M. I *was* home—doing the damned ironing. Now I had to continue ironing his shirts and worry about a beating I didn't deserve. I put the potatoes on and set the table. My mother came home and finished dinner. Jack had already been shipped out to live with my Aunt Florence, to get away from Lou, so there were just the four of us squeezed into the small breakfast nook. Butch and I sat inside with our backs to the corners, and my mother's and Lou's chairs were outside, where there was more room.

I hardly ever spoke at dinner or in Lou's presence at all, but this night an argument raged throughout dinner. Lou claimed I deserved punishment for not picking up the phone in time because I was ironing his shirts in the basement. We were both addressing my mother, not each other, which we never did if it could be avoided. Finally I exploded and said, "But I was here! I even called Waneta [Waneta Fender, my friend] and I spoke to Mrs. Fender. I asked her to have Waneta call me at home when she came in. Call her and ask her if you don't believe me," and then added insolently and probably hatefully, "Let *him* talk to her, too!" I had stepped over a line there. Lou was drinking his water and his face flared with anger. He threw his ice water across the table at me. I leaped up. I guess he thought I was going to hit him. He grabbed the glass milk bottle off the table and moved to hit me over the head with it, the milk spilling all over the table. I had a fork in my hand and, as I tried to hit the milk bottle away, the fork lodged in the fleshy part of his thumb in the palm. Blood spurted out over everything. He came at me, banging me against the wall on Butch's side. Butch was being slammed against the wall and I couldn't stand it that he was terrified, crying, and calling for us to stop, stop! I was trying to stop, but the bloody blows were landing everywhere. My mother finally pulled Lou off me. The fork was still lodged in his hand. I ran out to the street. My mother drove Lou to the hospital. He needed several stitches. He was furious, of course, but my beatings lessened after that. My mother still slapped me around, but they were starting to lose their taste for corporal punishment now that I was closer to their size.

I had several boyfriends at Cass. Ed McMullin was one. He was an artist, very intense, with white-blue eyes like a Samoyed, that looked like light was pouring through them. My other main boyfriend was Leo Parneghian. He was the center on the football team. I was captain of the cheerleaders. We were a natural couple. Once Leo came to pick me up for a date and as I answered the doorbell and admitted him, my mother came down the stairs from her bedroom. I was surprised to see her fully made up, wearing one of her best dresses. The three of us went into the den for a few minutes before Leo and I went out. I sat watching my mother smile coyly and chat demurely with Leo and thought, "My God, my mother is actually flirting with my date." Leo could see it, too, and flirted back obligingly. I felt horribly embarrassed for her. The next day my mother said, "Sometimes I wonder if Leo comes to see you or me." I said nothing. She was so transparent. But I did wonder why a mother would want her daughter jealous of her, because that was what I could feel her trying to do. She was competing with me. It took me years to understand that she envied me, envied my youth. I was just coming into all she was leaving behind, and I looked like her. She must have felt that whatever I had rightly belonged to her. She gave me her beauty and with her beauty I was getting all the attention she craved. The good part about that was because it was "her" beauty, I never identified with it. I had to develop something else that was mine. I had to identify with what I *did*, instead of how I looked. That has been a blessing in my life.

Even my voice is like my mother's. People couldn't tell us apart on the phone. Another of my boyfriends, Pat Harrington, had a wooden leg. He was lots of fun and I admired the way he handled himself. When we went to the beach, he unstrapped his wooden leg, left it on the blanket, and hopped down to the water. He seemed to have no embarrassment and just dealt with it matter-of-factly, and so then did I. But not my mother. She didn't like me going out with a one-legged boy. Suddenly Pat just stopped calling me and I couldn't understand why. We had been such good friends.

A few years ago my mother laughingly related how she had gotten rid of "that guy with the wooden leg. He called one time and I just pretended I was you and told him I didn't want him to call me anymore." She thought that was hilarious.

That was the problem—my mother never saw me as a separate person. She not only thought that I belonged to her, as her creation, but sometimes she seemed to think I actually was her or she was me. One of the reasons I was so eager to go to work and have my own money was because I wanted to be able to buy my own clothes. My mother would go downtown and come home with clothes that I had to wear whether I liked them or not. And I did not. The "in" style at that time was long corduroy hobble skirts, saddle shoes with bobbysocks, and a sweater, preferably angora. My mother bought me dresses at Lerner's that were not at all hip. I had a reputation to uphold in school. I couldn't wear those square dresses. So I would put one of them on at home, wear it to school, meet my best friend, Myrna Wood, in the girls' bathroom, and change into the clothes Myrna brought me. I went to great lengths not to look like my mother's version of me.

One of my first jobs after I obtained working papers was in Myrna's father's grocery store, bagging, weighing, and marking vegetables again. Mr. Wood was a very kind man, but a handsome muscular guy, who was in the produce department and one of my bosses, was after me sexually. I was fourteen and had no sexual experience except flirtations, spin the bottle, and other teenage fumbling. The summer I worked at the store, I was staying with Aunt Viola while my mother and Lou went to the lake for a vacation and I managed to persuade my mother to let me stay behind and work.

I took the streetcar home from Mr. Wood's store. It was a long ride and then a walk from the stop on Woodward to my aunt's apartment. That walk was in the dark and it was summer, so I guess the store was open late. One night *this* boss offered me a ride home. Why didn't I say no? I knew he was after me. He had come into the walk-in refrigerator on a few occasions when I'd gone in to get sacks of onions or potatoes to refill the bins. He'd made a pass at me each time and I'd learned to time my visits to the huge cold refrigerator when I could be sure he was busy and couldn't follow me.

So why did I get in his car? I think I just didn't know how to say no. I could when he grabbed me, but I didn't feel I had the right to anticipate trouble. I know I hesitated and he said, "Come on. I'm not going to touch you." I really wanted the ride and felt I could handle any problem that came up. I hated that walk from the streetcar stop to my aunt's apartment—it was a racially mixed area and at the time there was a lot of tension. I was glad for the opportunity to avoid that scary walk, but it was a dumb choice. This guy turned onto Aunt Viola's street, then quickly pulled the car into an alley behind Woodward, shut off the lights and engine, locked the doors, and grabbed me. I resisted him as best I could, but he was my boss and I didn't want to lose my job. He was very muscular and strong. I was afraid of him on every level, and more important, I had never learned how to say no. My mother didn't allow it. If she ever told me to do something I didn't want to do and I had the nerve to say no, she would look up from under her eyebrows and growl through clenched teeth, "Don't you say no to me, young lady." My mother's threats were always backed up, so I quickly learned that "no" was not a word in my vocabulary.

But here I was, a fourteen-year-old virgin about to be molested by a very strong man who meant business. He was trying to talk me into relenting, seduce me, and rape me, all at once. After a considerable struggle I finally managed to get the door unlocked and got away from him. I began the long walk down the dark street. He started the car and pulled alongside me, driving slowly, urging me to get back in the car, promising not to touch me. I prayed he wouldn't stop the car and drag me back in. He was trying to be nice now. I realized he was afraid I'd tell Mr. Wood, but he didn't have to worry. I'd always been bad, wrong, in need of punishment, and now that my sexuality was on the verge of erupting, I got a lot of attention for my looks and I was obviously creating trouble. It wasn't his fault. I felt deeply ashamed and hoped nobody found out. He had nothing to worry about. I wasn't going to tell on him.

I had a teacher for art composition named Don Brackett. He assigned us certain required drawings to teach us perspective, like a corner of the classroom or a hallway. But as usual I hated doing what I was told at school because I was forced to do that so much at home. On the day I was supposed to be drawing a corner of the room, I got bored and started drawing whatever I saw. As someone walked by I drew however much I could of him before he passed. A student sat on a stool sketching; I drew her. She moved. Someone else came and sat where she'd been. I'd draw the new figure right over the previous one. It was like a time-lapse, impressionistic drawing of the whole room. I shoved it in my sketchbook and forgot about it. When Mr. Brackett came around to view our sketchbooks I turned a page and revealed the unassigned sketch. Caught! I quickly hid it in the back. "Wait! Wait!" said Mr. Brackett. "Let me see that." *Oh no,* I thought, *I'm in trouble again.* But the teacher held it up and said, "That's good," and took it to the bulletin board and hung it for all to see. I was shocked. I did something I wasn't supposed to do, just because I felt like it, and I got praised? What could this mean? I carried that question in the back of my mind for more than twenty years, all the way to Lee Strasberg's acting class, where I finally learned the answer.

Cass Tech's school spirit was at fever pitch. Our basketball team was really good. We were winning many games. The bleachers were packed and the cheerleaders kept the fans stomping and shouting support. We actually went to the playoffs for the city championship. I was beside myself with joy. We were going to play Miller High School for the championship, the toughest team in the league. I had a big investment in this game, having seen Cass's athleticism transformed with the infusion of "spirit" we had mustered. Now we had a chance at the championship. The players had been playing their hearts out and I was so proud to lead the school in cheering them on. The morning of the big game, my mother heard me blow my nose and decided I was getting a cold. She said I couldn't cheer that night. What? We were playing in Detroit's equivalent of Madison Square Garden. Not be there? Impossible.

All day I begged and pleaded with my mother, but she insisted I couldn't go. It seemed to me that the more I tried to explain how important it was to me, the more firmly she became entrenched in her refusal. The crying and begging escalated close to hysterics. The more I said, "I'm captain of the team. I must be there," the more determined she was. Finally she went to my room and took my cheerleader's uniform away from me. Now I became determined to go—with or without her permission. I quieted down and made my plan. When I heard her in the kitchen, I searched her room for my uniform. It wasn't there. Then I tried my brother's room. Not there either. There was no place to hide it in the living room, so unless she had it with her in the kitchen, that left the dining room. I waited until I heard the water running in the sink. She couldn't see me from there. I tiptoed into the dining room and opened the door of the buffet, where she always hid our Christmas presents. There it was! I grabbed it and ran. I had enough money to take the bus downtown and arrive in time.

Cass didn't beat Miller High that night, but then few teams ever did. It was such an honor for us even to get into the playoffs. We cheered them until we were hoarse. I knew what was waiting for me at home, so I didn't return. I stayed with the co-captain of the cheerleaders, Selma Arkin, at her house. I called my mother and said, "I don't want you to worry, so I'm just calling to tell you I'm safe, but I'm not coming home until you promise not to beat me." The first day she said, "You get home here. I'm going to give you the licking of your life." She was furious. The second day she said, "I'm warning you. You better get home or, when I get a hold of you, you'll be sorry." She sounded angry, but not furious. The third day she said, "All right, come home. I promise I won't hit you." And she didn't. I had stopped the beating once and for all. At last, I'd won.

Every other summer, Lou and the other officers of the Fisher Wallpaper Company would meet to select the wallpaper designs for the next two years. The meeting was held near the summer home of Lou's boss, Mr. Drummond, on Lake Michigan near Holland, a town where the tulip festival was held each spring. In June my mother and Lou would pack up our car with all our suitcases and equipment and we'd make the long drive up to the cottage, traveling along Michigan's hilly roads that seemed like roller coasters to us kids. Once there, the men would go to work and the families would have a long, sunny summer at the beach. I loved our cottage. It had a giant tree growing straight through the front porch, and a creaking swing. There were never any books at home, but this cottage was furnished and had some books in it. Here I read *Thaïs* by Anatole France, *The Best Loved Plays of William Shakespeare,* as well as some popular novels like *Back Street* by Fannie Hurst. My love of reading started here on this creaking swing on rainy days and lying on a warm blanket in the soft sand in fair weather.

Butch was my charge, and we walked the boardwalk to the beach soon after breakfast every day. While Butch played with his pals, I spent the time reading and admiring the striking beauty of a girl I barely knew named Marlene Ederly and her easy grace as she walked with her boyfriend, the lifeguard. They seemed like a golden couple to me. They lived in Grand Rapids and, in my mind, they lived an ideal life. They didn't get beatings, I bet, or punished. They seemed good and blessed, as if they belonged in the sunshine, whereas I felt that even here under the blue sky, with the sound of the Great Lake lapping at the shore, the warm sun burnishing my body, that somehow I was a figure from the shadows who was carrying secret shame and a mass of unhealed wounds. A lifeguard would never be interested in me. I didn't feel lovable.

How was it then that one day in my seventeenth summer, while I was walking back from the beach on the boardwalk, a man with auburn hair and eyes, and lips like ripe fruit, should look at me with attraction lighting his eyes and say, "Had enough for one day?" I nodded and smiled as if I were a sunny girl. He was older—twenty-eight, I later learned—not a boy but a man, a handsome man, and as we walked on the narrow boards over the warm dunes, Butch running ahead, the man behind me, I could feel his eyes on my hips and thighs. Something moved and stirred in my body making me feel shy and my face burn with a smile I couldn't control. I felt embarrassed and wanted to run away. At a fork in the walk, he headed up and left and I down and right. I hurried home, pulled off my lamé bathing suit, and threw it on the floor, where it lay in a damp heap. I blamed it somehow for catching his interest and making me react in this embarrassing, exciting, sinful, mysterious manner. What had happened? What was my body doing? What was happening to me?

We saw each other again. And again. I made up excuses to get out of the cottage. He owned a little restaurant in Saugatuck and we drove over in his yellow Cadillac convertible. I couldn't take my eyes off him as he drove with his left arm on the window frame, barely touching the wheel with his long, light, freckled fingers. His hand held a lit cigarette and when he inhaled, his tongue flicked out of his open mouth. His legs were spread wide and his feet pointed out almost in fifth position. He didn't speak. Every once in a while, he turned his head toward me and smiled slyly, letting me know he knew I was watching him. I couldn't do anything else. He became the focus of my eyes, my mind, my desire. He was all I could think about.

Occasionally he would reach over and put his hand on my thigh and chuckle, striking an arc between us which could have melted metal. One day, in the midst of this tumultuous churning of desire, emotion, impulse, and containment, he said, "When are you going to let me make love to you?"

I answered haughtily, "I'm a virgin and I intend to stay that way until the day I get married." This was 1950. We said things like that then. He only smiled. He knew he had me. It was all over.

He had to explain everything to me. I still thought you got pregnant every time you had sex. I didn't know what birth control was; I'd never heard of it. Sex was not talked about, not if you were a good Catholic girl. Which I was. Or was I a bad Catholic girl? I know: good Catholic, bad girl. But it was all crumbling, fading, disappearing under the force of sexual desire. He wanted me. I wanted his wanting. Desire was consuming my virtue.

My legs were spread wide on a blanket on the beach under a black sky blinking with stars and streaking meteors. Over the curve of his shoulders as he entered me, I could see the Milky Way as he pulled me into the power of my sexuality. My fate was sealed. The church doors flew open, I ran from its pious restrictions and, like a brazen tart, hotfooted my way into the intoxicating land of sexual pleasure where all bets were off. There was no redemption possible for me now. I was bad and I liked it.

That night, when I went up to my room, I couldn't believe I'd actually done it. I had a small bedroom with a single bed in front of one of the windows whose sill was level with my mattress. There was no headboard, so many nights I would put my pillow onto the windowsill and even a little further out onto the roof of the front porch. I'd lie with my back on the mattress and my head out the window and look up at the stars. Down below, across the boardwalk, quaking aspen trees grew out of the sandy dunes in front of our cottage. They would shimmer in the moonlight and their silvery rustle in the gentle wind would lull me to sleep as Orion and friends made their slow-motion progress across the night skies.

That night when I came home, no longer a virgin, I placed my pillow out the window and watched the Big Dipper scoop up pails of night to wash over my sticky thighs. Chuck had pulled out at the moment of orgasm and deposited a gooey substance between my legs. He pushed up on his hands as this happened so that I was looking into his face as he came. His eyes seemed to roll back in their sockets under his fluttering lids. I wondered what that felt like. That must be the climax of all this, I thought. I didn't know enough about sex to wonder if I should feel that, too. I wasn't doing this because I wanted that feeling. I was doing it because Chuck wanted me to do it. I wanted to please him. I lay looking up at the sky wondering if we'd get married. Would our children have his beautiful auburn hair? Maybe red when they were little, turning dark red as they got older. I drifted off seeing myself at a screen door calling to a bunch of freckle-faced children to come in for dinner.

The day after the big event, I couldn't wait to see Chuck. I knew which house he was in and went up to the higher boardwalk and knocked on the screen door. A boy came to the door. "Is Mr. Harper in?" I asked.

"No," he said, "but Mrs. Harper is. Would you like to speak to her?"

"No, thank you," I mumbled, and hurried away with a hot face and pounding heart. He was married? Oh my God. I was having an affair with a married man! I couldn't believe he did this to me. He came by my house later. "You're married?" I exploded. His feathers did not ruffle.

"My wife and I are separated. We're getting a divorce," he said calmly. "I just invited her up so the kids could get a little sun."

"Kids?" I gasped. "You have children?" I was flabbergasted.

"Two," he said sweetly. "A boy and a girl."

We walked to his car and my head was muddled. When would he be divorced, I asked him. "Soon," he said, "it's all settled. I'm just waiting for the papers to go through."

Those papers never did go through. Chuck continued to tell me he was separated from his wife and waiting for the divorce to be final for the year and a half that we were together. For all I know he is still married. During the time I was with him, I learned that he'd spent a few years in jail for tax evasion. You'd think that might have been a clue, but I remember feeling that he'd had more life experience than I did and that made him even more attractive.

When we returned from the lake, I was supposed to go to night school to make up the science credits I was lacking, but by then I was already sliding down a thorny path with Chuck. My mother forbade me to see him, so I lied to her and told her I was going to night school, when in reality I was seeing Chuck every night. He moved down from Grand Rapids and got a job selling cars, and at the end of that year I still was minus a few credits to get a diploma, so I didn't graduate from high school.

I went to work for the J. L. Hudson Company, Detroit's largest department store, in the sign department. I was printing signs used in the store and worked all day as a printer getting my hands dark with ink and requiring extensive hand scrubbing at the end of the day. The scrub room was shared with the art department and, standing shoulder-to-shoulder over the huge sink, I came to know the fashion artists. Within two months, they told me of an opening in their department for a model and I got a new job modeling merchandise for the fashion artists as they drew the newspaper ads.

The day before my eighteenth birthday, I was having trouble walking. My toe was infected. My mother took me to the doctor's and he operated on it, bandaged my foot, and told me to go home and stay in bed with my foot elevated for at least three days. "Best to stay off it for a week," he said. I had always planned on leaving home on my eighteenth birthday, so I was very disappointed I would have to stay in bed on my birthday and leave a few days later when my toe had healed. But on the morning of December 7, 1950, my mother said something to me in that scolding, derisive, domineering tone she used when she spoke to her children, and I thought, *I just don't have to take this one more day.* With my foot bandaged up to the ankle, I hobbled out of bed, got my two suitcases down from the closet shelf, and began packing my clothes. My mother could hear me thumping about on my heel and came upstairs.

"What are you doing out of bed?" she asked in a surprised tone.

"Packing my things," I answered without looking at her.

"Why?"

Continuing to pack and still not looking at her, I answered, "Because I'm leaving home."

"But why?" Her voice was beginning to rise.

"Because I am eighteen today. You always said I was under your jurisdiction until I was eighteen." More packing. She started to cry, got angry, began to sputter. I just kept on packing.

Furious now, she blurted out, "If you leave here, I will disown you."

"Fine," I said.

Seeing that this was hardly a threat, she pulled out the heavy guns. "And I won't let you see Steve anymore."

For the first time I paused in my packing and looked at her directly. "Well, that would be very hard on me, but if that is the price I have to pay to get away from you, I'm willing to pay it." She didn't, of course, mean it; she was just desperate.

She left and went down the street and told her sister, Aunt Viola, who returned with her and tried to dissuade me from leaving. There was no force on earth that could have stopped me. I walked out of her house at 3277 Hazelwood, carrying my two suitcases to the bus stop on Dexter, hobbling on one foot, with blood filling the bandage on the other. I was out of there for good.

From this distance, looking at Edna walking away from the house, I'd like to be able to say she was leaving her mother. But it doesn't quite work that way. Some say that the way we enter the world, our birthing process, is a pattern that we repeat over and over in our lives, especially each time we face a crisis. My mother tells me that when she experienced the first of her labor pains with me, she was doing the laundry in the basement of her parents' apartment, where she had moved after my father left. She went upstairs and told her mother to call the doctor. She was in labor. She lifted her leg to get onto the bed and I jumped out. No one knew what to do. The doctor didn't arrive for an hour. In that time my mother lay on the bed with me between her legs, still connected to her by the umbilical cord. She had a blanket over me and I slept soundly until the doctor arrived to cut the cord.

When I left my mother's house in that same abrupt manner, I was still connected to her in a similar way. I had taken into myself her scolding, demeaning, berating voice and I could now continue the criticism myself. In psychological terms, I had introjected her. I got myself out of her house as I had gotten myself out of her womb, but as I hobbled away, bleeding from the very foot that carried me away from her, I was still attached to her through the umbilical cord of self-punishment. And it would be years before the doctor arrived to help me cut the cord.

I hadn't gotten my period for two months.

I moved in with Jackie Napier, one of the fashion artists, and stayed with her until I found my own place—a room in a boardinghouse. I didn't go to a doctor but I was pretty sure I was pregnant because I had morning sickness. I had to get off the bus in the morning to throw up my orange juice in the street. For the next three months I was in a dissociated state. I was something called "pregnant" and I had to do something about it, but at no time did I connect with what was happening inside. I never thought of it as a baby. I didn't think of it as a life growing inside of me, certainly not one with a soul or consciousness. I had to get rid of it and I never thought about what "it" was. I knew I didn't want it—that was as far as my thinking went. I told Jackie about my condition. She had gotten rid of some unwanted pregnancies with something, as I remember, called urgaphine. I bought some at the drugstore, but it only made me vomit, not miscarry.

I had to get some money from somewhere, but I didn't know where. Chuck wouldn't help. "Why don't you just have it?" he said. I knew I'd get no support from him. I was earning $35 a week. I'd die before I'd tell my mother and have her bash me over the head with that weapon. I didn't know what to do. Time went by. Too much time. I was beginning to spread. The merchandise was getting tight on me. I got to be three months pregnant, then four. I was desperate. I didn't know where to go or who to turn to. I still didn't consider having it. I also did not wonder what it was. I needed help, but I didn't know where to ask for it. Then I was five months pregnant and suddenly I looked it. Chuck worked with a guy named Al Mann. He liked me. I went out with him. I told him my problem. He said, "I'll give you the money, Edna." He did. Five hundred dollars.

Of course, in 1950 abortions were illegal. I don't remember how I found the doctor, but I did. He examined me. He said, "Oh, you're too far gone for an abortion. I'll have to induce birth." Whatever that meant. It sounded like another way of getting rid of it. He sent me to another doctor somewhere. I got on an operating table. He put a cold metal instrument inside of me. It hurt. It hurt a lot. Then he drove me to a house. A nurse's flat. Upstairs. I stayed there for three days, walking around her dining room table to "bring it on." It was March and cold outside. Old dead snow was stacked everywhere in dirty mounds. I walked and walked around and around her dining room table. On the third day, I got a pain. "This is it," the nurse said. We went upstairs. I got in bed. Labor. For hours. The doctor came. "Push. Push," he said. I grabbed the slats of the headboard behind me and pushed until I felt a mountain move and pass out of me in a great bloody whoosh.

It was out of me. I lay in a pool of blood on a rubber sheet. The blood coagulated and hardened on my skin. I slept in my own blood.

After a while, the nurse cleaned me up and moved me to the other bed in the room. The doctor came in the room and pulled up a chair beside me. The room was lit only by the light in the hall. He was asking me questions about myself. I can't remember now what they were. I only remember the last moment. He put his hand on my breast, jiggled it, and said, "Tell that bastard to use rubbers." He rose and left. I turned my face to the wall and cried in shame. Shame because I did not feel I had the right to object to his jiggling my breast. After all, who was I to object to anything after what I had just done?

A few years later I saw some photos showing the develement of the fetus month by month. I had never seen anything like that before. When I looked at the fetus in the fifth month I burst into tears. "Oh my God! It was already a baby!" I cried and cried. My mother's voice in my head said, "What did you think it was, dummy?" I didn't think.

That was the problem. I didn't think.

Back at the J. L. Hudson Company, I had told them I missed work for a few days because I had to have my tonsils out. I returned to work two dress sizes smaller. A tonsillectomy is a great way to lose weight—you can't eat, didn't you know that? I saw knowing ironic smirks pass around the Art Department, but so be it. Let them smirk.

My relationship with Chuck continued its downward spiral. I didn't know any psychological or even literary terms like sadomasochism, but I did know what was going on between us was tainted with something other than love. For instance, he liked to make me cry and then have sex with me while I was crying. The harder I was crying, the better. I discerned something there, but I didn't know what. And there was something intensely familiar about it.

Chuck was selling Packards in Royal Oak with another salesman named Bill Alexander, who was very kind to me. One day at the showroom, when

Chuck had stepped out for a minute, Bill said to me, seemingly out of nowhere, "Don't give yourself away completely, Edna. Always hold something back for yourself." I knew I wasn't doing that. I was in the grip of something I couldn't understand, but I could sense I was in danger.

Chuck once said that if he told me he would pick me up or meet me someplace, that he would be there. He might be late, but I should wait because he would definitely come. One day in late March, there was a brutal blizzard. Chuck called to say he'd pick me up after work and to wait for him in the Kresge store across from the side entrance of Hudson's. I finished work at five P.M., when the store closed. I walked through the empty store in dim light. The mannequins had been draped with muslin covers and stared with unmoving eyes as the wind howled outside. The employees exited through the side door and, as the security guard opened the door for me, a blast of cold air blew me back inside. Leaning into the wind, I crossed the icy street and ran into the neon-lit warmth of Kresge's. Sitting at the counter, I ordered a Coke. After an hour, I ordered a hot dog. At eight P.M. the store closed. It was still snowing when I walked outside. The manager locked the door and said good night to me. The door of the store was recessed from the street and had a canopy. It protected me from the falling snow and the wind, but not from the cold. My feet were dry because of the galoshes, but soon the cold of the wet cement penetrated them and crawled up through my feet and chilled my bones. Nine P.M. Still no Chuck. The streetcars were still running on Woodward, one block away, but infrequently. I had been waiting four hours.

Ellen Burstyn, remembering this scene, wonders what was going through the mind of Edna Rae Gillooly as she stood on a dark, deserted street in Detroit more than fifty years ago. Was she just watching the snow fall, thinking he'd come? He said to wait. He might be late, but he'd be there. There were no trees encased in ice on this snowy night. No groaning and tinkling of ice-covered branches. No full, shining moon. No sky could be seen. Only the snow piling up in the street and the closed side entrance of Hudson's department store in front of her. Downtown Detroit was empty. There was only the light from the streetlamp on Woodward a block away and the sound of the wind.

I want to speak to Edna. Tell her to go out on the lit street. Get out of this cold darkness. It's eleven P.M. He said he'd be there at five P.M. You've been waiting six hours, Edna. Go home. What if he shows up now? What does that tell you? Don't do this to yourself. Edna, can you hear me? I wish I could reach my long arm back through those years and pull you into the light of your becoming. But she can't hear me. She is deaf to my counsel. She is still on the path of descent and not yet ready to hear me calling to her.

At midnight Chuck arrived, seven hours after he said he would. His car slid over to the curb. He reached across the passenger seat and smiled a pleased reptilian grin. It was a game. He set her up for this and she took the bait. He had her completely in his power. As she pulled the door open, her teeth were chattering. She said nothing. She got in. She was a patsy. They both knew it.

But who knows? Perhaps she did hear me. In some dimension of being where time doesn't exist and the past and future flow together in an imminent present, perhaps our future can call to us, speak to us, and guide us toward our destiny. I don't know if she heard me. I do know that soon after this, Edna started making plans to get out of Detroit. Away from Chuck. Away from her past and into the future of which she'd always dreamed.

I sat in the dressing room that I shared with the other two models, Joanne Finnegan and Corky MacArthur. Two walls were mirrored from floor to ceiling, so it was hard to avoid seeing yourself. Nevertheless, I noticed that Joanne had a curious habit of changing her face whenever she caught her image in the mirror. She would tilt her head up, suck in her cheeks, and pucker her lips. She seemed to prefer that face to the one the rest of us saw. It was so instantaneous a change that I realized she never saw herself as the rest of us did. I began to wonder if I did that, too. Did I have a face I immediately switched on when I looked in the mirror? Do we all? And I wondered whether we had not only false faces, but false personalities that we hid behind. And if so, how would we know? How might we learn to see ourselves as we really are? All questions to add to my mental notebook of things I'd like to understand.

I was thinking about leaving Detroit and had talked it over with Joanne and Corky. I wanted to see the world. I really wanted to go to Europe, but I'd never been outside of Michigan and it seemed to me somehow unpatriotic or disloyal not to see America first. New York was still a scary idea. Los Angeles seemed a cliché. Chicago was too close to Detroit. I just wasn't sure. As I sat watching Joanne put rouge on her sucked-in cheeks, Corky walked into the dressing room, loosening her belt to get into her next change, and said, "I was just thinking, Edna. Neiman Marcus won the advertising award this year. That's where you should go—Dallas. They like your type there."

"What type is that?" I asked, not knowing I had one.

"The all-American girl," Corky said through the net that covered her head so she wouldn't ruin her hair and makeup as she pulled her next change over her head.

The all-American girl, I thought. Is that what I am? Okay, then, that's where I'll go. Dallas, Texas.

I got a second job. After a day's work at the J. L. Hudson Company, I'd grab a quick bite to eat and then go to work at the Patricia Stevens Modeling School, teaching modeling. I spent the next five months saving my money. With my employee's discount applied to marked-down clothes, I got myself a new wardrobe. By August I was ready to start out. I knew it was going to be an exciting trip. Dallas was my first stop, but in the years to come, I'd be spending time in New York, Hollywood, Paris, London, Rome, Israel, India, Iran, Morocco, Egypt, Cambodia, and Kenya. I boarded that Greyhound bus for Dallas with nothing but a one-way ticket, less than three dollars in cash, two suitcases of new clothes, and a whole lot of emotional baggage.

Posing for a camera club, around 1948.

PART II

On My Way

⁓

*He who would know the world, seek first within
his being's depths; he who would truly know
himself, develop interest in the world.*

RUDOLF STEINER

I wore a pink dress my mother had made for me. I thought it would be cool and wouldn't wrinkle on the thirty-six-hour trip from Detroit to Dallas. But it left my arms and chest exposed and I felt conspicuous as I stood in the Greyhound bus station watching the driver heave my bags into the belly of the bus. I hurried aboard and into a seat next to a window. I wanted to see everything there was to see. It was August 1951, and I was embarking on a new beginning. I'd never been outside of Michigan except for boarding school, never seen what the rest of the world looked like. But the movies told me there were mountains and mansions, waterfalls and elevated trains, tall buildings and exotic gardens, all kinds of magical marvels, and I wanted to see them all. We pulled out of the dark heat of the terminal into the blazing light of day.

Did I bring a book? I don't remember that I did. Certainly no camera. I wasn't a tourist; I was a traveler. I looked out the window for signs of change, because that was what I was after. We drove for hours through Michigan on highways without a single remarkable thing to see. We entered

Ohio, which looked just like Michigan. We stopped every few hours at dingy gas stations that had rest rooms and soft drinks. In one of them I asked a woman behind the counter for a Vernors.

"We don't have that here."

I must have registered surprise because she explained, "That's a Michigan drink."

We passed through Ohio and into Kentucky. Each time the bus came to a bridge, the driver stopped and opened the doors. The heat and the monotony intensified. By late afternoon we pulled into a large bus station in Louisville where we had an hour to wash up, have dinner, and change buses. At the counter I tried to find the cheapest item without mystery ingredients. I settled on a cheese sandwich.

"Cheese sandwich on white bread," I asked the girl behind the counter.

"Whaaat?" she drawled.

"A cheese sandwich on white bread," I repeated enunciating carefully.

"Whaaat?"

Hmm, what could be wrong here, I thought. Then I remembered the Vernors, but surely they have cheese and bread . . . maybe they don't call them sandwiches, I reasoned. I tried again.

"I would like a piece of cheese between two pieces of white bread."

The waitress had also been working on this problem.

"Do you mean *flowah* bread?" she asked.

"Flour bread? Why, yes, I guess I do."

Flour bread and no Vernors—did that count as change?

We managed the transfer of our baggage to the new bus and found our seats. Luckily I got a window again and we pulled out of Louisville into the heat of the evening. The windowpane cooled a bit from the wind outside and I leaned my damp forehead against it as we drove farther south. There was another stop around ten P.M. and then we settled in for the night. As night enveloped us one by one, the passengers disconnected their sight, hearing, and consciousness and sunk beneath the mysterious waters of deep sleep.

I woke up once to stretch out the crick in my neck and heard the sounds the other passengers were making as they slept. An old man across the aisle had his head back and his toothless mouth hung open emitting a hoarse rattle with each exhale. A few seats in front of him, a great gangly boy in overalls whimpered like a puppy in his sleep. All around me was the deep rhythmical breathing of this collection of souls. I drifted off, adding my breathing to the night song.

Hours passed and the light changed. The black went to gray. Again I stretched the sleep from my neck and arms. Pink entered the gray and strips of lavender seeped through. A bright apricot joined in. Other sounds of waking, stretching, yawning. People rising to the surface, cutting through the veil of night. Coughs here and there. No words yet. The *thwack* of a Zippo lighter, then the smell of smoke. All around us now a pink color on all sides and even layers of aquamarine. Then, in that glorious dawning, before any word had yet been spoken, the bus slowed and came to a stop. The doors clunked open, and as we felt the bus start up slowly, the bus driver said in a deep and reverent tone, "Ladies and gentlemen . . . the Mississippi River!"

We sat up in our seats, fully awake now, craning our necks to see the great gift that had just been presented to us. Our wheels rumbled over the bridge as we crossed this great river. It was smaller and muddier than I'd imagined, but it didn't matter. It was the mighty Mississippi and we were crossing over into a new part of the country, into a new life. The light changed. Everyone on the bus was glowing. I turned and looked behind me and from out the back window I saw the gorgeous hot orange ball of sunshine rising to bless us all. When I turned back, I saw the sun had burnished the shoulders and head of this kind bus driver whose job was just to drive us to Dallas, but whose generous soul had presented to us the miracle of crossing over into a new world, a new beginning.

And even so, I saw that that world would be lit from behind. Always what we are leaving behind will be the source of light and shadow of what we are going toward.

As the sun rose higher, so did the heat. We were in Arkansas. It was flat and dry. Long stretches with no trees. We passed a deserted bus stop with a broken screen door and a rusted Nehi sign dangling from one end. We passed broken-down trucks, goats in a dump. Fields where nothing seemed to be growing. An encampment of sorts, hundreds of shacks, open doors revealing dirt floors inside. Children were playing, their feet bare and their clothing in rags. A baby cried pitifully from somewhere and a skinny dog ran from a boy with a stick in his hand. A woman sat on a brown chair with its stuffing hanging out, her legs open and her hands hanging between her knees. Her face was long and her eyes sunken. As we whizzed by, her eyes caught mine. Just for a second, maybe two, my eyes looked into the eyes of poverty. In that swift look something shifted in me. Suddenly my life seemed privileged. True, I had no money, less than two dollars, in fact, but my purse jingled with possibilities. I was traveling in my pink dress and high heels to a new life. That woman wasn't going anywhere. She was trapped in a life whose future was just like her past.

When we got to Texarkana, the gateway to Texas, it was 105 degrees. I stood outside the bus station drinking a sarsaparilla. There were horses tied to the hitching posts that lined the dirt street. A cowboy near me was rolling a cigarette from a pouch of Bull Durham. There were few cars. It felt like a Western movie, but it wasn't. It was the West and I was in it.

In Arkansas I'd noticed the ladies' room doors in the little bus stations had a sign, "Whites Only," as did the drinking fountains. I grew curious where the non-whites went, so on one of the Texas stops I casually walked around the building and found the "Coloreds Only" door and drinking fountain. As dreary as these little stops were in the front, out back it was even dingier. When I saw those signs, I felt ashamed of my race and the way we treated fellow human beings. I didn't know what to do with the feelings aroused by these signs and the sights of poverty we passed, but they were acute, and remain alive in me today.

We drove all day through the desert heat of Texas and when we pulled into Dallas in the evening, the temperature was still over 100 degrees. I lugged my two suitcases to the hotel nearest the bus station. It was the first time I ever stayed in a hotel. I checked in with less than a dollar in my purse, but I felt sure I'd get a job the next day. After all, I was the all-American girl.

Once I got my suitcases into the room, I couldn't wait to go out and see Dallas. The hotel was not in a fancy part of town: penny arcades, tattoo parlors, burlesque houses, lots of neon lights, people walking arm in arm. Suddenly, I saw on the sidewalk a cockroach as big as a baby chipmunk. I looked around trying to catch someone's eye. Perhaps we should notify the authorities, call the Smithsonian? But everyone looked unconcerned. Then I saw why. There were lots of them. People were not only ignoring them, they were stepping on them, crunching them loudly like potato chips beneath their cowboy boots! I was in Texas all right. Big D! Even the cockroaches were big! I couldn't bring myself to step on them and I cut a circuitous path down the sidewalk for a few blocks before I wound my way back to the hotel and crawled into the clean bed.

Next morning, the temperature was 110 degrees and I discovered a major error in my plan. I'd come to Dallas in August because in Detroit the fashion shows for the new fall fashions are held that month. Dallas is way too hot in August and anyone who could afford to be thinking about fashion had left town for their summer home or cottage on a lake. The retail stores were dead in August. The very nice lady in the personnel department of Neiman Marcus suggested I come back in a month. A month? I couldn't last that long. I needed a job today! I spent the morning on the streets of Dallas just walking into stores asking if they needed a model, eventually lowering that to "help."

Then I spotted a Patricia Stevens Modeling School and I went inside and told them that I'd taught at the school in Detroit. This school was run by Patricia's brother, Patrick, who invited me into his office. I told him my story, how I'd made a mistake and come a month early. I asked him if he had any suggestions. He explained that they were not hiring for the same reason the stores weren't, but that the wholesale market was coming to town that very weekend and they hired models to show their lines to the local buyers. That was great news. Now I just had to last until the weekend. I didn't really know what to do with myself for a week in a strange city without money, so I walked the hot streets and came upon a bookstore that was having a sale. There were tables out on the street lined with books. One table had books for a dollar, then there was a fifty-cent table, and then a thirty-five-cent one. There I found T. S. Eliot's *Collected Poems 1909–1935*. It had a bright yellow jacket. I hold that book in my hand now. I have to wonder why Edna, an uneducated, green girl, selected this erudite poet to keep her company that lonely week. I imagine that his was probably the only name on the table she might have heard of and he was cheap!

At any rate, that thirty-five-cent purchase left me with my last thirty-five cents, which I decided to spend on dinner. I had passed a diner earlier in the day with a sign in the window advertising chili for thirty-five cents. I enjoyed a bowl of spicy chili, but when the check came, there was two cents tax on it and I had to apologize to the man behind the counter that I didn't have the tax.

Then I made a plan for the rest of the week. I didn't know you could sign the check for your meals in the coffee shop of the hotel, but I did know you could sign for room service. I think I saw that in the movies. I decided I would have one meal per day in my room for the rest of the week and put it on my hotel bill. By Saturday morning, when the salesmen were due to set up shop in their rooms at the two main hotels in town, the Baker and the Adolphus, I was one thin model.

I went from room to room at both hotels asking if anyone needed a model. Most of them had already hired their models or brought them with them. But in one room when I asked if they needed a model, the salesman answered, "I don't, but I know a guy over in the Southland Hotel that needs one." I didn't know it then, but I later learned that no reputable salesman showed at the Southland, just guys who couldn't afford the two big hotels. I went over to the smaller hotel down the street and found the salesman. I tried on his line of sportswear, which fit fine, and he offered me the job for a week at $25. I told him that I'd been presented with my hotel bill and it was $35. I had to earn at least that. He said he wasn't authorized to pay more than $25, but if I wanted to come back and meet the sales manager, who was due in at eight P.M., I could ask him. He suggested I have dinner with them and I was elated. A dinner out of the hotel, paid for by someone else! I returned at eight, made up, hair curled, in my best dress, excited, and hungry. The sales manager was short, balding, with a belly and a smelly cigar stuffed in his face. "How's that nightgown fit?"

"I didn't try on the lingerie. Only the sportswear," I said hesitantly.

"To hell with the sportswear. We can sell that ourselves. We need a model to sell the lingerie. Here, put this on."

I remember having a sad, wary feeling descend on me and settle in my stomach. I went into the bathroom, put on the nightgown, and modeled it for the sales manager, who sat on the couch with one arm over the back and the other holding his cigar. He peered at me through the smoke and said, "Put on that pink one."

I took the pink nightgown from the rack, saying nothing but feeling more uneasy. After I modeled the pink one, he took a puff of his cigar and said, "Let's see ya in the black one."

I could feel my face go red and hot. I said, "What's going on? You only have to see one garment to know if the line is going to fit."

He said, "Okay. Put your clothes on," making it sound somehow like I was naked. When I was dressed and combing my hair, there was a knock on the bathroom door. The salesman squeezed himself into the tiny room. He was examining his shoes at great length as he said, "Okay, the sales manager says you can have the job for thirty-five dollars for the week, but . . . ah . . . he'll ah . . . expect you to go out with him a few times."

"What does that mean, go out with him?"

Still looking at his shoes, he muttered, "Well . . . I guess . . . he'll expect you to go to bed with him."

I picked up my bag, scooped up all those nightgowns, and dropped them in the sales manager's lap as I said, "Thank you. But I'll never be that hungry." And I left.

But I was very hungry. Back at the hotel now, I discovered room service ended at eight. It was now close to nine and I still hadn't learned about signing for dinner in the coffee shop. So I didn't eat that day. Sunday morning, on my way out of the hotel, the manager stopped me in the lobby and asked when I was going to pay my bill. "Tonight," I answered him. "I'll pay you tonight." I stepped out into the blast furnace of Dallas in the throes of a searing heat wave, my stomach growling madly.

I went to the Baker Hotel first, and walked up and down the hallways. Many of the doors had signs outside, but the doors weren't open for business. I crossed the street to the Adolphus Hotel and it was the same thing. I asked the man at the desk when the salesmen opened their doors and was told that "the market opens at nine." It was only eight. I wasn't sure where to go, so I decided to stay there and wait. There was a beautiful sitting area in the lobby surrounded by graceful potted palms. I stepped onto the elegant Oriental carpet and saw tall upholstered chairs that looked like thrones. No one else was there. I selected a throne and was glad to feel that my feet did, in fact, touch the floor when I sat down.

After a little while a woman entered. She had a halo of white hair, was wearing a light summer dress, white shoes, and white lace gloves. She walked with a cane and seemed almost transparent. She selected a chair not too far from me. Once seated, she looked at me and said with a soft southern accent, "Good morning."

We chatted a while about the heat and I told her I had never experienced heat like this before. She asked me where I was from and soon I was telling her my whole story. When I got to the part about not having eaten since Friday, she said, "Oh, you must let me buy you breakfast."

Now, did I edge her into that invitation? I can't remember that I did. That is, I didn't calculate that if I said I was hungry, she would offer me food. But in the moment that I let it come out, did I hope she would offer? Probably. I was operating at the survival level and in that realm there is very little room for anything but the plain truth.

"Oh, I couldn't let you do that," I managed to say, but it was a faint protest.

At that moment this transparent being turned her mild, clear eyes to me and said, "Oh please, dear, don't deny me this. If you will allow me to buy you breakfast this morning, you will remember me for the rest of your life."

And so I have.

❧

Needless to say, I stuffed myself on "the kindness of this stranger" and with a belly full of bacon, pancakes, orange juice, and coffee, I thanked her heartily and set off to land the job I had to get that day for sure.

All the doors were open now. I inquired at each one, "Do you need a model?"

Floor after floor, I collected a string of no's that was weighing me down like a ball and chain. What would happen to me if I didn't pay my hotel bill that day?

Finally, at one door, in answer to my oft-repeated query, "Do you need a model?" a salesman replied, "Yes."

"You do?" I asked, excited.

The salesman laughed and said, "Yeah, if you can wear size 42½."

I burst into tears. The salesman was shocked and asked me what the matter was. I blurted out my story to him.

This whole scene I put into *Alice Doesn't Live Here Anymore,* where Alice is going from bar to bar looking for a job as a singer. In one bar the owner jokingly says, "Yes." When Alice realizes he's kidding, she bursts into tears and tells him her story. The owner, played by Murray Moston, keeps saying, "I don't even have a piano in here." Eventually he breaks down, gives her a job, and gets her a piano.

Well, this salesman had a friend in the building who did need a model. He called him on the phone and sent me down to him saying I was "a friend of the family." When I arrived in the room, that salesman was already showing a dress on a hanger to the buyer from Tiche Goettinger's. He said, "Here, put this on."

I came out of the bathroom in the dress, which fit perfectly. Size 7. I could have gotten into a 5. The buyer placed a big order and offered me a job at her store selling dresses after the market closed. The salesman, Carl, was so pleased with the big order, he was willing to advance me a week's salary.

I thanked him with my sexuality, which is what I used sex for at that time. Though I was indignant that anyone would be so crass as to offer me money or a job and expect me to go to bed with them, sex was my way of saying thank you.

Back at the hotel that night, I couldn't get my door open. The key wouldn't go in. I didn't understand what was wrong. A maid in a white uniform with ebony skin was getting sheets out of a closet a few doors down.

"Can you help me? I can't seem to get my key in the lock."

She tried inserting the key. When it wouldn't go in, she put her eyes to the lock and, straightening up, said in a lovely deep voice, "Honey, you been plugged."

"What does that mean?"

"Did you pay your rent?" she asked.

I thanked her and marched to the manager's office, waving my money in my hand, outraged. I was surprised to see my two suitcases against the wall behind his desk. Now I knew what would happen if I didn't pay my bill.

As I handed him the money, I said haughtily, "I told you I'd pay you tonight."

Soon I was selling dresses at Tiche's department store and sharing an apartment with three airline stewardesses who flew for Braniff Airlines.

During this period I went out with many of the young bachelors of Dallas, including Fenton Baker, Jr., whose father owned the Baker Hotel. Sitting in the Baker family's palatial living room, I wondered what they would think if they knew that a few weeks before I was wandering the halls of their hotel desperate to get a job so I wouldn't be put out on the street.

Texas was a dry state then, so whoever could afford it belonged to a private club, where rich people could drink all they wanted. One of the most exclusive clubs in Dallas was the Cipango Club where I was often taken on dates. It was here I had my first alcoholic drink, a French 75, made with brandy and champagne, a lethal combination I continued to drink until I learned better. I enjoyed the best food and wore the fancy dresses I'd bought with my employee's discount at Hudson's. If I didn't have a date, I didn't eat. But I always thanked them in my own way. My gratitude was downright promiscuous. The three stewardesses and I were seldom home and the refrigerator was always empty, except for a few items like Kraft parmesan cheese, a jar of olives, and some maraschino cherries.

When Thanksgiving came, all my bachelor friends disappeared into their families. It was my first Thanksgiving away from home and I was going to spend it alone. I couldn't afford a turkey dinner anywhere, but I found a White Castle within walking distance of the apartment and sat at the counter. I remember I ordered a twin burger and when it was put in front of me, I put my hands around the plate, looked down at these tiny little hamburgers in their warm buns and felt so content. I was not at my mother's table. I was not in Detroit. I was out in the world. All by myself. And I was free.

Sometime in this period, I got a job in Fort Worth at a store called Wally Williams. I lied about my age and experience and was given the position of fashion coordinator. I organized, produced, and narrated their fashion shows.

There I made friends with a customer named Dorothy Topalian. She was a tall woman in her forties who had once been a burlesque queen. She showed me clippings of her act. Her stage name had been Butch Bigby. One night, a stage-door Johnny presented his credentials. Mr. Surene Topalian was a wealthy Syrian businessman. Butch married him, moved to Damascus, and lived like an Arabian princess. After ten years of that life, Mrs. Topalian grew bored, left her husband, and now, past showgirl age, had moved back to her home, where she had enough money but not enough sex. At her age, she found it hard to attract men, so I became her decoy. We would go out to dinner at a local restaurant, Dorothy would case the joint, select the guy she wanted for the night, and say to me sweetly, "That one." I would then flirt with this stranger until he appeared at our table and I'd invite him to sit down. Then Dorothy took over and I took a fade. When I saw she had his interest, I'd excuse myself, go to the ladies' room to slowly repair my makeup. By the time I returned they were either going or gone.

I began pumping Dorothy for stories about New York. I had a record album (which I still have) called *Manhattan Tower.* It began, "It was raining the first time I saw my tower . . ." It was a romantic love affair with the whole New York experience and I started yearning to go there. One night Dorothy told me about a friend in New York named Carl Berger, whom she referred to as a crazy psychiatrist. She called him on the phone and introduced me. He said, "If you are a friend of Dorothy's, then you are a friend of mine. When you come to town, I'll take care of you. Just get here. I'll do all the rest." He did sound a bit crazy, the way he talked. His voice rose very high at the end of each sentence. I wasn't sure I'd ever call him, but I kept his number. Soon after, I was offered a job in Houston as fashion coordinator of Battlestein's department store. It was the same job I had in Fort Worth, but Battlestein's had a popular weekly fashion show on television. It had the highest rating of any local show in Texas. A television show! That sounded right to me.

I began dating a guy named Nick, who was a disc jockey who'd had a popular radio show that had just gone off the air when we met. I didn't last long in this job because Mrs. Battlestein took a dislike to me, complaining that I didn't wear a girdle. I was eighteen years old and a size 7. What did I need a girdle for? We parted ways and I had to think what my next move would be. I couldn't pay my rent, but Nick said he had a place for me. He drove me to a part of Houston I didn't know and installed me in his friend Betty's little frame house. Betty was a devoted fan of Nick's and was glad to do him the favor of taking me in. Betty was in her sixties, wore her house slippers with socks all day, and seemed a bit dimwitted. Nick left and I didn't see him for a few days until he returned with groceries for us. We spent some time in my bedroom, then he left again. I had no money, no job, I didn't know this part of town, and I didn't know what bus to take to get out of here to look for a job. The next time Nick brought groceries, I asked if he would take me into town to look for a job. He couldn't. He said he was busy. Another visit to my room and he was gone. It was dawning on me that I was a captive and Betty was my jailer. The next time Nick came I asked him to take me out for a ride. I was going stir-crazy. In the car I told him I needed to get out of there and get a job.

"What do you need a job for?"

"So I can earn some money," I explained.

"You got a roof over your head. I bring you food. What more do you want?" he shouted.

"I want my own money. I don't want to live with Betty. I want to get out of there."

Bam! He backhanded me in the face, hard. I went silent. I'd had enough experience with violence to know that no reaction was the best response. Don't rile him further, I thought. He took me back to Betty's and left. Now I really had to make a move. I didn't want to wait around for what would follow.

The next day I asked Betty if it would be all right if I took some bottles back so I could buy a pack of cigarettes. Frowning, she thought for a while and then said, "I don't think Nick would mind that."

I'd spotted a store a few blocks away when Nick and I had gone for that drive. I turned in the bottles and asked if I could use the man's phone. I didn't even consider calling my mother, but I thought my godfather, my uncle Dave, would help me out. The man in the store agreed to receive the wire for me and, next morning, I packed my bags and sneaked out with them before Betty woke up. I sat on them until the man came to open the store. When the wire came through he helped me get the cash.

By evening I was on a train to New York City. I had asked my uncle for just enough money to get me there. The trip took twelve hours. I had no money for food, but I carried with me *The Complete Plays of William Shakespeare* and read *Titus Andronicus*. When they ate the children baked in the pie, it made me feel queasy and killed my appetite. That helped me get to New York City on an empty stomach—that and some soldiers across the aisle from me who also had no money but carried a big bag of apples, which they kindly shared with me. Appropriately I arrived in the Big Apple with nothing in me but apples. When we pulled into Penn Station, I had forty-five cents in my bag and the phone number of a crazy psychiatrist.

March 19, 1952. Pennsylvania Station—people, many people moving fast. These people were in fast-forward, jostling, elbowing, surging. I was standing still in the midst of it, not knowing where to go, a suitcase in each hand. I spotted a newsstand. I got myself to it and asked the man with the newspapers (in my southwestern twangy drawl I'd picked up) where I could find a telephone. "Ovah dere," he growled and motioned with his head. I almost cried. Did I do something wrong? Why was he mad at me? I stood rooted to the spot, mouth open, wondering how I'd offended him. He looked up, was surprised to see me still standing there and repeated in a louder growl, "Ovah dere!" This time he jerked his thumb in the direction.

I put in my dime. It was eight A.M. The sleepy voice of the crazy psychiatrist answered. When I explained who I was and reminded him of our telephone conversation, he said groggily, "It's too early. Call me back in an hour. I'll be awake then," and he hung up. Now what?

I spotted a row of lockers not too far away. I could fit both suitcases in one for a quarter. That left me with only the dime I needed to call the crazy psychiatrist at nine o'clock. My stomach was growling. Hunger was taking over all my attention. I'd had nothing to eat since yesterday's apples. It was hard to think of anything else. I smelled coffee somewhere and moved toward it. There was a line of people from the cashier out through the door of the coffee shop. I got on line. I didn't have a plan. I was just going to order breakfast, stop this raging hunger, and then figure out what to do. A space opened up at the counter and I was next in line. I knew I had no right to that seat, but I took it. I read the menu in a high state of excitement and ordered breakfast. The coffee shop was packed and full of smoke. I don't remember who was on my right, but on my left was a pleasant-looking middle-aged man in a business suit and a tie.

I struck up a conversation with him. I told him in my newly acquired Texas accent that it was my first day in New York and I just couldn't believe the numbers of people, "all in a hurry, goin' so fast." I must've batted my eyelashes. We finished breakfast around the same time and I said good-bye to him and thanked him for all his good advice while I opened my bag and searched for my wallet. Oh no! I told him I'd left my wallet in a suitcase locked away. He reached for my check of $1.25 and said, "Here, I'll take it."

"Oh, that is so kind of you," I gushed. Once outside the door I said, "If you'll just walk with me to the lockers, I'll pay you back. They're just downstairs around the back, down that long hall . . ." I made it sound like Toledo, Ohio.

"Oh, that's all right," he said, and I thanked him profusely for his generosity. I never knew if the guy knew he'd been hustled or not, but hustled he was.

How did I feel about having done that? I felt daring! I felt like a criminal who had just pulled off a major heist. I felt jubilant I'd gotten away with it. I felt afraid the man was going to reappear with a policeman and arrest me. I felt ashamed I'd lied so shamelessly. I felt alive in the current of the river of life. I felt confident I could get along in the world. I felt guilty I'd taken advantage of that nice man's kindness and good manners. But most of all I felt full. I felt happy I wasn't hungry anymore. I felt ready to take on my next task.

When the crazy psychiatrist was fully awake he suggested I take a taxi to the Croydon Hotel, where he had booked a room for me. I said, "I don't have cab fare there."

"Call me back in ten minutes and I'll tell you what arrangements I've made," he said.

"I used my last dime for this call," I told him.

"Well . . . ah, just take a taxi to the Croydon and I'll arrange for the doorman to pay the fare."

I did that. In the cab I was pressed against the windows looking at the tall buildings. So many people, so many cars, huge apartment buildings to the left, a huge park to the right.

I'm going to like New York, I thought.

From my room in the Croydon Hotel on East 86th Street, I called the crazy psychiatrist and he asked me to come see him at six, when his office hours ended. I had the day to myself. I walked out onto the streets of New York and discovered a parade. Drums and bagpipes and majorettes marched down Fifth Avenue. My heart kept time with the thrum of the drums. I was elated. I felt like the parade was especially timed for my first day in New York. I turned to a stranger and asked what the parade was for.

"St. Patrick's Day," he said.

It *is* for me, I'm Irish—I'm part of this, too. I'm in New York City and I'm part of it, of the whole passing parade.

At six o'clock I was ushered into a spacious living room in a very large apartment to wait for Dr. Berger. Soon he bustled in, in a flurry of high energy. He looked like he was in his fifties; he had very little hair, was overweight, and wore large glasses that made his eyes look owlish. He told me to wait a minute longer while he got ready. In a few moments he called for me to come into his bedroom. All four walls were lined with books, and books were stacked in tall piles on the floor. There was a path to the bathroom and a path to the bed and one to a chair. Everywhere else there were books. On top of the stacks on the floor, there were many packs of Polaroid pictures held with rubber bands—hundreds of them. Dr. Berger was in bed. The bed was full of books, papers, a Polaroid camera, and other items.

He motioned me to a chair and began asking me questions about myself, which I answered, clutching my handbag. I felt very shy talking to this extremely eccentric man, whom I didn't know, while he was in his bed. His voice was pitched high in his throat and he had this disconcerting way of making it glide way up at the end of each sentence as though he were making a statement and then turning it into a question as if to say, *Yes? You agree? Isn't that right?* I found myself nodding a lot. He decided I needed a place to live and called a woman named Fritzi Schatel, who agreed to let me stay in her spare bedroom. Now I must have someone to show me around the city. He phoned a man he called The Baron. "No, no, no," Dr. Berger said. "This is a very nice girl. I promise you will like her. Francis, I'm sorry about that. I didn't realize she was an alcoholic! . . . . Well, this will make up for that. I'm truly sorry. Fine. Tomorrow then. At what time?"

So I had a place to stay and an escort to show me the city. I was all set.

"What kind of fanny do you have? Hmmm?" Carl asked, his voice sliding up through the ceiling, his eyes widening.

"Excuse me?" I stammered.

"Stand up," Carl commanded. I obeyed. "Turn around," he commanded again. I obeyed again, slowly. "Hmmm," he said. "Pull up your skirt. Let me see."

I turned back feeling frightened and unsure of what was happening. He saw my face and said, "I'm not going to hurt you. I just want to see it. And take a picture. Didn't Butch tell you? Hmmm? I'm a fanny man. Seeee?" He reached for a few stacks of Polaroids and held them out. Each picture was of a woman's bottom. No face, no legs, not even a back. Just the buttocks, one after another. Hundreds of them around the room.

And this man was a psychiatrist! I'd never encountered anything like this. I'd been afraid of him until now. He had seemed strange, but somehow powerful. Now I felt a little sorry for him. He seemed pathetic. Like *he* needed a psychiatrist.

He said, "I won't touch you. This is just my hobby. I love women's fannies. Hmmm?"

I felt embarrassed, but I did it. I added my Polaroided bottom to his collection. After all, I had said thank-you with my whole body for dinners.

Fritzi Schatel was a chanteuse from the cafés of Berlin. She had wiry gray hair that fell past her shoulders and must have once been a rich brown. She spoke in a deep voice through a veil of cigarette smoke. Her eyes were heavily lidded, and she had an air of old-world irony and wry sophistication. Her apartment on East 85th Street was in a brownstone with very high ceilings. Someone had built a sleeping loft over part of the living room that was reached by a ladder in the kitchen. It was big enough for a bed, a chest of drawers, and a nightstand with a lamp. It seemed cozy and romantic to me. I loved it. The kitchen was tiny, but large enough for Fritzi to make her dinner every night as well as a second meal that she cooked for the estranged husband of Marlene Dietrich, who lived a block away. Fritzi and Marlene had been friends in Berlin, but somehow in the dissolution of Marlene's marriage, Fritzi inherited the care and feeding of the ex-husband.

Fritzi was my first European friend. Baron Francis Von Kahler was the second and he became one of the most important and enduring friends of my life. Francis took me to my first Broadway play (*The Moon Is Blue,* with Barbara Bel Geddes), my first lecture (Arnold Toynbee at Town Hall), and my first panel discussion ("The Causes of War"). We met almost every Sunday on the terrace of the Museum of Modern Art for breakfast and the *New York Times,* reading whole columns to each other over coffee. At night, after my dates, I would join Francis and another German friend, Walter Henchel, at the Coffee Mill on 56th Street for a late-night coffee, and we'd share stories of our evenings. My relationship with Francis, who was in his fifties, was not a sexual one, but it was deep and intense. He was my first mentor. He often gave me books to read, such as *Zen in the Art of Archery* and *The Bhagavad Gita*. Francis enjoyed the presence of attractive women and never asked for anything in return but our company and conversation. He was a great friend.

He introduced me to a lovely couple, the Isaacs, who were also from Berlin. I didn't put it all together until later that they were all German Jews who had escaped Hitler. Francis told me that his grandfather was named Cohen and he was the first Austrian Jew to be given a title. Francis had been a lawyer in Berlin, but fled when Hitler came to power. In New York he sold insurance. But Francis was a clown at heart and always made us laugh.

My third European friend was a Romanian photographer, Jean Vasilescu, who had a studio on West 46th Street, where he lived with his cat, Pinko. Jean was an opera lover; he took me to the old Metropolitan Opera House, where we stood in the back and heard the great Chaliapin sing *Don Carlos*.

Jean took photos of me that I used to get modeling work. I answered an ad for chorus girls at the Old Nickelodeon and I got the job. It was to be a Gay Nineties revue and the choreographer was a girl who looked remarkably like me named Nona MacDonald. We rehearsed for a week and were set to open on the weekend. On Thursday the owner came in and said they had a party of men who were coming in that night and they were disappointed to learn that there would not be a line of girls. He asked us if we wouldn't mind doing him a favor and coming in and just sitting at the table with these guys. We agreed and that night joined a party of ten nice men. I ordered a French 75.

At my first sip I looked at one of the other girls and I saw the look on her face. We exchanged a silent communication. The owner was charging these guys for expensive drinks and serving us ginger ale, expecting us to cover for them. Looks darted among the girls and we all decided not to blow the whistle on our employers.

When the party was over I went to the owner and said, "When I order a drink, I expect to get it and not ginger ale while you charge the customer for the real thing."

Next day I was fired. Nona felt bad about it, so she introduced me to a choreographer named Boots McKenna who produced shows in three cities—Boston, Montreal, and New York. He said he could use another girl in each city. I preferred New York, but he cautioned me that this was not the best of the three clubs. Francis and I decided to see the show in New York before I chose, so we went downtown to the Old Rumanian. It was a huge place with few customers on a weeknight. A Sophie Tucker–style singer belted out some songs, a line of girls danced in a desultory way, and then a comic appeared. Playing to three tables in an empty barn is a comic's nightmare. I started laughing loudly and got the other tables laughing. Then I began bantering with the comic. There was a seltzer bottle on the table and I spritzed him at one point. We were doing an improvisation, though I didn't know what to call it at the time. Everyone, including the comic, was laughing. He looked like a man who had been rescued from comedy hell. When the show was over, he hurried to our table and breathlessly asked, "Who *are* you?" This became a refrain of Francis's for years. Whenever I said something that surprised or amused him in some way, he would narrow his eyes at me and say in a dramatic voice, "Who *are* you?" For years Francis ended most of his letters to me with that line. It was a very good question. Who was I? I certainly had no idea. But it was as if that comic recognized me. As if, had I answered "Ellen Burstyn," he would have said, "Oh! No wonder!" But there was no Ellen Burstyn then. Was there? I guess she was there in some nascent way. This is an idea that still intrigues me. My friend Jean Houston first introduced me to the word "entelechy." She said, "The entelechy of the oak tree is in the acorn." It's the realization of the full potential of the being already present in the seed. Aristotle coined the word. Jung uses it, too. So does Rupert Sheldrake. The idea that there is a life force in each of us, pulling us toward who we really are. Sheldrake refers to "future attractors." It is an idea that I see in action in my life.

I decided against the Old Rumanian and chose Montreal, the best club, although I had little experience except my dancing and acrobatics lessons as a teenager. Somewhere along the way, Boots and I started having an affair. He was fifty-two and I was nineteen, but I was a pushover for any man who actually seemed interested in me.

I had to rehearse in Boston, and the girls were very friendly and I loved rehearsing with them. I felt like I was fulfilling a dream spawned watching Betty Grable movies in Detroit. I was a hoofer in tights; I was in showbiz. When we "took five," most of the girls lit their cigarettes and put their long legs up on chairs. They looked so cool, I wanted to be just like them, so I accepted my first cigarette when they offered it to me. I was cool, all right, and I developed an addiction to tobacco that would take more than twenty years to break.

After two weeks of rehearsing with the dancers in Boston, Boots decided I could handle the more complex routines in the show at the Chez Paree. By the time we arrived in Montreal, I had changed my name to Keri Flynn, joined AFTRA, my first theatrical union, and was engaged to marry Boots McKenna, who was over thirty years older than me.

The line of dancers was excellent; real dancers, not showgirls. The lead dancer, Bernice, danced en pointe. She was a classical ballerina, but she had grown too tall for the ballet, so she did her pliés and pirouettes on the stage of the Chez Paree. We rehearsed a gaucho number with much foot stomping and finger clicking. I could fake my way through that one, but the second number was practically *Sleeping Beauty*. One of the featured acts for these two weeks was Ving Merlin and His Enchanted Strings. Ving was a classical violinist who had put together a nightclub act with six young pretty violinists all playing in various formations onstage. We were to be in flowing pink gowns and carry dummy white violins and weave in and out of the formations of Ving's girls while we did some very fancy footwork.

I began to have serious doubts that I was going to be able to pull this off. I wasn't sure I was even going to remember the routines. My kicks were high and I could do all the steps slowly, but I wasn't sure I could do it all up to speed.

Dress rehearsal was a mess, as usual. I prayed that the old adage the girls told me, "Good dress, bad show; bad dress, good show," was reliable. By opening night I was terrified. It was my first opening night except for high school and the fashion shows, and I thought the racing in my chest was probably bad for my health, but I didn't care as long as I didn't black out and fall off the stage. We came onstage to the exciting Spanish music in our black gaucho hats, stamping our little gaucho feet. I was so scared I must have looked like I was frozen, because at one point, when we grabbed hands and twirled each other around, the hand holding mine suddenly scratched my palm with its third finger in an obscene gesture that I remembered from grade school. It shocked me into focusing on the face I was twirling with. Lorraine! I snapped back to reality from the plane of fear I'd been vacated to. She smiled at me and I felt the ice on my face crack as I smiled back. Unfortunately, my mouth was so dry that when I smiled my lip stuck to my gum like Velcro and I did the rest of the number with my teeth bared by a hung-up lip.

As we came offstage, sweating and panting, into the kitchen, I pointed to my lip and made loud grunting sounds. Bernice grabbed a lemon and squeezed it into my mouth for irrigation. The other girls were trying to be sympathetic, but they were laughing too hard. Bernice showed me the bowl of lemon wedges that were kept on the counter for us and instructed me to suck on one every night before I went on. You can be sure that I did. Who knew that insufficient saliva was going to be a problem?

We dried off downstairs in the dressing room, touched up our makeup, got into our flowing pink chiffon, and affixed our tiaras onto our heads.

The stage manager came to our door and said, "Are the ladies of the ensemble ready?" His little joke, each show. It always elicited groans.

This was the one I was afraid of. There were many different formations around the stage, all choreographed to whirl around Ving and his girls. The stage was lit like moonlight and the blue light on our white violins made lovely patterns onstage. A violin in the wrong place would blow the whole intricate design. I was all right until about halfway through, when I suddenly went blank. What was the next step? Tracy was on my right shoulder. I felt her spin off upstage. I spun with her. Wrong! She ended in a pose upstage. I'd never been there before. Where should I be? Oh look, there's one girl on the stage right stairway, violin raised toward the stage. And the stage left stairway is empty! That's supposed to be me! Can I get there? No, I'll trip up Bernice who is jetéing all over the stage in between Ving's girls (who were playing their hearts out). Better stay here. How do I get to my next position? What is it? Can't remember. Here we go. Oh my God, I can't follow Tracy again. Oh good, they're forming a line. That's it. I belong next to Donna. Where is she? There! Okay. I'm back.

I felt so ashamed, but Boots was very understanding, and by the second show I was able to get control of myself and fall into line.

Once the show was stabilized, Boots went back to New York and I settled into the life of a chorus girl in Montreal.

After the show, we went to an all-night club that had a room upstairs reserved for performers in town. We'd congregate around two A.M. as all the clubs closed and everybody would do their act for the other performers. I remember Kaye Ballard singing, doing her Judy Garland imitation, and the comics Alan King, Alan Dale, and Charlotte Rae.

We went there every night and had something to eat and drink. We visited each other's tables. It was my introduction to the great camaraderie of show folk. Sometimes we stayed only an hour, but sometimes we stayed until dawn, and then we walked home in groups of two or three or four to our respective apartments while the rest of the world was just waking up.

I had moved in with an ex-dancer named Bonnie, who was married to a hockey player with the Montreal Canadiens. They rented me their spare bedroom. I was sleeping in a lot of spare rooms that year.

One evening, I was just waking up to go to work. I sat up in bed looking out the window at the people going home from work in the pink light of the setting sun. My arms over the pink coverlet, I felt very peaceful. I wondered, *Have I found where I belong? Is it that I'm not out of step with the rest of the world, I just need to work the other end of the clock? Am I a night person? Is that it?* I didn't know. I only knew that in the quiet evening of a foreign city, gazing from the window, I had my first tinge of a sense of belonging.

Temporary though it was, it stirred in me an awareness of what belonging felt like, and I longed to make it a permanent part of me.

One of the things that attracted the best dancers to the Chez Paree was that there was no mandatory mingling. The girls called it "mangling." If we were requested to join a party between shows, we'd peek out from behind a curtain and decide whether we liked the looks of the group. Often we sent our regrets and we'd either go out or, most often, hang out together in the dressing room with our legs up on the table and talk about boyfriends, husbands, babies, new additions on the house, and all the soft talk of women together.

We were often offered tips, but I never took one because I didn't like the idea of getting paid to socialize with someone. Except once, I did. I sat with a party of four very nice businessmen in the bicycle business. When I told them I had to go back to work, they offered me a tip. I declined, but asked them if there was any way I could get a bike from them for my brother in Detroit. They arranged to have their distributor there deliver a bicycle to my thirteen-year-old brother Steve. He'd never had one and somehow that bicycle arriving at my mother and stepfather's house for my brother symbolized for me that I'd done all right my first year away from home.

Boots and I decided I should leave Montreal and come back to New York and get married. It seemed like a good time for a visit to Detroit. So I went home for a two-week visit. If I hadn't done that, I probably would have had a very different life, but isn't that always the way? Each choice we make opens up a world of new possibilities while closing down another world.

In Detroit, I stayed with my mother and Lou. I called Bill Alexander, the salesman who had worked with Chuck and had been so kind to me. I thought he'd be happy to learn I was no longer with Chuck. He was. Then I told him that I'd become engaged to Boots, who was thirty-three years my senior. Bill invited me to his home and I met his wife, Jean Holtz, whom Bill always called Holtzy. I spent time with them and their friends. I saw people who were living a good life of friendship, potluck dinners, laughter, classical music, and literature. I just didn't know people lived like that. The day came for me to leave and return to my gypsy life. Jean went to work. Bill was going to drive me to the airport. My bags were all packed. I felt sad to be leaving, but there was something else, something just beneath the surface. Whatever it was, it was filling the room to the point of bursting. I didn't understand what was happening. I looked at Bill. He looked at me and then he kissed me. Bam! That was it. One kiss and my whole life changed. So did Bill's. No more fifty-two-year-old fiancé. No more Holtzy. No more New York. No more dancing. I was staying in Detroit and Bill and I were living together.

We found a beautiful spacious studio in a converted old mansion near Wayne State University. Bill was writing poetry and when he went to work selling cars, I walked over to the Detroit Institute of Art and filled my eyes with all the new beauty I was discovering and learning about. We spent our evenings browsing through a friend's used-book store for good buys. I was beginning to realize just how much I didn't know. It was getting embarrassing.

I'm not sure why now, perhaps it was from conversations with Bill, or maybe it was my age, or because I'd slowed my life down enough to realize it, but for whatever reason, it was at this time that I felt a deep need to find my father. My real father, Jack Gillooly. I needed to know him. I may have wanted some guidance or perhaps I realized that in almost marrying a fifty-two-year-old man, I was reaching for a father. I do remember that I wanted a man to see me with nonsexual eyes. I called my godfather, Uncle Dave, and asked him if he had a number for my father. They had always been friends. He gave it to me.

I had been vague with my mother about where I was living because I didn't want her to know I was living with Bill. But my mother was not one to be kept in the dark. One evening there was a knock on the door of our room and when I opened it, I was shocked to see my mother standing in the hallway. I said, "What are you doing here?"

"Looking for trouble," she said as she moved into the room.

"Well, you've found it." I closed the door and revealed Bill.

She shouted, "You!" and began hitting him with her purse.

Bill held up his hand and said in a stern voice, "Now, we'll have none of that!" And for some reason that stopped her. Wish I had tried that. There was some yelling and name calling.

I began to cry and then blurted out defiantly, "I'm going to see my father!"

My mother looked surprised and confused as she said, "Well, go see him. I don't care."

There was something about this exchange that I never understood until many years later when I received some photos from my brother Jack. They were in an envelope with a note from Genie, my father's last wife. After my father died, Genie sent these pictures to my brother. Three of them were pictures of me when I was about sixteen and posing for the Camera Club at Cass. On the back was a note from my mother, who sent them to my father, who left them to his wife, who sent them to my brother, who sent them to me. This circle took fifty-four years to complete. The note to my father read: "Edna looks like a real Gillooly, doesn't she? She's sixteen years old now and modeling. She could really use a father at this time in her life. Couldn't she come to see you? Nice eyes, huh?"

I was so surprised when I read it because I never knew that my mother tried to get my father to see me, or that she understood how much I needed a father.

I stepped out of the airplane—my first time on a plane—into the soft evening air of Atlanta in August, wearing the same pink dress my mother made, the one I'd worn a year before on the bus ride to Texas. My father was at the bottom of the stairs waiting for me. We said hello. We did not embrace. I got my first look at him and my heart dipped. He was so much shorter than I expected. We were probably around the same height, five foot seven, but I was wearing heels so I was looking down on him. He was wearing a short-sleeve rayon shirt with a Hawaiian motif of palm trees and bare-breasted women in hula skirts. I felt a swift, slight discomfort.

I don't remember what we talked about as we collected my bags and on the drive to his house, which was small and pleasant. I was shown to a bed on a sleeping porch off the living room. My father asked his wife, Adair, to make us drinks. Adair was seventeen when I was seven, so she must have been no more than twenty-nine at this time, but she looked older. She was very skinny and her blond hair was so thin I could see her scalp. She smoked constantly and looked wistful. She barely spoke above a whisper. I felt uncomfortable, nervous, excited, and very happy as my father sat down next to me and I saw Adair disappear into the house. He watched her go and then turned to me quickly and furtively grabbed me, kissed me, and thrust his tongue into my mouth. When he released me, he put both hands on my breasts, held them, fondled them, and said, "Oh, baby, you sure are stacked. Just like your mother."

I was frozen in place. Unable to move, to react. Stunned. That was the top layer. Under that was a stratum of shame, boiling, churning oozing into all crevices of my psyche, inflaming my recesses with loathing, self-loathing.

And further down, below the destructive forces of self-loathing was a substratum too dark, too inaccessible, except by years of archeology of the soul. In that lowly place lurked the worst demon of all. I call her Incestua. When I finally had the skill and courage to descend to her terrible realm, I found her dancing. Cymbals clanged. Conch shells bellowed. A whole orchestra blared the bellowing energy of the goddess of father love. "He wants me. He wants me. He wants me," she screamed as she stomped her terrible dance into the smoldering ruins of Edna's desire to be loved.

I was supposed to stay for two weeks. I didn't. But I stayed as long as I could—Maybe a week. Maybe ten days. During each day I was acting out my fantasy of what having a father was like. Scenes I'd observed of my friends with their fathers. I had him teach me to drive so I could say, "Dad, can I have the keys to the car?" I even called him Dad, which I didn't as a child. He was always Jack. I asked him to give me an allowance, which I'd never had, so I could spend it all at once and have him reprimand me so I could be contrite, then get him to give me more. I didn't need it. I got work while I was there modeling for newspaper ads and had my own money, but I was acting out my script. I took the money he gave me and bought a deep blue Clair McCardle dress and threw away the one my mother had made.

That was all during the day. At night, after Adair was asleep, he would creep into my bed with an erection, kiss me, and try to enter me. I always succeeded in making him get out of bed, but it wasn't easy.

After I'd been there around a week, Adair announced she was leaving to visit her parents in Grand Rapids, Michigan. I was going to be alone with my father in the house. "Why?" I asked her.

She said in her small, sweet, little voice, "I've always wanted to go home and visit my family, but I've never been able to because there would be no one to take care of Laddie [their collie] while your dad is at work. But now you're here."

I realize now that Adair was too timid to assume anyone would take care of her dog without asking. This couldn't have been her idea. She was being sent away.

Once I was alone with my father, his seduction escalated. I couldn't support my fantasy script any longer. I just had to leave. He didn't rape me, I'll say that for him. He didn't overpower me, which he probably could have done. He just used all the forces of flaming desire he could ignite in himself and in me. I knew that if I gave in to him, I'd regret it for the rest of my life. I managed to hold him off. I was furious that I had to. Deeply furious. I decided to squelch his advances for good. Calmly I said, "I came to see you because I thought you were the one man in the world who wouldn't try to get me in bed. Now I see you are just like all the others." Referring to his erection, I said disdainfully, "Now you better go jerk off in the toilet."

I called the airport, then a taxi, and I left. It was August in Atlanta, but I felt cold. Very cold.

Within three months I was married. At age nineteen, I became Edna Rae Alexander. No more Keri Flynn. No more Edna Gillooly. Bill and I rented a little house on Walnut Lake, near Pontiac, Michigan. Bill was at the showroom selling cars all day and I was home alone on a frozen lake surrounded by summer cottages that were empty all winter. I happily settled into the life of a housewife. After getting Bill off to work, I would clean house, do the laundry, try to have everything in order by early afternoon, and then I'd start reading. I'd read for a few hours, making notes of all the different words I didn't know. At four o'clock, there was a radio station from Canada that played classical music, but didn't announce the composer until the piece was finished. I listened every day, making notes like: Sounds like Beethoven—no, wait! This part sounds like Mozart—no, definitely Beethoven. Then when the piece was over, I would note the composer, conductor, and orchestra. After the radio show, I'd look up in the dictionary all the words I'd listed that day and write each one in a sentence.

Bill guided my reading. Soon I became obsessed with learning. The dictionary was my new best friend. My mind was growing and expanding. I was discovering how beautiful, complex, and intricate the world is—how little I knew about it, and how thrilling it was to learn. I fell in love with learning on a little frozen lake in Michigan.

One day I took the bus into Detroit because my old employer, the J. L. Hudson Company, was having a sale. I got myself two beautiful suits, a Balenciaga and a Dior, at less than half price. When the bill came, Bill went through the roof. "I'm not going to pay this!" he said. Well, I'd already worn the suits. I couldn't take them back.

I asked, "What do you expect me to do?"

"You're going to have to go to work," he said.

I registered with two different modeling agencies and was soon working steadily. Then that became a problem: I was bringing home more money than Bill. I said, "You're the one that told me to go to work!"

"Yeah, but I thought you'd get a job behind a counter or something. I didn't know you were going to start pulling in nine hundred a month!"

I stood there looking at him and remembering a letter to the editor I'd read in *Seventeen* magazine when I was a teenager. The writer asked if on a tennis date she should let the boy win. The columnist chastised her for assuming she was the better player, but never really answered her question. I just got the answer. Bill was a little shorter than me, so I always wore flat heels around him because the man "should" be taller. Now I felt too big. Too tall. Too much. I didn't fit. I began to yearn. Quietly, I yearned for a place where I didn't feel too big. A place like . . . New York. I wanted to go back to New York.

Soon after my brother Jack graduated from high school, he joined the army and was sent to Germany. This was only a few years after World War II and the United States still had occupation forces in Germany. Jack fell in love with a beautiful fraulein named Kitty. They were married, had their first daughter, Diane, and less than two years later, twin daughters, Maureen and Linda. In October they all sailed on a troop ship bound for New York harbor and provided me with a perfect excuse for a trip to New York to greet them on their arrival. Kitty and I had been corresponding, so I knew that she spoke English, but I thought it would make her feel not so far from home if, on her arrival in America, she were greeted in her native tongue, so I brought Francis, the Baron, with me. When the ship docked and thousands of soldiers disembarked down the gangplank, it was easy enough to spot them. Jack had a large baby basket on each arm and Kitty was holding the hand of my adorable little niece Diane, who was wearing a pink bonnet.

I pointed them out to the WAC on duty, who went up to Jack and could redirect him just by touching his elbow. It made me cry to see how the army had conditioned him to obey commands without question. He walked to where he was directed without knowing why, looking exhausted after the long trip with three children. I hadn't seen him for four years and burbled my emotional greeting all over Jack and Kitty. Kitty turned to Jack questioningly, and Jack said, "That's my sister." I hadn't managed to introduce myself. Then Francis stepped in and spoke German. I cooed to the babies and tried to speak to Diane, who spoke only German and looked very confused in this sea of strange crying, laughing faces around her. Somehow we all got disentangled and soon we were back in Detroit.

I'd spent a week in New York and now began to talk to Bill about both of us moving there someday. Bill didn't say no but felt he wanted to be prepared, save a little more money—maybe next year. I'd traded in my dreams of becoming an actress to be a housewife. Now this was beginning to seem like not such a good idea.

We attended a play at a small Detroit theater called the World Stage and I soon joined the company. I was cast in a small role in its next production, Chekhov's *Ivanov*.

I was modeling regularly by now, working often with cars, which is what you model in Detroit. We moved from Walnut Lake to an apartment in the city and I bought myself a piano. On time, of course. It was just a little spinet, but it was all mine. It meant a lot to me that I had the money to buy myself a piano. I did another production at the World Stage in early 1954, *Volpone*, in which I had the female lead.

I was very dedicated to being a good housewife, and I read books like *Your Own Home and How to Run It*, but soon Bill started not coming home from work. He'd call around eight o'clock and say, "Okay, I'm locking up. Get dinner ready." I'd make dinner, keep it warm, and start waiting. Around nine I'd call the bar down the street and ask for him. He'd come to the phone and say, "I stopped by for a drink. I'm just going out the door." That conversation would be repeated at ten, and then at eleven. In the meantime, I'd sit reading a book and drinking Jack Daniels on the rocks until I fell asleep. Bill came in after the bars closed at two A.M. Not only was I not in New York, and spending my nights alone, I was drinking too much. I decided to go back to New York. I'd find us an apartment, get settled, and Bill could come when he was ready, which he promised would be soon. I was ready now. I arrived back in New York on June 15, 1954. This time I stayed for good.

Within one month of my return, I'd signed a lease on an apartment, registered with Huntington Hartford's modeling agency, and found my way to Lee Strasberg. Lee was to become the most important influence in my life, but not for another ten years, when I would begin studying with him. Why didn't I start studying with him when I first met him in 1954? I wish I knew. But I do know that if Edna could have asked Ellen for advice, I would have said to her, "Lee is post-graduate work. Don't begin there. Go get some experience onstage, study with some other teachers, then, when you've got some sea legs, you'll be ready for Lee." I just don't know how Edna could have known that then, but that's what I did.

When Francis Von Kahler took me to see my first Broadway play, *The Moon Is Blue,* we sat in a box. As I looked down at the lighted stage, I was filled with deep pleasure. I knew I was looking at my future. Barbara Bel Geddes was the most magical creature I'd ever seen. I could feel the audience entranced by her charm. I understood that I did not know how to do what I could feel her do. But I also sensed that someday I would. Somehow, I was going to be on that stage and I would understand what to do or perhaps be, that would connect with the audience the way she was doing. I didn't know how I was going to learn it, just that I was. I had no plan. When I didn't go to Lee for ten years after I met him, I had no plan either. It just didn't feel right then, even though I understood that he was the greatest acting teacher in the world.

I spent the next three years modeling and became one of the illustrators' favorite models. They told me I had a "drawable head." I posed for paperback covers, magazine stories, and print ads for companies like IBM. By the fall of that first year back in New York, 1954, I landed a job on TV. Max Liebman was producing a big musical for television called *Satins and Spurs* starring Betty Hutton. There was a fashion-show scene in it and I was hired to be one of the models. My life was moving at a fast pace. I soon learned I needed to get away from New York for some quiet time. I began going to Sky Line Dude Ranch in Clinton Corners, New York, every weekend, leaving the noise and concrete of the city for the softness of the green hills where I roamed on the back of a palomino mare named Spice. After several months of riding Spice, I bought her and continued to keep her at the ranch. In the evenings we all square-danced and sat around the fire with Charlie, the horse trader, who told tall tales of horses "that could turn on a dime and give ya nine cents change."

At the ranch I met a TV announcer named Bob Williams, who was the spokesman for Old Gold cigarettes. Bill, who had promised to move to New York, never came. We spent our holidays together in Detroit and occasionally he'd come to New York for a few days to visit. We were still married and loved each other, and even though we never talked about it, we both lived as though we were single and in separate cities. Bob and I started dating and soon he bought a bay gelding from Charlie and we moved both our horses up to Bob's cabin in the Adirondacks. It was a coincidence when I got a call to audition for the *Jackie Gleason Show* that one of the sponsors was Old Gold cigarettes.

When I entered the studio for the on-camera audition, I saw every model in town. We were there all day waiting our turn before the camera. Jackie Gleason sat in the control booth behind a large one-way mirror. I was there for a few hours when in walked a model I'd never seen before. She was so beautiful my immediate thought was, "Well, if they're looking at girls like her, I might as well go home." I was wearing an aquamarine corduroy skirt over a crinoline petticoat and a striped shirt. She was wearing a slinky black dress with a plunging neckline and a slit up the front revealing her gorgeous legs. She wore black gloves, so nothing showed but her legs, her bosom, and that amazing face framed in dark curls. When she spoke she had a deep throaty voice that made me feel like Betty Boop. I had never run into her before and I was curious to know who she was. After a while I found myself standing next to this beauty. She aimed her dazzle at me and in her sultry voice said, "I hope they don't ask me to take off my gloves. I've got paint all over my hands." Suddenly this goddess morphed into human form as she told me she'd been painting her new apartment lilac when she got the call. She whipped out her swatches and asked me what I thought. "Beautiful," I murmured, the way any girl from Detroit would agree with anything Aphrodite was considering. What did I know? We both passed our auditions, were selected for the show, and we spent the rest of the Saturdays of 1956 and half of those of 1957 in CBS Studio 50 on Broadway and 53rd Street with one of the great comic geniuses of our time.

My new friend's real name was Blossom Plumb, but at the time she used the stage name Rebecca Sand, presumably because her real name sounded too threatrical. Blossom was not a model; she was an actress who was freelancing to support her two daughters that she was raising on her own. She had lived in Paris and spoke flawless French. She also spoke in poetic metaphor, and over the years I discovered that not everyone could understand what she was saying. I often was in a room with her when, after she spoke, people would turn to me quizzically and I would translate, "She means . . . ," as though she were speaking a foreign language. She was—not everyone speaks Metaphor. I considered her the most wondrous creature I'd ever met. Still do. She's my oldest friend.

That year on the Gleason show was the best training in comedy one could receive. Jackie didn't come into the theater until dress rehearsal in the late afternoon on the day of the show. He watched it on closed-circuit TV in his dressing room, with the producer, Jack Hurdle, playing Jackie's parts. Hurdle did a very good Gleason. Only one segment he didn't do and that was Jackie's stand-up routine. No one knew what that was going to be until Jackie did it live on air. That's how he kept it spontaneous and made all of us backstage laugh with the audience. I think he liked that surround-sound laughter. In rehearsal, that slot would be filled by one of the comics in town—Jack E. Leonard, Henny Youngman, Jack Carter, and others. They would drop by, hang out in the theater with us, do five minutes of jokes, then go next door to O'Reilly's, where we congregated on our dinner break. I remember Jack Carter sitting in our booth doing jokes for ten minutes, all the while tapping with a spoon on a glass. When he left, Blossom said, "Wasn't that amazing? He was looking for the rhythm."

Blossom and I were "lead-in girls." There were the Away We Go Girls at the beginning of the show, led by the gorgeous Elizabeth Allen. Then there were the June Taylor Dancers, and also the June Taylor Show Girls (who didn't dance but were all dolled up in gorgeous costumes), who each had a great close-up during the dance numbers. Then there were the "lead-in girls." We led into the commercials.

Although I introduced Bob Williams, who then did the commercial for Old Gold cigarettes, we weren't really working together as the commercials were done live from a different studio. But we often met after the show. Bob had a great voice and was an expert horseman, which I found very sexy. But that wasn't the real reason I was attracted to him. The real reason was that he was trouble. He had been brought up in an orphanage, was emotionally unstable, drank way too much, and was self-destructive. It's a gift. Some people have perfect pitch or photographic memories. Me? You could put me in a roomful of handsome, healthy guys, blindfold me, turn me around three times, and I would walk directly to the one guy in the room who was trouble and lay my head in the guillotine of his lap, smiling all the while like I'd finally come home.

Even though I'd started seeing a therapist in 1955, it would take many years before I stopped seeking out the pattern of relating to men that I learned at home. We are such curious beings. As much as we decry our early treatment at home, we just keep on repeating it because that's what we know. Those are the grooves laid down in our brains and until we take an active part in restructuring our brain patterns, we are doomed to repeat the horrors of the past.

In fact, it took a while for me to understand that I needed a therapist. The first thing I ever said to Bluma, my therapist, was, "I don't think I need therapy, my husband does. But he won't come, so I'm here."

Bluma wisely replied, through her cloud of cigarette smoke, "Well, why don't you tell me something about yourself and then we'll see."

That began my rescue from the morass of unconscious self-destruction and bad attitude I'd been floundering in most of my life. There was no quick cure. It's a process I've continued: bringing what's hidden in the shadows into the light of consciousness, recognizing the patterns, deepening the understanding, and literally taking responsibility for who I am.

It's too easy to blame the past for the present. We don't have to be victims of our conditioning. We just have to be willing to do the work of reprogramming ourselves. Only when I started answering questions Bluma carefully posed could I see what disaster there was in my wake—and also how I was cooperating with the disaster, recreating it every day of my life without any idea how to change. That seems to me what each of us must learn: how to let go of our habitual ways of being and give birth to our entelechy—our realized potential.

Jackie Gleason knew that Bob Williams and I had been dating and he often invited Bob to join us when he took a group of us out to dinner after the show. So one night at Toots Shor, a famous restaurant of that era, Bob didn't arrive for a while and Jackie decided to entertain the three of us girls with his psychic powers. He told us he was going to say one sentence to each of us that wouldn't mean anything to anyone else, but would have great significance to the one he was addressing. He did the other two girls first. Then he looked at me for a moment and said, "The guy on the beach." I almost fell off my chair. He had to be referring to Chuck Harper, with whom I'd had my first real sexual experience, but nobody in New York knew about that. I hadn't told Bob or anyone, so how could Jackie know? Lucky shot? Maybe. But why that specific thing to me? I froze. Said nothing. Couldn't believe it. He smiled that great knowing half-smile and knew he'd hit a bull's-eye. The other girls were quiet, too, so I guess he'd hit the mark with them also. Bob arrived and no one referred to what Jackie had done, but we were all pretty impressed.

Blossom and I, along with a dozen or so of the other girls, were invited to go with Gleason to Boston and ride in the motorcade that was to kick off a tuberculosis fundraising campaign. We were to travel in Jackie's private train. The morning of the trip, we arrived at the train station very early and none of us was really awake. We took seats in the first car of the train. We were facing the front, which had heavy velvet curtains the full width of the car. I was too sleepy to even notice that, but the moment the train started up and we lurched into our departure, those velvet curtains suddenly parted and behind them was a full Dixieland band. Waiters arrived immediately on cue with trays of grapefruit juice laced with vodka and the party was on! All the way to Boston the juice kept coming, the music played, and at one moment, one of the Away We Go Girls, Nancy, who had black hair, white skin, brilliant blue eyes, and a stunning figure, stood up in the aisle, dropped her coat, and adjusted her belt so that her bosom was even more conspicuous. She was a dazzling sight for all eyes. At which point one of the other girls said in a slightly disgusted voice, "Oh, put on your coat and sit down." We all howled with laughter. Needless to say, I cannot remember our arrival in Boston. The next thing I remember is getting ready to get in the convertible for the motorcade. Jackie assigned the cars. He motioned for me to sit next to him. There were three or four girls to a car. One in front, three riding high in back with feet on the backseat.

Jackie was wearing a white trench coat and he asked me if he looked like a "beached whale" in it. I was just telling him he looked dashing when someone from his office walked up with a serious expression on his face and said, "Jackie, we just got word, Tommy Dorsey died."

I saw Jackie's face contract in grief for one moment. Tommy Dorsey had been a friend of his.

Jackie said nothing. He just turned to our convertible and said, "Let's go!" He climbed up on the back of the car. I was on his right. Another girl on his left. The Away We Go Girls were in the car in front of us. The others behind us. We took off. We rode through the streets of Boston with people lining both sides of the street waving at Jackie and Jackie waving back. We passed under trees making dappled light on his face, as he went from light to shadow to light. When in the light I could detect a tear in his eye, but he was smiling, nodding, waving. Then some guy on the sidelines called, "Hey Jackie." Jackie turned, waved at the guy, and said, "How ya doin', pal?" The guy shouted, "Art Carney is funnier that you." Jackie just took the hit. Didn't respond. We drove on. The Great One smiling through his grief. But I couldn't take it. After a few moments, I said to Jackie, "You *let* Art Carney be funnier than you. Why do you do that?"

He said, "Because I don't want to have to be the funny one all the time. That way I can pick my shots."

I can't remember what else happened except we were so drunk on the train ride back, there was much drama. Jackie hypnotized some of the girls. It was another one of his parlor tricks. He did have amazing psychic powers and loved to play with them. I got emotional at one point, I can't remember why, but Blossom and I went off to a private roomette and I blubberingly confessed to her my abortion. Then she told me about hers.

I don't know if it was being on the Gleason show for that year, or seeing Bluma, or probably both, but a change began to occur in me. I remember the day it happened. It was no big deal. I got a new haircut—short and curly. My hair was dark then. I was wearing a black cashmere sweater and a fitted black skirt. I tied a bright red scarf around my neck. As I looked in the mirror of the hair salon, I actually looked good to myself. I don't remember ever having that feeling before. I went to rehearsal and entered the theater by the stage door on 53rd Street. I walked out on the stage to go into the house, where we all sat until our number and, as I approached the stairway, I felt everyone's eyes turn to me and the house got quiet. This was a room full of beauties and I wasn't by any means "the fairest of them all," not by a long shot. It was something new, confidence maybe, or self-acceptance. Whatever it was, for the first time I began to feel I might be carrying something of value. It wasn't long after that that I announced, first to Blossom and then to everyone else I knew, "I have made up my mind. I'm going to be an actress. I've decided to do a Broadway play this fall. Does anyone know how I can get an audition?" Well, someone did. And indeed I played a lead on Broadway that fall.

A friend introduced me to Phyllis Rabb, who worked for the William Morris Agency as a secretary. Phyllis was a smart, vivacious, slender, young New Yorker who said at dinner, "I know someone right now who is looking for a girl your type for a play. I'll send you up to see him." Within a few days I met Joe Hyman in his office, we had a nice chat, and he set an audition date and handed me the script of *Fair Game*, by Sam Locke.

It was the story of Susan Hammarlee from Chicago, who was married and lost her husband to a woman who was an intellectual. (We all know how often that happens!) She's come to New York to get an education so she can win back her husband. In the meantime she's going to make a living as a model to pay for her education. The first scene in the play is her arrival at her new apartment. It is her first day in New York.

I read that first scene for my audition. I entered the stage door of the Ethel Barrymore Theater on West 47th Street and walked to the backstage area. I'd never been backstage in a Broadway theater. There were other girls waiting in the wings to audition. The stage was lit only by a rehearsal light. Each auditioner read from the script. The other roles were being read by the stage manager. There were about three girls ahead of me. Then my name was called—"Edna Rae, you're next"—I walked onstage and looked out at the house. Blackness. I couldn't see anything at all. I could feel there were people there, but I didn't know who they were. I turned away from the vast darkness of the house to the light of the stage and got to work. I was nervous. My heart was racing. I looked around the empty stage. The stage manager stood holding the book, waiting for me to begin. I said to myself, "Okay. I'm in my first apartment, my first day in New York . . ." and suddenly I heard very clearly a voice inside my head: "No, you are on the stage of the Ethel Barrymore Theater, about to audition for your *first* Broadway play." I was shocked. Right. That's the reality. I don't have to make up anything. The feeling I have for the real situation, this first time on a Broadway stage, is the same feeling the character has for her first apartment in New York. Filled with real feelings for this day and all its implications of a new life, I began the scene.

Now, whose voice was it that spoke to me like that? It must have been mine. But it sounded like my voice today. It was the voice of a Method actress. What the voice said is the crux of the technique I wouldn't learn for years, which is basically to find what is real about the actual situation and really be with that. Those authentic feelings inform the fiction. But I didn't know that then. Some might say that it was "Zen Mind, Beginner's Mind." Shunryu Suzuki, in his wonderful book of that name, says that when you come to something fresh, you don't know enough to know how to do it wrong. You just do it and it's right. Later, as you lose beginner's mind, you have to take it all apart step by step. That was certainly what I did later when I studied with Strasberg. So maybe it was beginner's mind, but naming it doesn't solve the mystery for me. There was something about that voice . . . the way it interrupted what I was doing with that "No!" It was something other than me. There was an otherness that was addressing me. But it was in *my* head, so it couldn't be anyone else. So it had to be an "other me." Now, what on earth could that mean? These are the elements of the voice that were "other." The voice was calm; I was very nervous. It addressed me in the second person; it also said it was my *first* Broadway play, which implied more Broadway plays to come. A calm, knowing inner voice spoke to me and gave me the perfect direction for a scene, using techniques I hadn't yet learned, and infused me with a strength and assurance I didn't know I had. And it would speak to me again in the future. All of life is a mystery, but when that kind of otherness can speak to you and fill you with creativity, it becomes something more. It is a miracle.

I had my second and final audition a few weeks later when they had narrowed down their choice to me or Patricia Bosworth. I didn't know Patty then, but she went on to be a distinguished biographer of, among others, Montgomery Clift, Marlon Brando, and Diane Arbus. Today she serves on the board of directors of the Actors Studio and we work together all the time, but on that day in June of 1957, we were strangers to each other and competitors for a very choice role. I felt confident that this role was mine. At this audition I met the director, Paul Roberts, the author, Sam Locke, and Joe Hyman's close friend who was putting up all the money for this show, Moss Hart. I read a scene in the third act where Susan is out to dinner in a fancy restaurant with her boss, who later would be played by Sam Levene. A few years earlier Francis Von Kahler used to take me to a restaurant that had gypsy violinists, so rather than just sitting on a chair on a bare stage reading with the stage manager, I put myself in that restaurant and created gypsy violinists for myself. At the beginning of the scene I figured I was a little bit drunk, so as I listened to the imaginary music, I closed my eyes and swayed to it. Paul later told me that at that point, Sam leaned over to him and said, "What is she doing?" Paul sighed in deep pleasure and said, "She's listening to the music."

That, by the way, is also good Method acting, creating what the sensory reality would be, not just the words, but I don't question my knowing that. That didn't seem to come from anyplace mysterious. That was just what my native talent knew how to do. That really was beginner's mind.

Before I read I was standing in the back of the house with Patty. Paul Roberts came by on his way to the bathroom and introduced himself. After Patty's turn, I walked down the aisle and up some stairs to the stage. When I was finished and walked down the stairs again, Joe Hyman met me at the bottom, took my hand, and said, "Okay, have your agent call us tomorrow." I guess I must have stared at him blankly because I remember being puzzled by what he said. I thought, *Who's my agent and why should I have him call? Do I have an agent? Do I have to find one? Is Phyllis Rabb my agent?*

While all this was running through my head, I was murmuring, "Okay." Joe said, "You don't seem very excited."

"About what?" I stammered.

"We like you! You've got the part," he exclaimed. I finally got it. Then Sam Locke and Paul Roberts shook my hand. Moss Hart stood in his tweed jacket looking *très élégant.* "Who have you studied with?" he asked.

"No one," I blurted.

"Well, don't start now," he said. "You're a natural. Leave it alone." I would soon learn just how far being a "natural" would get me. Not that far. But that comes later.

I left the theater in a daze, jumped in a cab, and gave the driver Bluma's address. All the way to my appointment, I just kept repeating, "I got the part." Then I tried a different reading, "*I* got the part." Then, "I got the *part.*" In one way it was totally unbelievable and yet, at the same time, it felt like the unfolding of my destiny.

When I told Francis I'd landed a lead in a Broadway play, he didn't believe me. He said, "Nobody is going to give an unknown a lead in a Broadway play." He thought I was being sold a bill of goods. I assured him it was legit.

My mother had moved to California with my brother Steve after Lou's death a few years earlier and had been pressing me to come out for a visit. I'd promised her I'd come that summer. I called her on the phone and said, "Mom, looks like I can't visit you this summer. I just got the lead in a Broadway play."

"Oh, it's always something," she said in a disgusted voice.

After I hung up, I sat by the phone for a few minutes pondering her reaction. Finally I thought, *I don't think she understood what I said.* I called her back.

"Mom, did you understand what I said? I'm going to do a lead in a Broadway play."

"Well, what is it?" she asked. "Some amateur show or something?" Ah!

Now I realized the problem. How do you explain to someone who doesn't know what a Broadway show is?

"Have you ever heard of *My Fair Lady*?" I asked.

"Yeah."

"Well, it's like that, but without music."

Then she got it. "Oh," she said dubiously. "That's wonderful," still sounding like she'd prefer the visit.

Phyllis Rabb was secretary to Charlie Baker at William Morris. It turns out that she had sent me up to meet Joe Hyman on her own without telling her boss.

The day after my audition, Joe Hyman called Charlie Baker and said, "We like your girl."

Charlie was baffled. "What girl?" he asked.

"Edna Rae! We want her."

"Oh yes . . . good . . . glad you like her . . . can I call you back?" he stammered. He hung up and called his secretary. "Phyllis, do you know anything about an Edna Rae?"

Phyllis came into his office. "Yeah, I sent her up to see Joe Hyman. Why?"

"They want her," said Charlie.

"They want her for what? You mean for the understudy?" Phyllis asked incredulously.

"No," Charlie explained. "For the lead. They want her for the leading role."

Because of this, Phyllis was promoted from secretary to agent and was my agent for many years.

We began wardrobe fittings. All my costumes were being made for me. It was very exciting. Joe Hyman wanted to announce the casting in the papers, but he didn't like my name. We were sitting in his office. "It sounds unfinished," he said.

"It is. My last name is Gillooly. Use that," I said.

Joe smiled derisively. "They'll laugh you out of the theater with a name like that."

I held my tongue. After all, his name was Hyman.

Although I was born Edna Rae Gillooly, when I learned to write, the first name I wrote was Edna Francimore. My mother was Mrs. Schwartz, so in her circles I was known as Edna Schwartz, but I never called myself that. So I'd already had three names before I left home, plus my nickname Toots. When I danced in the chorus, I used Keri Flynn. I did a screen test under the name Erica Dean. My modeling name was Edna Rae. Obviously, all this name changing was symptomatic of a deeper process going on. I was searching for an identity, not just a name. Now that I'd found my way to Broadway, it seemed that perhaps I really was an actress. It wasn't just a fantasy anymore. It was a dream coming true. Suddenly, I wanted my own name. I wrote this letter to Joe Hyman:

Dear Mr. Hyman,

Everything I have accomplished in my life has been done by myself, with myself and for myself. I do not want the credit to go to someone else.

I remain,

Edna Rae Gillooly

Paul later told me Joe got a good laugh out of that. "What has she accomplished? Nothing." He couldn't have known the path I'd traveled from Detroit to his office door was indeed an accomplishment.

But I didn't persist. I gave in when he insisted I look for a new name. One of my friends at that time was Roger Price, the creator of a popular series of cartoons called "Droodles." One evening, we sat around playing with my name. Eventually we turned Edna into the more musical-sounding Ellen, and we tacked a "Mc" in front of Rae. And so it was Ellen McRae who was announced in the newspapers as playing the lead in *Fair Game*. I had three more names to go before I became Ellen Burstyn.

The rest of casting was completed. My boss in the wholesale dress market would be played by Sam Levene, and the salesman who worked for him and was my love interest was to be Bob Webber. He and Sam turned out to be the most toxic combination of personalities that walked a stage since Othello met Iago. Sam was a highly neurotic actor who once announced that any day he got through without having killed himself he considered a success. Bob was an ex-marine with an excess of testosterone and an obvious hostility to women. Once we got into rehearsals, he was always whispering in Sam's ear and stirring up trouble.

And I didn't help. I was a novice in a leading role, which caused resentment. At least it did in Bob, which he circulated throughout the company until it became the dominant group attitude toward me. To make matters worse, Paul, the director, was an alcoholic going through a divorce and very unhappy. Naturally I was attracted to him and didn't have enough sense to hide it. We decided not to consummate our love affair until after we opened, but everybody assumed we were in bed together, which caused more resentment. By the time we got to Philadelphia for our out-of-town tryout, no one in the cast was speaking to me. On opening night, the curtain went up at eight and didn't come down until eleven-thirty. And this was supposed to be a comedy! Only a handful of people were still in their seats at curtain call. Most had left groaning. Talk about third-act trouble. The rewrites started. We rehearsed new scenes during the day and inserted them at night. Sometimes new scenes wouldn't be ready to go in at night, so after rehearsing the new one all day, we'd do the old one at night. Sometimes it was new words, old moves; sometimes new moves, old words. At least the third act was getting shorter. Everyone's nerves were stretched to the breaking point. Moss Hart arrived from New York to help. His wife, Kitty Carlisle Hart, came to watch over him, as he'd had a heart attack and she didn't want him unnecessarily stressed.

All of a sudden, Paul was fired, but he stayed in Philadelphia to help his friend Sam Locke with the rewrites. Moss brought in a young man named Judd Horner as our new director. One day while giving notes, I asked a question. After Judd answered it, I heard a cast member ask someone, "What did she ask?" My question was repeated and the first guy made a face and said, "Oh, brother!" as if it was a really dumb question I'd asked. I felt a quaking occur. My body started shaking. I was losing it. The break was happening. At the end of Judd's notes, I asked to address the company. I stood up in front of them and said, "If you want to make comments about me, could you please do it where I can't see or hear them because it makes it hard for me to go on." I was crying.

Judd dismissed the company. Mary Alice Bayh, who played Bob's sister at the top of the show, came and put her arms around me and said to someone who was making a nasty comment, "Oh, don't! She just wants someone to be on her side." Then Bob Webber grabbed her and pulled her away from me. How I appreciated her kindness. It was true. The only one on my side had been Paul, and now he was gone.

Webber accused me of constantly upstaging him. When I was given that note, I had to ask what it meant. I grew so afraid to move, I learned to freeze like a store dummy unless I was speaking.

It was perfectly true I had little experience and no technique. All I had developed was grace, charm, and poise. Now even that faded. I was like a frightened automaton moving rigidly from mark to mark, remembering all my lines, the old ones and the never-ending new ones, but whatever quality I had that made them hire me was now lost. The play was getting better, but the leading lady was one sorry sight. One night as we came offstage, Herb Evers (later known as Jason Evers), who played my husband, stopped me as we left the stage and said, "Ellen, whatever you were doing at the beginning, you've got to get it back."

I covered my face and cried. I didn't know what it was I'd been doing or how to get it back. That natural thing Moss Hart had referred to can bloom in the atmosphere of a loving garden. But in the hell of an out-of-town tryout with a stressed-out, overworked cast led by two highly neurotic actors, technique was needed and I had zilch.

I had one thing going for me: I was gifted with a great memory. Throughout this ordeal, other actors had at one time or another dropped a line or gone up (showbiz lingo for going blank). But I never did. Not once. And whenever they did, I was able to save them, thank God. One night when an understudy came offstage, he said to me, "Ellen, I know everyone says you're an amateur, but after being onstage with you, I think you are the Rock of Gibraltar." A change began to occur. There wasn't a complete turnaround yet, but people were beginning to trust their own experience with me rather than Bob's manipulations.

At one of our last rehearsals, Sam came in and announced, "No more changes. We've got to freeze this show so we can begin playing it." And that ended the changes. Soon we left Philadelphia and headed for New York. We had one day to rehearse on the stage of the Longacre Theater before we did four days of previews.

My dressing room was on the first floor, just up a short flight of stairs from the stage door. Everyone had to pass it before going upstairs to the rest of the dressing rooms. I kept my door open except when changing. From the beginning, I've always been the first one into the theater. I usually get in three hours before curtain. I like to take my time getting ready and shift my focus from my life to the life of the character. So I was already at my dressing room table when the stage manager, Sterling Mace, entered the theater and stopped at my door. This surprised me because Sterling hadn't spoken to me during the whole time we were out of town. He didn't say anything. Just stood there. I said, "Hi." He didn't respond. I could tell he wanted to say something, so I said, "Come in."

He stepped into my dressing room but continued to stand, eyes downcast, poised on the edge of speech, but nothing came out. I put down the brush I'd been holding and turned to him. After a long, tense silence, he finally got out what he wanted to say and he looked right at me as he said, "If any group of people ever did to my daughter what these people have done to you, I would kill them." And he left.

That marked the real change. There were fourteen cast members in this play. Now, every one of them, except Bob Webber and Sam Levene, stopped by my door and said hello to me. The atmosphere lifted. I could breathe again. Who knows, maybe even something as ephemeral as charm might feel free to return to me. I may not have had any acting technique, but I sure as all hell was learning some survival skills. How to hang in until the tide changes, and until the Yin reaches its fullness and gives way to the Yang. The sun came out onstage. We were beginning to play.

Earlier in the summer I'd finally given up on the idea that Bill Alexander and I had any chance of reconciliation. In September, three days before rehearsals began, I flew to Mexico and got a divorce. We hadn't spoken to each other for months. My love affair with Bob Williams faded and I was falling in love with Paul Roberts. Nevertheless, on Friday, November 1, 1957, I sent Bill this telegram:

> *Dear Bill,*
>
> *Am opening on Broadway tonight. The lead in* Fair Game—*name is Ellen McRae. Very nervous. Needed to have some touch with you. Be with me between 8:00 and 11:00 please.*
>
> *Love,*
>
> *Ed*

Opening night was one of the worst rainstorms in New York history. It was pouring. Nobody could get a cab. Curtain time came and the theater was empty. I was calm enough, dressed and ready to go on, but they held the curtain for forty minutes, and in that time I became a nervous wreck. I hadn't yet learned to vocalize before a show. When I got onstage and opened my mouth to speak, my throat had closed. I had no voice. Just a little squeak which shocked me into getting hold of myself, and soon I managed to get my voice into its proper register. The play went well after that. We were zinging.

There was a party at Sardi's after the play. When the reviews came out in the Monday papers they praised Sam's "comic genius" and my "sensational figure." I was "the new girl in town." We were a hit.

Looking back, I am surprised to see how often I fell in and out of love. By April of 1957, I ended my relationship with Bob Williams and began seeing Howard Barnes, a radio executive at CBS. By November, I'd broken up with Howard and began my love affair with Paul Roberts, who was shortly to become my second husband. And Roger Price was a friend at the same time. I certainly wasn't shy of male companionship. But one does wonder what my idea of love was. Francis, in one of his letters to me, describes me as having "no sign of morality or immorality." I guess that is an accurate description. Once I had an affair and I was no longer going to be a virgin when I got married, my whole Catholic morality fell apart. I didn't really replace that structure with a new one for many years. I was so identified with being Catholic that when I slipped away from the Church, I didn't know what I was. What I knew then about religion was only its restrictions. And I didn't want to be restricted.

This was 1958, before the sexual revolution. But I seem to have let my sexuality rule my life. I was like a rabbit in the wild woods, food for all the other denizens of the forest, but my only concern seems to have been how to become a more delicious morsel.

Paul and I announced that we would be married in June. The New York newspaper headlines read CINDERELLA STORY, SHE'LL MARRY THE BOSS, UNKNOWN WALKS OFF WITH A LEAD ON BROADWAY AND NOW SHE'LL MARRY THE DIRECTOR, and HAPPY ENDING.

Happy ending? Hardly.

I knew that Paul drank a lot. I just didn't understand that he was an alcoholic. I never saw him drunk, though his hands shook so much in the morning he had to hold his first drink of the day with two hands. That should have been a clue, one would think, but I grew up around alcohol. My mother and Lou drank from early evening until bedtime. Most of the people I knew drank a lot; Paul just drank more. A lot more. But he was so charming and kind and he never seemed drunk. Also, he had two daughters—Cathy, age seven, and Cindy, age four—whom he adored and was heartbroken that his family was being dissolved. I thought his drinking was linked to this pain, which in due time would heal and he would drink less. I was wrong. He drank at least a fifth of Seagram's a day, sometimes a quart. I also drank at this time, but never during the day or when I was working, though afterwards I was only too happy to join in the fun.

My mother and Steve came to New York for the holidays during the run of *Fair Game*. I had been staying with Blossom. Roger Price let Steve, my mother, and me stay at his large apartment on Central Park West while he was out of town. After the first performance they saw, they came backstage and my mother said, "Oh, honey, I didn't understand what you were doing. This is terrific."

As I sat taking off my makeup, she said, "When I was carrying Jack, a woman said to me, that child is going to be somebody special. But she was wrong. It wasn't Jack. It was you." This story would grow over the years. Jack would be dropped, the woman would turn into a gypsy, and the line would become, "That child is going to be a great star someday." As the years went on and the story underwent its rewrites, my mother told it more and more often until finally she never met anyone without telling this tale, which by then she thoroughly believed.

The play closed in May. In July and August I did *Fair Game* in summer stock in New Jersey. By the time I returned to New York, Paul, who had been drinking even more than usual, had a complete physical collapse and was hospitalized. His doctor told him that he had to stop drinking. And he did, for a short while. Then he started again. Meanwhile, his first wife, Dell, went to Mexico for a divorce and Paul decided it was time for us to get married. I wrote in my diary on Sunday, September 14, 1958: "Beautiful glorious day—*Perfect*. Mrs. Paul Roberts (Bottstein)." Paul's full name was Paul Robert Bottstein, but he used only the first two of his names.

As soon as we were married, I tried to get pregnant—Paul and I wanted a son because he already had two daughters—but it just wasn't happening. By April I was seeing a Dr. Portnoy, who performed the very painful Ruben's test and announced that my tubes were closed. The only possible cure was a readministering of the test once a month for sixth months; sometimes the testing actually opened the blocked tubes. It didn't work for me and after six months, Dr. Portnoy advised me to adopt.

I went into a tailspin. This was the price I was to pay for my sin. I was never to carry a child again. I was wretchedly unhappy. I started drinking almost as much as Paul. Drinking and sleeping, that's what I did. I didn't get out of bed until four in the afternoon. I made the bed, tidied the apartment, bathed and dressed, and was ready for Paul when he got home at six. I made us drinks and dinner. After dinner, if we were not joining friends, we went to our neighborhood bar, Donohue's, sat at the bar with the other regulars and drank until the beautiful Irish bartender closed it down for the night. Then we staggered across Lexington Avenue at two in the morning, back to our apartment on 71st Street. One night I remember

I was so drunk, the sidewalk rose up like a wave and threw me against a lamppost, which broke my fall.

This went on for months. I was almost more ashamed of the sleeping than I was of the drinking. The drinking I shared with Paul and when we spent weekends with friends like the painter Alfred Leslie or Norman Mailer and his wife, Adele, everybody seemed to be having a great time as we emptied bottles right and left, going for broke and blotto. But nobody slept as much as I did. I didn't even tell Paul. I pretended I'd been up all day. I was a closet sleeper. I've been blessed with a pretty sunny nature and I seldom get depressed. That experience taught me that if I start sleeping too much, I'm depressed. But I didn't know that then, and I was so full of remorse, shame, guilt, and self-hatred that I added sloth to my list of deadly sins.

Finally I realized I was in trouble. I had stopped seeing Bluma, but I called her up and asked to see her again. I dragged my shipwrecked, sodden self down to her office in the Village and confessed my sorry state.

Bluma, as usual, gave me very good advice. She said, "Well, first of all, you have to get yourself out of bed. Make appointments that you know you won't break."

And so I did. I don't remember how I found my way there, but I went to Bellevue Hospital and volunteered as a "toy lady." There are children who require more daily medical attention than their parents can provide, so they live at Bellevue. Some are quadriplegic, some with braces on all their limbs, some confined to their hospital beds and connected to tubes. Some children have families that visit them regularly. Some are abandoned completely. The volunteer service has many different departments. One woman came every day and ironed the children's laundry, carefully pressing the ruffles on the girls' donated dresses so they didn't have to wear hospital gowns.

One day I was on an elevator in the hospital when it stopped at a floor and I noticed a beautiful little chapel. Intrigued, I stepped off the elevator and saw that this chapel was one of three on this floor. There was a Catholic, a Protestant, and a Jewish chapel, presumably where family members could go to pray for their loved ones. I stepped into each quiet sanctuary and was struck by the atmosphere in each of these spaces that had been carved out of this busy hospital. In a room near the elevator there was a long table around which were seated elderly men in hospital robes and slippers. Many were in wheelchairs. They were being served matzo ball soup by two volunteers, and I could tell by the serving dishes that they had brought the soup from their own kitchens. It was Passover.

I got on the elevator, very moved by the kindness of these women, and I rode up to the volunteers' office where I donned my toy lady's red smock and got my rolling tray of toys to bring to the children. I was on no rigid time schedule and I could take as long as I wanted with each child, showing them the toys and engaging in play with them. They always got excited to see a red smock come into their rooms, and soon the ones that could speak learned my name. These children were all so good-natured and brave, their little hands touched me with such warmth, that soon I began to heal and get out of bed, looking forward to spending my day with them. Perhaps I wouldn't be able to give birth to my own child, but there are so many children in the world needing love, it's really not all that hard to find a recipient for our love. And that's what it boils down to, finding someone to give all our love to so it doesn't clog up our hearts and turn us to stone.

I had been working with Paul at CBS radio doing the soap operas *Ma Perkins* and *Right to Happiness*. But they, along with my volunteer work at Bellevue, didn't fill my day. I decided it was time to take an acting class. Blossom had been studying with Stella Adler, so I went down to her school and spoke to her about taking a scene study class. Stella offered a three-year course, but I didn't think I needed that. After all, I'd already done a lead on Broadway, right? Wrong. I should have taken all the technique classes I could get. But that lesson was yet to come. Stella allowed me to join only the scene class. And so I began my training.

I had been in class for a couple of weeks and wanted to do a scene, but I didn't know who to work with. Blossom came to meet me after class one day and, as the other students filed out of the classroom, she pointed to a dark, curly-haired boy and said, "Ask him. He's good." Soon I introduced myself to this guy, who looked like a cast member of *West Side Story*. He had a sensitive, misunderstood, juvenile-delinquent kind of attractiveness. He said his name was Neil Nephew. I had selected a scene from Strindberg's *Easter,* and we began meeting every day to rehearse.

Paul, in the meantime, had been drinking heavily for about six months and then had another physical collapse that put him back in the hospital. This became a pattern. He would drink heavily for half a year, his body would fall apart, the doctor would hospitalize him and tell him he had to stop drinking or he'd be dead in no time. He'd give Paul a prescription for Librium to help him stay off the sauce. And it worked. But it also turned him into a zombie. He never laughed, seldom smiled, had no interest in sex. He became withdrawn and uncommunicative. After six months of this, he'd get fed up and want to loosen up and have some fun. He'd start drinking again. I tried to get him to go to A.A., but he wouldn't hear of it. He claimed he wasn't an alcoholic. I managed to drag him to one meeting, but he couldn't stand to be there and said he wasn't like those people. The pattern of our marriage was six months of fun and ribaldry, then total physical breakdown, followed by six months of judgmental, sexless, withdrawn sobriety.

I handled it fine until I found out I couldn't have children. That news hits you at the base of your femininity. Your very womanliness feels undermined.

I, who had always been a flirt and pursued by men, suddenly felt wobbly in my sexuality—unattractive, undesirable, and unlovable. I needed reassurance desperately.

As my rehearsals with Neil progressed, the space between us shrank and heated up. I was attracted to him and, more important, he wanted me. I didn't want to be unfaithful to my husband. I loved Paul, but I was in danger of getting what I needed—some stroking. One night as Paul was sitting in his chair, I went to him and sat at his feet. I told him that I needed loving. I said, "Even if you're not interested in sex right now, if you could just hold me, or even touch my hand or my hair, something, anything that communicates love." Paul said nothing. I began to cry in the silence. Then I said, "I'm asking you this because I know how much I need it and I'm afraid if you don't give it to me, I will get it somewhere else."

I had asked him to save me, but he couldn't. He didn't. Neil and I fell over the cliff. The scene from *Easter* that we were working on takes place on the Thursday before Easter. When we did the scene for Stella, it happened to be Holy Thursday. This synchronicity would play a significant and devastating part in our lives to come. After the scene Stella said, "Class, you have just been privileged to see the coming together of the perfect actress in the perfect role." She asked us to do the scene for her "Night of Scenes" at the close of the school year.

We did it again and it was flat, ordinary, nothing. Uninspired is what it was. Stella walked up to me at the party afterward, took my hand, looked deep into my eyes with those amazing liquid pools of hers, and after a moment she said, "Come, take my technique class."

She was right. My natural talent was there. The work could be fantastic, as it was when we did it in class. But I had no control over it. I couldn't summon it. I had no technique. Talent cannot be taught. But technique can. That was still ahead of me.

After Stella's class ended for the summer, I went out again in summer stock, this time in a comedy called *John Loves Mary*. We were to play three cities, including Detroit. James Garner had just finished his TV series *Maverick* and was a very popular star. In the first city we played, the theater was a huge tent with the stage in the center. The dressing rooms were in a separate tent in the back, behind the parking lot. So many people wanted Jim's autograph that there was no way to keep the crowd in order except to file them through my dressing room into Jim's and out his door. It never struck me as odd to see all these strangers lined up filing past me as I removed my makeup. Once in a while someone would say something complimentary to me, but mostly they chatted among themselves excited that they were about to meet "Maverick." I accepted this. He was a star; I was "the girl."

When the play went to Detroit, it was my first time back as an actress. The theater was in Northland, a shopping center in the suburbs. My extended family came to see the show, all my aunts and uncles. After the performance, Uncle Chuck came backstage and put his arms around me as he did when I was a child and stood in his warm embrace while he did the crossword puzzle. He held me, patted me on the back, and said, "Well, that was real good, Tootsie." No award or recognition I ever received was more meaningful to me than those loving words from my uncle Chuck. Could it possibly be that it was the first time I was ever told that something I did was good? It seems preposterous, but that's what it felt like to me. Of course Steve's face had beamed with pride, but my mother always managed to make my accomplishments her own product.

While I was on tour with *John Loves Mary*, Neil wrote me a letter and sent it to the office of my business manager, who, instead of sending it on to me, sent it home to Paul, who read it. The proverbial cat was out of the bag.

When Paul and I were next together we talked about it and I reminded him that I'd begged him to touch me. I explained how vulnerable I was; how much I needed affection, if not sex, and how much I would have preferred that he had been able to give that to me, but that I had been in desperate need of love and reassurance. Paul knew what I said was true and we decided to stay together. Not long after, I was offered a role in a pilot for a TV series that would be shot in Europe. I pleaded with Paul to go with me. I hoped we could make a fresh start and planned our trip like it was the honeymoon we'd never had.

The show was to begin shooting near Amsterdam and then move to the south of France. When I left Detroit my aim was to see the world. I'd completed the first circle with my return to Detroit as an actress, and was setting off to begin the second ring. I was battered, bruised, with very few of my illusions intact, but still trying to hold on to as many as possible. I requested that the company pay to have my husband and me sail there. This was a fantasy of mine from early Hollywood movies—Bette Davis or Joan Crawford at the rail of a ship, the moonlight shining on her floating chiffon as Charles Boyer lights a cigarette—that kind of thing. The fantasy did not include an injured marriage, an alcoholic husband, a reproductively obstructed heroine, or any of the other truths of my tarnished life. I tucked them into my denial kit and dissociated myself from them as I was fitted for my chiffon gowns at Saks Fifth Avenue. A brand-new wardrobe to begin a brand-new life with a trip to the Old World.

We stopped first in Southampton, England. Some passengers disembarked. Then we went on to Rotterdam, where we left the ship and traveled overland to Amsterdam. I was surprised how new Rotterdam looked. I expected to see old buildings. Then it was explained to me that Rotterdam had been leveled by the Germans in World War II—not a building left standing—so it was, in fact, a brand-new city in the Old World that had been completely rebuilt in the last fifteen years.

When the pilot for the series finished shooting in Holland, we headed for the south of France. There was a character who worked in that segment who always had a Chihuahua on his lap. It was discovered that there were no Chihuahuas available for rent in the south of France, so one was rented in Amsterdam to travel with us. The morning we were to leave, we gathered at the train station and I met the little dog for the first time, on a leash, shivering in terror on the busy platform. I quickly realized that the young assistant who had been assigned the care of the dog had no experience with animals and was quite chagrined to be given this responsibility. I offered to take the dog off his hands. He gladly surrendered his charge and I had an adorable pet for the rest of this particular adventure. Chihuahuas are so small that in this world of huge trains, cars, buses, noises, and giant people, they have a nearly parasitical relationship with their caregivers. Otherwise, they would be trampled to death. Consequently, they are extremely affectionate and grateful for the care they are given. When we began shooting, Paul returned to New York, so I was happy to have this sweet little body next to me in my empty bed.

On the *Rotterdam*, Paul and I had made friends with two Texas oilmen cousins, Bill and Jim Abeel. They were in France when we went there to shoot and I found them at La Colombe d'Or hotel in Saint-Paul-de-Vence. They had a visit for tea scheduled at the home of Marc Chagall and asked me to join them. Chagall's house was high up the mountain in the town of Vence. Madame Chagall greeted us and the first thing I noticed as we entered the house was a sketch of Chagall hanging on the wall to the left of the entrance, signed by Picasso. The house was eighteenth century or older, and built in the French country style with rough white walls, perhaps plaster over stone, with dark wooden beams and doors. The rooms were sparsely furnished and the chairs placed to contemplate the art on the walls, which was mostly paintings by other artists, like Matisse and contemporaries of Chagall. The artist himself was white-haired with penetrating merry eyes. He said a few polite words to the Texans and then motioned for me to come outside. Madame Chagall brought out our tea and went back in to talk to the Texans while Chagall and I sat outside at a table overlooking the Mediterranean. The hillside was terraced and planted with flowering fruit trees. Chagall's English was as poor as my French, but we managed a conversation. He wanted to know all about me. Where I lived, what I did, who I was, and what I aspired to be. He seemed genuinely interested in me and although I was extremely flattered, I couldn't imagine why. Only now that I am older and find myself more and more attracted to the unjaded freshness of young people do I begin to understand the keen interest of this great artist in a young girl. My memory of that day is seeing this white-haired man with the blue Mediterranean as a background, the flowering and fruited trees falling away behind him, and his blue eyes, those eyes that saw, truly saw, peering at me with merriment and sincere interest.

At some point on this first trip to Europe, I was staying in London and took a trip to Maidenhead and Henley-on-Thames, where I had the sense that I was coming home for the first time. It was not England necessarily that I was coming home to, but Europe, the Old World. It had to do with time. I remember going to a tavern that had a feeling of age unlike anything I'd ever experienced. The tavern, the thick dark oak table at which I sat, had been there while Shakespeare was alive. I touched the table reverently and imagined all the hands that had touched it before me. All the lives, all the stories, all the deaths. I felt them all present in a continuum of which I was a part. I was conscious of this being one moment in time and in this moment I was actual and alive. I realized that this table was older than my whole country. It was as if a curtain opened at the back of the stage that was the theater of my mind, revealing a far deeper space than I had ever imagined. In fact there was no longer a wall at the back of the stage, but an opening onto the infinite night where stars were born and died in the ever-present majesty of Chronos. The moment recorded itself the way those moments of clear consciousness do, filling me with a love of and a connection to the past that is a continuing presence in the play of my life.

When I returned home, I told Paul I wanted a dog, a Dalmatian. We located a breeder with a new litter in Connecticut and drove up to see him. We walked into the kitchen; five Dalmatian puppies were in a pen. I sat on the floor. The pen was opened. Four puppies ran past me. One puppy ran to me, jumped on my lap, and nipped my nose. No questions asked. She'd picked me. I named her Daisy Mae after Li'l Abner's girlfriend with the polka-dot blouse. She became my closest friend and helper for the next seven years and, in several ways, she was one of my most important teachers.

Paul had another physical collapse and went back in the hospital, back on Librium, and consequently was in a period of nondrinking and nonaffection. But this time I had Daisy Mae to love, care for, and talk to when I felt alone. Paul and I investigated adoption, but at that time all adoptions were through the social services of religious organizations. Because we were considered a mixed marriage (he was Jewish) and was not a member of a church or synagogue, we were not desirable candidates for adopting. That door, too, was closed to me. Daisy Mae became the willing recipient of all my maternal impulses.

It was at Donohue's bar that I met Jack Wilson, one of the regulars, who did the *New York Times* crossword puzzle every Sunday. I decided to try it myself one Sunday, but I couldn't get one word. So I began looking up things in the dictionary, the encyclopedia, *Roget's Thesaurus,* the *Reader's Encyclopedia,* anything I needed to come up with the solution. That began a habit of doing the *New York Times* crossword puzzle every Sunday. At the beginning, I worked on it all week. It was almost a year before I finished an entire puzzle. Later I would start doing the daily puzzle, too. Diving into these reference books was my real education. I became deeply engaged in learning. I would look up something to do with a bridge and discover there were only three main types of bridges. Then I'd fill up a notebook with pages on the history of bridges. I still have the notebooks, of course, with my habit of saving, collecting, and filing.

All of this searching for words led me into study of all kinds. Bill Alexander had introduced me to literature and I became an inveterate reader, but now I developed a thirst to understand the world. Belief had fallen away from me and I stood poised on the edge of the mystery, naked and hungry. I was drawn to the behaviorists. Konrad Lorenz's *King Solomon's Ring* was the beginning. Then I read Nikolaas Tinbergen and the other naturalists who were approaching understanding reality through the study of nature. I came across archaeology as if I had discovered a discarded shard from a lost civilization. That led me to anthropology and the study of my own species. Deeper and deeper into history, the Romans, the Greeks, the Egyptians. What was I looking for in all that deep diving? I couldn't have articulated it then, but I know what I was searching for was simply the meaning of life. ("What *is* it all about, Alfie?") I was floundering. I didn't know why I was alive or what I was supposed to do with the fact that I was alive. I didn't know how life came about. Life on the planet Earth, I mean. I had lost my faith, that's for sure, but I was aware, as Sartre said, of "a God-shaped hole in my heart."

I'm reminded of a story: Mullah Nazrudin is searching the street by a streetlight. A friend comes along and asks, "What are you searching for?"

Mullah Nazrudin replies, "My key, I've lost it."

"Did you lose it here?" asks his friend.

"No," explains Mullah Nazrudin, "I lost it over there, but there is more light here."

Like Mullah Nazrudin, I continued to search among the ruins of the past for the key to the present, never thinking to look where I had lost it, in that God-shaped hole in my heart.

Paul got offered a job in California. His old friend Tom McDermot was running Four Star, a company formed by Dick Powell, David Niven, Charles Boyer, and Agnes Moorehead. The last three had mostly faded from active participation, so Dick Powell brought in as CEO McDermot, who offered Paul the chance to be an executive in charge of production of their TV shows. Paul was pretty bored with directing radio soap operas in New York and was ready to move into TV, so he really wanted to take the offer. I did not want to leave New York, despite the possibility of working in film. I did not want to live in Los Angeles, but I had no choice: Paul was the head of the household. He was the boss. We moved to California in late 1960.

I didn't transplant easily. We lived in a motel on Santa Monica and Doheny for two weeks. Paul went to work every day and I cried. I cried all day. It all looked wrong to me: the trees, the flowers, the architecture, the streets, the people. We found a furnished house in the mountains on the valley side of Mulholland, the road on top of the mountain that divides Los Angeles from the San Fernando Valley. The house had a pool and a small garden. I thought I might feel better if I could just have a lilac bush. I drove to the nursery and asked the man for a lilac bush. He said, almost sadly, "Oh no, lilacs don't grow here." I felt the area around my midsection sink a bit.

"Why not?" I asked timidly, almost afraid of the answer.

"Well, actually," the man explained, "they have gotten them to grow by grafting them onto a native rootstock, but they have no smell."

"How come?" I asked feebly.

"Oh, they need a long dormant season to develop their characteristic aroma," he said kindly.

The tears bubbled up and out. My whole body trembled. "I know how they feel," I said, helplessly exposed to this stranger with a shocked expression on his face, as if to say, *What happened? I thought we were talking about lilacs here.* I ran back to the car, gripped the steering wheel, and cried.

There I was, feeling uprooted and transplanted to an alien terrain, having no understanding of why I was in this semitropical, desertlike, artificial atmosphere, when I discovered that the adoption laws were different in California than in New York, and here I could get a baby! I could be a mother at last. Paul and I began to investigate the process.

In the meantime, my frustrated maternal instincts were running wild and Daisy Mae wasn't enough. I turned the small garden into an animal yard. I bought two rabbits and a guinea pig, and soon after that a baby goat that I fed from a bottle.

As we moved ahead with adoption proceedings, I began to have doubts. What if I didn't love this baby? What if he were very different from me, or he looked funny, or had some hereditary disease or quirks? Would I still be able to love him? That was my worry. I didn't share it with Paul. He was really going through this for me. He already had children. I didn't want him to know I had doubts, but they were, in fact, gnawing at me.

Then Daisy got pregnant. I'd not had her spayed. I just couldn't. She had come in heat soon after we arrived in the house. I didn't think she'd gotten out, but she had all the signs. Her nipples were growing and she was gaining weight. The vet confirmed it. He gave a date when we should expect the puppies. He said he could feel at least four in there. But the day came and went and no puppies arrived. I took Daisy back to the vet. He examined her again and this time proclaimed he no longer felt any puppies, that she'd had a false pregnancy. I was stunned, but I understood how she felt. I took her home and was busy doing something in the living room when Daisy came in the room and spoke to me in a way she had that was not quite a bark, but talking, making noises and shifting her weight on all fours, back and forth. I knew that she wanted something, but I didn't know what it was. I asked, "What is it, Daisy?"

More shifting of feet and her talking sounds. I walked to the kitchen to check her water bowl. It was full. She'd eaten. It wasn't that. I asked again what it was. She went to the door of the shop off the kitchen and stood there excitedly talking to me. I didn't have a clue. She went into the shop and turned to me, wagging her tail enthusiastically. I entered the shop, but saw nothing but tools. She went to a particular counter and looked up pointedly. I just didn't get it, but obviously she wanted something, so I picked her up, put her on the counter, and said, "Show me. What is it?"

She stood on her hind legs and put her feet on the center of three shelves and stretched herself up as high as she could, pointing with her nose to the top shelf, where I'd put some stuffed animals. "Is this what you want?" I asked, bringing down the bear. No, she motioned, still pointing. I lifted down the stuffed striped tiger. "This?" I asked. Yes! That's it. The stuffed tiger! She quickly took it by the scruff of its neck, jumped off the counter, and ran to the bedroom. I followed her. There was a large table in the bedroom with an open space under it. She got under it and lay down with the tiger held between her front paws and looked out at me. She had adopted a baby. She didn't care if it had stripes instead of spots. It was her baby and she made a nest for it and stayed there for ten days, not coming out except to move her bowels quickly, then return to her nest, where she licked her baby just as she would have done her own puppy. I had to bring her water and food bowls there and leave them. I sat on the edge of my bed facing her nest, watching her mother this stuffed tiger and I knew I was watching a miracle in action. This dog had read my fears and doubts and taught me in her own way that the instinct to mother is so powerful, it will prevail. Doubts and worry come and go, but mothering goes on. I turned to my other great teacher, the dictionary, and looked up the word "mother." There I learned that the first definition of the word "mother" is a verb. Daisy showed me that you become the noun by doing the verb.

Soon Paul and I made contact with a lawyer who had a client who was an unwed mother. We made an arrangement to pay for the girl's last two months of pregnancy, when she could no longer work, and for the delivery. I wished very hard for the baby to be a boy, so afraid was I to repeat the relationship I had with my mother.

August 31, 1961, was the happiest day of my life. My son was born in the morning and eight hours later he was transferred from the nurse's arms into my own. He was a pink, fat, hungry, little creature who surpassed the two ounces I'd been told to feed him in no time, and was gobbling up eight ounces per feeding. Daisy Mae was very happy I'd taken her advice but was only worried that I didn't seem to understand how important licking was. Puppies are stimulated to eat, breathe, and defecate by their mother's licking. Without it, they could lose their tenuous grip on life. That's why Daisy didn't leave her nest for ten days. That's how long it takes for the pups to remember to stay alive on their own. Daisy kept demonstrating this to me by uncovering my baby's feet and then licking them while she looked up at me, meaningfully. "Lick them," she communicated to me. "You've got to lick them!"

I named my baby Jefferson Jack Roberts. Roberts didn't sound like a last name to me, so I thought I'd give him a weighty first name. But I called him Skipper because with all the little animals we had in our menagerie, I thought of him as the skipper of the Ark. (I'd tried to name him Noah, but Paul balked, which Jefferson thanks him for.) "Mom, women love my name," he informed me when he was around sixteen years old.

I adored being a mother. Jeff's early childhood was the happiest time of my life. We had six months before the adoption became final and we were investigated several times in those six months. Paul was in a non-drinking phase, so had no way to handle the tension of the investigation. He would sweat profusely as the social worker asked us questions. I saw her make note of Paul continually wiping his beaded brow. But we passed and on April 23, 1962, I wrote in my diary, *Went to court and my son became J. J. Roberts—legally.*

It wasn't as if the moment the nurse put the baby in my arms he became *mine*, my baby, I'm a mother. That's it. The nurse carried the baby down in the elevator, through the hallway, to a doorway that opened onto the parking lot. For insurance purposes I couldn't receive the baby until I was out of the hospital. The nurse handed the baby through the doorway and placed him in my arms. Thirty years later, I learned the term: a liminal experience. Liminal (I think from the Latin for "doorway") is a doorway that once you pass through you are changed. You've entered another realm. The realm was motherhood. I was very attuned to what was happening to me inside. And I stayed open and aware to my impulses and feelings in this new realm I'd entered. I wanted to be conscious of the whole process. When I looked down at the brand-new human being in my arms, I was moved by the perfection of the tiny hands and toes, the sweetness of his little lips, his closed eyes fluttering at the change of light, but I felt no different yet than I would feel about any other newborn baby that I held. That difference would come slowly in the next few weeks. It would come as I held him, feeding him his bottle, and he would look in my eyes as I gazed at him. I could feel the love flow between us as surely as the milk flowed from the bottle I held to his hungry mouth. It would come as I held him on my lap facing me, supporting his head with my two hands and he moved his arms and kicked his legs rhythmically in time to the music I played for him. It was the most beautiful dance I'd ever seen. It would come when I was feeding him one day and he made a noise and I said, "Nah, you're puttin' me on," and he smiled at the joke. I was so impressed—he recognized humor! And it wasn't gas, it was a smile! As the love between us grew each day, he became the most important person in the world to me. In a very short time I came to love him unconditionally. Not for anything he did, but just for what he was.

When Skipper was around two months old, I went for an audition and was sitting in the outer office waiting to be asked in to read. There was a young actor also there to audition and he kept leaping out of his seat and rushing down the hall to make a phone call. He finally apologized for his hyper behavior, but explained that his wife was in labor. I asked if it was his first child. He said it was and I told him my baby was only two months old. We got into a conversation about the thrill of being a parent. Then he asked, "How was your labor? Did you have a hard time?"

I thought for a moment trying to remember my labor and I just couldn't remember it. I did remember a novel I'd read many years ago where the heroine is about to give birth and another character explains that it is very painful, but you soon forget it and I thought, well that turns out to be true after all. I've forgotten all about my labor. I said to the actor, "Isn't that funny, they say you forget the pain and . . ." Then suddenly I remembered, "Oh, oh," I said startled. "I wasn't there."

The actor's face registered equal parts of surprise and incomprehension. "I mean," I sputtered, "my baby's adopted." I had completely forgotten. But completely. Then I knew it had happened: the verb had become the noun.

After three months, I resumed acting. I averaged about one TV show a month that year. Each show took from three to five days to shoot. The rest of the time I was home enjoying being a mother. But as happy as I was being a mother, other areas of my life were in trouble. Shortly after Skip's adoption became final, Paul started drinking heavily again.

He was a kind, good man and I always loved him. But his drinking was a real problem that he just wasn't ready to face.

Even so, in those last months of our marriage, with my ability to dissociate, I didn't realize how unhappy I was. Paul had to tell me. One night, we'd had some neighborhood friends over for dinner and when they left, I might have leaped up and begun washing the dishes. Or I might have turned to Paul and said something. I might have kept the balloon of pretense in the air with the slightest tap, but I didn't. I just sat there and didn't move. Paul was sitting across from me. Between us there was just a moment, a tiny moment of silence when the balloon slowly drifted to the ground. Then Paul said quietly, "You're unhappy, aren't you?"

I nodded.

"Do you want a divorce?"

Again I nodded.

And that was the end of it. The end of my second marriage.

I never asked for anything from either of my husbands. No lawyers were necessary. I flew to Mexico for both divorces. We just sorted through the detritus of the marriages and said, "I want this," "You can keep that," and so forth. I found a house in Laurel Canyon and sent for my furniture, which had been in storage for a year in New York. I looked forward to living with my own things again—especially my piano.

By June 1962, I'd moved into my own place with my nine-month-old baby. I was supporting us both by working on television shows. Neil, the acting student, had moved to California in the meantime and we began seeing each other regularly. He shared an apartment with his friend Henry Madden, who was the beau of Shelley Winters. We became a frequent foursome. One night we gathered at Shelley's apartment to watch a show I was in. Shelley had a way of inviting us to dinner, then sitting in the living room like a diva while I cooked dinner in the kitchen. Just as the show came on, I was pouring coffee from Shelley's silver coffeepot, when the whole pot fell off the handle. I was still holding it in my hand as the coffee ran out of the pot, soaking into Shelley's white rug. I spent most of the show on my hands and knees scrubbing the rug and trying to calm Shelley. Years later, Shelley would refer to the time I "spilled coffee on her rug."

"I didn't spill it," I shouted. "Your coffeepot fell off the handle!" But in Shelley's history, I spilled the coffee.

No one saw the show, but afterward Shelley offered this opinion. "You look like nothing ever happened to you. You should pierce your ears, lower your neckline, and go to Lee Strasberg." I was stunned that anyone could possibly think I looked like nothing had ever happened to me! With my life? But now that I think about it, she was right.

Henry was six foot four and an Irish-American Catholic two-fisted drinker. He had a beautiful singing voice, was madly handsome, and wildly self-destructive. Neil, on the other hand, was a funny Long Island Jewish, boyish charmer. They were both actors and writers. Quite a pair. We had nothing but hilarious fun for about five years. Then the other side of all that hilarity began to reveal itself when everything slowly descended and went deep down into the dark.

But in 1962 we were young and in love. Neil was determined that Skipper's first word would be "Neil." He coached him regularly, repeating his name over and over. Skipper's actual first word was "cookie," but his second was "Nee." For months he called Neil "Nee" and when he finally got around to my name, he called me "Money." Soon Neil was spending more time at my house than in his apartment and we began to mention the word marriage. I was twice burned, but that seems not to have deterred me and I did want my son to grow up with a father. Neil seemed to love him and even wrote a song for him using only words Skip could say. It went "G G G go go go outside. G go go go go outside. G go go go outside. Yes everybody go outside. Bye bye, bye bye car. Bye bye bye bye car. Bye bye bye bye car," et cetera. When he played it, Skip would stand at the piano, hands on the piano bench, and dance up and down. That is one of my most tender memories of Neil and Skip together.

As we discussed marriage, Neil held up a cautionary finger and said, "I win on a bump." That was vernacular for "I'm the boss." I was six years older. We were in my house, with my furniture. I paid all the bills and was responsible for running the house. He didn't work, brought in no money to the forming family, and seldom would in the years to come, but I agreed to this arrangement. He would be "boss" because after all, he was the man. It would take ten years and a whole paradigm shift for me to question this assumption.

Soon after Neil and I got together, Neil made friends with Bob Rafelson, who would later direct *Five Easy Pieces* and *The King of Marvin Gardens*. But at this time Bob was an associate producer in television. The guys decided to get together with their "old ladies," a hip term that I always deplored. I met Bob's wife, Toby, who was five months pregnant, and we became friends. Those marriages are long gone and other tragedies injected into our psychic streams, but Toby and I are still close and loving friends, though when we met, we had no idea how deeply we would affect each other's lives. They had a son, Peter, who was only a few months older than Jeff, so we had much in common and often took our kids to the park together. The day their daughter was born, Bob, Neil, and I visited Toby in the hospital and saw Julie, an adorable little pink package with lips like ripe cherries.

In the meantime, I was working. That year I did guest shots on *Perry Mason, The Real McCoys, Dobie Gillis,* and *Kraft Television Theater.* I was shooting at Universal on November 22, 1963, when, while sitting in the makeup chair, in the morning, being made up by Bob Dawn, someone rushed into the room and said, "President Kennedy has just been shot." I leaped out of the chair, as did all the others. We ran out into the hallway of the building. We turned on the radio and listened for news as the car carrying our president sped to the hospital. We paced the halls waiting for word. A black maid in a white uniform was crying. I went to her and though we had never met, we embraced and held each other, sobbing as word came that our president was dead. All work stopped. We proceeded to the set, everyone in tears. A moment of silence was requested. We all stood on the set, our sobs filling the silence. Then we were released to go home. Neil and I had only one car at the time, mine, so he had dropped me off that morning. I didn't know what to do with myself. He hadn't answered the phone. I was on the Universal lot just wandering about lost and sad and then there he was. Neil walked toward me and held me. He had this uncanny way of finding me in a crisis. This wouldn't be the last time he did it. You couldn't always count on Neil to do what you wished, but he often would surprise you and be there when the chips were down.

Neil wasn't getting any work at all, so Bob Rafelson encouraged him to start writing scripts. It would be a while before he sold anything and that would be to Bob, who was doing a circus show on TV starring Cornel Wilde. Bob cast me in an episode as a photographer for the circus. The other guest star of that episode was Jack Palance as a lion tamer. It was on this set that I had one of the most moving experiences of my life. The set was full of circus people and one of them was raising a baby chimpanzee, who was only four months old and wearing diapers and baby clothes, including a crocheted bonnet. The owner was about to feed her from a bottle and I asked if I might do it. The owner, glad to be relieved of his duty, handed the baby to me and I fed her as she gazed into my eyes and rested her tiny hand on my breast and squeezed it gently as though the milk were coming from there. Scientists tell us that oxytocin gets released when a mother nurses, but I know that it also gets released when you feed a baby a bottle. That chemical is the transporter of love through the eyes of the mother and child, but it doesn't even have to be a human baby. I could feel it happen as I fed this little chimp.

Neil and I started studying with Jeff Corey, an acting teacher in Los Angeles, and it was here that I began to have a glimmer of the resources that were available to me artistically that I hadn't yet explored. Neil and I often worked together in class and we prepared a scene from *Talk to Me Like the Rain and I Will Listen*. In that scene I relate a story. I chose to do it sitting at a window and watching the rain slide down the pane. The picture of what I was envisioning formed in the pattern of the rain so it was as though I were seeing the whole story in the window in front of me. Now, we were on a bare stage, no rain, no window, but I had created one for myself. In the critique afterward, Jeff Corey said that he had seen the window, seen the rain, and was very excited by what I'd done. He used it as an example to the class that "if the actor really sees something, even though it's not there, the audience will see it, too." Jeff was not as complimentary about Neil's work and it was the beginning rumbles of a problem that would eventually engulf us. Neil's hero was Marlon Brando. He copied him. It was what was wrong with his acting. He was always trying to do Marlon, so he never was able to act from his own center.

In Jeff Corey's class I began to explore some deeper areas in my acting. Until then I had mostly played light comedies. But in the theater in New York I had seen some great acting. I saw Julie Harris play Joan of Arc. I'd seen the great Kim Stanley in *Freud,* and Uta Hagen in *Who's Afraid of Virginia Woolf?* These actresses had made me experience something profound as I sat in the theater. What they were doing was important. It had meaning—depth. They weren't just up there being pretty, cute, and admired. They were saying something. They took you places you hadn't been before. They made you understand something about the human condition. Something hidden. Something beyond what the text said. Something that they knew! And when you saw their performances, you knew it, too. Could I do that? Did I know anything? Was I capable of penetrating that deeply into a character? I wanted to find out.

I decided to work on a scene from *Virginia Woolf.* Martha is a complex character and she is very aggressive with her husband. I didn't ask Neil to play George. I didn't want to lash out at my own husband the way Martha did at hers. I began rehearsing the scene with another actor in class, Bill Jordan. As I worked on Martha, an image rose up in me of a bullfighter. I decided to go with it. I played Martha like a bullfighter who was taunting her husband the bull, trying to get a rise out of him, to make him charge her. It was very effective. I think the conventional way to play Martha, like a drunken ball-buster, is a trap one can easily fall into, but playing her like a bullfighter, a toreador, gave her cunning and focus and a deadly intention along with a heightened flair. I entered Martha. I could feel her inside of me. She was like a room in me that I kept locked and sealed. I didn't want to go there. But as a bullfighter, I had an image that allowed me to enter that space in myself where the Martha in me lived.

All space is in us. All those many rooms. Our egos will not always permit us to accept that. It keeps us out with lines like, "Oh, I could never do that to anyone," but if we can find just the right metaphor to wrap our egos in, they will allow us to enter those hidden rooms. For me, the metaphor was the bullfighter. Once I was in that room, Martha spoke out clearly using my voice.

Then one night I dreamed as Martha. In the dream, I was Martha, talking to my husband, George, when suddenly I woke up. Neil had gotten out of the bed and had gone into the bathroom. I saw the empty bed and felt abandoned and called out loudly, "George?" As soon as I did, I knew that was wrong. I said to myself, *No, wait! I'm not Martha. I'm an actress playing Martha. I am* . . . And then there was a pause. An empty space with no name. I knew I was an actress. I just didn't know which actress I was. My identity as an actress seemed deeper or more real than my personality. It was as though I were a soul poised on the edge of a new incarnation, having separated from her past life—whatever that was—and not yet having taken on her new one, but knew only one thing—my mission in this life: I am an actress.

After shooting a racing car movie, *Pit Stop,* my next feature was a teenage beach party movie starring Jimmy Darren and Pamela Tiffin called *For Those Who Think Young.* It was not too memorable.

And then I finally got cast in a big-budget, Hollywood-studio movie called *Goodbye Charlie,* directed by Vincente Minnelli and starring Debbie Reynolds, Tony Curtis, and Walter Matthau. I was costarring. This was the big time. The movie is about a womanizer named Charlie who dies and comes back to life in the body of a woman and has to suffer the indignities that he put women through when he was a man. Debbie Reynolds played Charlie as a woman. The small role of Charlie as a man who gets killed in the first scene hadn't yet been cast. One day Neil and Henry Madden came to visit me on the set. When Minnelli saw Henry's good looks, he quickly cast him as Charlie. I was being photographed in a pretty costume that day and the photographer asked Neil to step in for a few shots. This picture of Neil and me defines how mismatched we were. We don't look anything like a couple. Seeing that picture of two anonymous people, I would never be able to imagine what their relationship would be. They surely don't look like husband and wife.

Vincente Minnelli, father of Liza, ex-husband of Judy Garland, was a strange bird. He directed some of the biggest pictures in Hollywood: *Meet Me in St. Louis* with his wife, Judy; *An American in Paris,* one of the best musicals of all time; *Gigi*; and many others. At this point in his career he was a bit past his prime, married to a woman named Lee Anderson, but his manner seemed campy, if not downright androgynous. There is a strange phenomenon that happens on sets with some directors in which they will zero in on one member of the cast who then becomes the whipping boy. It's never a star, but someone in a supporting or lesser position, and they go after them, taking out all their frustrations on that one person. I've only been chosen for this ignominious designation once in my career, and it was in this film. Minnelli seemed to be polite to everyone on the set but me. He railed at me, humiliating me at every opportunity. The first day on the set, I began to say my lines and Minnelli joined in, saying them, too, so I stopped. Then he'd say, "Say it. Say the line." I'd begin, and then he'd join in, so I would stop. Then he'd yell, "Say the line! Say the line!" I just couldn't imagine he wanted me to say the line with him at the same time. But that's what he wanted. Over and over until I had his rhythm and there was nothing left of mine. I was doing his performance of the character.

I had stopped smoking nine months before we began shooting, but one day after one of Minnelli's tirades at me, I was sitting on the set trying to collect myself and keep from crying when a hand with a muscular arm put a lit cigarette in front of my face. It was a crew guy letting me know I wasn't alone. I didn't want to smoke, but I was so in need of the friendly gesture, I took it gratefully and inhaled his kindness into my lungs.

To me the most remarkable thing about this film was Walter Matthau's choice of accent. He played a character that he decided had been born in Hungary, grew up in Brooklyn, so had a Hungarian-Brooklyn accent that he tried to cover by adopting an English accent. When I remarked on it to

Walter, he said, "Yeah, I'm doing a triple." It was amazing to see when he chose to forget the British and let the Brooklyn come through and when he fell into his native Hungarian. What a feat!

Tony Curtis was extremely funny and much smarter than I would have predicted from the movies I'd seen him in when I was a teenager in Detroit.

I offered to cue Debbie once when she was running lines on set and I held her script for her and read her cues. I noticed that she had written in the margin of one of her speeches, "little cat smile." I realized in that moment the difference in training if you come up through film or through the theater. She was choreographing her facial expressions whereas a stage actress would be orchestrating the emotions that were behind the smile.

I don't know how conscious I was of the discrepancy between the level of work I was doing in class and the kind of roles I was doing on film. I only know that one day, wearing a wig that had been designed by Sydney Guilaroff for Shirley MacLaine in another film, wearing a dress designed for me by Edith Head, and my face painted by Bill Reynolds, Debbie's brother, I felt like I had been assembled on the production line into this character. All these different departments had plunked their work unto me. And to top it off, I was doing an imitation of Vincente Minnelli!

So there I was, this manufactured creature sitting quietly on the set waiting to be called, when a thought ambled across the empty set of my mind: *Well, this is it. The big time. I'm costarring in a Twentieth Century–Fox movie starring Debbie Reynolds. Next step is I'll be playing her part.* There was a pause and then "the voice" spoke and said clearly and rather flatly, "I don't want it."

And that was it. Out of nowhere, my life changed again. I could see where I was going. I could see where my career was headed and I didn't like it. It was time. Time to move back to New York. Time for me to take Shelley's advice and study with Lee Strasberg. I was ready. Much of the furniture I had with me had traveled from Detroit to New York to California. Now I was backtracking, returning to New York. It didn't seem right to keep carting all this stuff around. Especially the biggest pieces. I decided to off-load some of it. It was time to sell my piano. I put an ad in the paper and found a buyer. He came with a friend and loaded it onto their truck. I sat on the couch feeling sad and reflecting on all the houses and apartments it had been in, the marriages it had survived; how it was the first major purchase I'd ever made and now I was selling it. I felt disloyal, as if it were a trusting friend being jettisoned. While I was mushing around in all this slushy sentiment, Skippy was watching what the men were doing with avid interest. He was now past two, toddling about and talking pretty well, although still saying things like "plano" for piano. He stood on the porch watching the men load the piano on the truck; stood while it pulled away, and watched it go out of sight. Then he toddled back into the living room, went to the spot where the piano had been, bent down and examined carefully the bare floor full of absence of piano, got up, and ran to me, where I sat sullenly on the couch. He lifted his pudgy open hands to shoulder level, his fingers stretched wide, palms up; looked at me with eyes wide open and said this poem:

"Plano all gone.
Find a new star."

That's what he said. And that's what I did.

Me as Sally in *The King of Marvin Gardens*.
She was one of my favorite characters.

PART III

Arriving

─❧─

Talent is not only something you are born with,
it's what you allow yourself to go through,
what you permit yourself to experience,
to perceive, and the work you do.

Elia Kazan

N eil and I were married in New York in 1964. Present at our civil ceremony were Neil's parents, Flo and Hank; Blossom as my maid of honor; and Flo's brother Brad as Neil's best man. A word here about Neil's family. Flo's maiden name was Boobis and they were a very tight tribe, all talented in weird ways. For instance, Brad was a painter. His technique was impeccable, but his artistry was unsophisticated and even corny. (He painted Churchill as a clown with one tear on his cheek and Hemingway as a bullfighter.) Brad also played the piano and he and Neil wrote songs together. Neil adored him. Flo's other brother was Nadie Boobis, also a musician. He and his band used to play bar mitzvahs. Nadie put out an album of his music with a Latin beat called *Oi Vay Olé*. Flo herself had aspirations to be a singer and pianist. She developed a nightclub act, had eight-by-ten glossies made of herself in a sequined strapless evening gown standing at a mike, and signed with her theatrical name, Roza Lind. In their home on Long Island, which had a marble floor with a sunken Oriental rug in the center of the living room, was a baby grand piano with a microphone on a boom stand. We would sit in the living room, Flo would sing into the mike in a cocktail lounge breathy voice "Fly Me to the Moon" and other favorites. As far as I know, she only got to sing once in an actual cocktail lounge. As long as I knew her, Roza Lind's black sequined strapless evening gown hung in the closet in mothballs waiting for her chance at stardom.

Flo's husband, whose family name in Poland was Burstyn and was later changed in immigration to Bernstein, called himself Hank Bernard. He worked on Seventh Avenue selling "piece goods," but he had secret, or not so secret, dreams of being an actor. I saw him in an amateur production of *Death of a Salesman* that I can only say was poignant in his revelation of unfulfilled yearnings.

Anyway, that was the wedding party that assembled in downtown New York in the justice of the peace's office on November 12, 1964. We sat outside his office in an empty courtroom waiting our turn to be called. I was sitting with Blossom and was very nervous about tying the knot for the third time. The doors to the office opened, a clerk came out and called, "Bernstein." At the moment our turn was announced, I began to get the giggles. Now, Blossom and I were notorious gigglers. When one of us went, the other would catch it and we'd be sent into paroxysms of teary laughter. The moment I felt this urge to laugh rise up in me, I looked at Blossom and said, "Oh, no." She gave me a steadying squeeze on the arm as I walked into the judge's chambers, fighting with every ounce of strength to control this fit of laughter waiting to explode. Neil and I stood before the judge. Flo and Hank stood behind Neil, Blossom and Brad behind me. I was holding a bouquet of flowers, rigid with the effort not to laugh. Then the judge opened his mouth and I was dead in the water. He had the strangest, most affected, unnatural, funny delivery I had ever heard in my life. I thought, *Oh, no. Please, God,* but my body started shaking and tears ran from my eyes, moistening the glue of my false eyelashes, which then ran down my cheeks. I plucked them off, laughing helplessly. I turned to Blossom for support and saw her bent in half, waging her own silent struggle not to laugh. Brad was flat against the wall, also crying with repressed laughter. I turned the other way for help from Flo and Hank. They were standing in stony silence, radiating disapproval. I turned to Neil, as the judge droned on. Neil pointed to the wall.

I asked, "What?"

"Focus on the wallpaper," he offered. I turned to the wallpaper and examined it hard, still laughing and crying. I was hysterical, when suddenly there was a shocking silence. The judge had stopped talking. I thought he was refusing to go on. I turned to the judge and said, "I'm sorry."

Neil leaned toward me and said in a confidential tone, "You're supposed to say 'I do.' "

"Oh, yes," I blurted. "Of course. I mean, sure. I mean, I do." I was still both laughing and crying.

Then the judge asked Neil if he would take me as his wife, Neil promptly said, "I do," and we were pronounced man and wife.

We moved into Neil's parents' house on Long Island until we could find an apartment in New York. I got work right away shooting a commercial. I remember being in a makeup room with Eddie Calahan doing my hair when Neil burst in and told me he'd signed a two-year lease on an apartment. "Without me looking at it?" I asked, stunned by the idea of spending two years in a place I'd never seen.

"There was no time," Neil said in excitement. "We were going to lose it if we waited. My father said it was too good. It would be gone. So I took it."

When I saw the apartment my heart sank. I'd never lived in an elevator building. I'd always lived on the first or second floor, and that's what I liked; it made me feel grounded. The view is also important to me. I need some sky, a garden, or at least a tree. I had no such view here. If I leaned out the kitchen window and looked way down West 77th Street, two blocks away I could just make out the upper portions of the trees around the Museum of Natural History. I spent much time over the next two years hanging out that window. I like to see the sun rise every morning or set at night; I like to see the moon rise and to know what phase of the moon we are in. I love to see trees through the full cycle of bloom—changing color, dropping their leaves, and going into dormancy until the first chartreuse buds come out in the spring. I am connected to the cycles of the natural world. I'm attuned to them. None of that mattered to Neil. But it was too late. He'd signed the lease. So I moved into an apartment that I hated and paid for with my earnings for two years. Neil was writing a novel. Skip had his own bedroom and we had the other one. Neil needed a place to write. I installed a drape over a section of the bedroom and closed it off for his office. But he hadn't given up on acting completely. He still had aspirations of being the next Marlon Brando. When I signed up for Lee Strasberg's class, Neil did, too.

At that time, 1964, Lee was holding his classes in a studio behind Carnegie Hall. You signed up for two classes a week—one exercise and scene class with Lee and one scene study class with his wife, Paula. Lee asked for a commitment of at least six weeks because he felt it took that long to understand what the classes were about so that one could make an informed decision on whether or not to continue. He was right. The first weeks I didn't understand the classes at all. Several actors would work at the same time. There was one guy who was obviously being a chicken pecking at food (turned out it was a pigeon). Another girl was looking close up into a mirror, singing to herself in a sultry way and crying. Another older woman seemed to be taking an imaginary shower and rubbing soap between her legs. One guy was on his hands and knees doing something I couldn't understand, but it was obviously very moving to him because he was crying like a baby. The whole lot of them looked crazy to me. I wanted to laugh out loud. I looked around the room to see if anyone else was suppressing a giggle as I was. Everyone was dead serious. I couldn't imagine what any of this had to do with acting. Then Lee brought the exercise to an end and criticized each one as though what they were doing made any sense at all. I was baffled. I would have left the class right then, but I had made that promise to stay for six weeks. I attended the scene study class taught by Paula. She was a short, heavy, fair-skinned, red-headed woman in a black muumuu. The scenes didn't seem all that good to me and I didn't quite understand her comments afterward. She praised things I didn't see and seemed to criticize the very things that I thought looked pretty good. I just didn't get it. But I thought before I left I ought to give it a go, so I signed up to do an exercise for Lee and a scene for Paula. The first exer-

cise everyone was asked to do was to create whatever you had for breakfast, a cup of coffee, a glass of juice, whatever you normally drank every
morning. I was a coffee drinker at the time, so I went to work at home creating my imaginary mug. When I felt I had it, I got to be one of the five
crazy people up there. I sat in my chair and held out my left hand and
imagined a cup sitting on it. With my right hand I traced the rim of the
cup. I let my finger move down the handle until I could define its shape.
Then slowly I wrapped my fingers around the handle and tried to lift the
cup off my left hand into my right hand. But when I did, I lost the whole
thing. The cup had no weight. Damn! I had to start all over, holding the
cup with my left, bouncing it gently up and down. Yes, there's the weight,
I can feel it. Now I can feel the rim again. During all of this, the other four
people were going through various intensities of sobbing, sighing, laughing, and grunting. I never took my eyes off the cup. After about twenty
minutes, in my peripheral vision I saw Lee sitting in the front row, lifting
up the five-by-seven white cards with an actor's name on each and going
through them until he came to the name he was looking for. Then he said,
"Ellen, keep on doing what you are doing, but just answer my questions."

There was a pause and I felt the focus of the room shift to me. I tried
to continue concentrating on my cup, but I began to get a little nervous.
What was he going to ask me?

"Do you ride horses?"

Oh man, this was from left field. Where was he going with this one?

"I used to," I answered, still trying to feel my cup, which no longer had
coffee in it. I tried to get it back.

"When you rode, did you ride well?" he asked, seemingly innocently.

"Pretty well," I said. "I used to own my own horse."

"Well," said Lee with the precision of a surgeon. "You don't have to ride
that cup."

I paused. My hands remained poised, but they trembled. What had he
just said? I looked at him. My exercise was over, but I found I couldn't drop
my hands. The cup had become too real. I had to set it down on an imaginary table. My heart was pounding. I looked at him. He said to me gently, "What would happen if you made a mistake?"

Tears rose. What was happening to me? I was losing it. The room got deathly quiet. He said in the kindest way, "Go on, make a mistake!"

I shattered, broke, chunks of my mask, my persona fell to the floor. My bare skin, or what was under it, was exposed to the air for the first time like the pink skin under a peeled scab. He pierced me with his gaze. He saw me. He knew me. He gave me permission to make a mistake. And I would not be punished or beaten. I could risk something. Anything. I might even risk not pleasing him. He said it was okay. I could be whatever I am. I could . . . I could . . . He said that I could even . . . be . . . myself. I cried for two weeks.

I didn't know what to do. I had learned survival techniques—how to please, how to be charming and cute, to split from what was painful, to dissociate from what I didn't want to feel, to hide behind a persona that worked for me. Now Lee was telling me I didn't have to do any of that anymore. Lee's genius, and he was a genius, was that he could say what his X-ray vision perceived, in words that had deep meaning only to the person he was addressing. I don't know if what he said to me had meaning to anyone else in the world, but those words were like a sword of truth that pierced my heart and opened me to a new world. I just didn't know what to do instead. I tried explaining this to Neil.

"Well," Neil said softly, "maybe you can just consider that personality you built to be a temporary thing, like a crutch, and now you can put it down because you don't need it anymore."

I stopped crying. That's it, I thought. I don't need it anymore. Now I'll find out who I am without all of that.

And that began my new life. Lee told me that the first step was the willingness to make a mistake, to suffer the humiliation of daring to risk, to grow. I just had no idea how terrified I was not to be perfect. "Addiction to perfection," Marion Woodman, the famous Jungian analyst and writer, would teach us later. I had it. And it wasn't that I thought I was ever perfect or anywhere near it; it was that I thought I *should* be perfect, but was so far from it that I needed to hide the fact. I felt that I was just plain wrong. Essentially wrong, bad, unacceptable, shameful. That was really it. I was ashamed of myself. And that's what had to be hidden. That's what was behind the mask. And somehow by telling me that I did not have to ride that cup, he freed me. By telling me that I could make a mistake, he communicated to me that there was not some mark that I was required to hit and it was unacceptable to miss. He was telling me that I didn't have to pretend anymore. People say, "But isn't the point of acting to pretend to be someone else—to submerge yourself and just become the character?" The answer is a paradox. You cannot move your persona from yourself to the character's without first locating yourself, and from that site you make the move. If you are hiding not only your self, but *from* your self, you don't have a chance for a true creative impulse.

Lee discerned something in me. Something that I formed many years before. A way of coping with my situation at home, a way of dealing with my sexuality and my talent. It was a way that was not truthful. When my mother said, "Pick up the rug, Edna, and do your tap dance," dutifully I did. I did my tap dance for my mother's friends. And I was still doing it. This was what the voice meant when it said, "I don't want it." It didn't want me to go on tap dancing anymore. In Jeff Corey's class, I had begun to ascertain another way. This is what I came to Lee to learn. I thought it was another way to act. He quickly let me know it was another way to *be*.

This was when I finally had the answer to the question I asked in my art class when Don Brackett tacked up my drawing on the bulletin board. It had come from a true creative impulse, not from a desire to please or to get a good grade.

For our first scene in Lee's class, we were to choose one that was "close to us," "not a stretch," "a simple scene." So without a trace of irony, I chose Joan of Arc. I don't remember the scene at all, just that I felt I understood Joan hearing voices. She heard two. I had heard one. I'd heard it twice. So that was why I felt the role was "not a stretch." After the scene, Lee chastised me for my selection and at some point asked, "Can you hear something we can't hear?" I was leaning forward, my elbow on my knee, chin cupped in my hand. I nodded my head, thinking of the voice that had spoken to me. Lee said in a surprised tone, his voice rising a bit, "You can?" Suddenly, his question put me in doubt. I mean, I could hear something when it spoke to me, but he meant now, right now. I listened. The class

was still. I could hear only the sound of the air conditioner. I listened further. I detected a sound just behind the air conditioner, another sound, almost like white sound or the sound behind sound. I had just got there, just
heard it for the space of a second, when I was interrupted by Lee saying,
"Ahh, but that's different." That's all I remember of this incident, but it
etched itself into my actor/artist's knowing. I did hear something different.
I hadn't moved. My chin was still cupped in my hand. Nothing had
changed but the quality of my listening and he saw it! He could *see* me *hear*!
Now, that not only taught me something about him and how precise were
his powers of observation, it taught me something about the level of reality that an actor must create onstage. "The voice" that had spoken to me
was a memory that helped me to understand Joan, but that was in the past.
I had to hear something now, in the present, onstage. It didn't have to be
St. Michael or St. Catherine or even my "voice." It just had to be something *real*, active in the moment, and then that would be seen, communicated, and experienced by the audience. There is an engagement—I would
later feel it as a communion between the actor and the audience—that requires an active doing in the present moment of time. Yesterday's memories are not active. They must be brought into the senses and enlivened in
the present. That way, the witness can "see me hear." It was a great lesson.

Another lesson comes to mind concerning Joan of Arc. In the early seventies at the Actors Studio in California, a visiting actress from England
who was not a member had somehow gotten working privileges and was
playing Joan in a scene from *The Lark*. She was not an accomplished actress and she played Joan like a cheeky bird. It was painful to watch. After
the scene was over, she and the other actor pulled up chairs and waited ex-
pectantly for the praise of the master. There was a moment of quiet, then
Lee addressed the girl. "Have you had any training in sense memory?"

"Yes." She nodded her head, her pretty blond curls bobbing up
and down.

"Could you create a candle for me?"

"Right now?" she asked innocently, even happily.

"Yes, right now," said Lee, also seemingly innocently.

She used her hands to define the shape of an imaginary candle. When she thought she had it, she looked at Lee sweetly and smiled.

"Is it lit?" he asked.

"No." She pouted.

"Light it," Lee instructed.

She went through the motions of lighting a candle, put down the matches and looked at Lee, pleased.

"Hold one finger over it," he said.

She did.

"Can you feel the heat?" he asked.

She nodded vigorously.

"Now lower your finger into the flame and hold it there."

Her smile dropped.

"That's right," Lee snapped. "She put her whole body into the flame. Now you think about that before you ever play Joan again."

We never saw her again.

Neil did a scene for Lee and it was brutal. At one point he dropped his keys accidentally on purpose. He made a point of looking surprised before he picked them up. I don't remember now what that was supposed to signify, but it was something Neil liked and he must have thought it was something Brando would do. After the scene, Lee lit into Neil. At one point he said in a very stern voice, "What are you doing? You drop your keys on a particular line. You bend down to pick them up on another line. That kind of acting went out forty years ago." Afterward Neil said, "I was thinking, *Gee, is this as bad as I think it is?* I'd almost talked myself out of it being that bad until after, when people started coming up to me and saying things to make me feel better. Then I knew it really was that bad."

I never thought of Lee as being cruel, as others did. He was very truthful. When your ego prevented you from hearing the truth, Lee was willing to cut through your ego. Years later when I was teaching, I said to Lee one day, "Sometimes when I'm teaching, something will occur to me to say, but I know it will hurt the person's feelings and I hesitate to say it."

Lee answered, "You must be like a surgeon. When a surgeon has to cut, he doesn't say, 'Oh, this is going to hurt.' No, he just cuts." And he made a chop with his hand. That's what I saw him do. Cut through the defenses of a person. Did he succeed? Not always. Many times he did. But only if the person, the actor, was willing to move beyond his ego-defended ignorance and really learn. I have discovered that the only position from which one can learn is the position of not knowing. From there you say, "Teach me." Then the teacher can teach. I was blessed to be able to stand in that place. Whatever are the ingredients of that blessing, I don't know. I just know Neil didn't have it. I don't think it was talent he was missing. I think it was the ability to be authentic. He copied Brando and he didn't seem to be able to give that up. He never learned what was behind his own mask. Was it that his ego was so frail that he needed to imitate Marlon because that was all he could do? I don't know. I just know he never found his way home to his own center. And that would be his undoing.

Reading over my diaries for 1964 and 1965, I'm amazed at all I was doing. Going to the Strasbergs' classes twice a week during the day and another in the evening. I was also doing commercials. I had a 5 Day Deodorant commercial running on *The Tonight Show*. I attended a dance class with Blossom who had moved into our building. And I was raising a three-year-old!

By June 1965, my notes tell me, "Lee said my work is progressing. Good! Have intensified as he recommended and should keep it up. Assigned me a private moment." Lee might not ask an actor to do a private moment for years. In this difficult exercise you select an activity that you would only do in private, so you learn to be private, even intimate, while you are being observed. When an actor finally is able to accomplish this, he or she can begin to be real onstage. Not only to act naturally, but to be real.

Although I attended classes three times per week, I got to work only once every six weeks. I wasn't satisfied with that, so at Lee's suggestion I enrolled in Peggy Feury's class, which was taught in the same building behind Carnegie Hall. Peggy was an excellent teacher, though she had narcolepsy and would sometimes doze off while actors were doing a scene. When they finished, she would criticize the scene lucidly, as though she'd been awake the whole time. She was a fine teacher despite her disease, which eventually killed her when she fell asleep while driving on a California highway. Peggy used to say, "When you encounter a problem in a scene, something you don't understand or know how to play, don't just slide over it. Work on it until it is solved. It's like crossing a river on stepping stones. You can't just say I'll pass over this stone because I don't like it or understand where to step on it. Solve it before you go on to the next one or you'll find yourself in the river. And when it's solved, you say 'Okay, I've got that one. Now let me go on to the next one.' And *never* say, 'Oh yes, I've encountered this problem before, I know how to solve this. Because if you solve a problem in a way you've solved it before, that becomes a mannerism! It's why, with some actors, if you've seen them a few times, everything they do seems familiar. They're putting new wine in old bottles. Every character you play is a brand-new human being and must be created like nothing you've ever done before."

I got cast in a daytime soap opera called *The Doctors*. I met with the producers and writers and we discussed what kind of a doctor I would be. I became Kate Bartok, head of the hospital's research lab, hot on the trail of unlocking the key to the genetic code. During the run of the show, the genetic code was actually broken and soon all strands of the DNA molecule would be named. The writers sent down a script where I was still hard at work trying to break the code. I went into the office and said, "Hey guys, you can't go on with this storyline. It's in all the papers. It's the biggest news in science. Kate has to be devastated that she was so close to making history and missed it. We've got to find me a new storyline." I can't remember what they came up with, but it didn't matter; it was incidental to the romance I was involved in on the show.

After the rehearsal one day I went to meet a friend for a drink in a bar in the theater district. There was a theater across the street with its lights on. As I sat in a booth waiting and looking out the window, the lights of the theater went out. Moments later I realized the lights had also gone out in the bar. And down the whole street. It was a blackout! On the street I found a police officer and asked how extensive it was. "All the way up to Sixty-fifth Street," he informed me. I later learned the blackout extended to Maine. The whole East Coast was blanketed in darkness. There I was in Times Square with no lights, no signs, no streetlights, just darkness descending on the early evening. It was magical. There were no strangers. Everyone was talking to each other. I went into a grocery store and bought candles and matches. Traffic was brought to a standstill. I walked over to Joe Allen's. Joe was there and gave me a table. As actors arrived at their theaters and discovered there would be no shows playing on Broadway that night, they all headed for Joe Allen's. The gas stove in the kitchen was working, so a bunch of us stood around the stove and held candles aloft for the chef, who slapped steaks on the grill until they were gone. Suddenly I heard Neil's voice nearby say, "Babe, what do I want to eat?"

"How did you know how to find me?" I gasped.

"I figured you'd come here. What do I want?" he asked.

"Get a steak while they last," I suggested, still holding my candle.

Fortunately, it wasn't the housekeeper's night off, so Skippy was safe at home.

We sat at the table for hours, friends coming and joining us, standing around. Some recited their parts for each other. By eleven we left Joe's, and in total darkness Neil and I walked the twenty blocks home, hand in hand, looking at the bright stars over the darkened New York City. Neil and I fought a lot, but on nights like this, we were just hand in hand in love.

While I was on *The Doctors*, I still went to class regularly. I was learning sense memory and used my time on the show to practice it. It was quite thrilling to be doing acting exercises while doing a story *live* in front of millions of viewers. I found a way to use the exercise logically. For example, I had to play a scene where I stepped out on a balcony at night, so I transformed the padded walls of the NBC studio into a star-strewn sky. My key light became the moon and I could even see Orion as I played the scene.

But live television has certain perils. One of them is the terror, which reaches almost obsessive intensity, that you are suddenly going to lose your mind, turn to the camera, and speak every obscenity you can think of. There were times when I would be in the middle of a scene and the demon would rise up in me. It was just a thought. What if it happened right now? And the terror would come and I'd have to fight for control. I was so relieved a few years later when I read an interview with an actor who referred to this as a common fear of all stage actors. The fear of suddenly walking downstage to the apron and hurling invective at the audience.

Another nightmare of live television is to have a hacking cough that the character doesn't have. I was still a smoker in those days and thanks to my many illnesses of the throat and chest, I was prey to any bug that got near my throat. I developed a terrible cough while I was on the show and, in one particularly awful phase, I had a stagehand hidden under Dr. Matt Powers's desk with little cups of honey, lemon, and warm water. Every time the red light went off on my camera, I'd swig my honey and lemon while the other actor was speaking and then I'd quickly compose myself before my camera went back on.

On the day of the first space walk, some of the cast and crew ran up to the newsroom at NBC to watch, but I was too focused on the script that day to take the time. Of course now I'm sorry I didn't, but doing forty pages of memorized text for a live show is no small feat. And we'd get the script only the day before. At four in the afternoon we'd have a reading sitting around a table. The next day we'd have a blocking rehearsal, a dress rehearsal, and then do the show. After the table reading, I'd spend every waking moment right up to dress rehearsal memorizing the forty pages, but as time went by, I relaxed into my character and the storyline and gradually I got to the point that I never looked at the script after table reading and blocking rehearsal. I think doing this developed my memory. I always had a good one, but this gave me confidence in it. Years later, I visited John Gielgud backstage in London, where I saw him perform in Pinter's *No Man's Land* with Ralph Richardson. That's when he told me that memory is a muscle. He said, "You must develop it. I memorize something every day. If I'm not working on a role, then I memorize a poem, or at the very least a column of newspaper print."

There was something about the theme music coming up at the end of *The Doctors* that made Skippy cry. He'd watch me on the show, then at the end, the moment he heard the theme, he'd begin wailing and Neil or our housekeeper would have to quickly turn the sound down to stop his tears. When I asked him about it he'd say, "Mommy go away." At some point, we'd taped a week of shows so that I was able to watch the show with him at home. When the music came up he began to cry. I asked, "Why are you crying, honey?"

His eyes still on the screen, he said through tears, "Mommy go away."

I touched him gently and said, "Mommy not go away. Mommy right here." He looked at me surprised, then back to the screen rather confused, back and forth from me to the screen, processing a problem only an actor's child has to learn, and then he got it.

Finally, after two years in that apartment I hated, our lease was up. Dr. Kate had been written out of *The Doctors* to make way for an actress who was returning from maternity leave. Neil decided we should live in California. I did not want to go back there. But I was moved to California by a husband for the second time. I had agreed that he would win on a bump. This was the bump. But this time I had a condition—I would move back to California if we could fulfill a longtime dream of mine and camp across the country on our way there!

Blossom had gotten married to her third husband, Maurice Tuchman, the curator of modern art at the Los Angeles County Museum, and had moved with her two daughters to California. She and Maurice were living in a duplex on Orchid Avenue in Hollywood and she told me there was a house next door for rent; they would move into the house and give us their duplex. So we put everything in storage again, bought a Volkswagen van, and took Skipper, Daisy Mae the Dalmatian, our Persian cat Georgie Baby, and set out.

I had planned the trip with the help of the Automobile Association of America and gotten a TripTik to chart our route each day, visiting as many Native American communities as possible. We drove through North Carolina, Mississippi, Oklahoma, and Arkansas. In New Mexico we drove from one end to the other because I wanted to visit Carlsbad Caverns, where we had the amazing experience of total silence in complete darkness eight hundred feet below the surface, sitting among the stalactites and sta-lagmites. We passed a small town called Silver City and about fifty miles later stopped at a general store in a place called Tuba City. There were a few Native Americans sitting outside the store. Our New York license plates attracted a lot of attention. A Native American man approached me and asked if I was from New York. I said yes, and he asked if I would read a letter to him. Clearly I was not the first person to read it to him, but from his expression, I understood that he couldn't hear it often enough. His daughter had left New Mexico and was working as a nurse in a hospital in New York. When I finished the letter his eyes had a far-off look. I asked if he knew where New York was. He didn't. I got out my large map of the United States and showed him Tuba City on the map. Then I asked him if he'd ever been to Silver City. He had. I showed him the distance from Tuba City to Silver City, just an eighth of an inch away on the map. Then I moved my finger across the country to New York. He traced his finger back to Tuba City, to Silver City, and with his nose only inches from the map, he slowly traveled the whole route across the country to New York City. He did this several times. Then he straightened up, looked me in the eye and smiled. "Thank you," he said. "Thank you."

We visited the Hopi, Navajo, and Apache homelands. The Hopi were very welcoming and the Navajo were cordial, but the Apaches, who had the reputation of being fierce warriors, let us know we were on their land and the sooner we moved on, the better. We didn't wait to see what might happen if we didn't. I was looking forward to visiting the Grand Canyon, which I'd never seen. But when we got close, Neil became possessed with the idea of getting to California and drove straight on. I can't remember now how many hours it was, but it was way past safe. Over twelve, I think, with no stops except to refuel and walk Daisy Mae. We arrived in California one bedraggled family.

We took about two months settling into our new digs. It was a three-story duplex in the Hollywood Hills; Maurice and Blossom's house was a few steps up the hill, where they lived with Blossom's two daughters, Rebecca and Cathy. Blossom and I had been living close to each other since we met on the Gleason show in 1956. We were like sisters, with all the complex mixture of love, admiration, and competition. Fortunately, our husbands liked each other and we spent many happy hours together, including late nights of drinking and partying.

By August I got a job on a television show called *Time Tunnel*, produced by Irwin Allen and directed by Bill Hale. Each week a fictional drama was set within a historical event. My episode was about the eruption of the volcano on the island of Krakatoa. It was called "The Crack of Doom." We had just three days to shoot this half-hour episode and on the third day we were nowhere near finished. By lunchtime word came down that we absolutely could not go over. We had to shoot everything we could and stop on time. Anything that wasn't shot wouldn't be in the show. But how would the show make sense? No one knew. With ten minutes left in the shooting day, we'd gotten everything but the eruption of the volcano. The scene was set up, but there was no way to get a master shot and coverage. What were they thinking? With five minutes to go, Irwin Allen appeared on the set with a pot and a wooden spoon. He placed all the actors and extras at the foot of the volcano, then shouted, "Okay! When I hit the pot with the spoon, you all jump to the right. When I hit it again, you jump to the left." And that was the climax of the story of the largest volcanic eruption ever heard or witnessed on the planet earth. I was paid $1,000 for three days' work and went home exhausted.

I climbed the many stairs up to our pink three-storied duplex, opened the door, and saw Neil sitting in front of a blaring television, watching a baseball game. There were empty beer cans around him and several very full ashtrays. He called brightly over the roar of the crowd, "Hi, babe! What's for dinner?" I felt something tickle my mind. I didn't ask, "What's wrong with this picture?" It was just a sinking feeling that not only was I going to have to whip up something out of nothing in the kitchen because, of course, I hadn't had time to shop, I was going to have to empty those ashtrays and clean up the living room. And I was going to have to do this cheerfully without any complaints because if a wife chose to have a career, it shouldn't interfere with her domestic duties, which must always be a priority. The fact that I was supporting the family should not be used as an excuse for shirking my duties because, after all, Neil would be working if he could get work and I shouldn't rub it in that I could. That would be demoralizing and humiliating for him and I didn't want to be one of those "ball-cutting women."

I found some pasta in the cupboard and made the special sauce I'd invented that I knew Neil liked. As I was cooking, Neil entered the kitchen and said, "And we're out of toilet paper, too."

In 1966, I got a running part on a Western television series called *Iron Horse*, starring Dale Robertson. All day I wore high-button shoes, long petticoats, and high-necked costumes in 120-degree heat on the Columbia backlot in the San Fernando Valley. I was in the nineteenth century by day and dealing with Neil's outrageous, cool, turned-on behavior at night.

He was smoking a lot of marijuana, playing Beatles songs on his guitar, riding his motorcycle, and trying to convince me we should embrace the counterculture. And I did, to a point, but I stopped short of free love and having sex with other couples. Soon Neil began experimenting with LSD. We attended a love-in at a park called Elysian Fields. There, I saw twin babies about ten months old left on a blanket studying the patterns the leaves made as they trembled before the sun. I looked at their eyes and gasped when I realized they were stoned. They looked as if they'd been given a tiny tab of LSD while their parents went off to make love not war. While I believed in the part of the movement that was opposing the Vietnam War, I couldn't go so far as to believe any good could come from drugging babies or by completely "dropping out." I was too motivated for that. Or I guess I was ambitious, that dreaded thing no woman was ever supposed to be called.

An episode of *Iron Horse* was directed by the 1940s film star Paul Henreid. One week we had an actor playing a bad guy who really scared me. I made a point of remembering his name: Gene Hackman. Years later he played my husband who left me for Ann-Margret in *Twice in a Lifetime*.

We spent a lot of time with Toby and Bob Rafelson and their friends Bruce Dern and Jack Nicholson, who were still unknowns. Neil did a biker movie with Bruce and Jack called *The Rebel Rousers*. Neil chose to be "the Jew" as his Hells Angel character and wore a Star of David on his motorcycle jacket. Bruce's then wife, Diane Ladd, was in the film, too.

Bruce was one of the actors to open a West Coast Actors Studio. The others were Lee Grant, Jack Garfein, Mark Rydell, and Peggy Feury. They moderated the sessions and made arrangements with Lee Strasberg to come to the West Coast when the studio in New York closed each summer. Bruce also taught privately, and Neil and I joined his class. On the first day, Diane Ladd came to class wearing a full-length mink coat. Bruce had everyone go onstage and gave each of us a task. After a while he motioned for me to come over then whispered in my ear, "Make everyone sit down." He didn't say how to do this, so I went to everyone individually and whispered, "Bruce said to sit down." Everyone dutifully sat back down in the house. Except Diane. She knew Bruce's exercises and refused my instructions. The stage was bare except for Diane in her mink coat and me. I stood there trying to figure out how to complete my task. I considered my options and seized upon the first one. I tackled her, brought her right to the ground. Boy, was she mad! She stood up and went up to Bruce and in her southern accent said, "Bruce! You bettah tell yaw students that they ah not allowed to hurt anybody in this class or I swear to God, if that ever happens again, I'm gonna kill her!"

Well, I was just completing my task. Of course, I had no idea she was five months pregnant. Laura Elizabeth Dern was born four months later weighing seven pounds, eight ounces. Neil and I went to St. John's Hospital to view her the day after she was born. I was relieved to see she was in perfect health and suffered no lasting effects of my flying tackle.

Bob Rafelson had the idea to create a television series about a band similar to the Beatles. He hired four young actor/musicians and called them the Monkees. The series was a huge hit, and so was the band. They gave a sellout concert at the Hollywood Bowl. Bob hired Neil as story editor for the show. For the first time since we were married, we both had steady jobs. Bob, along with his partners Burt Schneider and Steve Blauner, formed a production company called BBS. They had offices on a small lot next to Paramount's. I loved to go there and visit Neil in his office. When Neil got work as an actor, it was usually as a juvenile delinquent or a young hood, often Italian or Puerto Rican. Now he had his very own office and every time I dropped by to visit him, I felt so proud of him and happy that he had at last found his way—thanks to Bob, of course, who was always a big promoter of his friends, including Nicholson, Dennis Hopper, and Peter Fonda. It was a wild time. Full of creativity, energy, and drugs. There was so much going on then that I made this plea in my diary entry for July 15, 1967: *Nobody nothing—Just Neil and Skip and me. Please.*

But it didn't slow down; it accelerated. We were in Bruce's class and attending Actors Studio West as observers with working privileges. By November, we began to get involved in politics. We attended a meeting called Dissenting Democrats and joined a group called STOP, an acronym for Speakers and Talent Organized for Peace. It was founded by an actress named Leslie Parrish. We attended meetings every week for six months and heard lectures on different aspects of the Vietnam War. There were about a dozen or so members who were training to be speakers against the war. Of these members, a few of us became close friends. Fred Haines, who wrote the screenplay for *Ulysses*, and his wife, Francey, a beautiful Irish lass that Fred met while they were shooting the film in Ireland. Fred and Francey figured importantly in my life for the next decade. Also Sylvia and Leo Wolfe, who were not in show business, but were like *mishpuchah* to me and some of the other STOP members. We frequently congregated at their house in Cheviot Hills during this time. Also Naomi Newman, a beautiful opera singer, drama therapist, actress, writer, and ultimately director of the Traveling Jewish Theater. We were all very tight friends. We went through the training together, and now as the 1968 political campaign heated up, we were out making antiwar speeches wherever a speaker was needed, from Rotary Club luncheons to bowling alleys. Very often, an organization would have two speakers at their functions: a dove and a hawk. We were the doves.

Then the Actors Studio started an outreach program in Watts. Neil and I, with six-year-old Skipper, went to George Washington Carver Park in Watts and taught theater games to the neighborhood kids. Skipper was the only white child there and the black kids were fascinated by his soft blond hair. They would smile lovingly as they played with him like a doll, and Skipper would go into a trance as they stroked his silky curls.

I did an exercise where I had a little girl who was about ten years old hold a bottle of fingernail polish behind her back. I asked her to tell me what it said on the label. I assumed she would be able to feel the shape of the bottle and say "nail polish." But she just kept saying that she couldn't. I repeatedly told her she could, and urged her on. She finally said, "My mind dudn't go that far."

Not getting it, I said, "Sure it does. Feel the shape of what you're holding, feel the paper on the bottle, now picture what the words on it say."

Again she repeated, "My mind dudn't go that far."

As I persisted, a little girl, no older than five or six, came up to me and whispered, "She mean she can't read."

It just hadn't occurred to me. The child was so embarrassed, she couldn't come out and say in front of all the other kids, "I can't read." But what a poetic and brilliant way she found of expressing the tragedy of illiteracy. Of course, her mind *could* go that far if someone had taken the time to guide it.

In June 1967, Daisy Mae died giving birth to ten puppies. I had never had her spayed. She carried my fertility for me, the fertility that I had killed off. She got pregnant many times, and this was a double litter—five white pups and five black. Blossom pointed out to me that Daisy didn't look right a few days before she was due, but I didn't listen. I thought Blossom was being an alarmist. Then suddenly I saw what she meant. Daisy *didn't* look right. She looked too big, too heavy, too tired. I took her to the vet. He decided she needed help with the puppies and he allowed me into the operating room while he took them out by C-section. I stroked Daisy's head and comforted her. She was very weak. Finally all ten puppies were out and the doctor was sewing her up. Looking into Daisy's eyes that were looking back into mine, I saw her light dimming. I asked the vet, "Is she all right?"

He answered casually, "She's fine. She's lost a lot of blood, is all. She'll be okay." He went on stitching her up. I didn't believe him. Her look was telling me she was not all right. As she held my gaze, her light went out. Just like the dot of light diminishing on an old television screen when it's turned off. It fades, then is gone. She was gone. I couldn't speak. I covered my mouth with both hands and backed away from her, sobbing, my eyes still on her. The doctor looked up surprised, sutures in hand. Then he looked at Daisy Mae and back to me with an astonished look on his face. He stopped sewing. My beloved friend was dead. She died giving birth for me, as she had so many times. I couldn't have felt more responsible for her death.

I took home her ten puppies and bottle-fed them. But they got distemper because the immunity to it is administered through the mother's milk. One by one, they died. We were able to save only two of them, Bernard and Ralph. We had them both for six months until one day I thoughtlessly said in front of them to a friend that Ralph was not as smart as Bernard. The next day Ralph left home and we were never able to find him. Since then I have been very careful what I say in front of dogs. They may not be able to speak, but they understand more than we give them credit for. Bernard lived over ten years and grew to be one of the most eccentric and interesting canines I've ever shared my life with.

A word here about Bernard. He never knew any mother but me. Our relationship was unusually close and he was a unique dog. For instance, he loved classical music and would sit on a chair during his favorite pieces and sing—really sing. He also loved opera, but he never sang with another singer; he would just sit on a chair listening, cocking his head from side to side. His favorite piece was Beethoven's Fifth Piano Concerto, the second movement. I played it for him years later as he lay dying in my arms.

In December, we drove to San Francisco for the wedding of my mother to Winsor Meals. We stayed on for the holidays, which were unpleasant. Winsor took my brothers out for a drive and stayed away too long, in my mother's view. They arrived back just in time for dinner. As we were all seated, my mother came from the kitchen, scowling, carrying the turkey, plopped it on the table so hard the bird bounced off the platter, and she said in an angry tone, "There! There's your goddamn Christmas dinner!" And walked out. We all sat glumly in silence for a few minutes, everyone's appetite quietly tiptoeing from the room. I vowed never to have another Christmas ruined by my mother. I kept the vow until she got too old for my conscience to allow it, but most of my adult life I avoided my mother on holidays.

In addition to the STOP meetings, studying the history of Vietnam, and teaching in Watts, I auditioned for the Actors Studio with Neil, doing a scene from *Cat on a Hot Tin Roof.* I had done a preliminary audition in New York and had not passed. Rumor had it that Lee got angry with the judges for not passing me, but they didn't like my scene selection. After this second preliminary, Neil and I were passed and booked for a final audition on February 10. I passed and became a member of the Actors Studio, but Neil didn't, which was very painful for him. He did get into the playwright's unit, so we could continue attending sessions together.

In February 1968, we met with the California Democratic Council and had lunch with Congressman Edmund "Pat" Brown, who was later to become governor of California. We were all hoping Robert Kennedy would declare his candidacy for president, but in the meantime Senator Eugene McCarthy declared his, and as he was an opponent of the war in Vietnam, STOP pledged our support to him. After the New Hampshire primary on March 15, it became clear that President Lyndon Johnson was vulnerable and Bobby declared his candidacy. We were in a quandary. In our hearts we all wanted Bobby, but we were officially committed to Senator McCarthy. After a few weeks, and with much discussion and guidance from the California Democratic Council, it was decided that we'd be loyal to McCarthy until the California primary, which Bobby was expected to win. At that time, it would be clear that Bobby had the better chance at the nomination, McCarthy would most likely step aside, and we'd switch our support to Bobby. That was our plan.

On April 5, we were scheduled to attend a fundraising luncheon given in honor of McCarthy. The day before, on April 4, Neil and I planned a day at the beach with Skipper. I'd set my clock radio to get me up so I could pack our lunches. At eight A.M. I was still sound asleep when the radio came on with the full, rich voice of Martin Luther King Jr. saying, "I am not afraid! For I have been to the mountain and I've seen the other side and mine eyes have seen the glory of the coming of the Lord!" I sat straight up in bed and said, "They're going to kill Dr. King today."

Neil was in the bathroom shaving and leaned out the door. "What?" he asked.

"When is that march in Memphis?"

Neil answered, "Tomorrow."

I said quietly, "That's funny, I saw him being shot today."

I didn't know what to make of this. I didn't know if it was a premonition or a bad dream. We proceeded to the beach. It was a foggy day. We lay on our blanket reading. Skipper played nearby in the sand. Suddenly without any previous thought, I said, "We have to go. We have to get to the radio. Dr. King has just been shot."

We gathered up our things quickly and got in our van. I turned on the radio. The station came on, but there was no sound. We had tuned into a pause. Then the announcer's voice said gravely, "Ladies and gentlemen, Dr. Martin Luther King has just been shot in Memphis, Tennessee." We drove home in anguish. I don't know how such things can be. I feel that I got that message from Dr. King's voice, which makes me wonder if he didn't know what was coming himself, and that's why he was telling us that he was not afraid, for his eyes had, indeed, seen the glory of the coming of the Lord.

The next day at the McCarthy luncheon, we passed out black armbands and everyone wore them as a sign of mourning. We all ached with grief, but the black community couldn't contain their outrage, and rioting broke out in cities across the country.

April 14 was Easter Sunday. I wanted to observe Dr. King's passing, but not with white people. I chose, among the many black preachers I saw on television, to attend the Easter services of Reverend Samuels of Grace Episcopal Church in downtown Los Angeles. I asked Blossom, Neil, and

Maurice to go with me. On Easter Eve, we stayed up all night to drive downtown for the sunrise service, but Neil and Maurice backed out, so Blossom and I drove downtown together in the dark.

We got to the church as the sky turned to light gray. The congregation was arriving. However, they were not entering the church but walking around to the back. Blossom and I fell in step beside them. We all went to an open field behind the church. There was a grassy rise where everyone gathered. A piano had been brought out and sat incongruously on the hill. Soon a thin man wearing a navy blue suit sat down at the piano. The whites of his eyes shone like beacons. He began to play softly, wandering arpeggios over mournful chords. We stood in a circle swaying gently to the soul-filled music. Blossom and I were the only white people present, but nobody seemed to question our being there.

There was no sermon at this sunrise ceremony, just a group of people sedately dressed, the women in hats and gloves, purses over their arms, the men in suits and ties of navy, black, or brown, standing quietly in a loose circle, swaying gently to the sad sounds of the piano in the early dawn light.

As the light began to lift, the music responded. The dark chords lightened the clouds to shades of red. Was the light leading the music or the other way around? The piano player was pounding his heel against the ground. As the tempo quickened, my heart did, too. Something was stirring in me. It felt like something new. I could feel it rising in me. I couldn't hold it back. A pair of hands near me began a steady clap. We all joined in. A voice called out. Someone began singing. I wanted to shout. I was caught up in it, whatever it was. We were swaying and clapping and bringing it about. But what was it? I didn't know at all. Then suddenly, there it was! Over there! The hot orange ball was peering over the edge of the earth, answering our call. It seemed we had done it. We had brought the sun up! The piano player was Apollo and we were with him in his chariot pulling Helios, the sun, into his rise. We could see his golden light shining in each other's eyes. He is risen! The sun is risen. Great God Almighty, the Son is risen!

I understood then what a sunrise ceremony is. It isn't something one observes or attends, but a participation mystery that one enters into and experiences the manifestation of divinity. Be it God the Father, Helios the sun, or the Holy Sacred Ghost of our fallen leader.

Apollo not only pulls the sun up into the sky every morning, he is a god of music as he showed himself this day, and the god of prophecy, too, announcing his judgment through his priestess, the sibyl, who speaks the god's words without knowing why or how. And as the archer god who shoots his arrows from afar, he is the god of sudden death. Like Dr. King's death. And being a god associated with spring, he is the god of the re-greening of the earth each year, therefore, the god of Resurrection as Jesus later became. All this was present on this Easter day. Oh, rapture! Oh, Glory! The glory of the coming of the Lord!

The music decrescendoed and brought our heart rates down. It dwindled to a stop. There was only silence in the shining light. Then from an unseen signal, everyone crossed and clasped hands. Together we sang:

We shall overcome
We shall overcome
Deep in my heart
I do believe
We shall overcome
Someday.

In May, Neil and I decided to take a break and go with the Rafelsons and our kids to some cabins in Kings Canyon National Park. We walked among the giant sequoias during the day. At night, after we put the kids to bed, we got high. Bob brought some psilocybin. I'd never taken any drug stronger than marijuana, but I decided to try it. The four of us sat in the Rafelsons' cabin and we ingested the drug. Soon everyone seemed to be having a very good time—that is, everyone except me. Very often when we got together, Bob and Neil would do impromptu routines with Toby and me as their audience, so it was not unusual that I said nothing. But what was going on inside me was a nightmare. The drug was way too strong and I was trapped inside it and couldn't speak or signal that I was in trouble. After a while Neil turned to me and said, "Are you okay?" I couldn't answer. I looked at him and prayed that he could see I definitely was not okay.

Bob laughed and said, "She's fine." No, no, I thought, don't believe him. I'm not fine. But still I couldn't speak or move. It was as if I were sealed in plastic. I tried to communicate to Neil through my eyes. He looked at me. I saw him see me. He read me. He said, "No, I don't think she is." Thank God, I thought. He took my hand and led me outside into the night. There were a million stars over the tops of the giant trees. He touched my shoulder and pointed up to the stars. "Look at the stars," he told me. I held on to my life by a thread of starlight. And I cried. I didn't take my eyes off the stars, but I cried and cried. Maybe I was crying for Dr. King, or for the country and all the uproar. I could have been crying for what I felt coming. Who knows? There were no thoughts, really. It felt as if the drug had opened some long-sealed tomb and inside were all the lost tears of my whole life, all that I had denied, ignored, and disowned. Once they were lost, but now they were found.

Robert Kennedy's campaign was gaining strength. He was surely going to win the California primary on June 5. On that day, STOP members were in McCarthy's California headquarters when he conceded. We admired the senator deeply. He was the first person in the federal government who had the courage to speak out against the war and declare himself a candidate on that basis. It was his strong showing in New Hampshire that changed Kennedy's mind about running and let Johnson know he was in trouble. McCarthy had made a valiant effort. He made it possible for the antiwar movement to penetrate the establishment. The truth was that he paved the way for Robert Kennedy to win the nomination and defeat Richard Nixon, the likely Republican nominee. The STOP members left McCarthy head-quarters ready to pledge our support to Senator Kennedy the next day. Neil and I were in our car driving away from the hotel when we heard the news on the radio that Robert Kennedy had been shot. I wailed at the top of my lungs, "No, no, no," and cried all the way home.

The hope of Camelot lay in a pool of blood. Dr. King's dream was shattered in a million pieces. We would never be the same. We carry those three assassinations in our collective soul. We may overcome them someday, but I don't believe we have yet. I know I haven't.

In the seven years since we'd been together, Neil had struggled as an actor and hadn't been able to sell his writing except once to our friend Bob Rafelson, but now that he had the first steady job since we got together and was coming into his own, he seemed at last to be enjoying himself. He wasn't going to be the next Marlon Brando, but at least he was working. The work was creative and he was paying his own way in the world. At STOP meetings Neil would entertain everyone with his one-liners, and now that the establishment of the Democratic Party seemed to be backing Vice President Hubert Humphrey, who supported the war, STOP redoubled our efforts for Senator McCarthy. Neil and I were busier than ever, writing letters, getting petitions signed, and calling in to radio shows.

As we got closer to convention time in August, STOP appealed to the California Democratic Council, or the CDC as it was called, to get some of us credentials to attend the convention in Chicago. They responded with one pass for STOP's founder, Leslie Parrish. We were so involved in this campaign that we didn't want to be left out, so Neil and I decided to go to Chicago on our own. We'd work the lobbies and bars, find out where the delegates hung out, and do whatever we could to convince them to vote for the peace plank in the platform and to nominate McCarthy.

Many people had already given up on "the system," as it was referred to. They joined antiestablishment groups like the Yippies and others that made up the whole counterculture, whose motto was "Turn on, tune in, and drop out." That was often an appealing idea. Neil was smoking grass regularly and had taken a few acid trips. My drug of choice was still alcohol, and though I did smoke a joint sometimes with Neil, I was never tempted to "drop out." Neil and I made the choice to work within the system. We proceeded to Chicago.

We got a room at the Sherman Hotel on Clark and Randolph Streets. Most of the delegates were staying a few blocks away at the Hilton, and it was there that the rules committee was meeting, as well as all the other committees. Across the street in Grant Park, the protesters were gathering. Neil and I took a walk through the hundreds of hippies, flower children, and antiwar protesters. In many ways we felt more kinship with this group than with the politicos across the street, but we'd made our choice—for the moment anyway.

By August 25, the hotels were packed with delegates and in the park the protesters had swelled to over five thousand. The tension was building. Mayor Daley called in extra police to enforce the eleven P.M. curfew he imposed on the park. National Guard troops were standing by in case of trouble. And of course in that highly charged situation, there couldn't be anything but trouble. When it erupted, it was mayhem. The police, at Mayor Daley's order, moved in and started beating and clubbing protesters; hundreds were arrested. Neil and I were watching from a window high up in the Hilton at McCarthy headquarters.

The next day at the amphitheater, Mayor Daley officially opened the convention. As the speeches were delivered on the floor of the convention, there were just as many being given in Grant Park and other places around Chicago by Julian Bond, Rennie Davis, Terry Southern, Norman Mailer, Abbie Hoffman, William Burroughs, and Allen Ginsberg. There were really two conventions—one in the amphitheater and one in the streets—and Mayor Daley was determined to thwart the one in the streets. Somehow Neil and I managed to get credentials to get into the convention, though Mayor Daley's people stopped us from getting onto the floor. We wanted to be there to cheer any candidate who spoke out against the war, especially Senator McCarthy. But the mayor was running the convention like his own private party.

We went back to McCarthy headquarters. At some point we had a few minutes alone with the senator. He thanked us for our support, but warned us not to expect too much. He said, "The peace plank will be defeated and Hubert Humphrey will get the nomination on the first ballot." We heard him, but we just didn't want to believe him. We knew when and where the platform committee was meeting to vote on the peace plank. We sat outside the door on the floor in the hallway at the Hilton with dozens of others waiting for word. Suddenly the door flew open and an angry young blond woman burst out into the hallway. We could see the committee meeting breaking up inside.

"What happened?" we yelled as she stormed down the hallway.

"It was defeated," she called out angrily. Everyone jumped to their feet. That was it. Months of effort, for nothing. We lost! It was over. We caught up with our contact in the CDC.

"What now?" we asked.

"Join the protesters in the streets. That's all we can do."

I glanced at Neil and headed toward the front doors of the Hilton. Suddenly Neil grabbed my arm. "Where are you going?"

"To the street, like he said."

"No, I want to talk to you," and he pulled me in the opposite direction.

"What? What do you want to talk to me about? Where are we going?" He was pushing, pulling, shoving me out a side door. He wouldn't answer me. Once out on the street, I demanded to know where we were going.

"To our hotel," he answered. "I just want to talk this over with you." He seemed very nervous.

"Talk to me now," I pleaded. "What is it?"

"Come on. I'll tell you in the hotel."

When we finally got to our room, I turned on him angrily and said, "Okay. What? What do you want to talk about?"

He didn't answer me, just pulled our suitcases out and began throwing our things into them. "We're getting out of here."

"No! I don't want to. I want to join the people in the streets!"

He went on quickly packing, refusing to explain why we were leaving. He snapped the suitcases shut and said, "Let's go!"

"I don't want to go," I cried. "I want to stay here and continue what we started."

He tried to push me out the door. We struggled. Then he grabbed me and said in an intense voice, "Listen to me! Mayor Daley is about to declare martial law. He's going to ring this city with the National Guard and make this a police state. We'll never get out. We have to go now! Before it's too late!" And he shoved me hard out the door. I was crying, begging him all the way downstairs not to run, to stay and fight for what we believed in. But he wasn't listening. He was very agitated, dragged me out of the hotel, and pushed me into a cab. He told the cabdriver to take us to the train station.

"The train station? Where are we going?" He put his hands over my mouth. In a few blocks he told the driver to let us out. He was leaving a false trail so they couldn't track us.

Track us? Who? Who would want to track us?

"Come on," he said and shoved me into another cab. He told the driver to take us to the nearest car rental place. Soon we were in a rented car, driving furiously out of Chicago, out of Illinois. We crossed into Wisconsin as night fell. By then I was silent and cold with fury. I couldn't believe he ran, and even worse, that he'd made me run. He found a lonely motel on a remote road. The only sound was the chirping of crickets. I didn't know where I was. He turned on the television. Senator Abraham Ribicoff was denouncing "the Gestapo tactics in the streets." Mayor Daley was shouting at him from the floor.

Then we saw what was happening in the streets. The police were clubbing protesters and throwing their bleeding bodies into paddy wagons. The crowd began chanting, "The whole world is watching. The whole world is watching."

I ached to be there with them. It felt so cowardly to be sitting safely in a motel room watching it on television. I sat silently crying: feeling shame that we weren't there, sympathy for the people being bloodied, and agony for our country that we had come to this. Neil was crying too, then suddenly he stood and walked close to the television and joined in the chanting, "The whole world is watching." And in that moment I hated him, with a feeling like cold steel around my heart.

"Don't you dare!" I said. "Don't you dare join in, you coward."

There are very few times in my life that I have really wanted to hurt someone. This time I did. I wanted to plunge a sword right through his craven heart. Later, when I finally understood how sick he was and that this was his first real paranoid attack, I would come to regret those cruel words.

We flew home to Los Angeles the next day, just in time for Skippy's seventh birthday.

Hubert Humphrey was nominated on the first ballot and lost the election by 500,000 votes to Richard Nixon, who by June of the following year ordered the beginning of withdrawal of our troops from Vietnam.

In November, we went to New York for the opening of Rafelson's first feature, *Head.* It was a somewhat surrealistic film about the Monkees, very imaginatively done. Neil and I stayed at the Croydon Hotel, the same hotel I'd stayed in when I first arrived in New York in 1952. It was here that Neil turned violent with me for the first time. I don't remember what we fought about. We were fighting all the time by then. I just remember being on my back on the bed with Neil sitting on me and slapping me hard in the face, first on one side, then the other, repeatedly. I was so furious at this violation that I turned off, dissociated, and just watched him do it in cold defiance. I didn't cry or struggle, I just looked him in the eye until he saw me watching him. Then he got off me. I stood up and confronted him with blood pouring from both nostrils. I wanted him to know how hard he'd been hitting me. As I shouted angry words at him, his face twitched in remorse. I guess that's what I was after.

My diary has a notation in this same week to go to the Gotham Book Store to buy a copy of *Psychological Commentaries on the Teaching of Gurdjieff and Ouspensky* by Maurice Nicoll. I had been introduced to the work of Gurdjieff the previous year by an actor when I was at the Actors Studio. For the next few years, almost everything I read was by one of the Gurdjieff students who had spent time with him at the Institute of Harmonious Development in France. Gurdjieff was an enigmatic teacher who had appeared in Europe from the Caucasus and had established a school outside Paris, where he taught people from all over the world his system of inner work. It was Gurdjieff's teachings that opened my eyes to the fact that not all spiritual work takes place within the boundaries of a church or temple.

Mark Rydell had me read for a picture he was going to make with Steve

McQueen called *The Reivers*. I had done three readings for that film, and Mark let me know that I was his first choice for the role, but McQueen had casting approval, so my fourth audition would be for him. In the meantime Mark asked me to read with the young kids who were auditioning and I gladly obliged. I felt as if this part was mine. I'd been acting for ten years in radio, on television, on Broadway; I'd made three minor pictures and been studying diligently with Jeff Corey, Stella Adler, Peggy Feury, Bruce Dern, and Lee Strasberg. I'd improved my craft. The feedback I got was encouraging, but I hadn't yet been able to "break through," to get that one film that would ensure that I wouldn't have to struggle for the next job. I thought this would be my big break, but Steve McQueen didn't agree. He liked another girl better. I was devastated. I couldn't stop crying for days.

Neil recently had gotten involved with a circle of friends he called "my gang." He asked if he could invite them over to cheer me up. I was desperate and ready for anybody to lift my spirits, so I agreed. Two of his friends arrived and they did in fact cheer me up. I actually laughed with them and soon I was able to put the whole thing in perspective. It was a job, for God's sake, not the end of the world or even my career. Neil's gang, two or three at a time, began spending a lot of time at our house.

Then the Monkees went off the air and Neil was out of work again. Not long after, he got a job as story editor for Dino De Laurentiis. We were moving to Rome! At last, I was going somewhere! From there I would be able to visit Florence, Naples, Venice, and the rest of Europe. And we had friends there. Bob Rudelson, an actor/writer we knew from Jeff Corey's class, had married a beautiful actress named Lelia Goldoni and they were living in London. Fred and Francey Haines from STOP had moved to Paris because Fred was writing the screenplay for a film adaptation of Henry Miller's novel *Tropic of Cancer*. Of course I was hoping to play Mona, Henry Miller's wife in the story, and Fred had recommended me to the producer, Joseph Strick.

We left for Europe in January 1969, with high hopes that were dashed right away. We missed our original flight, Bernard in his crate was nearly left behind as unchecked baggage, and then our own luggage was lost. We arrived in Rome without so much as a toothbrush. We proceeded to the hotel, only to learn it wouldn't admit dogs. The manager allowed us to stay long enough for our bags to be delivered the following day. It was a trying situation that wasn't helped by the way Neil was treating me. Finally I said to him, "Look! You're acting like your family is a lot of extra baggage you're dragging around and you'd much rather be here alone. If that's how you feel, I want you to say so right now and I will take the dog and the kid and get on the next plane home." There was silence. I took that as an answer and then said, "If that's not what you want, then stop treating me like dog shit. I don't want to be spoken to in that tone."

Soon we found a spacious apartment in Parioli, a residential section near the Borghese Gardens. We enrolled Skipper in St. George's School of England and we seemed to be settling into a normal life. But by the end of January, Neil took an acid trip in the Vatican, whose effects weren't apparent for a while.

In late February, on a golden afternoon, we took a carriage ride down the Appian Way, the ancient highway of classical Rome. The sun was low in the sky and its gold light was polishing the pink, yellow, and ochre buildings. The dome of St. Peter's glistened in the distance. Neil held out his hand to help me into the carriage. I sat down on the old leather seat and Neil sat beside me, a soft smile on his face. The driver picked up the reins and turned the carriage down the road. Neil leaned forward to look at something over my shoulder and at that moment the sun's rays kissed Neil's face with an angelic light. His brown curls were burnished with golden tips. His skin was like a ripe apricot drinking in the sun. His brown eyes radiated golden light. He looked so beautiful I almost burst into tears. Something clutched at my heart, a deep sadness welled up inside of me, and I reached for his hand. He put his arm around me and I lay my head on his shoulder. We rode down the ancient road in silence, the clomp of the horse's hooves echoing on the old stones as they had for centuries. On that ride there was only beauty and love. So why did I feel so sad? For years I thought it was a premonition of what was to come.

Sometimes I wonder if premonitions are not simply a breaking through of the truth that we already know, but are in denial about. Of course I might not have been so successful in my denial if Neil had told me that during his acid trip in the Vatican he'd had a vision where he saw himself as John the Baptist whose mission it was to reveal to the world that the second coming of Christ was upon us.

In April I got a call from Fred Haines in Paris to come meet Joe Strick and read for the part of Mona in *Tropic of Cancer.* When I arrived I found Fred very dispirited because Joe had rewritten his script and Fred said he was going to demand his name be taken off the picture. Francey, too, was not feeling well. I read for Joe and he offered me the role.

Mona leaves Henry early in the story, so it wasn't a big part, but Mona was an important character. Mona is based on June, Henry's real wife, who was the main focus in the other books, *Sexus, Plexus,* and *Nexus.* I read all three of these books in preparation for the role.

Looking back at 1969, I see the strands of my fate coming together in an almost ordered way. I'd been introduced to Gurdjieff and his system for awakening from the normal sleeping state of everyday unconsciousness, to the conscious evolution of the "inner man." I'd been brought to Europe and introduced to the classic civilizations and the artists of ancient Greece, Rome, and the Renaissance. I had a part in a film based on a book by one of the greatest writers of the twentieth century, an erotic, lyrical, amoral, witty, bawdy, profound, brilliant, shocking genius I never would have found my way to otherwise. I visited all the museums and archeological sites of Rome, and now was going to be on location in Paris, that city of cities that had inspired not only Henry Miller, but Scott Fitzgerald, Ernest Hemingway, Gertrude Stein, Victor Hugo, and on and on. I was reeling with excitement. I was fulfilling the dream I had as I rode out of Detroit on the Greyhound bus.

Fred got over his pique at Joe Strick and was making a documentary on Henry Miller and the shooting of *Tropic.* Henry arrived from America and came to the set regularly. One day at lunch at a picnic table outside the house we were shooting in, Henry said to Fred, "I was sorry you didn't use that part of the book where I met the prostitute in the café for breakfast and we used to discuss all the great books of the world's literature."

After a long pause, Fred said, "Actually, that's not in the book, Henry."

"It's not?" Henry asked in surprise.

"No, it's not," Fred answered gently.

"Oooh, I thought I put that in the book. I always meant to. We met each morning. There she'd be sitting at the same table at an outdoor café. I'd sit near her and we'd talk about Balzac and Tolstoy and Dante. Oh, I'm sorry that wasn't in the book. I always thought it was in there."

I asked Henry if he was still in contact with his ex-wife June. "I called her a few years ago and went to see her in her little apartment in New York," he said. "But I couldn't stay. It was too upsetting for me."

"What was upsetting, Henry?"

"Why, she was an old woman! A little old lady in her basement apartment! I had to leave. She'd put out a beautiful spread for me and everything—but I couldn't eat it. I had to get out of there!"

As he said this, gesturing with his trembling age-spotted hands, his faded blue eyes brimmed with tears and spilled over onto his old man's cheeks.

In the summer of 1969, Neil drove Skip and Bernard to Paris to stay with me until I finished shooting. I had a few days off and the American astronauts were about to land on the moon. I decided I didn't want to observe this historic occasion on French television. I wanted to hear it in English. We called Bob and Lelia Rudelson in London and asked if we could come for a visit. London was suffering from a rare hot spell and we all sat around the Rudelsons' flat in our skivvies drinking ice water with an electric fan aimed at us as we watched man set his foot on the goddess Luna for the very first time.

We drove down in our little red convertible to Newhaven and took the ferry to Dieppe and got back to Paris just in time to see Neil Armstrong, Buzz Aldrin, and Michael Collins return safely to Earth as we watched on the television in the hotel bar. When they emerged from their space capsule, everyone in the bar cheered, then sent us a bottle of champagne. We were the only Americans in the bar and they asked that we accept, as representatives of our country, a gift from them representing the people of France. We tearfully accepted their gift and stood as the whole bar toasted us for the remarkable achievement of the American space program.

The next day in my diary, I wrote: *I have decided to devote the next nine months to my career. The picture* (Tropic) *opens in March. I am going to concentrate on getting work until April. If after that time my career isn't secure enough for me to get the kind of pictures or plays that I want, I shall not continue.*

Back in Rome I was taking the bus each day to the Colosseum and sitting on the old stone benches reading Robert Graves's *I, Claudius.* I was in the middle of "Claudius the God" when Neil had a meeting with Dino and they suddenly terminated their relationship. Neil had been writing a screenplay of Thomas Mann's *Joseph and His Brothers.* I take it Dino was dissatisfied, but Neil never told me about it.

We returned to Los Angeles. On September 16, I wrote in my diary: *It's time to find a teacher . . . I don't know what the next step is, but I know I am ready for it. I am getting my house in order—all houses—literal, physical, and spiritual. I am at the end of something. I know a teacher is in order now . . .*

Reading Gurdjieff introduced me to the idea of a teacher, but I didn't know how to go about finding one or how to recognize a good one if I bumped into him on the street. But there is an old Sufi saying: "When the student is ready, the teacher appears." Apparently, I wasn't ready just yet.

Bob Rafelson was preparing *Five Easy Pieces* and I desperately wanted the part of Rayette. I developed a complicated plan of getting his casting agent, Fred Roos, to introduce me as Colleen Bernstein from Dallas, Texas. I wore a black wig, went in with an accent, pretended I was some other actress, not me, and I seem to recall bringing in some props, including some nuts I cracked and ate during the reading. Bobby got a big kick out of my effort. Then he hired Karen Black. I was beyond disappointed. I was crushed. I wrote on November 1: *If spring comes without my having done another picture, I am going to quit. This business has had as much of me as I can give it. Maybe we'll try New York for a while—maybe just give up and go back home.*

On Wednesday, December 24, 1969, at noon, I had an appointment to meet Paul Mazursky and Larry Tucker at Columbia about a movie they were making called *Alex in Wonderland*. Paul Mazursky and Larry Tucker had had a big success with *Bob & Carol & Ted & Alice,* and this was to be their next film. They wrote and produced together and Paul directed. The script was about a Hollywood director who has a big success with his first film and can now do almost anything he wants and is facing all the creative, moral choices of being in that position. It was a funny, well-written script, and I read for the part of the director's wife, Beth. The reading went well and I felt I had a good chance of getting this role. However, they hadn't yet cast the leading role of Alex, and they had to do that before they cast his wife.

Right after the New Year, Neil, Skip, and I were in San Diego on a short vacation. I was waiting for word from Mazursky. On January 5, Paul called and said they were testing Henry Jaglom for Alex. I knew Henry through the Rafelsons. I didn't know him well, but I knew he grew up with lots of money and I had a real attitude about him. The atmosphere between us had always been chilly. Henry has since become a successful director and we've become friends, but back then I had my doubts about him, though I agreed to go forward.

It was during this time that I changed my name for the last time. Neil had stopped calling himself Neil Nephew and was using his grandfather's name, Burstyn. Legally we were Mr. and Mrs. Bernstein. Skip used Bernstein at school, but professionally I was known as Ellen McRae. I wanted all of us to use the same name. One day in early January, Joe Strick tracked me down in Mazursky's production office. He was calling from Paris. He said they were laying in the credits and wanted to know which name he should use—McRae or Burstyn? It was one of those moments I remember with crystalline clarity. I had a feeling that this was the end of all the name changing. Whichever name I picked now, I would carry for the rest of my life. My marriage was very shaky; my husband was in a volatile state. It didn't seem the right time to make this choice, but, right or not, this was the time. There was a pause when all the reality flowed and flashed through my mind. I couldn't vote against my marriage—I had to give it a vote of confidence despite what I felt. "Make it Ellen Burstyn," I said.

Soon after, Henry and I rehearsed together and it was very strained. Paul asked that we bring our real relationship out into the open and talk about it so that we could build from there. We rehearsed two more days, and then Paul shot a screen test.

A few days later, Paul called and said that Henry and I didn't "go so good together" and asked me to recommend another actor. I suggested he see Neil for the role. What was I thinking? We had been in so many acting classes together, I knew his limitations as an actor. Early on when Bob Rafelson was producing television shows, there was a role in one of them for a young motorcyclist. Neil thought he was perfect for it and worked on it for weeks before he auditioned for Bob. Bob wanted Neil to get the part and worked on it with him, yet the role went to another actor. It was soon after this that Bob began to encourage Neil to write. Neil did begin writing then, but he still had dreams of being a movie star.

We read for Paul again on January 16. I wrote in my diary: *Neil opened the interview by asking Paul if he'd ever seen God. It went on from there. I drifted into a dream.* I dissociated—left my body and went vague, pretended I wasn't embarrassed by my husband's lecture on personally knowing the face of God.

Paul let Neil down easy. He called and said they'd decided against Neil because he looked too young, but they were still very high on me. They cast Donald Sutherland in the role of Alex, and Paul cast Neil in a small role as a friend of Alex. My diary also records all-night crying jags around this time. Though I don't write what I was crying about, it seems I knew on some level that in fact my husband was crazy, but I stayed in denial as long as I could.

Had Neil's sickness been constant or if he were suffering, it might have been more difficult to hide the truth from myself, but there were too many good days for that. Neil was expansive, energetic, and full of ideas. One day in January the California sky had been swept clean of smog. After Skip went to school, we got in our car, put the top down, and rode together under the blue sky. We ended up at the Rafelsons, had breakfast in Toby's cozy kitchen, talked, then put on some music and danced. Neil told Bob about the script he was writing and Bob told me about a script by Charles Eastman in which there was a part for me. He asked if he could call Charles and recommend me. It was a happy day.

But there were other kinds of days. Like our night during the session at the Actors Studio West when Neil got up from his chair beside me and sat beside a beautiful actress, put his arm around her, and spent the session nuzzling her and whispering in her ear. I felt embarrassed and humiliated. At home when I protested, Neil raged at me, calling me oppressive and a jealous crazy bitch. Then he stormed out and didn't come back that night.

I was cast in Mazursky's movie *Alex in Wonderland,* then went to meet Mike Nichols, who had seen *Tropic of Cancer* at a screening and was considering me for a part in *Carnal Knowledge* (which went to Ann-Margret). But there was definitely action in my career. I was about to pop. I could feel it. It felt as if I was coming into my own.

As Neil struggled with my success, our fights grew more frequent. He became convinced that his gang carried the energy of the Christ. Jesus was coming back to earth, not as one person, but as a group. He developed a whole theology around this idea.

I was so worried, I urged him to go to a therapist, but he refused. He said he was enlightened, not sick; I was just too stubborn to see it. Just as Neil had idealized his uncle Brad and considered him the world's greatest painter as well as songwriter, he now idealized his gang and saw them as not only the world's greatest artists, but as the world's saviors.

We started filming *Alex* on May 11, 1970. Donald Sutherland and I worked well together, and Paul Mazursky was a wonderful director. I loved the work. This was what I'd wanted for years, a good part in a wonderful script with a creative director, playing opposite an excellent actor. Is it any wonder I was in denial about the effect my success was having on Neil? I knew he was restless, frustrated, envious, and desperate. I just didn't allow myself to see that he was, in fact, crazy. How could I? The implications were too horrible.

On June 11, Donald and I were shooting a scene in the Los Angeles airport. We were one flight up behind a glass wall. Neil was below us, on the ground, unaware we could see him. He was pacing back and forth talking to himself in an agitated manner. He seemed about to burst. As Donald and I stood watching him, Donald made the observation that he looked like a caged lion. I said something mild to lighten the moment. Donald said strongly, "No! I'm telling you, that's a caged lion!" I was startled at the force in his tone.

The company moved out to Malibu. The first scene we shot there was to be a party at Alex's house with some of our friends, one of whom gets into an argument with Alex. This was the scene in which Neil appears. He again was in an agitated state, walking around and talking to himself under his breath. I tried to calm him. He ranted about "having to do it, this was his chance."

"Just do your work, Neil," I said. I knew he was thinking about doing something. I just wasn't sure what. It was a big scene. Three cameras were set up: one on Donald, one on me, and a master shot that included everybody. I was holding a child actress on my lap, who played our younger daughter. When the scene started, the actor who was supposed to get into the fight with Alex started shouting. Neil was sitting next to him and told him to stop shouting in his ear. And then he persisted. Every time the actor tried to get the argument going with Alex, Neil would interrupt him and point to his ear. Soon that actor and Neil began to fight. Neil stood and started shouting. The actor was so angry he stormed off the set. The young actress playing my daughter looked up at me, frightened, wondering what was happening. I took her hand and led her off the set. The cameras were still rolling. Neil walked to my empty chair and sat down facing my camera. Looking directly into it, he said, "I have come here today to tell you that Jesus Christ is alive and living in Van Nuys." I don't remember what else he said, but he went on for a while, all three cameras rolling, as he explained that he was the reincarnation of John the Baptist. When he finally slowed to a stop, Paul called, "Okay, everyone, that's a wrap. See you on Monday."

There were probably a hundred people present, including the cast, crew, and extras. Nobody spoke as the crew began breaking down the lights and we headed for our trailers. A friend of Paul's, a former Catholic monk, was playing one of Alex's friends in the film. As I walked silently to my trailer, he came up to me and said, "Your husband is in deep trouble. Get him to a doctor."

There it was, the truth. In my face. All my avoidance collapsed in a heap. Neil was in deep trouble. He needed help fast and he didn't know it. He had to be put into a hospital and I had to do it. I didn't want to commit him against his will; the image of Neil being led away in a straitjacket was too awful. I had to talk him into admitting himself.

I called Fred Haines, who suggested we come to his house in Laurel Canyon and he would try to talk Neil into admitting himself. On the way to Fred and Francey's house, Neil told me that the day before, when he was considering whether or not to "do it," a raindrop landed on his shoulder and he knew that this was a message from God that he must do it. At the Haines house, Fred invited Neil out for a walk while I stayed with Francey, who had just returned from Ireland, where she had gone for a diagnosis of her mysterious symptoms of blindness and lameness. Multiple sclerosis was suspected and was shortly confirmed. Francey's father was the head of a hospital in Dublin and while there, he'd given Francey some pills to take home with her, to help her stay calm in the face of her illness. My whole body was trembling with worry and fear for Neil. Francey offered me one of her Librium and I took it.

Francey and I sat in her living room discussing her illness and Neil's. About twenty minutes after I took the Librium, I suddenly said in surprise, "Oh! I just felt that Librium drop." I had taken LSD only twice, but I used the term "drop," which was always used when the user felt the drug activate in the system. I asked Francey if there was any chance she'd given me acid by mistake. She assured me that this was one of the pills her father had given her and couldn't possibly be anything but Librium. Then why was my body experiencing all the same things I'd felt when I'd taken acid? I got scared. Something was very wrong and I didn't think Francey in her fragile condition should have to deal with it. I called our mutual friend Naomi and asked her to come right over. She was there within a few minutes. By that time I could barely control myself. When I went to the door to admit Naomi, my legs gave way, I fell on her, and said crying, "I'm so glad you're here."

She got me into Fred and Francey's bed and under the covers, where I proceeded to scream, cry, moan, and howl for hours. I was in a kind of terrified dream state in which huge blocks of color would move toward me and smash me into another huge block of color, and then another, repeatedly.

At some point, my eyes opened for a moment and I saw Daisy Mae, my Dalmatian. That is, I could discern her form—not her body—beside the bed. I could see her tongue hanging out the side of her mouth as it would when she was worried or anxious. She had come back from the other side to be with me. I could feel her presence, her love, and concern. Then I was back into the screeching darkness.

Neil and Fred returned and I heard Naomi say, "She's been like this for hours." Then I retreated inside the screaming once again, though I heard someone shouting my name. It was far, far away. Someone was calling me. I wanted to rise to the surface where my name was being called, but it seemed so far above me. But if I could just make the effort, I could reach it. If only I could make the howling stop. It sounded like wolves. I was able to remember that I was at Fred and Francey's house. In Laurel Canyon. Were there wolves there? Coyotes, there were coyotes. I then broke through to the surface. As I did, I realized the howling was coming from my throat. I looked up into Neil's face. He was sitting on me; his face inches from mine, shouting my name. Fred, Francey, and Naomi were standing around the bed looking worried. Neil held me. "She's all right. She'll be okay," he said. Then to me, "You're going to be okay. That's just what it took to break through your resistance. You have a very strong will, babe. But now, you're on the other side with us. Now we're together. Come on, let's go see my gang."

It's true, I had no resistance. To anything. I whimpered for a while in his arms and soon was able to get out of bed and even walk. But before we went to join his gang, we had to pick up Skippy, who had returned to L.A. from a class trip up north. Neil drove our convertible to Skip's school and I lay with my head on the back of the seat, letting the wind dry my swollen face.

When we got to the school, we learned that Skip had been sick the entire drive home. As I'd been going through my ordeal, my son had had diarrhea. He got in the car and we drove to the house in the valley where the gang lived.

Once there, we went to the backyard and lay down in the grass. My head was resting on Neil's chest. Skip was curled up into the curve of my body. My hand was stroking his soft blond curls. We were so happy to be together.

All was peaceful. I felt as if we were a pride of lions after filling ourselves on a good kill, lolling in the summer sun, digesting all we had taken into ourselves. I could hear the insect world clicking and whirring beneath us, a far-off airplane droned by, autos in the distance. Up close I could feel Neil's chest expand with each breath. We were together, happily together. I'm fine with all of it, I thought. As long as we can curl against his body and be a family.

That lasted for about a day. Twenty-four hours later, reality started reassembling itself and my mind came back together. Neil would later say fiercely to me, "You crossed over for one day! One day! And then you had to go back! You just couldn't stick it, could you? I'll never forgive you for that! Never!"

I would later learn that what had happened to me that day had happened to other people, too. It's called an "unscheduled voyage." An acid trip without acid. The body, once having experienced the effects of acid, retains some memory of it and under the right circumstances, recreates it. Mine did that time. And perhaps Neil's did all the time, or often. There were times that Neil seemed perfectly sane, albeit eccentric. It was part of his charm. He was quirky. But at other times he could be a raging maniac. Those times would grow more frequent and impossible to tolerate.

And why those huge blocks of menacing color? I don't know why they were envisioned that way, but it does seem to me now that each one represented a different force at work in my life. My blossoming career smashed me into my husband's fragile, deteriorating ego, which pushed me up against my son who loved his daddy and for whom I desperately wanted to provide a happy home. But I guess I really didn't know what one looked like. I had tried to deny the truth, to protect myself from it, and instead had succeeded only in letting the pressure build underground until it exploded in a geyser of reality that broke through all my defenses and shattered my mind into a million psychedelic shards of screaming pain.

"Samsara" is the Buddhist word for the inevitable state of confusion and blind repetitious behavior suffered by all sentient beings who have not yet realized the nature of their own minds and thereby gained the release of enlightenment.

I surely had not done that. The more I struggled to free myself, the more entangled I became.

Even after all of that, I still seemed to hold out hope that Neil would get better, that somehow it was all going to go away, that he would wake up one day and realize that his group was not his or anyone else's savior, and that he was not John the Baptist. I thought someone was going to be able to get through to him—to the old Neil, who must still be alive in there somewhere. Many people were trying besides me: Bob Rafelson and his partner Burt Schneider, Mark Rydell, and our friend Fred Haines. Everyone was trying to convince him that he was sick and needed help.

I consulted many therapists and psychiatrists during this period and it is shocking to me now how little good advice I got. There was one doctor who spoke plain truth to me. He was in Beverly Hills and had come highly recommended, but when I got him on the phone, he said he didn't have time to take on any new patients. When I told him the John the Baptist story, he said, "Oh, okay. You've got a real problem. I'll see you once. Come see me after hours and I'll advise you what to do."

When I met with him, he gave it to me straight. "Many people take even more LSD than your husband without any bad side effects," he said. "But we've found that there are some people whose bodies seem to become LSD factories and they keep on producing the acid all the time. They stay on a continual acid trip. It sounds like your husband is one of them."

"What happens to them?" I asked.

"The prognosis is not good. I have one patient like that who's been in the hospital for two years and he shows no sign of 'coming down.'"

"What should I do?"

"Get out," he said. "Save yourself and save your kid. There's nothing you can do for your husband."

I thanked him, though I knew I wasn't going to take his advice. Neil was sick. I wouldn't leave him if he had a physical illness. Why would I desert him because he had a mental illness?

I've always loved camping and suggested we buy a camper so we could get away sometimes into the high mountains with the big trees. We found a used one-ton Chevy cab-over camper and bought it with my earnings from *Alex*. A few days after we finished filming I suggested we take a trip. Neil refused to leave his group. I said I'd go alone. Neil insisted that I not take the camper. At least some part of me understood that I had to get away and *retreat*. So I sent Skippy to stay with Adela, our housekeeper, and boarded a bus to the San Ysidro Ranch outside of Santa Barbara. I spent four days in a cabin by myself and tried to figure out what to do with my life. I brought along a notebook and filled it with possibilities, including, surprisingly, giving up my life as I knew it and moving back to Detroit with Skip.

One night I went to the restaurant on the ranch for dinner and eavesdropped on the conversation at the next table. An older man, a younger woman, and a European youth were discussing reincarnation, past lives, and other mystical topics. I yearned to join them, but I didn't have the nerve to intrude. But I stopped at their table, made one remark, and then took a seat at the bar and ordered a drink. Then the young man came and asked me to join them. The older man (he was eighty-two) was from Canada, an economist by profession, who had lived in India, China, and Japan. He'd traveled the world, knew about Sufism, Zen, yoga, Gurdjieff, and Ouspensky, whose books I'd been studying for the past year. I was very impressed. He was the kind of person I'd so often read about, but never had actually met. I asked him how I could go about finding a teacher, and he promised me that my teacher would appear. In the meantime, he said that I should make contact with "my higher self" every morning, that I should make notes and later—not now, I was still too green—use them to write.

I never saw this man again, but he was the first living mystic I ever met, and to me he was a numinous being. I tucked him into the back of the files of my memory until now, as I search through the very notes he instructed me to take, and he is resurrected in me along with all the idealization and naive fervor I felt at the time. My life at home was on a steeply descending road to hell. This stranger, met one night in an inn, threw me a lifeline. He promised me I'd meet my teacher. In less than a year, I did, and he also gave me very good advice about contacting my higher self every morning. In the meantime, I had to return to Los Angeles and my tumultuous life.

One of the worst ideas any of us ever had was for Neil's parents, Hank and Flo, to come from New York and for us to camp our way up to Lake Tahoe, where my mother and her husband, Winsor, had rented a condominium for the summer. *A family vacation!* Were we all mad? Neil was raging the whole way. I was sniffling. Hank and Flo were rigid. When we arrived at the place in Tahoe, my mother greeted us by asking us to wipe our feet before we entered. Neil shouted, "This is my vacation. Don't you dare boss me around." My mother burst into tears and ran into the kitchen. I ran after her. We spent four days in a collective nightmare. Neil was ordering everyone around in a ranting fit and all the while shouting about God. Everyone was in tears or holed up in their bedrooms. Flo and Hank retreated into silence. Neil's insanity was all over us everywhere. There wasn't a moment of peace. I spent the whole time in tears.

And for the first time, Neil brought Skippy into it. Somehow we had managed to have our fights when he couldn't observe. This time Neil started including him. When we got back to Los Angeles, I said to Neil, "Don't you ever drag him into this again. That is off limits. Either commit to that or leave!" It was sort of like a bizarre international agreement that says I can bomb you to death, but we agree not to use chemical warfare on innocent bystanders.

During the month of August, back in L.A. the situation deteriorated more dangerously still. One day's fight escalated to the point that I dissociated. My body went limp. I got suddenly very tired. I went to the living room and crawled onto the couch. Neil followed, shouting. I was aware of his voice growing louder and more persistent, shouting, "Stop this bullshit! You are a bad girl. That's what you are." Then twice he slapped me hard on the ass. "You need a spanking," he screamed. I saw he was justifying more violence. I got up and ran up the stairs. He came after me. I was terrified. I ran into the kitchen to find a way to protect myself. He shouted viciously, "If you get a knife, I'll kill you!" and he knocked me to the floor, sat on me, pinning my shoulders down with his knees, and picked up my head between his hands. I knew he was about to pound my head into the floor. This number had been pulled on me before by all the bullies I'd ever lived with—my mother not the least—so I knew that resistance enrages bullies when they're mad. I went limp and grew very calm, just as I used to with my mother. And from that vantage point, I observed his red face, its skin hanging down, the spittle collecting in the corners of his mouth, and his hatred of me choking the cords in his neck. I knew that I could no longer subject myself to his cruelty. This monster that Neil had become was not the Neil I loved. When he let me up off the floor, I went crying into the bedroom, and he said in a voice hoarse with hatred, "I'm sorry, Ellen. I had to do that because I love you."

So once again I got Skip to the safety and calm of Adela's house, got in the camper, and drove away. I didn't know where I was going. I was just getting *away*. I needed time to get centered and think. After a couple hours, I found a campground and pulled into its empty parking lot. When I got out of the truck, there was blissful silence. The only sound I could hear was the breeze soughing in the tall pine trees—and the far-off sound of rushing water. I set off toward the sound. My dog, Bernard, was with me. As we entered the woods, the sound got louder and louder until we came to a wide rushing stream. I stood on the edge and noticed a large flat boulder in the center, upriver a bit. I walked to it and found stepping stones out to the boulder. Bernard was investigating the shore as I made my way to the center of the river. Once there, I found the sun shining on my face and I sat on the warm flat rock with my eyes closed and the water rushing past me on all sides. I sat like that for a long time, trying to ease the hot clutching pain from my heart. Soon I was crying away all the rage and trying desperately to figure out what to do. Suddenly I felt something. Something was calling to me, trying to get my attention. My eyes popped open and there on the opposite bank in a meadow was a beautiful being in tree form whose limbs and leaves were dancing in the light. The tree, it seemed, was calling to me. It reminded me that all of this drama I was immersed in was not all there was to life. There were also dancing trees and sparkling rivers, warm rocks, and sweet sunshine. I felt completely present. The chatter of my mind was stilled. Behind the chatter was a peaceful, calm spaciousness. I sat on the warm rock in the midst of the rushing river and knew with quiet certainty that "this too shall pass."

When I returned to Los Angeles my life was there waiting, and I fell back into it. At least on the outer level. Inside, I was awakening.

A film was being made about Lenny Bruce, one of Neil's heroes. He was convinced he was the only person who could play Lenny. In September 1970 he managed to get sent up for the role and the director showed interest in him. They were going to screen-test him. I prayed he'd get it. On December 21, during his screen test, I sat on our terrace and prayed for him to get the role. I chanted his name and Lenny Bruce's for an hour. If he ever had a chance of getting that part, he ruined it on the test. He did his John the Baptist number.

He didn't get the part. Dustin Hoffman played Lenny.

My life with Neil was disintegrating. We had very little money left of the paycheck from *Alex* in July. Neil had been preaching to all of our friends that he was the reincarnation of John the Baptist and it was his job to announce the second coming of the Christ. As our friends' patience ran out and they refused to listen anymore, Neil began going into the streets and preaching to strangers his remedy for the problems of the world, which seemed to be to believe in him and his gang as the next incarnation of the Christ.

Neil's craziness and violence escalated to a point that was unbearable, and I asked him to leave. He packed a few things and got a room at the Ocean View Hotel in Venice. I felt devastated when he moved out, but I'd grown too frightened to be able to sleep in bed with him. Neil's mother, Flo, called from New York to tell me that I was responsible for what was happening to Neil, that by working I robbed Neil of his masculinity.

Bob Rafelson's company was producing a film based on Larry McMurtry's novel *The Last Picture Show*. It was to be directed by a new-comer named Peter Bogdanovich, who had previously directed a film called *Targets*. I was asked to read for the part of a waitress named Genevieve. As I read the script I saw there were two other roles I could play: Ruth Popper, the coach's meek wife, and the lusty Lois Farrow. I preferred the part of Lois. I met Peter in his office along with Polly Platt, who was his wife, part-ner, and the film's art director. I read the part of the waitress. Then Peter said, "Would you mind reading the part of Ruth?"

I said, "No, if then you'll let me read for Lois Farrow. That's the part I want." I read Ruth for him and then Lois.

When I finished, Peter said, "Okay. We know you're in the movie. Now we just have to figure out which part you play."

Months later, Peter and I were talking about auditions in general and I said, "It must be hard when someone is reading for you and you can tell after the first few minutes if they're any good or not, but you have to let them go on reading till the end of the scene."

"You can tell before that," Peter said. "You can tell when they walk through the door."

"How?" I asked.

"Really good actresses have a mysterious solidity about them," he said.

I thought that was an intriguing phrase. I wouldn't think of something solid as mysterious; something more amorphous would be mysterious. But used the way Peter did in regard to that elusive thing, talent, I could see how its presence could give someone a solidity. Talent and where it comes from are great mysteries.

Did I feel solid? In my life I was in turmoil, but when I acted, I felt more sure-footed. The year before, sometime in 1969 maybe, or perhaps earlier, Neil and I were studying in Bruce Dern's class. I did a scene from the Nikos Kazantzakis novel *The Last Temptation of Christ,* in which I played Mary Magdalene. I remember that Bruce made me play the scene in my underwear. It was a scene with Jesus in which He is about to go to the desert for forty days and Mary Magdalene is furious with him for running away and hiding. She berates him to stay and basically she's saying, "Deal with it! Deal with me! Get real! Get into your body and stop escaping!"

After the scene Bruce said to me, "Now, get it. You are one of the five best actresses in America. I'll name them," and he counted them on his fingers. "There is Kim Stanley, Geraldine Page, Julie Harris, Maureen Stapleton, and you."

That should be enough to give a person a mysterious solidity. I just can't remember actually believing him.

Peter reported that he was having an easier time casting Lois than Ruth and that I might have to play Ruth Popper. He urged me to play her. "That's the Academy Award role," he said.

"I don't care," I said. "I just don't want to be her."

I couldn't tell him that I was just too miserable in my own life to take on someone more unhappy than I was. Lois was unhappy, too, but she was on top of it, she wasn't letting it get her down. I wanted to go to that place. I wanted to learn from my character how to do what I couldn't do in my life.

There was to be a great revelation at a Rosh Hashanah party at our house. Everything was to become clear. Neil invited Paul Mazursky, Mark Rydell (who brought his friend, a psychiatrist), Fred and Francey Haines, the Rafelsons, and Bert Schneider. Neil's gang came and showed a film about the cathedral at Chartres. But whatever was supposed to occur, didn't. Nothing happened. Neil was devastated and spent the next day crying. I spent the day on the phone with friends and Neil's family trying to figure out how to get him into a hospital. Everyone had a different opinion. His family was divided. His father said, "Just leave him." His mother said, "Put him in right now." His sister, Donna, called in hysterics. "If you commit my brother, don't you ever bring Skippy up here again!" She hung up on me.

On October 3, Peter called to give me the part of Lois. He'd found Cloris Leachman to play Ruth. Rehearsals were to start the following week. We were to rehearse a week in Los Angeles, then a week in Texas, then I'd be home until the end of October. I would then be away for a month. In the past when I went out of town, I'd leave Skip with Neil and Adela, whom Skip loved. For the first time, I didn't want to leave him with Neil. I didn't trust him with our nine-year-old son. I was afraid of him. My heart started racing when he got near me. My body was telling me I was in danger, even if I thought I still loved him. Again I told Neil to leave. Now, all of a sudden, he wouldn't. He became a maniac.

Fortunately, Skip's school took all the kids away to camp for the two weeks I was to be in Dallas. We moved to Wichita Falls on October 12 and had dinner with the company at Mayo's Steak House. We got into our Texas accents and stayed in them the whole time. I wrote my one-word first impression of everybody.

Tim Bottoms is very sensitive.
Cybill Shepherd is sweet.
Jeff Bridges is well-mannered.
Ben Johnson is real.
Cloris Leachman is fine china.
Polly Platt is energetic.
Peter Bogdanovich is polished.

The next day we drove around Wichita Falls, then to Anarene, which is the model for Archer City, the town in the story. After rehearsal we sat and talked to three local kids. When Jeff Bridges asked the boys what they did for fun around here, one of the boys, who we'll call Johnny, leaned on the back legs of his chair and answered, "Whup niggers." No one in our group moved. We froze. Johnny added, "That's about all there is to do."

None of us spoke about this, but I felt a resolve travel through us like an electric current that said, "All right, young man, we will take on your education." And we did. And it turned out not to be such a difficult task. The poison that had been planted in that young man's mind was like a brain tumor that was operable. We were the surgeon's knife that lifted it right out cleanly and restored his brain to its innate sweetness. By the time we left town, Johnny said to us, "You know what you folks have done? You've made me unfit to live in my own hometown."

He was right. We took him with us. He brought his girlfriend and they lived with me for about a year. He got work as a stand-in and is still in the film business.

We were all relatively unknown at the time. Cloris and I had been acting for fifteen or twenty years, but we were certainly not famous. Eileen Brennan had had some success in musicals, but she was not all that well known. Ben Johnson was a real cowboy who'd worked for years with John Wayne in Westerns. And Jeff Bridges, Tim Bottoms, and Cybill Shepherd were brand-new. I don't think anyone with the exception of Peter and Polly, had any idea what a rare collection we were. At least not until the first reading of the screenplay. We sat around a large oval table in a bare room of the hotel. Partway through the reading, it dawned on me that this was something special. The quality of the writing lifted off the page and the actors were relating to each other—for real. The characters were coming alive. The story unfolded—the town, Archer City—became peopled with families—us. We were in it and we were it. Something in the room seemed to deepen, and at the same time grow brighter—the yearning, the love, disappointment, the humanity. It was so moving, so exciting.

The last words were read. We closed our scripts. There was a moment of silence. Then somebody said in an almost awed voice, "You know, this could be a good movie."

I turned to Peter. He had a half-smile on his face and his whiskers twitched, as he savored the taste of that canary he had just swallowed.

On October 16, 1970, I wrote in my journal:

Incredible night. Tim, Jeff, Eileen, Johnny, and his girlfriend all went to a dance. Later Tim in his room—reminded me I will always have the dawn. And all the time the rain came down. Later in my room after everyone left, Jeff stayed. He's just unimaginably sweet and straight—a nice boy. A really good dear person. If Skip could ever get to that place, I'd really be happy. But so mature. The kids are so open. I love them. Cybill is shy. She's not sure of the world, but when she feels safe, she's like a morning glory. I wish I were twenty now instead of when I was. This is a much better time. Better. More real. More loving. I would like them all to spend the night with me just sleeping near, warm and sweet. I feel nicer with them than I have for a long time. Jeff left his tapes. I'm listening now to Joan Baez. I will listen until I fall asleep. I don't want to feel bad anymore.

I did my first scene of *The Last Picture Show* on October 31, 1970. Peter shot in sequence as much as possible, so for a change I began with my entrance in the picture, in my convertible, dark glasses on, a scarf on my head and when I see Apilene, my sometime lover, I flip him the bird. Excellent entrance.

Shooting went well. We all got along and spent our down time with each other. We had to. We were staying in a Ramada Inn beside a highway outside of Wichita Falls. There was nothing else around there. None of us had cars. After work or when we weren't called, we hung out in the hotel getting high, singing, laughing, and talking. Cloris's husband of twenty years was leaving her for a younger woman. I asked Cloris how old the girl was. She answered with great emphasis, "She fiiiinally turned twenty-one!" Cloris and I spent a lot of time bemoaning our collapsing marriages, telling stories to each other in rage, in tears, in pain, but always in our Texas accents.

We were all fond of Polly, Peter's wife. Peter was falling in love with Cybill before our eyes; Polly could see it happening, too. I've got to hand it to Peter—he didn't sneak around. He was very up front. When he and Cybill decided to find out what was going on between them, Peter told Polly that he and Cybill were going off for a weekend together. Polly stayed with us at the Ramada and grappled with her fate—just as Cloris and I were doing.

Reading my diaries for this period, I'm amazed to learn that I was still in denial about just how serious Neil's mental illness was. When I had two weeks off from shooting, I flew home to be with Neil, still hoping that somehow he had come to his senses. In retrospect, I was as deluded as my husband. But I guess I was still carrying in my heart the love I originally felt for Neil, plus the hope that somehow I could preserve our family. Skip loved his daddy and I couldn't bear the thought that he was going to have to endure the same pain of a broken home that I had. I did not want to repeat that pattern, but what was the option? For my son to live with an insane father? When I got home, I found Neil crazier than ever. Previously, although Neil's actions were obviously mad, his demeanor seemed normal. Now he looked like a madman, talking to himself and laughing maniacally; his eyes had a wild expression and he spoke in an unnaturally lowered voice. He neither looked nor sounded like the old Neil. Some might even say he appeared to be possessed.

When I came home for this visit, Neil came in at two A.M. raging. He was wild, violent, and brutal. He demanded sex. When I refused, he raped me, then kept his hands around my throat throughout the night, threatening to strangle me if I tried to move away from him. This went on for eight hours. I was terrified he was going to kill me. By the afternoon of the following day he was calm, but I would never again lose the fear that he was going to kill me. As soon as Neil left, I called the police and reported that I'd been raped, my life threatened, and I was frightened that my husband was going to kill me. The policeman said, "We don't mix in domestic matters."

"Even if he threatened to kill me?"

"That's right," he said.

"What do you do?"

"When a crime has been committed, we catch the criminal."

"But I was raped!"

"By your husband."

"And that's not a crime?"

"No."

Soon the women's movement would succeed in getting the laws

changed so that sexual assaults included spouses. But in 1970 married women were still the property of their husbands, who could do with them as they chose. Two days later, I had to fly back to Texas to complete the rest of my scenes for *The Last Picture Show*. I got Skip's assignments from school and took him with me.

We shot a scene that began with me sitting in my living room in front of the television; my husband is asleep beside me. I'm bored, flipping through a magazine without looking at it. I hear a car pull up and recognize it as the sound of my lover Abilene's car. I get up excited, walk to the door to greet him. The door opens and my daughter, Jacey (Cybill), enters. I'm disappointed it's not Abilene's car I'd heard, then realize I was right, it was his car. And he's just dropped off my daughter. As she stands there, I realize she's just had sex with him. My first reaction is jealousy, and then quickly—oh my God—my baby's not a virgin anymore! It was all one shot in just a few seconds with no lines. While we were waiting for the lighting to be completed, I went over to Peter and said, "Peter, I have eight different reactions here and no line."

Peter grinned sweetly, almost innocently, and said, "I know."

"Well, how the hell am I supposed to do that?"

He said quietly, "Put everything else out of your mind and just think the thoughts of the character and the camera will read your mind." That's what I did. And he was right. That lesson has served me well.

Jeff Bridges was so kind to my son. He spent a lot of time with him and when Jeff's brother, Beau, came for a visit, they took Skip out to play touch football, only to discover he didn't know how to throw a football. The Bridges brothers teaching my nine-year-old son how to hold a football was just a moment in time, but it was a symbol of all the love and attention my son had been denied because he had a crazy father.

Jeff's birthday was the fourth of December and mine was the seventh. I finished shooting on the fifth, so Jeff and I threw a party for the crew at the Ramada Inn on the sixth. During our time there, we had made friends with most of the staff, many of whom joined us in our rooms when we got together. The cook's name was Sam and he invited me into the kitchen to show me the cake he'd made for me. When I thanked him profusely, he said, "I was glad to do it. After all, when was the last time you had a happy birthday?" I looked in his eyes, astonished that he'd seen through my laughing mask. Feeling suddenly exposed, I burst into tears. Then he said, "Anytime you want to give up this life, know that I will have a home for you here. For you and your son."

I stood leaning on the cold, stainless-steel counter in the kitchen of the Ramada Inn on a highway near Wichita Falls, Texas, on the eve of my thirty-eighth birthday, crying helplessly, feeling totally stripped of all pretense and received this great gift from a man I barely knew but would always remember.

After our party, Cloris, Jeff, Johnny, and some of the waiters came to my room and we continued our revelry until dawn. The cast had grown so close to each other; there was such camaraderie throughout the company, I was reluctant to leave them and return to my real life. And which was my real life, after all? This harmonious creative effort filled with love and respect, or the insanity waiting for me at home?

The next day, December seventh, reluctant to leave, Jeff took Skip and me riding for one last time together. Sam the cook came along to help us find some horses to ride and we finally found some for rent in the late afternoon. We rode through a glorious Texas sunset and then drove back to the Ramada Inn, where Cloris was waiting with a bottle of wine for my birthday. After tearful good-byes all around and promises to stay connected, Cloris drove Skip and me to the airport and walked us onto the small plane. As soon as we left the ground, the stewardess announced over the loudspeaker, "Texas International and friends of Ellen want to wish her a happy birthday." Of course I burst into tears.

I thought I would be friends with these people for the rest of my life. And we are friends whenever we see each other. We are in each other's hearts in a way that is special to these circumstances of coming together, having an intense, creative, intimate relationship, and then saying goodbye. Over the years I've gotten used to the idea that this incredible intensity was temporary. That we would fall in love with each other and then it would be over. We return to our lives, but we do take a vital memory with us. I can't see Cloris or Jeff or Cybill in a film or at an opening, or even by chance in a restaurant, without feeling I'm seeing someone who was once very important to me, and that I remember so fondly. Like a cousin who was close when you were a child, then moved away to another part of the country.

My time in Texas woke me up. Though I would occasionally fall back into the dream that there was still hope for Neil, I was awake enough to begin making plans for a life without him. It took me a long time to understand that he was psychotic and that his behavior was beyond his control and was not going to go away, even with therapy. Neil vacillated between absolute certainty that it was his mission in life to save the world, and days spent in agony, crying and moaning, "I don't know. I don't know. Maybe I just made it all up."

In January 1971, he took our camper and disappeared. He was gone for a week and I was about to report him to the police as a missing person when he came home in tears asking to be taken to the hospital. I got him admitted to UCLA Medical Clinic and breathed a sigh of relief that at last he was going to get treatment. But once in the hospital, he got angry at me. The whole thing was my fault. It was my inability to accept that the Messiah had come that was the problem. I was the enemy—me and my ego. Neil told me not to come to the hospital anymore. He didn't want to see me. It was my fault that he was in there.

I was living on unemployment. The money I earned on *The Last Picture Show* had paid most of our debts, but by mid-January I was counting every penny wondering how I was going to make it to my next job. Suddenly, checks started bouncing. I thought there must be some mistake and went to the bank to look at the cancelled checks. I found that Neil had been cashing checks forging my signature. When I protested, I learned the only way the bank would return the money was if I pressed charges—meaning that I'd have to have Neil arrested and taken from the mental hospital to the jail. I couldn't do that, but I was now penniless. Finally I realized that my son and I were in a jam that Neil had created and I had better get myself out of it and stay out.

It was at this point that I let go. I withdrew my support and told Neil, "Fine, don't see me. You're in a hospital. Work it out. Sink or swim."

Within a few days, Neil got himself out of the hospital "against medical advice." He now decided that he was no longer John the Baptist, but
Christ himself. The next I heard from him was on January 31 when he
called at ten A.M. from Waikiki Beach in Honolulu. He was very agitated
and in tears. He said he was sent to Hawaii to commit a murder so as to
become a martyr, but he couldn't go through with it. There was a dragnet
out for him. He was turning himself in to the police. I called Naomi in a
panic and told her the story. She said in a deep voice, "Oh, he's having a
real paranoid attack."

"Is that what it is?" I quieted down. My heart had been racing. Now it
made sense. I called Neil's doctor at the UCLA Medical Clinic, and then
began to make arrangements to get him back. When Neil called, he said
once he got to the police station he'd changed his mind.

It was hard for me to sort out what was paranoiac delusion and what
actually happened. I would learn that there definitely was an incident at a
party where Neil received a knife wound. The people did press charges and
accuse him of attempted murder, but they later dropped the charges when
they learned Neil was a mental patient.

Neil decided to stay in Hawaii because everyone liked him there. He
said he planned to live on the beach. The doctor advised me to get him
committed in Hawaii and then make plans to have him transferred to Los
Angeles County Hospital. I called a hospital in Honolulu. They took the
report and said they'd notify the police to be on the lookout for him. I had
no money to pay for plane fare to Hawaii, but was able to borrow some
from Neil's uncle so I could fly to Hawaii to bring him back.

Neil called and said he was leaving Honolulu and going to Hilo and
that he'd meet me in the Hilo airport in the morning. While making my
ticket arrangements with the airline, for a reason I no longer remember, I
disclosed my situation to the ticket agent. Soon I got a call back from the
airline saying that I could not bring a mental patient onto an airplane. At
that moment I felt a tiger rise up in me and I said, "Look, I've got a big
problem to deal with and what I need is help, not hindrance. I'm getting
on that plane and getting my husband home to a hospital. Don't try and
stop me!" The woman on the other end was silent. I had no idea what to

expect, but I was now in high gear and determined to deal with whatever had to be dealt with.

I spent the night in an airport hotel in Honolulu and flew into Hilo, arriving at seven A.M. The Hilo airport was small and had walls only on three sides. The fourth side was open. Outside were lush tropical gardens and palm trees. Neil was there as promised with his guitar strapped to his back. We had a little time until our flight left for Honolulu. I was praying the airline would let me board with Neil, who seemed quite placid. He was tanned and his brown curls were tipped with gold. He greeted me sweetly and kissed me. Then he tried to get me to leave the airport with him. I refused. He explained that we were in Paradise and he knew that if I walked with him outside and we made love in the Garden of Eden that I would surely get pregnant. I refused and he started backing out the open side of the airport, beckoning to me the whole way, saying, "Come on, come on."

I sat down on a chair in the waiting room as panic rose up inside me. I was afraid to go with him, afraid of losing him, afraid of making a scene that would cinch the airline's refusal to let us on a plane. As he backed down the road, his eyes on me, I had to do something that wouldn't make him run and I had to do it fast. He was approaching the main road. I took out a cigarette and asked a passing stranger for a light. As Neil watched and the man held out his lighter, I said in a quiet voice, "I'm in trouble. I need help. Get me a policeman fast."

The stranger said, "What?"

I repeated quickly as I puffed on my cigarette. "Get a policeman. It's an emergency. I need help fast."

The man returned in a minute with a security guard. I told him I needed to stop my husband. He was a mental patient and he was running away. We started toward Neil as the guard called on his walkie-talkie. As we approached Neil, a police car pulled up behind him. I was shaking from my head to my feet, but Neil was very calm. As the two police emerged from their car, drawing their guns, Neil put a comforting arm around me and said to them sweetly, "Aah, that's all right, officers. My wife is just upset because she can't have children. That's okay. I'll take care of her."

The police nodded. Their faces cleared with understanding and they put their guns back in their holsters. They believed him! Of course! I was hysterical. He was protecting me! Despite my trembling and fear, I steadied my voice and instructed them to call the detective at the Honolulu police station and verify that Neil had been there yesterday.

The police didn't know whom to believe. One of them looked from me to Neil and said, "Your wife seems pretty upset, Neil. Why don't we go down to the station and get this straightened out?" We both got into the police car and went to the station. Once there, the police called in a psychiatrist, who interviewed us separately and agreed that Neil needed hospitalization. There was no mental hospital in Hilo, so he was placed in a local hospital until we could get him transferred to Kaneohe Mental Hospital in Honolulu. The doctor who admitted Neil was very kind when he explained gently that the law insisted that he be kept in a locked room with bars on the windows. When we entered the room, Neil looked at the bars and started crying. He took his guitar, sat on the bed, and began playing and singing "The Birth of the Blues." When he sang the line, "And from a jail came the wail / Of a downhearted frail," tears streaming down his face, he looked so beautiful and helpless, I ached for him.

We stayed in this hospital for three days until we found a police officer who wanted to travel to Honolulu. Neil was now a certified mental patient and could travel only if handcuffed to a police escort.

In Hilo we were met by a police car and taken to Kaneohe State Hospital. I spent the day with Neil while he was evaluated and interviewed by an admissions nurse.

There were many beds, some filled with people lying quietly, some empty, and others with people sitting on them who looked as if they were trying to remember where they'd left their souls. Neil was interviewed by a doctor who was very perceptive and very helpful to me, who finally helped me to understand what was happening to my husband. He explained that Neil's delusions were not the insanity. The delusional system is constructed to keep the person from experiencing the despair of true insanity. He said by keeping Neil in the hospital on medication long enough, the delusional system would finally collapse. At that point he would actually experience his insanity and it would be so uncomfortable for him, he'd do anything to get away from it. Only then could he be treated. Talk therapy wasn't going to do a thing as long as he had his delusions as protection from the painful truth.

I left the hospital at the end of the day feeling calmer and more hopeful than I'd felt in a long time. I had almost no money left to pay for a hotel room and no credit cards. (We'd never established credit anywhere.) A policeman took me to a pleasant hotel and instructed the manager to give me a room for as long as I needed it. The manager escorted me down the hall and walked me into a room that was used as a broom closet. The scrub pails and mops were stored there, but it had large windows that looked out on some palm trees. The manager had a cot set up for me and this is where I slept for the next few days.

I remember the first breakfast I had at that hotel. I was sitting in the dining room having ordered ham and eggs, and when the plate was placed in front of me, along with the ham and eggs there was a slice of fresh pineapple with a small orchid sitting in the round hole of the cored pineapple. The purple of the orchid surrounded by the yellow of the fresh pineapple was so beautiful, simple, sweet, and natural in comparison to all the sordid things my eyes had been seeing for the last few days, it was like a little gift to remind me of the beauty of life. I just sat there, looking down at it, my hair shielding my face on either side and watched the little orchid tremble each time a tear landed on it.

I spent all day with Neil at the hospital, traveling there by bus. Because the weather was ideal and the grounds so beautiful, we spent most of each day lying in the grass with Neil's head on my lap as I stroked his forehead or read to him. Sometimes he played his guitar softly. Other patients approached us from time to time. Some seemed almost normal, but many were agitated. One young man described what was wrong with him this way: "I went out the door, but I was back in, so I went out again, but I was back in again. Every time I got in, I was out, then when I was out, I was in. Then I realized I was in a revolving door and out was in and in was out. There was no difference, just in and out, not in or out."

As we sat on the lush green lawn, I saw a young Asian girl in a pink dress walking very quickly toward us. When she was about ten feet away, she stopped abruptly as though she had bumped into an unseen barrier.

"May I approach?" she requested formally.

I nodded and said, "Yes."

She took a few more steps, then dropped to her knees. We introduced ourselves. She asked Neil why he was here, a question the patients frequently asked each other. Neil replied slowly, "Oh, I guess because I thought I was Jesus Christ."

The girl sat quietly for a moment, her small hands folded in her lap. Then she asked, "Neil, did you take some LSD?"

"Yes," he answered, and she moved on.

We had arrived at Kaneohe on Friday. The doctor who was going to handle Neil's case was due on Monday, but he didn't show up. We waited all day. Neil grew more agitated as the day dragged on. I'd been bringing him food from nearby restaurants because he didn't like the hospital food. As it got close to dinnertime, he asked me to go get him some teriyaki. I left him sitting on a bench under a huge old tree. When I returned, the bench was empty. I checked inside. Nothing. He was gone.

The hospital asked one of the patients with driving privileges to take me in the jeep to see if we could find Neil. He drove me all over Honolulu for hours. We never found him.

At this point, I'd been away from home for nine days. Skippy was staying with Naomi and her daughters. I had to get back home. I made arrangements to take a very early flight the next morning and took a bus out to an airport motel for the night.

The next day, February 9, 1971, I went to the desk to check out. The manager said, "Are you flying to Los Angeles this morning? Well, you better check with your airline. They've had a big earthquake there."

I tried calling Naomi's house. All circuits to Los Angeles were busy. On the television, with no pictures of the devastation yet, the newscaster made it sound as if Los Angeles were gone! A major catastrophe! I raced to the airport, my heart pounding. I tried every pay phone I passed to get through to Los Angeles. All circuits were still busy. At the gate while I waited for the plane, I learned that most of the other passengers who were waiting with me were wives of soldiers who had just completed a week of R&R and were returning to combat in Vietnam. Most of the wives had children back in Los Angeles. Everyone was frantic. We couldn't wait to get on the plane and back to our children. Suddenly an airline official appeared and announced that the flight was cancelled. There was one stunned moment of silence and then tears and protests from all sides. I remember thinking, "Wait a minute here. Just hold on. This script is overwritten. I need the writer on the set, please."

I was traveling with only a carry-on bag. Inside I had a small bottle of Jack Daniel's. I used the deep cap as a cup and after taking a slug myself, I went around the waiting room offering some to the other women. Few refused. We all drank from the same cup. After all, we were all in the same boat.

Soon a man managed to get through to his family. He came away from the phones and announced to all of us, "It's okay. It's not as bad as they're making it sound on TV." We settled down then, slightly buzzy from our breakfast of Jack Daniel's.

Eventually I got back to L.A. Neil was still in Hawaii. Both his parents and Bob Rafelson at different times went to Hawaii to bring him back, but he refused to come. He was happy there, he said. I was on the phone daily with him, with them, with doctors. He was in the hospital. He was out. He loved me. He hated me. He was Jesus himself. He was sick and wanted to get better and come home and take care of us. He was coming. No, we should come there and live on the beach with him. Up down in out yes no. I was glad he was gone. I was bereft. I loved him. I'd had it.

I awoke one morning at dawn a few weeks after I'd returned home, turned over in bed, and saw the rim of the blood-red sun lifting through the hazy skyline of Los Angeles. I stretched my whole body like a waking cat and heard my inner voice say, "Ah, another wonderful day without Neil." I bolted upright in bed. I was actually enjoying life without him. I couldn't have been more surprised.

As the weeks passed, I experienced what life without Neil meant. It was good. Whatever spell I'd been under began to lift and I was living in peace with my son, taking care of him and myself without the constant drama imposed on our lives by Neil. It dawned on me that I was a single parent and that I was going to have to fill both roles of mother and father for my son. During this period he refused to answer to Skippy anymore. He liked his name, Jefferson, and insisted that he be called that or Jeff. I can't help but wonder if his decision wasn't influenced by his time with Jeff Bridges. He was going through a hard time, but he was hiding behind a tough mask. I focused on getting him to own his feelings and finally he broke into floods of tears and confessed he was sad for two reasons—because Daisy had died and because "Daddy isn't here." He cried and cried. I held him and kissed him, so glad that at last he didn't have to play the tough guy.

When Jeff told me he wanted to go fishing, my first reaction was resistance. I used to go out in the boat with my mother and Lou when they fished, but I just sat in the sun and stared at the lake. I didn't like threading the worm on the hook and I certainly didn't like seeing the fish caught with the hook in its lip or worse, having swallowed it. And when the fish wiggled free and flopped in the bottom of the boat, its eye wild with the struggle for life, I just couldn't bear it. But I had that image of the Bridges brothers teaching my ten-year-old how to hold a football and I didn't want my son to be denied anything just because he had a sick father. I decided I had to go fishing. And anyway, I'd started reading *Moby Dick* and was just approaching the confrontation between Captain Ahab and the Great White Whale. Why not read those chapters at sea? Perfect. I'd noticed an advertisement for sports fishing at Paradise Cove, north of Malibu, and planned a day at sea with my boy. He'd catch fish while I read *Moby Dick*.

I packed up our cooler with food and drinks for the day and headed for the beach with Jeff. He was very excited. So was I. It had been a difficult month. Now I was heading away from all that and out to sea on a beautiful day with my son in happy anticipation of catching some fish. As we boarded the large boat with about twenty other people, the captain showed me the sonar he used, which informed him when the boat was over a large school of fish so he could tell everyone to drop their lines. Each line had at least half a dozen large baited hooks on it. It would be almost impossible *not* to catch a fish. Some sport fishing! But it served my purpose and as Jeff got his bait for his hooks, I found a nice seat on the starboard side, stashed our cooler underneath it, and settled down to continue my journey with Ishmael under the command of the mad Captain Ahab. The sailors up-anchored and as we pulled away from land, I opened my book and read:

The Symphony. It was a clear steel-blue day. The firmaments of air and sea were hardly separable in that all-pervading azure; only, the pensive air was transparently pure and soft, with a woman's look, and the robust and man-like sea heaved with long, strong, lingering swells, as Samson's chest in his sleep.

Hither, and thither, on high, glided the snow-white wings of small, unspeckled birds; these were the gentle thoughts of the feminine air; but to and fro in the deeps, far down in the bottomless blue, rushed mighty Leviathans, sword-fish, and sharks; and these were the strong, troubled, murderous thinkings of the masculine sea.

Then I heard, "Thar she blows. Thar she blows." For one moment I was disoriented. Had I conjured that call from the ship's loudspeaker? Had the captain noticed my book and decided to play a joke? No! It was a whale straight out to sea in front of us. The captain said over the loudspeaker that he would get as close as he could without scaring the whale and then cut his engines. Feeling I was inside the center of a miracle, I read on.

I kept reading until the captain silenced the engines and the forward motion of the boat kept us moving ever closer to the great Leviathan lolling in the blue waters off the coast, not of moody Nantucket, but pretty, sunny California. As we approached the whale, I saw its eye see me. We held each other in our gaze. We sailed slowly past him, so close we almost brushed his body. I could see his blowhole looking like a giant belly button on the top of his head. The hole opened and closed a few times. Then spouted. His spume shot up in a great fountain of sea-smelling spray and landed on me and my open book. We drifted past the great calm whale who had risen up from the depths of the sea with a message for me.

I looked down at the dampened page and read:

Is Ahab, Ahab? Is it I, God, or who, that lifts this arm? But if the great sun move not of himself; but is as an errand-boy in heaven; nor one single star can revolve, but by some invisible power; how then can this one small heartbeat; this one small brain think thoughts; unless God does that beating, does that thinking, does that living and not I. By heaven, man, we are turned round and round in this world, like yonder windlass, and Fate is the handspike. And all the time, lo! That smiling sky, and this unsounded sea!

That's it, then? It's God. It's all God. Not any more here than there. Not more in this person or that—not more on land or sea or in those people or me—all of it everywhere is Him, is Her, is blessing.

My boy caught fish. Many fish. And he was happy.

I hadn't yet begun the Jungian explorations that would give me a framework in which I could appreciate this event. But I did seem to understand it in my own way, which was not intellectually but emotionally. Later that day I went to a party, got high, and had what I recorded in my diary as: *a very big moment. Screaming soundlessly—tears. Hit some kind of understanding of my own stature. Had a concept of dignity that was organic. It just didn't seem necessary to go any further down. It seemed time to surface and in my own way.*

I don't know if I would use those same words today—"stature" and "dignity." I think I would express it in terms of valuing my Self—not the small self—the ego—but the Self as Jung defines it—the central organizing principle of the psyche, one of whose symbols is the Leviathan, the whale. It had risen up before me on this day and I felt its awesome power rising up *in* me as well. I was ready to "surface in my own way."

Two weeks later I was walking down a Los Angeles street with an actor friend of mine named Warren Miller. A man was walking toward us who looked at Warren as if he knew him. They said hello and we stopped. Warren felt he knew the man, too, and asked his name—it was Art Kunkin. They spent a few minutes trying to figure out how they knew each other and finally decided that they didn't. In the meantime I observed that

Kunkin, who was the editor of a Los Angeles alternative weekly called *The Free Press*, was carrying one of the six volumes of *The Psychological Commentaries on the Teaching of Gurdjieff and Ouspensky*. I had been studying these works for over a year. As the men prepared to take their leave of each other, I asked, "Enjoying the books?"

"Yeah," he said. "Do you know them?"

"I've been studying them."

"So have I," replied Kunkin.

"Do you have a teacher?" I asked.

"No," he says. "I've been looking for one."

"So have I. If you find one, will you let me know?"

"Yes, and you do the same."

We exchanged phone numbers and parted.

Soon the idea of having a spiritual teacher or a guru would be popularized and one could be found most anywhere, especially in Los Angeles. But in early 1971, it was not so common, and to me, who was still trying to limp back to a spiritual path after wandering in the wilderness for years after resigning from conventional religion, it was a downright radical and exotic idea. I knew that Gurdjieff had been a profound teacher for the people who studied with him. But Gurdjieff was long dead. Although I was studying his system by myself, he made it clear that "the work" couldn't really be done alone. It should be done in a group and with a guide. But where was such a group and who would be that guide?

From my reading I learned that Gurdjieff had been associated with the Sufis, an ancient mystical sect, but did they still exist? I didn't know. But I was drawn to one of the central concepts as I understood it: that the usual state of mankind was a kind of sleepwalking. That there was a way to wake up from this state and to come into consciousness—the awakened state. Gurdjieff said that we are not one person, but there are many different people inside us and they're all in conflict. There is the person who wants to stop smoking and the one who is addicted to cigarettes. There is the one who wants to leave an abusive spouse and the one who can't separate from him, etc. All these unorchestrated voices speak at once in disharmony and cacophony. The first step in coming into consciousness is to appoint just one of those inner beings as witness. You don't try to change anything straight off; you simply give one aspect of yourself the job of observing all the others. I had begun that process. Of course, I'd forget. I'd fall back to sleep. I'd go hours and then remember that I'd forgotten to witness, but slowly I remembered for longer and longer stretches. Later I realized that what is actually occurring in this process is learning how to detach from the emotions. Most of the time we are inside our own ego and completely identified with it. We believe that we know who we are. We are the one who is having all these reactions to everything around us. The "I" that gets offended, upset, angered, resentful. The one whose feelings get hurt. The one who feels threatened or jealous or, conversely, pleased with oneself, the holier-than-thou one, or the superior one. That's all our ego and it is possible, by appointing one "I" as an observer, to step away from all that, and that first step is huge. Once you practice that step over and over, and see yourself as you are in reaction, that very seeing, without judgment or name-calling, just plain seeing, is the beginning.

That's where I was at this point. I was at the beginning.

Peter Bogdanovich showed me a rough cut of *The Last Picture Show* and I thought it looked really good. But you never know. I had high hopes for *Alex in Wonderland* and the critics pretty much buried it. I tried hard not to have expectations or to hope for too much, but I was feeling more confident than I'd felt in a long time.

Jefferson and I drove up to San Francisco to spend Easter with my mother and Winsor. Once there, my mother told me about a luncheon she'd attended given by a sporting goods company. During the luncheon the company had a spokesperson get up and tell the women about her camping trip and all the funny things that happened with her family on the outing. My mother recounted a few of her anecdotes and then said, "She had us all laughing so hard, I thought, gee, that would be a good job for Ellen."

I said, "I'm an actress, Mom."

Turning her back to me, my mother tossed over her shoulder casually, "Yeah, but you really haven't done anything with that, have you?"

Those jabs from my mother I'd always received as body blows. I would explode in fury, lash out, cry, and walk out, slamming the door behind me. This time I came to a full stop. I observed my body. I could feel my heart rate accelerate, my face flush. I held out my hand in front of me; it was trembling. I was angry, that was clear. But why? My mother didn't understand the business. She didn't know how close I was to success. She couldn't understand the kind of effort I'd been making and the progress I was experiencing. Why did I expect her to? As soon as I asked the question, I flashed back to St. Mary's Academy, standing onstage as Little Miss Muffet, and hearing a woman's voice from the darkness of the auditorium say, "Isn't she adorable?" and me standing there hoping my mother heard it. I was thirty-eight years old and I was still looking for my mother's approval.

I told myself not to judge, just to observe. That was all I was required to do.

It's the ego that gets wounded. It's the soul that grows when it doesn't identify with the ego.

In May of 1971 I was painting the ceiling of Jeff's bedroom when the phone rang. I got down off the ladder and ran across the tacky newspaper to the phone. It was Art Kunkin.

"If you can be at my house in one hour, I'll take you with us. There's a Sufi in town from England giving a talk out in Downey."

I stood there, roller in hand, paint on my hair and face, ceiling half white and half blue, took one moment to run through all the reasons there were to say no and then said, "Yes."

I remember this so clearly because my life took a whole new direction from that moment on, but first I had to say yes to it. It wasn't convenient in any way for me to stop in the middle of this project and just leave the mess, clean myself up, get dressed, and be at Art's in one hour, but my yearning was stronger than the inconvenience. And what was I yearning for? I was yearning to change my life, my inner life as well as my tumultuous outer life; yearning to find a way, my way, to a spiritual life. I could not embrace the religious institutions I'd known, but there was that in me that longed to relate to life in a way that was meaningful. I did not understand life itself. Why I was here, where I came from, what I was supposed to do in the time I was on the planet. How was I to realize my full potential? Was it as an actress, a mother, a citizen? Or was there another dimension of being that every now and then I intuited? All those strange happenings I'd experienced in my life—from my earliest memory of the bird in the wall that my mother heard when my brother Jack was sick, to the inner voice that spoke to me so clearly, to knowing when Dr. King was going to be killed, to the whale coming out to greet me like a miracle from the depths—these events seemed to indicate a greater range and depth of reality than the feel-taste-touch world that my five senses told me was all that existed. I knew there was more, but I did not know how to access those other realms. And yet I wanted to. I yearned to. And so I said, "Yes."

Art took me to an average suburban house. In the living room and dining room, about seventy-five folding chairs had been set up. People were milling about talking quietly. I could recognize the Sufi right away. He was wearing a long brown woolen robe, like a cassock. He was tall, fair, freckled, with startling blue eyes; his hair was reddish gold, thinning, and standing away from his head in soft curls. The light shining through them gave him a slightly angelic air, and yet he was very much in his body. His hands were large and looked strong. To me he looked like a Scottish laird ready to go tramping across the moors.

I saw where he would be sitting and took a chair directly in front of him in the second row. I didn't want to miss anything. He had a beautiful voice and an aristocratic English accent. His name was Reshad Feild. He was a healer and a dowser. He had been employed by Scotland Yard to dowse for buried bodies. The human body, being 98 percent water, pulls the dowsing stick right to the ground when a body is below the surface. He talked about the principles of healing and how he was able to read people by looking at their auras. He described the ancient Eastern system of the chakras, the energy centers of the body, the color of each and its function. As he moved from the base of the spine chakra up to the number-two chakra, which is where the sexual energy is, he said, "That's where most of our troubles are. If that energy center isn't clear, that's where we find relationship problems, a distortion of sexual energy into the power drive, and ambition. You can be sure that most overachievers have trouble in the number-two chakra!"

The third chakra, located near the solar plexus, he said, is where we take in solar energy. The first three chakras make up "the lower man." The fourth chakra, the heart chakra, is the beginning of the higher man. Between these two chakras, three and four, there is a veil that must be penetrated. A shock must be delivered for the energy to rise between the third and the fourth. "How do you catch a unicorn?" Reshad asked. "First you find a virgin, then the unicorn will lay its head in the lap of the virgin. It is the penetration of the virgin by the unicorn that raises man from the lower, unconscious, into the heart, the beginning of higher or conscious man." He paused here, letting each of us ponder the meaning of that parable for ourselves. Then he went on. Above the heart is the fifth, or throat, the gateway to spirit, then the sixth chakra, the third eye, which is where we take in sidereal energy from the stars, and finally the seventh chakra, the top of the head, the highest energy of totally realized man.

I sat listening to all of this with my face streaming with tears. Some time later Reshad asked why I had been crying. I said, "I just remember as I sat listening to you, I felt I had come home." And that was it. Reshad was telling me that there was another dimension of being; that it had been known for thousands of years; one could learn about it and work with it. My intuition had told me this, but I had wanted to really understand it. I wanted to know.

At some point in his talk, Reshad noted that he always wore brown because it contained all the colors of the chakras mixed together. I remembered getting dressed hurriedly that morning. Although I was just throwing things on, I did notice at one point that I was grabbing for a brown suede skirt, a brown shirt, a brown vest, and brown boots. I'd never worn those items together before and wondered why I was doing it. Now I realized I was dressing myself in Reshad's color, hoping he'd recognize me. During a break, I spoke to him, told him my husband was schizophrenic, and asked if he could look at his aura and do a healing on him because Reshad had spoken about doing long-distance healing. "Not without his permission," he answered. "He has to ask for healing. I never impose anything on a person they don't want."

Then he told me a story. "When I was very new at this, a woman came to me and asked if I could help her mother. She'd been bedridden for many years. I did some long-distance work on her and was able to help her. When her mother was well, the woman told her that she had spoken to me and I'd been working on her. Her mother asked to see me. So I visited the mother in her home. This is what she told me. 'For many years, I was an invalid, but I was not unhappy. My daughter took care of me and my friends came every day to visit with me and bring me gifts of food they'd prepared, flowers from their garden. They'd sit by my bedside for a while and talk to me; sometimes we even played games. Now I am well and nobody comes, not even my daughter. I am alone. Who are you to judge how another person's life should be?' "

(I later used this understanding in a scene in *Resurrection* when adoring brothers bring in their invalid sister for a healing and, looking at her, I realize that the girl's illness is the way she gets love and caring and she doesn't really want to get well. So I say that I can't help her.)

When I got home that night, Neil, who had returned from Hawaii, was there. I told him about Reshad and asked if he'd go with me the following day. I brought Neil to the talk, but not only did he not want Reshad to "look at him," he was very disruptive—speaking out while Reshad was talking and announcing that he was the Messiah. I felt terrible that I had brought disruption to Reshad's talk, and during the break I went up to him to apologize. He said, "Listen, I woke up three times during the night. That never happens to me. And it had something to do with you." He tapped my hands with his index finger. He said he must see me in London. I told him that my friends, the Rudelsons, who lived in London had just called me the week before to invite me to visit them, and my other friends, the Haineses, were in Basel trying to raise funds to make a film of *Steppenwolf,* so I had two reasons to go to Europe already, and was planning a trip there. He gave me his number in London and said his instinct told him that I must come. I knew that already. I made plans to leave for London in mid-June, though I had no money to pay for the trip. Within two days I was sent on an audition for a *Gunsmoke* episode and got the part. I earned enough money to pay for plane tickets for Jeff and me and to cover our stay.

On June 4, while in Utah shooting *Gunsmoke*, I made this entry in my diary: *I'm doing good work in this show. I really understand how to act now. I don't smoke—drink little—have lots of energy—do yoga breathing when necessary. I am relaxed and absolutely confident.*

That certainly was a new attitude for me. That episode was on television the other day and I watched it, more than thirty years after I made it. It's such a strange experience watching your young, thin, pretty self, while you sit on your sofa icing your arthritic knee, feeling every one of those years and probably the same number of added pounds on your aging body. There you are just blooming, your fresh petals unfolding before your own eyes even as you feel your current petals dropping around you. Beauty is a temporary state, but that which we accomplish by real effort abides.

I called Reshad as soon as we arrived in London, only to discover that he'd just left town with his group for a long weekend at Glastonbury. So Jeff and I had a pleasant few days in London together, going to museums and visiting with Bob and Lelia Rudelson and their son Aaron Jack, whom we hadn't seen since our visit with them to watch the moon landing. They had a nice flat very close to a riding stable. Jeff was obsessed with riding during this period, so we signed him up for rides every day. When Reshad returned with his group, we met and he told me that he was due to go on a much needed retreat on the Isle of Wight the following weekend and then shortly he would be leaving to teach a healing seminar in Pir Vilayat's Sufi camp on top of the Alps. He looked at me with his amazingly clear blue eyes and a half smile and said, "Well, now that you're here, what do I do with you?" I loved his voice. He could do anything he wanted with me, as far as I was concerned. The next day he told me he'd discussed the question with his teacher, "The Turk," who suggested he take me with him on retreat. The Rudelsons invited Jeff to stay with them and continue his riding lessons, so I left with Reshad for the Isle of Wight.

I thought I was in paradise. We were picked up by a vicar in a tweed jacket. He spoke with a crisp upper-class accent and was called simply Kenny. We were driven to the seventeenth-century estate of two maiden sisters in their seventies. The house was immense and the gardens gave way to a natural woodland. The most enchanting element of the whole scene was the hundreds of wild rabbits that tended the lawn, hopping away from us without fear for a few steps, then settling down to more grass munching. As we walked up the old stone stairs to the house, Kenny took his leave and the sisters came out to greet us. They were aristocratic, charming, and very welcoming. Inside, the rooms were spacious. The walls hung with ancestral paintings. Old Aubusson carpets on the oak floors. Vast quietness except for the tick of a huge grandfather clock. Reshad and I were shown to our rooms on the second floor and told what times meals would be served. I was in a world I'd seen in films. It was quiet, peaceful, very old, and very, very romantic. I had no idea what this retreat would be like. I was just open to it and I felt enchanted by the atmosphere.

In the afternoon I was sitting in one of the window seats in the parlor watching the rabbits at work when one of the sisters rolled a mahogany tea cart into the room. I took a seat on the settee she indicated and she asked me, with a large smile that showed all her teeth, "China or India?" I didn't have a clue what she was asking, but assumed it had something to do with tea, so I took a shot and replied, "India," then waited to see what would happen next.

Tea! Oh! I see. Tea from India as opposed to China. I only knew about Lipton or Tetley. She served little chocolate-covered wheat biscuits. At dinner I admired the most delicious bread I'd ever eaten and the next morning, one of the sisters showed me the grinder they used to grind the fresh wheat to bake the bread in their old stone oven. After dinner we retired to the chapel. There Kenny had a stack of letters from people who wanted healing. Reshad, the two sisters, and I sat in the quiet stone chapel as Kenny read the letters to us, told us their first names, where they lived, their ailments, and when he finished, we all sat in silence and prayed for these people. Kenny was an Anglican minister. At the end of the silent healing prayers, he said a prayer out loud and the session was over. It was very simple and dignified. As we walked back to the parlor, I noticed a tremor in my body. I thought it was strange, but I said nothing about it. Kenny and Reshad were chatting quietly as they walked behind me. But the tremor didn't go away. It grew stronger. Soon, my whole body was violently shaking. I got scared. I turned and faced Reshad and Kenny. "I'm shaking," I said. I had no idea why. Reshad and Kenny looked at me, surprised, and then Reshad said, "Oh, for goodness sake, why didn't you tell me you're so sensitive?" He approached me and started moving his hands as though wiping something off my whole body, but his hands didn't touch me. Kenny stood on the other side of me, the two of them wiping away whatever it was.

"What is it?" I asked, totally perplexed.

"Why, you've picked up all the neggies, love. You'll be good as new in a minute."

Sure enough, as they continued the wiping (of my aura, it turns out), the shaking subsided.

The next morning after breakfast, Reshad and I sat with Kenny on the stone porch basking in the sun. Reshad and the vicar were swapping healing stories the way some men trade fishing or hunting tales. "I had an interesting case last year," Kenny said. "A young couple called me. They lived in Chicago. The man's mother went to hospital at death's door three times, but each time she was in hospital, the patient in the other bed died and his mother recovered. Finally, she did die, but every time the couple made love, the ceiling in their room turned black and a horrible smell filled the air."

Reshad asked pleasantly, "What did you do?"

Kenny took a sip of orange juice from the glass in his hand. "Oh, I just flew over there and helped the old woman finally let go."

"What do you call that?" I asked in astonishment.

"Psychic vampirism," Kenny explained in the same tone he might have used had he said "indigestion."

That afternoon Reshad and I took a walk along the shore. Small smooth stones crunched underfoot. The energy between us was both charged and peaceful—sexually charged, spiritually peaceful. He asked me how good an actress I was. "Well, one of my acting teachers once told me that I was one of the five best actresses in America," I said.

Reshad stopped and looked directly at me. "All right. Here is your first Sufi test. When you go back to America, you are to become one of the five most famous actresses in America," and he tapped my hand with the side of his forefinger again. Then he bent down and picked up a stone and handed it to me. "Here," he said placing it in my hand. It was perfectly heart-shaped. We walked until we came to a jetty and sat in silence on a large warm rock as the sinking sun turned our faces pink. We sat without speaking for a long time and I thought, *He's not meant to be my teacher. He has so many people that take from him. I'm here to give to him.* As I wondered whether to tell him that, he turned to me and said, "I bow to you. I bow to the God within you." We walked back to the house hand in hand. What was happening here? I felt flushed, happy, excited, and shy. I felt as if I was falling in love.

When we returned to London, I met the teacher that Reshad called the Turk. His name was Bulent Rauf. He was a large man in his fifties with an air of deep calm. We sat in his kitchen drinking tea from a glass. "Why have you come?" he asked.

"To learn how to be of service," I responded without thinking, and surprised myself.

"Aah!" he said.

He asked me many questions. One of them prompted me to tell him about wearing all brown that day I met Reshad in his brown cassock. "I see," he said slowly. "Tell me . . ." he paused trying to remember my name.

"Ellen," I offered.

"Yes," he said. "I have trouble remembering that. It's not your real name."

"No," I said. "I changed it. My real name is Edna."

"No, that's not a good name for you either. If I were to name you, I would name you Hadiya. It means She Who Is Guided. Do you like that name?"

I tried it on for a moment, then said, "Yes."

"Good," he smiled. "That is your true name."

Later Reshad would teach me that Hadi means "the guide" in Arabic. The feminine passive is Hadiya—she who is guided. But because we are all both masculine and feminine, in my case I was also in my latent nature "the guide." I would later learn that Hadiya was the first wife of Muhammad. She was older than the prophet (many years older than I was to Reshad) and she was his patron who encouraged and supported him in his mission.

Reshad had a partner in his healing and group work, a beautiful, dark-haired, sparkly-eyed Cockney whose Sufi name was Siddiqa. She and Reshad had been having a love affair for some time, which Reshad had not told Bulent. Now Reshad felt his feelings for me were complicating his relationship with Siddiqa and it was time to confess the situation to Bulent. He returned from his meeting with Bulent the next day and announced, "He's put me on celibacy for three months."

At my next meeting with Bulent, he asked me about my marriage. I told him about Neil's psychosis and the form it took. He wanted to know if the marriage was still viable. Was I going to continue in it? Did I still love Neil? To all those questions the answer was a quick "no." Bulent sat at the table looking off into space and then said quietly, "When Reshad returned from America this trip, I said to myself, 'But where is the wife?' I realized that I had seen him marrying an American." He paused a moment and then looked at me. "Now, here you are."

Bulent told me that I should accompany Reshad to Pir Vilayat's camp in the Alps above Chamonix. "After that, if you still want to go on, you'll travel to Istanbul with Reshad to my home, where I'll be. After Istanbul, if you still want to go on, you go back to America, close off your life there, and return to your new life, the wife of the sheikh. Do you know what it means to be the wife of the sheikh?"

"No," I said.

"The sheikh is the teacher, the spiritual teacher of his group—the shepherd of the flock, so to speak. But when the people come to the sheikh's house, they are always greeted first by his wife. She welcomes them into his presence. She provides the loving atmosphere into which they will enter for instruction. The teaching is sometimes difficult, it can even be harsh if that's what is needed, so the pupil must be received in love. Can you do that?"

"Yes," I said without hesitation.

Long silence.

Then I asked, "Is there anything I must do to prepare for this? Learn Sanskrit—or something?"

"No."

"What about Siddiqa?" I asked.

"I'll take her to Turkey with me."

So that was that. I was climbing the Alps, going to Istanbul, divorcing my husband, selling off everything I owned, and moving to London to become the wife of the sheikh. But what about becoming one of the five most famous actresses in the country? Was I supposed to do that, too?

The Last Picture Show was scheduled to open at the New York Film Festival in three months.

I had been to the church where Reshad met with his group and seen him working with Siddiqa, who was a very accomplished healer herself. At the end of Reshad's talk, the group sang and chanted together, Reshad playing drums and Siddiqa the tambourine. The songs and chants were sometimes in English, but more often in Arabic or Hindi.

After one of the meetings, Reshad told me that Siddiqa and I must "work it out." She was his partner in "the work," and the work must not suffer because of our relationship. On the weekend the whole group was going out to Sawyre Farm in the countryside. I was to come and listen attentively for the correct moment in time to have a talk with Siddiqa.

Jeff and I took a bus the next day, riding with Reshad's secretary, Jo. Her Sufi name was Jezeba. On the ride she told me she was the daughter of a doctor and had grown up in a leper colony in Africa. I couldn't imagine such a childhood.

"Why?" she asked. "I'm going back soon. As soon as I can get a replacement for myself for Reshad."

"Why are you going back?" I asked incredulously.

She looked at me with kind eyes.

"I miss the lepers," she explained.

I had visions in my mind of horribly disfigured people from a film I'd seen. "What do you miss about them in particular?"

"Their sense of humor. Their compassion. Their humanity," she replied.

I could feel at this moment my own prejudice, preconceptions, and ignorance. I felt like my brain was being held in a rushing stream and cleansed with pure clean water.

Sawyre Farm was a sixteenth-century farm that Reshad bought with the other people in his meditation group. They were in the process of restoring the main house and barn and turning them into a healing center. The day I arrived everyone came for the dedication of a dome built inside the old cruciform barn. Many people were already staying at the farm, sleeping on mattresses on the floor. On this day about fifty people were there. A river ran through the property. On the other side was a hill that rose straight up from the river and was covered with tall grass. Sitting with Jeff, facing the hill and listening to Reshad and the others sing, I wondered where Siddiqa was and when the right moment would come to talk to her. Suddenly, she was right in front of me, up on the hill, only her head visible, moving through the tall grass. I leapt to my feet. Jeff wanted to come with me, so we both climbed the hill. I found Siddiqa and sat down near her without speaking. Jeff sat for a few minutes and then wandered off. Siddiqa lay down in the grass. Without a word I lay down beside her and we both stared straight up at the fast-moving white clouds. Soon I could feel Siddiqa was crying. I took her hand. She clasped it tightly and began crying harder. Great deep sobs. We lay like that for what seemed like an hour; side by side, staring at the sky, holding tight our hands, Siddiqa crying and crying because the man she loved, had loved for years, was turning away from her and toward another woman whose hand she was hanging on to for dear life. After a while her sobs subsided. She lay there quietly, tears still sliding down her temples and dampening her hair. Still not a word had been spoken. There were only the sounds of the birds, the breeze through the grasses, and the distant sound of voices down the hill.

Finally, out of the silence, in her Cockney accent, Siddiqa asked, "Do

I know you?" We both laughed and laughed. We'd been gone, I think it really had been an hour, when suddenly we heard Reshad nearby calling Siddiqa's name. She whispered quickly, "Put a circle of fire around us so he can't find us." And she closed her eyes hard and giggled. She looked about six years old.

Then I heard Reshad call my name. He had others with him. "Where could they be?" He sounded worried. They were getting closer. I couldn't do it. I sat up. In a moment he was standing looking down at us and he said in a slightly scolding tone, "Why didn't you answer?"

What could I say? "Because Siddiqa said we should build a circle of fire around us and she's the one whose heart is breaking"? Or, "Because this is what the right moment of time looks like to two women in this situation." Any answers I could think of, I couldn't say. I only knew that Siddiqa and I had the talk he'd asked for. True, it was wordless, but we understood each other. We were not enemies. She would be able to go on doing "the work" with him. There was no strain between us. We had connected in a uniquely feminine way and we sat in the grass looking up into the face of the man we both loved who wanted an answer for our behavior. We had no answer. We stood up like two chastened children and followed "the man" down the hill.

Back in London, Reshad left to go up to Pir Vilayat's Sufi camp in the Alps while I made my preparations to travel there a few days later. Gurdjieff had been a Sufi, but I knew very little about Sufism itself except that it had originated as the mystical branch of Islam and over the centuries had grown to include all religions. That's what interested me; its followers searched for the truth in all religions.

Reshad had given me a list of equipment to bring, which included a backpack, a sleeping bag, an air mattress, and a Swiss Army knife. This camp had no facilities—whatever I would need for two weeks on top of a mountain I was going to have to carry up on my back. I bought a brown plaid Irish blanket and cut a slit in the center for my head to go through. Lelia helped me edge the opening with brown yarn. This would be my parka and at night it would be an extra blanket. At that time I had very long blond hair that I washed every day. There were no bathrooms up there, just a couple of rigged outdoor showers with freezing cold water. People kept their bathing to a minimum. Clearly this adventure couldn't support my glamorous hair. On an impulse, I ducked into a hair salon on a London street and said, "Is there anyone free right now to give me a haircut?"

As I sat in a chair and the man snapped a cape around me, he asked, "How much do you want taken off?"

"All of it." I smiled. "Give me the shortest haircut you can."

The man picked my hair up off my shoulders and stroked it in his hand. "Are you sure?" he asked with a pained look. I nodded.

He took off about a foot of long blond curls that floated gently to the floor. It felt good. I wanted to be stripped down to the bare essentials. I was climbing a mountain looking for the meaning of life. And whatever was nonessential would become a heavy burden on the climb. It all had to go—powder, paints, perfumes, and false pride.

One of the concepts in the Gurdjieff work is to know your different selves. To refrain from identifying with one particular self. For example, the self who has vanity. Of course I have vanity, but it was this experience that helped me to be able to separate from it. The work is to know that there is a self who can at times experience vanity and at other times choose to step away from it and let go of it.

My hair was cut off; Jeff was happy to stay with the Rudelsons and go riding every day; I had my backpack stuffed and was breaking in my new mountain-climbing boots when I got a phone call from Jezeba in Chamonix. Reshad had asked her to tell me that Pir Vilayat said I was not to come to the camp, ostensibly because the cut-off age was thirty-five and I was thirty-eight. But that made no sense. Was that the real reason?

I didn't know what to do. I called Bulent. He said in a sympathetic voice, "And you've come so far." Then he told me that the Friedlanders, Ira and Barbara, were due in that night. They were very close friends of Pir Vilayat's. Why didn't I ride with them?

I decided to go.

All the way to Chamonix I wondered how I was going to introduce myself to Pir Vilayat and tell him I had disobeyed him as an introduction to our relationship. I was also worried that Reshad would be angry at me. But all that fear dissolved when we pulled into the station at dawn. He was at the station to greet us. He embraced me and held me tightly as he said, "Thank you for coming."

We had coffee and croissants at an outdoor café in the charming old town. Then we walked to the teleferique station, where we boarded the cable car that would take us up as far as it went. We would then hike the rest of the way to Camp des Aigles. I felt like a pilgrim. I was.

Reshad and I boarded the teleferique with the others. It had glass walls on all sides. The front of the car filled up fast with people who were eager to see where they were going. Reshad and I stood looking out the back window facing what we were leaving behind. As the car rose, the station where we boarded rapidly disappeared and there was only green grass and alpine wildflowers tumbling away under our feet. I felt very quiet inside. Reshad, sensing my mood, said softly, "It's a long way from Los Angeles."

I answered, without looking at him, "It's an even longer way from Detroit."

We stepped out of the car into the station. There were restrooms, a restaurant, running water, and electricity. This was as high as any of that went. From this point up, there was only the world as God made it. We sat on the terrace and had some more coffee. Then we started up. Straight up.

We began the nearly vertical climb on a crest that faced Mont Blanc, named because its peak at 15,782 feet is always covered in snow. There was a kind of jagged path that wound its way up to the crest we were climbing, but it was steep and rugged, and at this altitude I was gasping for oxygen under the weight of my backpack. When we finally reached the top of this crest, I was panting like a dog.

All the way up I was looking into the face of the mountain. With my last gasping step I saw that I was on a wide plateau dominated on one side by the looming Mont Blanc. In other directions all I could see were breathtaking vistas of Alpine peaks. Camp consisted of several big tents, each sleeping about ten people. There was one permanent structure, a shepherd's hut made of rocks where the cooking was done, and a few early arrivals had staked out a space on the floor with their sleeping bags. Reshad

had his own private tent, as did Pir Vilayat, who was nowhere in sight. People milled about getting settled. A Sufi named Aeolia showed me to her tent and I blew up my air mattress, rolled out my sleeping bag, and set up my toilet articles beside me. I still didn't know how I was going to introduce myself to Pir. I just planned "to listen for the right moment in time," as Reshad would say, and speak from my heart. I went into the hut where dinner was being prepared and volunteered to help. I was instantly put to work. Dinner was served at two long tables outside. Everyone filled their plates, then sat on the ground facing out toward the inexpressibly beautiful vistas in every direction. The air and light both were crystal clear and dazzling. The food was good and the atmosphere calm. I couldn't imagine a more idyllic heaven.

After dinner, as the sun dropped quickly behind a peak, the temperature fell considerably. Everyone hustled into the shepherd's hut with its warm stove. With the whole camp packed into one small room, you could hardly move. I spotted Pir Vilayat across the room. He was Indian, in his sixties, spare of frame, with gray hair and beard, and the piercing eyes of an eagle. *Now*, I thought. *This is the time.* Guitars and drums were being played, everyone singing, a kind of spiritual rollicking atmosphere. New people arriving. Old friends greeting each other. Much hugging and bowing. People all tangled up with each other. I fought to get across the room, but it was impossible: There was nowhere to put your foot without stepping on a leg. Then I couldn't see him anymore. He was gone. I'd missed my chance.

I stepped outside into the night. From this height and without any artificial light, the sky looked unimaginably huge, dark, immense, filled with carefully delineated constellations of stars and glimpses of distant galaxies. I was awestruck. Then a star moved at some speed from far on my left in an arc over my head and down to my right. I couldn't imagine what I was seeing. I grabbed a passing sleeve.

"Look," I pointed. "What is it?"

"That's a satellite," a kind young voice said.

To see a man-made object travel 180 degrees across the vault of the immeasurable sky in seconds flat is to actually glimpse the cocreation of

God's world and ours in two different rhythms—man-made time traveling fast against the background of slow-moving infinity.

I crawled into my sleeping bag, teeth chattering, thankful for the air bag
between me and the rock of the ground.

In the morning, after breakfast, there was a meeting to assign jobs. I
still hadn't introduced myself and confessed to Pir (which means "teacher")
that I was here without his permission. I hoped now would be the right
moment.

There were many jobs to be done. Latrines dug and concealed. Three
meals a day prepared for seventy-five people, then cleanup afterward.
Someone was designated to take names of volunteers for each cooking
and cleanup crew so they would be rotated. Crews were designated to go
down the mountain to the teleferique station each day with the donkeys,
load them up with water, bring them back up, and dump the water in our
inflatable swimming pool reservoir.

Then Pir said, "Then there is the job that nobody wants. We need someone who will get up a half hour before everyone else and put the water on
to heat so that there will be tea for the whole camp when we all rise at
five A.M."

Silence. No volunteers.

I raised my hand. "I'll take that job."

"What is your name?" Pir asked.

I stood up. "I am Hadiya." He nodded.

I sat back down. I'd done it. When I saw Reshad privately, he smiled
and said, "Well done."

"But how am I going to do it?" I asked desperately. "I didn't bring an
alarm clock. And even if I did, I couldn't use it. I'm in a tent with ten other
people. What am I going to do?"

"When you go to sleep tonight, set your inner clock for four-thirty A.M.
and you'll wake up," Reshad said. "You'll see."

As I crawled into my cold sleeping bag that night, I prayed Reshad's
method would work. It did. I've never used an alarm clock again.

At four-thirty, I crawled out of my sleeping bag and laced up my hik-
ing boots as the others peacefully slept. It was still dark in the tent with

slits of faint light seeping under the tent edges. I lifted the flap and stepped out into the most glorious sight my eyes ever beheld.

Directly in front of me was the magnificent snow-covered Mont Blanc. But it wasn't white. It was a gleaming pink. I was standing on top of a pastel world. The sky all around was painted in every conceivable soft and bright color. I stood for one moment in the hushed silence gazing up at the pink mountain, feeling as though I was a baby lying in the crib of the world with an immense, loving mother smiling down on me. At last I moved quietly through the still camp and filled the heavy pails with water, brought them to the shepherd's hut, and emptied them into the big pots on the stove. Everyone else was asleep. I stepped outside into the silence of camp and watched the bright orange sun rise in the east from behind an Alpine peak. It was perfect and I had it all to myself. It seemed like a great gift I was given for doing the job that nobody wanted.

Later, after tea, we all climbed the nearest peak that was higher than the camp. On a grassy plain, we did yoga and then Pir sat facing us on a raised platform. He instructed us to lie on the ground on our backs with our arms and legs stretched out so we each formed a five-pointed star. Our heads were the fifth point. I did this, feeling the thick green plants between my back and the rock. I looked up into the brilliant sky that stretched uninterrupted forever. Pir said, "Now see yourself lying here on your back looking up into the sky. Feel your body relax and sink into the mountain, now keeping your eyes open. See the vastness of the sky and yourself looking up into it." He translated what he'd just said into French and German. He could have translated into eight languages if need be, but there were only three needed for this group. I lay there quietly, peacefully waiting for him to return to English. When he did, his soft voice said, "Now, seeing yourself clearly lying here relaxed on top of this mountain looking up into the sky, remember that the earth is round, so you are also plastered against the surface of the earth, looking *down* into the sky."

I felt as if I was going to fall off the top of this mountain and fall right down into the sky below me. Why didn't I? Gravity, of course. I'd always taken it for granted, but "in space there is no up or down," as Buckminster Fuller wrote, "there is only toward the earth or away from the earth."

Gravity sucks us toward the earth; otherwise we would fall down into the sky. It was more thrilling to experience than any ride I'd ever been on. But the most profound part, beyond the physical sensation, was the shift I felt inside my mind. By seeing the reality of the earth as a round ball, all my assumptions were jostled free and turned upside down and around.

I mentally drifted off the earth and away from it out into space. From that perspective I was able to see our planet as a round spaceship covered by a film of life—trees, crystals, fish, animals, and human beings.

Reshad taught me that the sound "Hu" is the most sacred name of God in Arabic. It is the name for the Holy Spirit. That spirit of God comes into man and manifests on planet Earth. We are not just man. We are Hu + Man. God being on Earth in man is a human being.

Reshad was very busy with his healing classes, but we did take one hike together. There were peaks all around us, some lower than we were, some higher. We headed for the highest peak on the crest we were on. We wanted to see the view from the absolute top. We hiked for about twenty minutes, and then began the climb.

Many years ago, when I was doing the Jackie Gleason show, I came across the phrase, "Alps on Alps arise." I used to say it to Blossom all the time, meaning that you just manage to get past one damn problem when there's another one to overcome. It was years before I tracked down the phrase. It's from Alexander Pope's "Essay on Criticism." I found it in the verse that begins, "A little learning is a dangerous thing," and it describes the folly of embarking on a path of learning and thinking that with the early lessons we have come to some final understanding. But in truth, each thing we learn leads us to the next. The verse ends, "Hills peep o'er hills and Alps on Alps arise."

Reshad and I finally attained the top of the peak and with our last few steps we saw a higher peak reveal itself. We were nowhere near the top. The line burst through my panting breath. "Oh! Alps on Alps arise! I see!"

Kinesthetically, in my whole body I experienced that any understanding is just one more step toward a larger world to further understand.

For instance, I'd come to the great realization that there is no us and them, there is only God manifesting in human form; that when I yell at my foe, I am yelling at God, I am forgetting that the person I'm facing is made up of God stuff whether he/she knows it or not. With my feet planted firmly on that peak of understanding, I stand facing the Alp that was hidden behind it. It stares back at me searing my heart with its question, "Then what is evil?"

The other day I read a definition I liked: "Evil is matter without spirit." I continue to grapple with that question daily. I'm still climbing that Alp.

Another building was being built near the hut, one where Pir could sleep off the ground. Stones were needed to be brought down from the mountain. We made a human chain up to where there were many fallen rocks. Large speakers, which were powered by a portable generator, were aimed up the mountain and, as we passed each rock to the person next to us, we kept rhythm to the inspired music of the Misa Criolla, which is the Catholic Mass in Creole. Music was always a part of Pir Vilayet's teaching, as it had been his father's. His whole family were musicians. Pir was a cellist. His father, Hazrat Inayat Khan, was a singer of sacred Indian songs of such accomplishment and mastery that, for his talent alone, he was considered a saint in India.

We looked into each other's eyes as we received each heavy rock, then again as we passed it to the next person, practically dancing to the sacred strains. It was a beautiful day, the perfect temperature, not too hot for this heavy work. It was just seventy-five souls passing rocks in the Alps on a fine day to sacred music. That's all. But that day lives in my heart like a song.

As the hut was cleaned at the end of a meal, preparations began immediately for the next meal. It took that long to cook for seventy-five people. As we bustled about preparing breakfast the first day, I noticed a young heavyset woman with long red hair lolling in her sleeping bag on the floor reading a book. All the other sleeping bags were empty. Everyone was out working, studying, or taking a class. Just this one idler was there reading her book. I didn't pay much attention to her until hours later, when we got the food on the table and began to serve. The first spoon of cereal I ladled out landed in her bowl. The next time I was on cooking crew I was preparing dinner with Aeolia. We had large burlap sacks of potatoes and carrots between our legs and we were paring them for hours. Again the red-head was the only other person in the hut. And again she was on her side reading a book. It bugged me. I said to Aeolia, "Did you ever notice that the person who does the least work is the first in line for food?"

Without looking up, Aeolia said, "Oh, she's just doing what she does, just like you're just doing what you do. She would be as uncomfortable working as you'd be not working." It was a profound lesson in nonjudgment. Alps on Alps arise.

On the fourth morning, Pir Vilayat during an instruction said, "Don't worry if you don't get this right away; it's quite difficult, but keep practicing and it will come." Our eyes were closed and he guided us through the meditation. But I got it right away, because it was just like sense memory that Lee Strasberg taught. The training of the mind for one thing trains the mind in many things. It's all focus, concentration, directed will, visualization, relaxation, and breathing.

I was standing gazing at Mont Blanc, marveling at this insight, when I heard the donkeys coming up the mountain loaded with their heavy jugs of water on either side. The team of Sufis leading them reached the top and one of the young men called out, "Is there an Ellen Bernstein here?"

Surprised, I called out, "Over here." He handed me a piece of paper on which was written: "Call immediately. Jeff fell off a horse on head. Severely bruised." Reshad was standing nearby talking to Pir Vilayat. I went up to him in tears and said, "I must leave. My son has been hurt." As I started to dash off, they stopped me and asked for details. It was arranged for me to be driven directly to the Geneva airport. Reshad sat with me in the backseat. At the airport he handled everything. I called Lelia with my heart pounding. She told me Jeff didn't have a concussion, but he was very banged up. She said, "I think you should come back." I said, "I'm calling you from the airport. I'll be on the next plane to London." Reshad told me later that, as I walked away from him and Pir to go to my tent to get my things, Pir said, "I told her not to come."

Back in London, when the Rudelsons' door opened, Jeff was standing there beside Bob and Lelia. He was a mess. I dropped to my knees and, after embracing him, examined his face. Half his face was normal. The other half was three times its usual size. It was one huge scab. His eye was sealed closed, half his mouth was closed by the scab. On one side he looked like a little boy, on the other side, a little monster.

In the living room I held him on my lap as he described with difficulty from his half-sealed mouth how somebody had ridden by and slapped his horse on the back. His horse had bucked, reared, thrown him, and then, with his foot caught in the stirrup, dragged him on his face along the gravel path. My heart ached with guilt that I hadn't been there when he got hurt. And I couldn't help but wonder if he would not have gotten hurt had I been there.

The next day I took him to the doctor, who examined him and announced, "There'll be a good deal of scarring. We'll need to graft some skin." I felt my heart plop into the pit that once was my stomach.

"Where will you take the skin from?"

"His hip, I should think. I guess about three times ought to do it. Bring him back in ten days and we'll see how he's doing."

Reshad called from the teleferique in the evening. When I told him the doctor's prognosis, Reshad said, "Take him to Rosemary Russell. Here's her number. Call her and tell her I said that she should see you. Also, with your permission, I am going to make him our patient for the long-distance healing aspect of the class. The group will work on him for the rest of the camp. Do you agree?"

"Of course. Please," I said.

Jeff and I rode a bus out to a charming cottage with a beautiful rose garden. Rosemary Russell was in her seventies, white-haired and with a mischievous smile. We sat on her chintz-covered couch while she served us tea. I expected her to touch Jeff or pray over him or God knows what, but I didn't expect her to ask for "a snippet of his hair." That was pretty close to the nail parings voodoo practitioners use. I must have looked concerned when I said, "His hair?" because she flashed me a big smile and said, "That's right, I'm an electronic witch."

She pulled back a curtain at the end of the room to reveal a large black console box with dials. She said, "I just put any part of his body here and it registers his vibrations. Then I tune it up to the healing vibration. And that's it. It's called radionics."

On the bus ride back to the Rudelsons' flat, I remembered something Reshad had said to me at his first lecture. I'd told him that I wanted to change my life. He answered, "If you want to change your life, you must change your being. Your being attracts your life."

"How do you change your being?" I asked.

"You must change your vibration."

He later talked about how each person vibrates at a different frequency of the electromagnetic field. People keep attracting other people and events that are vibrating at that same frequency. That's how patterns keep repeating in one's life. One way to change your vibration is through meditation. Another way is attuning with sound, which the Hindus call mantra and Muslims call wasifa. Christian prayer and chanting like the Gregorian chants work that way, too.

Now I was to believe that not only was there a healing vibration, but a mechanical device could attune one part of the body to that vibration and the rest of the body would be healed miles away. Could this possibly work? Looking at my little boy's face, I was too desperate to be skeptical.

Ten days later, the scab was gone. Jeff's eye was open. His lips unsealed. His face was normal size. One half was white and the other bright red, but he had no other visible scars. The doctor examined him, amazed, and said, "I never would have believed that face could heal like that in ten days."

"I took him to a healer."

"Who did you take him to?"

"Rosemary Russell."

"Oh, yes! She's terribly good!" he said in his crisp British accent.

Seeing Jeff's and the doctor's faces after ten days confirmed more than anything that the world and the people and forces in it are more strange, mysterious, and miraculous than our limited minds allow us to comprehend. To disbelieve or hold tightly to a cynical attitude serves only to keep miracles at bay.

During the time I was in London with Jeff, Neil called from California saying he wanted to try again. He said he was down off the Messiah kick and just wanted his family back. I told him I had no more tries left. I said that I wanted a divorce.

Rereading my 1971 diary, I learned that my encounter and time with Reshad served the purpose in my life of helping me separate from Neil. I still hadn't learned how to be alone. I still thought of myself as a helpmate to a man. Despite my ability to support myself as an independent person, I'd always ended one relationship and immediately begun another. On occasion, they overlapped. Reading the '69, '70, and '71 diaries, I get so impatient with myself for vacillating between understanding Neil's illness and the kind of delusion that gave rise to entries like: *I guess my husband is a crackpot, but he's awfully cute.* I just couldn't let go. And I certainly couldn't without having another man present onto whom I could transfer all my projections. In Jungian terms, I'd projected my animus, my inner male self, onto Neil and felt complete only with him. When that relationship faltered because of Neil's psychosis, I hadn't yet learned how to withdraw my projections from Neil and stand alone. I had to transfer them to Reshad temporarily and wait until I could then withdraw them from him. That was to come, but we still had a bumpy road to travel together. I never had a strong inner male figure. That's what having a father builds in the girl child. And without it, I had to build it inside of myself, by myself. I hadn't even begun.

Two weeks later, I traveled back to Chamonix, this time with my son and his brand-new face. I hadn't told Reshad when I was coming, but still he met me at the station and embraced me warmly. Jeff and I spent the night in Chamonix and the next morning went up the mountain together for the last day of camp. Jeff was presented to Reshad's healing class, who had been working on him the whole time they were up there. They were all smiles when they saw the result of their efforts.

On Sunday morning Pir Vilayat was conducting the Universal Worship Service outdoors. An altar had been set up on a plateau. This service was designed by Pir's father, Hazrat Inayat Khan. A candle is lit to each of the major religions of the world and on the table in front of each candle is the holy book of that religion. Each service is based on a theme. It might be love, union, fidelity, devotion, intention, redemption, or any of the great universal themes. Then there is a reading from the sacred books. The service is a beautiful living demonstration of the fact that all the books say the same things about these themes. The truth lives in all of the religions and speaks clearly from their holy books. The only difference is in the dogma, the rules, the presentation. The truth does not change. If it is truly the truth and not some lesser idea, it is universal, no matter its form.

At the end of the service came the initiation. I had asked to be initiated. There were three people who stepped forward before me. Pir asked a few questions, raised his hands over their heads, and showered them with the "baraka," the blessings of all those who had gone before. Then I stepped forward. I looked into his kind, sensitive face with the eyes of an eagle. His glance was penetrating. In my peripheral vision, I saw the Alps on all sides and the endless blue sky. Then something strange happened. The Alps fell away. My body fell away, too. My vision closed down like a lens. I could see only his face; then only his eyes. There was no mountain; no other people, just the two of us in a strange space out of time. I could feel tears rising in me, but I didn't know why. As Pir lifted his hands to bless me, I saw they were trembling. I was streaming with tears. Then the world returned. Mont Blanc came back into view. I could feel my feet on the ground. The other people reappeared. I didn't know what happened. Had that same thing occurred to the initiates before me? Is that just what an initiation was like? Or was that as momentous as it felt to me? After it was over, one of the Sufis came up to me and said, "I've seen many initiations. I've never seen anything like that." I didn't ask what he saw, but I sure know what I felt. It was powerful.

Later, Pir Vilayat motioned me aside and said, "Hadiya, during your initiation, I saw you in a previous incarnation. I was with Genghis Khan's army. You were there."

I thanked him but asked him no questions about it, even though I was bursting with them. I was speechless.

Soon we were going to leave. I felt panicked. I knew I'd probably never come back here. I'd learned so much, felt so much, but I could hardly stand to go. I decided I had to say good-bye to Mont Blanc. I left Jeff listening to someone playing guitar and I walked down to a favorite perch of mine, out on a ledge. You have to be very careful because there are so many different ground levels all around you, your peripheral vision keeps picking up too many contradictory signals and actually creates an imbalance and you get dizzy. You can't let your eyes scan as you move. You have to keep your eyes on the peak your feet are moving on, then stand still and scan. Finally I got down to my perch and sat cross-legged, facing right into the heart of Mont Blanc. I closed my eyes and deepened my breathing. After a few minutes, I felt the ache of departure rise into my chest. Inside I said, "Mountain, I don't want to leave you. What do I do?"

And very clearly, inside of me, the mountain spoke and said, "Take me with you."

And so I did.

At the end of camp, Reshad was taking a small group on retreat, so Jeff and I boarded a train for Basel to visit Francey and Fred Haines. On the train I thought about all that had happened in the last few weeks, particularly what Pir had said to me about being together in Genghis Khan's army. Did I believe in reincarnation? When I looked inside, I couldn't find a real belief in it. What I found instead was an interest in the possibility. For instance, I'd done much research on Joan of Arc and one of the things that impressed me most was how she had led the French army to victory in two early battles. She'd shown such an uncanny understanding of military strategy that the generals paid attention and altered their plan of attack. How was it that an illiterate farm girl without any sophistication or exposure to battle had been able to do that? What if reincarnation were an actuality and she had been a general in another life? What if she had been Genghis Khan himself? Or Alexander or Napoleon, and in this life, the great warrior is trapped in a simple peasant girl's body and life? When the voices spoke to her, they could be vestiges of her memory of a past life. Couldn't they? Why not? It really didn't matter to me so much if reincarnation was true or not. I don't like to believe in things unless I have a knowing about them in myself. For instance, if I had actual memories of past lives, then I'd say I believed in reincarnation. But to use it as a possible explanation for a mystery we don't understand, like Joan's military sophistication, *that* appealed to me creatively. I never did get to play Joan (except that one time in Lee Strasberg's class), but the idea of playing her as a great warrior from another time living through a young farm girl's life is very appealing to me. I wish I'd had the chance to try that interpretation.

After our visit in Basel with Fred and Francey Haines, Jeff and I took the train back up to Chamonix to meet Reshad and the group he'd taken on retreat. We all had lunch in a quaint old restaurant. There were around ten young Sufis, all fresh-faced and full of laughter after the rigors of a retreat outdoors in the Alps.

We sat at a long table. I was on Reshad's right with Jeff beside me. Reshad asked Jeff a question and he murmured a shy answer. Then Jeff turned to me and whispered, "I've never talked to a holy man before." I laughed out loud at the innocence of his acceptance of Reshad as a holy man. Did I accept him that way? I'm not sure. A teacher, yes, he was that. But I was too sexually attracted to him to think of him as a holy man. Bulent put him on celibacy for this period so we never acted on the sexual energy between us. But I was full of desire for him.

After lunch we said good-bye to the others and set off on what I hoped would be a great adventure. I was going to Istanbul. Just saying the word I could hear the tinkle of camel bells and the clomp of donkeys carrying bags of spices through the Souk.

We were going to Bulent's home, which I was sure had a sweeping view of the Bosporus. I would be trained to be the wife of the sheikh and live a pure life with all those beautiful seekers of truth. I didn't think these thoughts, but they were fleeting images in my imagination. At last my life would have a purpose.

Then reality slowly descended like a kind fog, gently shrouding my illusions and replacing my pretty dreams with the simple truth of what it would mean to be the wife of a sheikh.

We loaded our small rented car with our many bags. A young Sufi called La Tif drove with Reshad beside him. Jeff and I were squeezed into the backseat. We bumped along through the hot summer with no air conditioning. We were to drive through Switzerland, Yugoslavia, and on to Turkey. Reshad told La Tif and me that we were to ask him questions. I would tape-record his answers, and by the time we arrived in Turkey, he'd have the material for the book he planned to write. Once a question was asked, Reshad "went upstairs" and no one was allowed to say a word or Reshad would be "brought down." That was all right for La Tif and me, but it's hard for a nine-year-old boy to stay absolutely silent for hours on end in the backseat of a hot car, bumping about in a foreign country. Each time Jeff said something like, "Mom, I'm thirsty," Reshad would get cranky and insist I "simply must" control my son. Our first day was not going well.

We spent the night in a motel in Trieste. At dinner Reshad asked us to ask him a question. I asked, "Do other people see the chakras as you do?"

Reshad said brusquely, "That is not a real question."

Exhausted after the long dusty trip, I burst into tears and said, "I don't understand. You say ask a question, any question at all, then when I do, you condemn it as not real."

Reshad got furious and roared at me, "Stop being so dramatic! I can't bear it!"

I stopped crying immediately and said, "I should stop being dramatic? You are the most dramatic person I've ever met."

"Really?" Reshad said mildly and humorously. "Then that must be why I can't bear it in you."

But I was very confused about what a "real" question was. I tried to come up with one that pleased him, but he didn't seem pleased no matter how hard I tried. Looking back, I see why Reshad didn't like my question; it had a tinge of doubt in it. I was questioning his knowledge, trying to verify what he'd said. That's not the kind of question he was looking for. He wanted a question that assumed he knew the answer; that had faith in his knowing. The question I asked shows me that I had some doubts about him. That's what made him flare up, my lack of faith in him. But I didn't discern that then. I was simply confused.

The next day we drove south down the coast of Yugoslavia. By early evening I asked if we could stop for the night at a hotel I spotted. Reshad pulled out his pendulum and asked it "if it was intended that we spend the night there." The pendulum immediately swung in a counterclockwise direction indicating "no." Jeff was exhausted; so was I. Couldn't we just pull into a hotel for the night without consulting a damn pendulum?

Reshad asked the pendulum if there were a place nearby where we were meant to stay. We got a clockwise "yes." Then Reshad asked if it were a hotel. We got a "no."

"A motel?"

"Yes."

"Did the motel begin with an 'A'?"

"No."

" 'B'?"

"No."

On through the alphabet, the pendulum always swinging counterclockwise, until Reshad said "E." Suddenly the pendulum slowed, then reversed itself and swung clockwise.

Reshad stopped. "All right. We're to look for a motel whose name begins with E."

I cannot explain this, but very shortly, the road curved and we came to a sign that read, "The E Motel." Not the Edison or Edwardian. The E Motel.

We spent the night there.

The next morning Reshad and I walked away from the building and out to an open spot surrounded by tall grass. We sat on two rocks in the early-morning sun and meditated together. Sitting quietly listening to the birdsong and chirping of the insects, a sentence rose in my mind. In one of his talks Reshad had quoted St. Francis saying, "What you are looking for is what is looking." It was such a profound statement and I thought I understood it, but it kept dancing around my mind flirting with my attention.

If I had really understood it, I would have stopped dead in my tracks and asked myself what it was I was looking for. The answer on the deepest level was that I was searching for God, but God was within all the time. Not in Istanbul, or in the role of the wife of a sheikh, or in Reshad's approval. All those outer things that I was looking to for meaning in my life were not what I was looking for. I was looking for that which was urging me to understand ultimate reality.

There is a story by the Persian mystic Rumi that goes like this: A man prays to God for years asking God to answer his longing to know Him, but he never hears an answer and the man finally gives up praying. After he is dead, he meets God and asks God why he never answered his prayer when he longed so to know Him. And God answered, "But I did. I was there in the longing."

We drove south along the Adriatic and about a hundred kilometers north of Dubrovnik we found a hotel on a little island. Reshad decided we were to stay there for a few days to work on his book. It was August and searing hot. Jeff and I shared a room. We spent the afternoons lying in our twin beds not daring to move in the sweltering still air. I could feel the sweat rolling down the sides of my body as I lay there listening to the never-ending and maddening sound of the cicadas. Around sunset we rose, had dinner, then stayed up late working on "the book." And again in the early morning we tried another session.

At one point Reshad gave me his socks to wash. I stood at the tiny sink in our room, rinsing out his socks, feeling the heat, wondering if my son, who was miserable, was going to make it to Istanbul. I thought, "Is this it? Is this the life of the wife of a sheikh?"

At dinner Reshad asked me what was wrong. He said the atmosphere was tense. There was no flow. He couldn't work on the book unless it was cleared up.

I told him that Jeff was unhappy, and I was torn between my care for him and trying to fulfill what was expected of me.

Reshad was relieved I shared my feelings with him. And having told him how I truly felt, knowing I was no longer so interested in the role of the wife of the sheikh, owning up to my own truth, a real question arose in me. It was, "If what you are looking for is what is looking, then why is it so difficult to find?"

Reshad sat up straight and said, "Aaah." He was pleased. But that was no longer important to me. What was important to me was my son.

The next day we agreed that it wasn't working. Reshad decided to consult the *I Ching*. The reading all but said, "Go home, Ellen. Take your kid and get out of here."

And so I did. Jeff and I flew from Zagreb to London and in a few days we were back in Los Angeles.

In the six weeks I'd been in Europe:

I had climbed the mountain.

Reshad healed me of Neil.

Pir Vilayat had initiated me in a blaze of mystical light.

I had come down into the valley of my life with a mountain in my heart, romantic notions of Istanbul falling away along with my illusions about Reshad.

I had returned home with my son and his brand-new face.

All my money was gone.

I went into a depression.

But not for long.

We arrived back in Los Angeles on August 11 and I saw Neil that same day. I felt revulsion.

Now I know that revulsion is an instinctual reaction to psychosis. Sometimes an animal will growl at or run from a person who has the smell of insanity about them. So while I was away, the veil had lifted. I was no longer enthralled by Neil; love is a powerful shield from our instincts of self-preservation. When that shield was dissolved, I was left with the dog of truth. I felt revulsion. My instincts were functioning.

I was out of money again, and I was out of work. Without an outlet for my creative energy, I slid down into that old valley of despond. After the exhilaration I'd just experienced, one would think I had some protection from the feelings that overwhelmed me and pulled me down into the darkness of depression. But over the years I've come to observe that any truly enlightening experience is followed by a heaviness as you leave the realm of spirit and reenter the world of matter. Jung's research into alchemy found it was called the nigredo. It is a natural part of that process and soon will transmute into the next stage. And it did.

Reshad called and said he wanted me to organize an American lecture tour for him. I threw myself into the task with full steam. Shortly afterward I got a job—two days on a television show for $1,000. Great! I could pay the rent!

Bob Rafelson gave me the script for the next film he was going to make, *The King of Marvin Gardens*. It would star Jack Nicholson and Bruce Dern. There was a part in it of a character named Sally. I was still smarting from not having gotten Rayette in *Five Easy Pieces*. I hoped he wasn't going to get my hopes up again for nothing. I wrote in my diary, "Either I play Sally or he dies."

I went to New York on October 2 for the screening of *The Last Picture Show* at the New York Film Festival and did my first-ever press conference, along with Peter Bogdanovich, Larry McMurtry, and Ben Johnson. The audience loved the film. So did the critics. It was hailed as a masterpiece. After the film, BBS had a party at Elaine's. I called Henry Madden and asked him to escort me. By now Henry had broken up his long-term relationship with Shelley Winters and we'd always liked each other. But at the party, I was in a strange mood. I was where I'd always longed to be. I had played a very good role in a great film. This was the top, wasn't it? Or near it, anyway. I was up there. I was a success. I should be happy, exultant. But I felt strangely low, troubled. Henry and I stayed at Elaine's until everyone left and then I began to cry. Henry took me in a cab to his apartment on Park Avenue and I cried until dawn. Finally I fell asleep on Henry's floor and didn't wake up until ten A.M. I cried until three in the afternoon, then went back to my hotel.

As I remember it now, it was just tears, no words or even thoughts. Henry didn't ask me what I was crying about. It probably seemed normal to him. You struggle your whole life for success. You attain it. But then you're miserable. It would make sense to a black Irishman. I'm just not sure it makes sense to me. Was I crying because I was successful? Because I didn't think I deserved it? That doesn't seem like it. That I probably would be able to get work more easily in the future? That I might never again have to worry about paying the rent? Doesn't sound so bad to me. But I don't think the tears were for what lay ahead. I think I may have been crying for what was behind me. All the loss, the mistakes, the things I'd done that I wished I hadn't, the tries that failed. Perhaps that's what it was. Now that I was successful, I could cry for all my failures. Failures of judgment, of choices, of courage, but most of all, my failures of love. I stood, if not on *the* pinnacle of success, certainly *a* pinnacle, and I stood alone.

In November I met with James Brooks, who hired me to shoot a movie for television called *Thursday's Game* in which I was to play Gene Wilder's wife. Cloris Leachman was in it, too, playing Bob Newhart's wife. It was a very funny film. We had a great time shooting it and I earned $10,000 for four weeks' work. It seemed like a million to me.

Bob Rafelson finally told me I got the part of Sally in *King of Marvin Gardens*. I was ecstatic. On December 1, we started shooting in Atlantic City. I left Jeff at home with Adela, and Johnny, the young Texan from *The Last Picture Show*. He'd recently sent for his girlfriend and they were married. I let them stay at my house. Johnny was great with Jeff and I knew he'd love to have Johnny stay with him while I was away. On December 12, Neil called me in Atlantic City from Los Angeles, saying he was going to Seattle and he wanted to take Jeff with him. I said no.

Two days later, Neil called Jeff and asked him to go for a hamburger. They left together and never returned. Johnny waited until one A.M. and then called to tell me that he thought Jeff had been abducted.

I called the police in Los Angeles, in Seattle; finally I called the FBI, only to discover that none of them would help me. Neil had adopted Jeff; he was his legal guardian. He had the right to take him. There was no crime committed. Oh, if only I had divorced him sooner.

I called Steve Blauner, who was producing *The King of Marvin Gardens*. He got on the case right away. By nighttime he'd been able to find Neil in

Seattle and talk to him. Bob Rafelson also spoke to Neil. Neil told Bob that Seattle was a better place for Jeff. I had a few hysterical fits, but Bob calmed me down by pointing out that this whole episode was Neil's way of trying to distract me and Bob while making a film together—something that Neil had always hoped to do with Bob. It was sheer envy on Neil's part. Bob said, "Don't let him win." I was determined to stay centered, do my work, get my son back, and start divorce proceedings immediately.

I didn't really think Neil would hurt Jeff, but I knew Bob was right and Neil would go to any lengths to disrupt our film.

Jeff called me at two A.M. to ask if I would buy him a drum set. He sounded very happy. He was getting attention from his dad that he sorely needed. I was touched by the happiness in Jeff's voice, but furious that Neil was telling him to call me in the middle of the night when I had to get up at five A.M.

I spoke to Neil's parents. Negotiations for Jeff's return were going on between them and my friend Jim Butler, a lawyer in Los Angeles. My great fear was that Neil would disappear and take Jeff with him. Hank said Neil was going to bring Jeff home to Los Angeles. I flew back to Los Angeles on Saturday, December 18. When I called Seattle, Neil had gone. Nobody knew where.

I was sitting in Jim Butler's law office on Sunday when we got a call from Hank saying Jeff would be returned to me that day. Next came a call from Neil telling me I should fly to Seattle to get him. This continued for hours. No sooner would I be assured that Jeff was flying to Los Angeles than I was being told I had to fly to Seattle. I could tell Neil would love it if he could actually have Jeff and me fly past each other in the sky going in opposite directions. Finally between Hank in New York, Jim Butler in California, dealing with Neil in Seattle, Jeff was put on a plane for Los Angeles.

Blossom and her daughter Cathy went to the airport with me. I wasn't sure if Neil hadn't pulled some trick until I actually saw Jeff in the flesh. I was pacing in the airport holding my stomach, which felt as if it was in a vise. I tried to breathe and stay calm, but it was impossible. I just wanted my son back. And then there he was. He came down the ramp wearing

Neil's big brown leather flight jacket. His face was beaming. He'd had a great time and he said happily, "Hi, Mom," as though nothing had happened. I embraced him, wanting so desperately to feel him in my arms, while at the same time I was flooded with anger at him. I guess I'd been so sick with worry that I expected he knew that, or was as unhappy as I was, or missed me—or what? I don't know.

On Monday, Jeff and I flew back to Atlantic City together. I couldn't let him out of my sight. Being a single parent wasn't going to be easy, especially with Neil's psychosis mixed into the situation, but I was going to be dealing with all that for a long time.

The King of Marvin Gardens is the story of two brothers, played by Jack Nicholson and Bruce Dern. Bob Rafelson has a brother, Don, so he was somehow compelled to explore the relationship between brothers, as he had in *Five Easy Pieces*. My character, Sally, was a woman who lives off men. When the film opens, the man she is living off of is the brother played by Bruce Dern. She has a stepdaughter she's raising, played by the young and heartbreakingly beautiful Julie Robinson.

On December 23, we were shooting the scene in the Atlantic City Convention Hall where the four of us stage a mock Miss America pageant and crown Julie Miss America. Then we were to jump in a golf cart and drive off. Bruce was the driver. Julie was to climb in the backseat and I was, too, with Jack's help. When Jack sat down beside Bruce in front, that was Bruce's cue to take off. But Jack forgot to help me and hopped into the front seat before Julie and I were settled. There was no back on the cart, so when Bruce took off fast, I fell off to the side. Having done acrobatics as a teenager, I knew how to fall, so I wasn't worried about myself as I went down, but I kept my eyes on Julie as she went over backward like a doll. I could see that her shoulders took the brunt of the blow before her head smashed into the solid concrete floor. If she had landed headfirst, I think she would have been killed. We all ran to her and she was rushed to the hospital. Although she was badly hurt, the X-rays showed no fracture or concussion. I suffered only a nastily bruised arm and body aches, but I was fine. Julie stayed in the hospital for a day or so. The next day we just did pick-up shots, and then it was Christmas Eve.

We were in a Howard Johnson's hotel. They had a big Christmas tree in the lobby and BBS had a turkey dinner for everyone who hadn't gone home. I called my mother for Christmas and heard that my godfather, my uncle Dave in Detroit, had cancer. He was the one who sent me fifty dollars when I needed it to escape from Texas back in the fifties. I called my mother's sister, his ex-wife, my aunt Mildred, to get the phone number of my uncle. My aunt confessed to me that she also had cancer, but asked me not to tell my mother. She was planning a visit to my mother in March and wanted to tell her herself. We had a week off, so I decided to fly to Detroit and visit with both my aunt and uncle for the last time.

While in Detroit, I called Bill Alexander, my first husband. I hadn't seen Bill in fifteen years and hadn't been back to Detroit since I'd left. Bill and I stayed up until four A.M. talking about books, as we always did, as well as our lives and all that had happened to us since we were last together. The next day we drove to the Detroit Institute of Art and visited the Diego Rivera murals I've loved since I was a child. We had a look at the top-floor turret studio where we used to live. I asked Bill to take me to Hazelwood so I could visit the houses in which I'd grown up. I remember when I was a child, the adults used to worry about any neighbor selling to a black family because "the neighborhood would go down." Why? I once asked. "Because they don't take care of their homes," was the answer. We drove down Hazelwood, which was now an African American neighborhood, and saw the living reality of the ignorance of prejudice. All the houses were well cared for, the gardens tended, the lawns mowed. Children were playing ball in the street, just as we had. It looked like a dreamscape to me. I've dreamed so often of this street. It lives in my psyche like one of those streets on the backlot of a big movie studio. To actually revisit it was almost surreal. It was real to me inside, surreal to actually stand there in the flesh. The most astounding thing was there was a very tall maple tree towering over the roofs of the two houses I'd lived in. It stood on the front lawn of 3277, but also shaded the roof of 3271, which was next door. That tree was not there when I lived there. It had grown in my absence. I stood gazing at it and saw how much time had passed. How much life I'd lived. The door of 3277 opened and a pleasant-looking, middle-aged man stepped outside and looked at my white face quizzically. I smiled at him and said, "I used to live here."

"Is that right?" He smiled. "Would you like to come in?"

"Thank you. I would."

Bill waited in the car as I stepped inside a smaller version of my memory. I've read about other people having this same experience, of going to their childhood home and it looking so small. It is a remarkable phenomenon. After all, when I left home I was eighteen years old, fully grown. It's not like I was a child and everything was physically bigger in proportion to my size. I was adult size. I stood there realizing the size of my life, how it had expanded, taken in more. I'd seen the wide-open spaces of Texas, the opulence of the Vatican, the magnificence of the Grand Canyon, and the Atlantic Ocean. My eyes, my seeing, my point of view is what had grown larger, what made these rooms seem so tiny. I looked out the dining-room window at the backyard. I could see myself sitting on the top step of the back porch eating tomatoes from the garden, licking the juice off my arm. I could hear my mother's footsteps upstairs and smell my stepfather's cigarette smoke, see my brothers coming through the door. The owner of the house stood by me smiling quietly as he allowed my life in this house to come alive for me. I thanked him for his kindness and left his home and my own childhood.

The next day, Bill took Jeff bowling. When they returned Jeff asked if he could stay at Bill's house when I went back to work. Bill suggested I consider the request carefully because if Jeff stayed with him, he would become attached to Bill and that would involve certain decisions on my part. I wasn't sure exactly what he meant, but I promised I'd think about it and see if I could clarify my feelings. Bill put us on a plane for Philadelphia. As we waited in the airport for the limo to take us to Atlantic City, Jeff found a toy store to browse in. I bought the *Philadelphia Inquirer* and settled down on a wooden bench to read. An article about the New York Film Critics caught my eye and as I read, I was startled to see my name, Ellen Burstyn, listed as Best Actress in a Supporting Role in *The Last Picture Show*.

I couldn't believe it. I'd actually won an award. I felt so excited, I wanted to share the news with someone. I turned and looked at the stranger sitting next to me. He had a kind, nearly blue-black face.

"Excuse me," I said to him. I pointed to my name under the heading "New York Film Critics."

"See that?" I asked.

He nodded.

"That's me."

"Well, congratulations," he said, nodding his head. He flashed a big, beautiful, white-toothed smile at me.

"Thank you." I smiled, nodding in rhythm with him.

"How about that?" he said.

"Yeah," I said. We continued nodding and smiling together.

"Well," he said, beaming at me. "You got your name in the newspaper."

As Chris MacNeil in *The Exorcist*.

PART IV

In the Thick of It

*The fate of the world hangs by a thin thread
and that thread is the human psyche.*

CARL JUNG

In the first months of 1971, I completed work on *The King of Marvin Gardens*; Neil attempted to sabotage the shooting; I won awards for my acting; fame took up residence in my life; Jefferson was exploring his new relationship with my first husband, Bill; I tried to serve divorce papers on Neil, who I was convinced was capable of anything in his derangement; and I met William Friedkin.

All of these threads were intertwined and weaving a pattern for the next decade of my life, but I could not see the pattern. I was inside of it. I was caught, trapped within the forces at work, all the while naively chirping about how well things were going. There was much darkness ahead of me, but for the moment I was enjoying the light shining on my closed eyes.

I was still shooting *The King of Marvin Gardens* in Atlantic City, staying at a Howard Johnson's hotel. There was a private dining room off the lobby where the whole company ate meals together. On January 7, I was sitting in the dining room talking with the producer, Steve Blauner, and his wife. Jeff was beside me. Toby Rafelson rushed in from the lobby to tell me that Neil had just entered the hotel. I panicked, grabbed Jeff's hand, and bolted through the swinging doors that led into the huge kitchen of the hotel. I didn't know where I was headed—anywhere away from Neil. Startled chefs and kitchen help lifted their heads to stare at us as we ran the length of the kitchen and out the back door to a stairway. I didn't want to go to our room or any room where Neil might look for us. We ran up the back stairs and I found the room of Julie's boyfriend, Lenny Holtzer, who fortunately was in and let us hide out there.

I was determined to stay focused on my work, but in order to do that, I had to make sure Jeff was safe from Neil. I spent the rest of the day making plans to sneak Jeff out the back of the hotel, into a limo for the Philadelphia airport, and onto a plane for Detroit, where Bill would meet us. I'd fly back the next day. I wasn't scheduled to work that day, so there was time to execute the plan. But once on the plane in Philadelphia, strapped in my seat beside Jeff and with a martini on the way, a stewardess brought me a message that the schedule had been changed and I had to shoot the next day. Jeff and I talked it over; he said he was not afraid to fly alone to Detroit, so I kissed him good-bye and got off the plane. Bill met him and he stayed in Detroit for the rest of the shoot.

When I got back to the hotel, I discovered Bruce Dern had managed to get Neil on a bus for New York, but not before Neil convinced Bruce that all his problems were my fault. This put a strain on my relations with Bruce for the rest of the shoot.

There was a big scene ahead in which Sally decides that her stepdaughter is now her meal ticket, and she takes her fancy clothes down to the beach, makes a huge bonfire, and burns everything. Then she buries her false eyelashes and cuts off her hair. We shot the scene all day up to the haircutting part. Bob wanted to see all the footage to make sure it was good before I cut off my hair because afterward it would be impossible to reshoot anything. I wore a fall over my hair for most of the picture, but it was the same length as my hair, so when I cut it, I'd be cutting my own hair with it. Often scenes like this are faked so the actress doesn't have to cut off her own hair.

But I wanted to. I knew there would be a realism to the scene if I were chopping off my own long hair that would be difficult to equal if I were only cutting the fall.

When working onstage, there often is a moment of communication between the actor and the audience that I call communion. It's as though the actor's soul extends and opens to the audience so that their souls join. When acting on film without an audience present, it is difficult to achieve this communion. But on the day we shot this scene I did. I felt the camera on me and through its lens, I time-traveled to the audience in the future. I opened to them and felt them move through time and into the lens of the camera and connect with me—in communion. Later, when I sat in the audience watching this scene at the New York Film Festival, I felt it happen. That was when I discovered that communion is not an event that is time bound if it's done with full consciousness.

When I finished the haircutting scene, I walked up the beach and saw Julie sitting on the wooden steps of the boardwalk. She was huddled in a blanket and staring into space with a dazed look. I spoke to her and she murmured a reply without looking at me.

"Jules, you all right?" I asked.

She continued to stare, but nodded her head slowly. "I'm fine," she said in a barely audible voice. I walked on with an uneasy feeling.

Julie and I had connecting rooms. I opened the door between our rooms and listened for her arrival. After a while she came in and I entered her room, again asking if she were all right.

She said, "I'm okay. Just a little weird, that's all. The fire on the beach, the smell of the gasoline cans. It brought me back to when I was a child. I was in the backyard and my father was doing something with gasoline and he threw one of the cans over his shoulder, not realizing I was standing there."

She was doused with gasoline that somehow ignited. Her shocked father then threw himself on her burning body. She spent the next six months in bed, her father coming to her room every day after work and spending the entire evening until bedtime with her. His guilt and overcompensation set up a dynamic that strained the whole family. Julie seemed far away and distant as she told me this story as though in a trance. Within two years, beautiful young Julie Robinson would burn to death in a mysterious fire that erupted through the electrical outlets of her apartment as she slept. No one else was even injured in the fire.

The next day I was to leave for New York to attend the presentation of the New York Film Critics Awards. Bob Rafelson came in and told me Neil had just checked into the hotel again. My limo wasn't scheduled to leave until seven P.M., but as Jack Nicholson was leaving sooner, he offered me a ride. I ran up the back stairs, packed a few things, and dashed out the back door to Jack's waiting limo, leaving Neil to search for me in Atlantic City. I was glad he was there. I'd been afraid he might crash the awards ceremony and make a scene. His arrival in Atlantic City told me he was unaware of the event, and I could breathe more easily.

Henry Madden was supposed to escort me to the awards, but he came down with the flu. I went alone. I'd never been to anything like that before. Many celebrities, famous people, and critics. I felt shy and out of place. I couldn't think of what to say. I felt panicked. Peter Falk stopped by my table to congratulate me. I said to him, "I don't know what to say. My mind is a blank. Can you think of something for me to say?"

Peter thought for a moment and said, "Yes. Say, 'Consider Peter Falk for all future roles.'"

Anne Jackson and Eli Wallach presented me with the award. I told the story of asking Peter what to say and repeated his line. It got a big laugh and I sat down. Not very gracious, but the best I could do. It would take me about ten years or so to do better. Playing a character I'd learned, but facing an audience as myself? I didn't have a clue.

Back in Atlantic City the next day, there were several notes from Neil waiting for me. One of them was signed "Jesus Christ Superstar."

I found out that Neil's father, Hank, had come to the hotel and paid his bill for a week and had assured the manager that Neil was a good boy and not dangerous. I was very uneasy. Steve Blauner told me to ignore him, that he'd spoken to the chief of police and that if Neil made one false move, I could sign a paper and have him committed. That made me feel a little better, but I was still worried. I knew Neil was there for one reason only, to sabotage the film and my work with Bob. I couldn't help but wonder what diabolical means he might employ. I had one scene left. I had to shoot and kill Jason, Bruce Dern's character. I became frightened that Neil would find a way to switch the prop gun for a real gun. (Paranoia can be contagious.) I spoke to the prop man and told him to keep the gun with him at all times. Not to let it out of his sight. The next day we spent the whole day on the shooting of Jason. Sally is deranged in this scene and her state of mind joined my fears; I was in an altered state. After shooting Jason, I went to the bathroom to turn off the running shower, but it wouldn't go off. I tearfully begged the shower to turn off. That's still in the film. But then, when I turned to exit the bathroom and return to where Jason's body lay, I closed the bathroom door because I thought the sound of the running water would ruin the soundtrack.

Bob yelled "Cut."

"Why did you cut?" I asked.

"Because the door has tape all over it." When I closed the door, I had revealed the electrical lines taped to the other side. I wished Bob had let it run and just cut away to Jack or Julie, then come back to me when I was away from the door. I knew I was in a state that would have been perfect for the last speech and I didn't know if I could get it back. My technique wasn't yet developed enough to know how to access and repeat what had risen up in me when the water wouldn't go off. How to get right back into that state of being—not copy it, but actually bring it back to life like Lazarus and be alive in it again.

I don't think I succeeded, but nevertheless, when we finished the day's shooting, Jack Nicholson announced, "This woman has just put in the most remarkable day's work I've ever seen." He led the applause and the whole crew joined in.

I was finished in the picture. Julie was supposed to go on after this scene and return with Jack's character back home to Philadelphia. But she turned up for shooting on this day with all her hair cut off, save for one long strand in the back. Bob was furious and cut her out of the rest of the picture.

"Well, maybe she cut her hair off after Sally did at the bonfire," I suggested.

Bob smiled and said, "No. Only one haircutting scene per picture."

I never understood why Jules did that, but she was acting very strange by this time and was too remote for me to find out. I did ask her why she did it, but she only answered in a misty tone, "Because I felt like it."

Jeff was still in Detroit with Bill, who had enrolled him in school. Jeff hated it and Bill and I had a terrible conversation because Jeff didn't want to go to school. I flew to Detroit, got Jeff, and we returned to Los Angeles. My fantasy about Bill helping me raise Jeff as "our son" was crumbling.

In early February we flew to San Francisco for a visit with my mother and Winsor. My mother lived in Walnut Creek, less than an hour from San Francisco, where *The Last Picture Show* had played for weeks, but she didn't bother to make the drive. She said, "We'll wait till it comes out here." Now, months after it opened, it finally came to Walnut Creek and they went to see it. "Winsor and I finally got to see *The Last Picture Show*," she said.

I waited. Silence. Nothing.

Finally, I asked, "Did you like it?"

Without looking at me, she tossed casually over her shoulder, "Winsor liked *Summer of '42* better."

That was it. I had received awards from the New York Film Critics and the National Film Critics, and a Golden Globe nomination for my performance, but from my mother? I didn't even get a pat on the back. I always thought that she delivered these body blows because she just didn't know any better. Later I would understand that they were intentional. She needed to hurt me because her envy was so painful to her. She had to lash out at what she deemed the source of her envy—me.

One day she and I were talking about reincarnation and she said, "Well, in the next life, I'd like to come back as a bird or a butterfly."

"I don't think that's how it works, Mom," I said. "My understanding of reincarnation is that you are always evolving to a higher, more complex

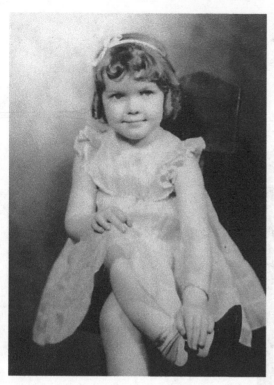

Me at around
four or five years old.

Me and my mother.
I'm about fourteen here.

My mother's friend Mary Amperin,
Jack with our dog Rusty, my mother,
Steve (kneeling), and a very glum
me. I can tell from my expression
that my stepfather was
taking the picture.

My cousin Carmen, me, my
brother Jack, and my brother
"Butch" in our Easter outfits.
My mother made mine—brown
tweed with kelly green trim.

The cheerleading team of Cass Tech High in Detroit, around 1950. The star on my arm meant I was the captain.

I used to pose for camera clubs. I'm around fifteen or sixteen here, and still in Detroit.

At a Ford Motor Company display at the Michigan State Fair; I'm third from the left. We long-skirts had lines to speak; the short-skirts handed out brochures.

FORDOMATIC DRIV

TOUCH AND

Edna Rae
WITH
HARTFORD

My first composite for
modeling, around 1954.

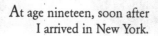

At age nineteen, soon after
I arrived in New York.

A modeling photo,
New York, about 1955.

A modeling photo. I'm about twenty-three
and living in New York.

My first TV appearance, with
Betty Hutton in *Satins and Spurs,*
at the opening of New York's first
color TV studio in 1954; Mayor
Robert Wagner is at center.

Neil and me on the set of
Goodbye Charlie in 1964.
We don't look much like
a couple, do we?

With Jefferson wearing
the elf outfit I made for him
one Halloween.

With my beloved
Dalmatian, Daisy Mae.

At the premiere of
The Last Picture Show with
Peter Bogdanovich and
Cybill Shepherd in 1971.

From *The Last Picture Show*.

With Cloris Leachman.

In *Tropic of Cancer*, 1970.

From *The King of Marvin Gardens*, 1972.

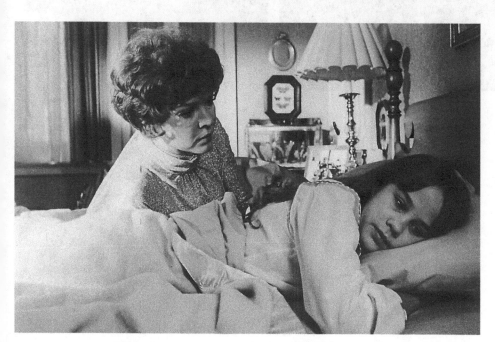

With Linda Blair in a scene from *The Exorcist*, 1973.

On Broadway with
Charles Grodin in *Same Time,
Next Year*, 1974.

With Jefferson backstage
on the opening night of
Same Time, Next Year.

With Lee Strasberg at his
80th birthday party.

On the set of *Alice Doesn't Live Here Anymore*
with director Martin Scorsese, 1974.

With Sir John Gielgud and Dirk Bogarde in *Providence*, 1977.

With Buckminster Fuller, sailing off the coast of Maine.

With Alan Alda
in the film version of
Same Time, Next Year,
1978.

My mother was
an extra in *Resurrection*.

In *Resurrection*, 1980.

With Eva Le Gallienne
in *Resurrection*.

On the set of *Silence of the North*, 1980. (The baby next to me is a doll.)

My mother, Steve, me, and Jack at Jack's daughter's wedding.
I think we were all pretty high.

One of our productions of *A Midsummer Night's Dream* at the Stone House, with me as Titania and Bill Smith as Bottom, in the early 1980s.

With Steve at my
sixtieth birthday party, 1992.

In the one-woman play
Shirley Valentine, 1989.

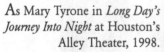

As Carrie in
The Trip to Bountiful, 1993.

As Mary Tyrone in *Long Day's
Journey Into Night* at Houston's
Alley Theater, 1998.

Vagabonding on a street in New York
with Sensei Bernie Glassman.

A Christmas card for 1999. That's me with the
big mouth, holding Emily and dog Molly.
Tricia is on Jeff's lap.

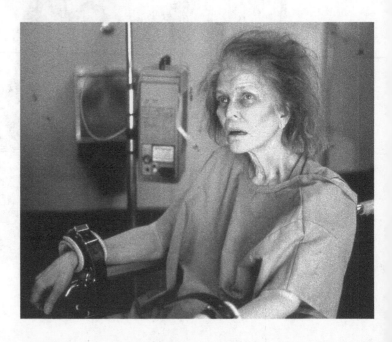

As Sara Goldfarb in
Requiem for a Dream, 2000.

life-form. You don't ever go backwards. And once you evolve to a human being, you are here to learn lessons your soul needs to learn, and if you don't learn them you come back and have to repeat those lessons all over again."

My mother said, "Then I'm going to have to live my whole life over again because I haven't learned one goddamn thing."

I was stunned that she would say such a thing and deeply saddened that she felt that way. At the same time I was a little impressed that she could be so unguarded, if only for that brief moment.

My friend Jim Butler wasn't a divorce lawyer, but he offered to handle my divorce for me. I had very little money at the time. He drew up the papers and we tried to serve Neil during the time I was in Atlantic City and New York, but Neil always managed to elude them.

Back in Los Angeles, I started looking for work. I was offered a movie with John Wayne, which I turned down because I didn't like the script. I was being considered for a few films that were being cast, but the big casting coup was for the lead in *The Exorcist*. I had read the book and knew this would be a challenging role in a big movie. Warner Bros. was interested in me and set up a meeting with the director, Bill Friedkin. I called Friedkin's office and told him I felt meetings in offices were stilted and formal. I asked if he would mind coming to my home. He agreed and our meeting was set for February 23. On February 22, the Oscar nominations were announced. I didn't want to get caught up in waiting for my name to be announced, so I asked a friend to drive to the beach with me that day. I sat quietly staring at the ocean; I meditated and prayed that I stay in touch with what was real and eternal, and not get swept away by what was illusionary and ephemeral. Not that this was easy. This is when I learned the lesson that temptation does not appear to us as an evil-looking devil in a red suit. That is something we run from. Temptation appears to us in the guise of our desires, all the glitter and glamour of distractions that keep us from focusing on what is eternal. This day made me wonder about Jesus in the wilderness. How did the devil appear to him? As a gourmet chef come to end his fast? A beautiful woman to please his body? Or was it something even more insidious? Like something that would be most debilitating of all? Something that would cause him to fall into spiritual pride, which, for Jesus, I can imagine, would be the deadliest of all sins, as well as the greatest temptation. This is not to say that delaying my knowing whether I got a nomination was in any way to be compared to Jesus' time in the desert. But just that when you choose not to identify with the immediate flow of events—not to get caught up in the world's attention, be it praise or approbation—you create a space, a space where you can sit quietly; a kind of time out of time when you just might wander in the desert with Jesus for a few minutes and contemplate what it might have been like for him, instead of greedily lapping up the feast set before you that's sure to lure you into the sin of gluttony for illusion.

In the afternoon when I walked into my house, it was filled with dozens of bouquets of flowers, and Adela had a long list of phone messages. That's how I knew I'd been nominated.

Cloris Leachman and Ben Johnson were nominated, too. When I won the New York Film Critics Award, the first person I called was Cloris. She said, "This might be hard for you to believe, but I am as happy that you won as I would be if I won myself." I told her that it was not hard for me to believe because I felt the same way. Now I called her to congratulate her on her nomination. We were truly happy for each other. This was very important to me, because it belied the stereotype of women, especially actresses, as jealous cats, but I also think because after all the competition I'd felt from my mother, it was good to have a female friend who wanted the best for me and wasn't threatened by my getting it.

Bill Friedkin came for tea the next day at four P.M. and we chatted in my living room for two hours. I liked him. He was smart, cultured, knowledgeable. He had a vacuum-packed quality—high energy, but concentrated and contained. He also had a great sense of humor. He'd seen *The Last Picture Show* as well as *Alex in Wonderland* and seemed genuinely interested in me. At the end of our meeting, he said, "I'm not going to string you along on this, Ellen. Frankly, it's between you and Anne Bancroft. I'm leaving tomorrow for ten days location scouting in Georgetown and then

I'm going to New York to meet Bancroft. I'll make up my mind right away and let you know."

I thanked him for his candor and he left.

Three weeks later Billy called me from New York. "Bancroft is out," he said. "I ran into her on the street shopping, and she looked rotten."

"Well, Billy, that's not fair," I said. "I look pretty rotten when I'm shopping, too."

Billy said, "These are the jokes! That's the way it goes!"

In the three weeks in which I was waiting for Billy to call, I was visited by Bill Alexander. He was thinking about selling his business and moving to Los Angeles. I think he was considering whether he could fit into my life in Los Angeles, and at some point he must have decided that he couldn't because he left abruptly and returned to Detroit. Jefferson was crushed and couldn't understand what happened. It awoke in him his feelings about Neil. He was crying a lot, and I finally said to him, "Okay, you ain't got a conventional setup of a mommy and daddy in a nice little house. You gonna cry about it or make the best of it and have substitutes like I do?" He really responded to that. We packed up the car and headed for Sequoia National Park, where we took a cabin for a few days and licked our wounds in the quiet of the ancient trees. Jeff loved the trip and we came home happy.

Hank called from New York to say that Neil was hitchhiking across the country and I should expect to see him. I still hadn't managed to serve him with divorce papers, so although I was uneasy, even fearful of his heading our way, I hoped that this time we could manage to get the papers served. For Jeff's safety, I had to get Neil legally disconnected from him.

Bill Friedkin asked that I meet with William Peter Blatty, the author of *The Exorcist*. Again I requested we not meet in an office and Blatty suggested a little park in the Valley. We met there and sat on the grass talking. The first thing he said to me after we shook hands was, "I feel this is kismet." Soon I was in negotiations with Warner Bros. to play Chris MacNeil in *The Exorcist*.

Two days after my meeting with Blatty, Neil walked up to the front door of our home. Per Jim Butler's instructions, I admitted him calmly, invited him in, and offered to make him some coffee. As he sat in the living room, I ducked out of the kitchen and into the bedroom and called Jim's office to notify him that Neil was there. Jim was in court, but his staff would round up the papers and someone to serve them. I was instructed to keep Neil there until someone arrived. It took four hours for all that to happen. During that time, Neil was quite calm, as he could be when he was not in the midst of a paranoid attack. I don't remember what we talked about during that period, except that I asked about his family. I'd heard that his grandmother and his uncle Brad had died recently on the same day.

I do remember one moment in this conversation because it was the second time I intentionally tried to hurt Neil. We were talking lightly when Neil referred to our sex life with a twinkle in his mad eyes. It was my cue to engage in sentimental appreciation of our sexual adventures. But I was in no frame of mind to engage in any hint of sex talk that might make him reach for me. So when he asked for my agreement that our sex was always great, I wrapped my sword in a cloak of nonchalance and said that I didn't think it was.

"Really?" he asked surprised. "I always thought we had a great sex life."

"So did I," I said, dropping the cloak, and aiming my sword directly at his heart, "but now that I've had other lovers, I see that it wasn't much." I meant to wound, and I did. I would spend the next thirty years grappling with the shame of intentionally hurting a sick man.

Eventually the young man from Jim's office arrived. He handed the papers to Neil, who took them innocently and then was told that he had just been officially served with divorce papers.

Neil looked at me with surprise and disappointment on his face. "Oh, I see," he said. "You were just keeping me here for this."

I nodded.

I remember that moment so clearly. It wasn't so much that I intended to hurt Neil; it's more that I was willing to, or some part of me rose up and put that sword in my hand. It really wasn't him I was thinking about. It was myself and the game I was no longer willing to play.

This was my dark side in action. It's always difficult for me to admit to my dark side—it doesn't fit with my self-image, yet it can be a powerful ally. Bringing that dark side into the light as an ally, keeping it at hand and conscious to call on, not for evil, but for my own spiritual work and psychological health, actually creates more love and light in my life. It's like marshaling all your forces to do what you have to do. And I had to do it. But there was hell to pay: It sent Neil into a full-blown paranoid attack.

The next day a journalist and photographer from *Life* magazine arrived for an interview and photo shoot. I had just admitted them into the living room when suddenly Neil appeared in a rage calling me a cunt and whore, yelling that I had opened my cunt to every man in town. I called the police. Neil left. So did *Life* magazine. Neil then went to Bob Rafelson's office and hid in the bathroom. When Bob came in, Neil jumped him, accusing Bob of having sex with me. He threatened to "get" everyone who had slept with me in the past year.

I spent the day trying to get Neil committed. I went to the police, the hospital. I was told he had a right to his privacy. I called his family to see if they would help get Neil into a hospital. His mother yelled at me, "If you persist in trying to take my son from me, I'll see to it that your son is taken from you." I was chilled to the bone that she would be willing to wreak her vengeance on her own grandson.

I went to the district attorney's office and filed formal petitions to have him hospitalized. But they would have to see Neil behave in a way that was a threat to his own life or mine. I said, "You mean, if he tries to kill me I should call you and keep him doing it until you arrive?"

"That's right," they said helpfully.

A few days later, I spoke at Valley State College. *Life* magazine came to photograph that. I gave the interviewer the name and number to call at the county hospital in case Neil showed up. I was now under siege. I was afraid he would turn up anytime, anywhere.

The next day Bill Blatty took Jeff and me out to visit Tippi Hedren and her husband, Noel Marshall, who had just established a compound for wild animals. They had a pride of five lions they had raised since birth in their home in Sherman Oaks. The cubs were now eight months old, full grown and too big to keep at their house, so they were moved to the compound in Thousand Oaks and were living in a large cage. When we arrived, Noel

and Tippi entered the cage and the cubs jumped all over them. I stayed outside, a little cautious about being in a confined space with five lions. They
were let out of the cage and leapt happily about, enjoying their freedom.
We walked for a while through the trees until we came to a clearing with
some picnic tables. Lunch was brought out and we sat at the tables
with Tippi and Noel's kids and their friends. It's a little disconcerting to
eat with lions trying to snatch your ham sandwich. They'd put their giant
paws on the table and try to grab some food. Noel would punch them hard
and make them get down. I'd been used to eating with dogs with bad manners, but protecting my food from hungry lions was a new one.

After lunch we headed toward the cages. We were walking along a dirt
path overhung by trees when suddenly one of the lions leapt from a branch
onto Jeff, knocked him to the ground, and pretended to maul him. As I
screamed, Noel pulled the lion off as he assured us it was how lions played.
It was one of their jokes. Some joke. Jeff did not join in on the joke. He
took it very seriously, repeating over and over, "Why me?"

When the lions were rounded up into their cage, Tippi discovered that
one of the cubs, a female named Nidra, had gotten wet while they were
out playing. She decided not to let the young lion sleep outside that night.
She put her in the car and took her back to their house. When we arrived
there for dinner, Jeff was playing with all of the many kids present. I was
sitting on the couch in the living room. Nidra was roaming around the
house like a giant house cat when suddenly she jumped on the sofa and,
laying her head in my lap, grabbed my thumb and began to suck it as she
soothed herself to sleep. The roof of her mouth was like very rough sand-
paper, I have the singular pleasure of reporting. Not too many people have
this information who have lived to disclose it. Several times as she slept I
tried to retrieve my thumb, but each time I did, Nidra grasped at it and
held it fast as she sucked herself back into lion dreamland.

Easter Sunday was the following week and the Friday after that was the
court date for our divorce hearing. With Neil now completely identified
with Jesus Christ, I was anxious about what he might do to reveal his assumed divinity. I decided I'd better get Jeff to a safe place. Bill Alexander

invited him to Detroit for his Easter vacation. I was happy to have Jeff in a place where Neil couldn't get at him.

On April 4, Jim Butler told me he'd spoken to Neil's cousin, a lawyer named Toots, who was going to represent Neil in court. He said he planned to ask for visitation rights. I said I'd be surprised if that was all he did. I was right. The next day in court Neil's lawyer asked for complete custody of Jeff, stating that I was an unfit mother and asking the court to subpoena my psychiatric records. Jim stepped forward and offered a personal observation to the judge that he'd never seen a better relationship between a mother and son. Neil also asked for the $10,000 that BBS was giving me (all the leading actors in *The Last Picture Show* were given a small percentage point). I had no money in the bank, I owned no home, and I was the sole support of my son. I was asking for nothing from Neil except to be legally divorced. I was shocked at his behavior, but even more so at his family, whom I knew to be behind this. The court ordered Neil to submit to psychiatric examination and reappear in court in seven weeks.

The Academy Awards ceremony was five days away and I was struggling to achieve clarity about the whole competitive Oscar circus. I decided not to attend the ceremonies. Not because I didn't want to win, but because I did. I could feel just how strong in me the desire was and it didn't seem healthy. It was like a greedy animal that I knew needed to be tamed. The only way I could think to tame it was to detach myself from that desire and not go. It seemed like a spiritual test not to lust after winning.

At the time, that was my thinking. But I must ask now, was it not also guilt?

In the culture in which I grew up, a woman was supposed to be shorter than a man, make less money, have less, say less, and be less. And any woman who did not stay within that boundary was a castrator; she would emasculate a man, ruin him, perhaps even drive him crazy. Is that what I'd done? I don't think I asked myself any of these questions consciously; however, they may have been roiling beneath the surface and affecting my decisions without my knowledge.

I did not attend the Academy Awards ceremony.

I struggled with the decision until the last moment. I even attended the rehearsals. I saw my name pinned to the seat where I would sit. Something about it seemed so cruel. Each one of the names pinned to a seat represented a life that had fought to get to the point where they were doing good work in a good film. Five of us in each category were cited, but only one would win. The others would be losers. It seemed so unfair. And a loser by dint of one vote or a thousand. Didn't matter. A loser. It just didn't feel right to me. When I called the producer of the Oscar ceremonies and told him I wasn't going to attend, he said, "But what if you win?"

"Then I'd like Cloris to accept for me," I answered.

"Oh, no," he said sounding slightly horrified. "We can't have any losers on stage."

And there it was.

But Cloris wasn't a loser. She won! I was home watching it on television with my friends and I felt so happy for her. Bill Alexander called immediately from Detroit to console me. I tried to convince him that it wasn't necessary. That, in fact, I was having a great night with my friends because it felt like a graduation day for me.

The next night I had dinner with Cloris. She was radiant with happiness. Many people came to our table congratulating her and I felt deeply pleased for her. There was a freedom in this. I had broken free of bonds that had been tied around me when I was very young. It was the notion that whatever someone has, especially another woman, means that I have less. That was certainly one of my mother's covert messages. But I had just discovered that I was not less than I was, no matter whose shelf the trophy sat on. I was still me. I was intact. Cloris and I talked about all this and she told me that Ann-Margret, who also was nominated and had won the Golden Globe for her wonderful work in *Carnal Knowledge*, sat behind her at the Oscar ceremony. She had brought her father out of a nursing home to sit beside her. Cloris said that when her name was called, Ann-Margret took her father's hand and said, "I'm sorry, Daddy."

With Billy's support and help, my contract for *The Exorcist* was finally set.

I began work on the character of Chris MacNeil by writing her history. I decided she was a dancer. She got into acting after being a gypsy on Broadway. Only later did I learn that Bill Blatty had modeled the character of Chris on his friend Shirley MacLaine who, in fact, became an actress by the same route I had intuited. There must have been clues in the writing, but I'll be darned if I could tell you what they are.

Jeff had put on a lot of weight during the past year and was beginning to be teased at school for being fat. He didn't want to go to school. I took him to a child psychologist named June Bauer. I waited in her outer office reading volume 9 of *The Collected Works of Carl Jung*. I'd recently set a goal for myself to read all of his work. Volume 9 is on archetypes and the collective unconscious. I expected to have a full fifty minutes to read, but after ten minutes, the door opened and Jeff came out in tears. June said that would be all for the day, but she'd like to see me privately for a moment. I went into her office and she told me that the moment she asked Jeff about his father, he burst into tears. I quickly filled her in on Neil's illness. She asked me if I'd told Jeff his father was mentally ill.

"No, I thought I should protect 'the father image' in Jeff's eyes," I said.

"Well, you've got to level with him," she said. "He's got to know the truth so he can begin to deal with it."

Of course. The truth. Why hadn't I thought of it? It's always the answer.

I'll never forget his face when I finally told him that his father was crazy. The light literally dawned all over his features. Clarity cleansed his sweet face. He understood. Now it all made sense. His father was ill. Mentally ill. He sat quietly beside me, working it out for himself. He looked profoundly relieved.

Jeff continued to see June Bauer twice a week. She gave me very good advice about Jeff's weight problem. "He's built a wall around himself for protection," she said. "There's nothing you can do about it; only make it worse. When he's ready to give it up, he will." She was right, but it would take a few years for Jeff to be ready.

I was the first person Billy cast in *The Exorcist* and he was now casting the other roles. I was already into my regimen to get ready to play Chris MacNeil. I was dieting, going to yoga, ballet classes, tap dancing, and swimming. Chris was a movie star and I wanted to look like one. I had a few months to work on it and I did succeed in getting thinner than I'd been in years by the time shooting started. But weight has always been my bête noire and my diaries are full of all my efforts to stick to my latest diet. Over the years, I've given up grass, tobacco, and alcohol, but I couldn't give up food. That one demands you learn moderation and I don't seem to have been equipped with that skill. It's all or nothing. I'm still working on it.

Friedkin, Blatty, and I flew to New York to read with auditioners. Also on the plane were Francis Coppola and Cloris. We had a party in the air.

In New York I'd arranged for Henry Madden to read for Father Karras, but Henry was nervous and the meeting with Billy didn't go well. I squirmed between them and was glad when the meeting was over. I read with some actresses for the role of my assistant. Billy rejected them. One of them was an unknown actress named Jill Clayburgh. I thought she was terrific, but Billy shook his head. I couldn't understand why he didn't like her. Now, of course, I realize why Billy couldn't hire the young, beautiful Clayburgh to play my assistant. She looked more like a movie star than I did.

A few days later I read with Stacy Keach, who was really wonderful. Billy liked him a lot, too. He was thrilled to see the scene come alive. Yet he wasn't a hundred percent sure. Later that day I met Linda Blair, whom Billy was considering for the part of my daughter, Regan. The next day we did her screen test. I found that she did her best acting if we moved away from the script a bit and she played the scene in her own words. She got looser then and really came alive.

Billy and I visited some designer showrooms and settled on Oscar de la Renta to do the clothes. It was a good choice. When *The Exorcist* was rereleased in 2001, the clothes were so classic they hardly seemed dated, even though it was twenty-five years later.

While we were in New York we saw *That Championship Season* on Broadway, a play written by Jason Miller. Jason was an actor and a playwright. I got the feeling that Billy didn't really believe that an actor could play Father Karras, that being an actor precluded having the depth needed for the role. I felt that Billy respected Jason more than most actors because he was also a writer. He decided to have Jason do a screen test. We returned to Los Angeles.

After the stimulation of Billy's creative energy and my growing love affair with Henry Madden while I was in New York, the appearance of Neil jumping out of the bushes at me as soon as I got back home was like a splash of cold water on a flushed face.

One morning at eight, Jeff was playing next door and Neil appeared at the front door demanding I let him in. I called Jim Butler immediately and refused to open the door. Neil smashed through the French doors and I ran out the dining room door into the street in my nightgown. A neighbor appeared with a robe and stayed with me until the police arrived, having been called by Jim. They took Neil away. I packed up the cats and my dog, and Jeff and I moved in with Leo and Sylvia Wolfe, my friends from STOP.

I went to UCLA to see the doctor who had conducted the court-ordered psychiatric examination of Neil. He wanted to test me and Jeff, too. I told him he could test me all he wanted, but I refused to allow Jeff to be put through any more than he'd already been through. I suggested he speak to June Bauer, the therapist he was seeing.

Jason Miller arrived in Los Angeles for his screen test. He called me from his hotel and wanted me to come pick him up and go to dinner. I suggested he call a cab. He replied, "Get your ass over here." I actually responded to that and said okay. Then when I hung up, I stood and replayed my long history of responding to remarks like that. I called him back and told him I was going to bed. The next day I had lunch with Billy and Jason at Sorrentino's restaurant. After, we walked to the set where Jason would do his test. Later Jason and I spent a few hours together in a Mexican restaurant where he made a pass at me. I would have considered it unprofessional if he were about to test for a role playing the love interest in the movie. But a priest? Later I would realize how troubled and self-destructive Jason was.

The next night Bill Friedkin called at dinnertime and said that I must see Francis Ford Coppola's new white Mercedes stretch limousine. Francis and Billy picked me up. We ate at an old Los Angeles restaurant called the Pacific Dining Car. Francis bought two bottles of great champagne. One we broke on the limo for christening; the other was opened and a small group of us sipped champagne in the back as we drove. The roof was opened and we stood on the seats with our heads and arms out the top of the roof singing "Hooray for Hollywood." I felt like I was playing Zelda Fitzgerald as we drove up Hollywood Boulevard. Then we went to the Fez restaurant to watch the belly dancers.

The next day we took Francis's limo to Freddie Fields's house to watch a screening of a Steve McQueen film. After the party Billy and I got in the long white limousine to go to the Whiskey A Go Go with Francis. Driving down Sunset Boulevard, we pulled alongside a car with Peter Bogdanovich and Cybill Shepherd. They'd been at the party, too. Billy rolled down the window of the limo and shouted across to Peter's car, "*French Connection*, five Academy Awards." We raced on. Suddenly Peter zoomed by us shouting out his window, "*Last Picture Show*, best movie since *Citizen Kane*." Francis told the driver to catch up. As he stood on the seat putting his head through the roof, he shouted, "*The Godfather*, one hundred fifty million dollars."

They were all screaming with laughter, with success, and with the promise of what would become a classic decade in film history.

We were back in court on June 22 and 23. This is my diary entry for June 23:

Went to court. Neil looked terrible. People were staring at the crazy man. It broke my heart to see him like that. I couldn't look at him. The court awarded me complete custody until such time as Neil receives psychiatric treatment and a new report submitted to the court saying that he is no longer psychotic. Then he can have reasonable visitation rights. He hummed while the judgment was read into the record—I guess to show his nonchalance and to cover his craziness. Of course, it only made him look crazier. I was sent to the cafeteria by Jim to avoid Neil until the lawyers finished talking. Then his lawyer brought

Neil into the cafeteria and sat him at the table next to me. I moved. Had a hard time controlling my tears. The dam was leaking. I drove to Toby's. Cried for a few hours. She gave me Valium and Percodan for my headache. Woke up better, but Jeff is sick. Fever close to 105. Put him to bed. He was delirious all night. Bad dreams.

Had little sleep because Jeff was so disturbed all night. Took him to doctors. Verdict? Tonsillitis. Gave him penicillin. Fever finally broke in evening. Deliriums ended.

It is clear now that Jeff got sick when some dramatic event was taking place with Neil and me. When there is emotional stress, the resistance gets lowered and the body can succumb to illness. I can't tell from the diary entries whether I had any inkling of that then, but I can see how true it is as I follow the path of my life backward, trying to make sense of it all. It makes me wonder what I am not understanding in the present that will later be clear as I look back from the future.

My diary entry for June 23 concludes this way: *Neil does want half of my piece of* The Last Picture Show. *Jim says I should just give it to him and get it over with. Pay off. Buy out. I never asked for alimony or anything from my husbands. Now I must pay. How weird.*

I gave it to him.

Finally on June 29, I left Hollywood for New York, where we would be shooting *The Exorcist*. With me were Adela and her two daughters; my dog, Bernard (Daisy Mae's son); Georgie Baby, the Persian cat Neil bought for me; and Moses, a cat that Jeff had brought home in a box from a shopping mall.

"Why Moses?" I'd asked.

"Because he's an orphan," my eight-year-old son explained.

Jeff didn't fly with us. He and his new tutor, Mark, had planned a camping trip across country and wouldn't arrive in New York for another two weeks.

With one month before shooting was scheduled to start, there was much to do. Among other things, I wanted to chart Chris's consciousness. I wanted her to begin the film unawakened to any other realm of existence except the material, the world that she perceived with her five senses. Slowly, during the course of the film, she would be forced to confront the existence of a far greater mystery. I wanted her to do battle completely ill-equipped to deal with the malevolent forces of the unseen world. So I selected a good-luck charm that she always wore: a small horseshoe dangling on her wrist. I wore it in every scene.

I was better equipped than Chris was. I knew that we were entering the lion's den. I did not think for a moment that we could focus all our creative energies on a major battle between the forces of good and evil without attracting some very powerful energies to the enterprise. Before I left California I saw Reshad and asked him to give me some prayers and practices to keep myself spiritually strong during the filming. He made a tape for me to play at the beginning of each day. It contained a series of prayers and a guided meditation.

The company had rented F&B Ceco Studios on West 55th Street and Tenth Avenue. This studio once belonged to Twentieth Century–Fox and it was here that I'd done my first screen test in 1956 for Gregory Ratoff's film *The Fifth Season*. On the first floor were two soundstages. Stage I was the interior of the furnished house Chris MacNeil has rented during her stay in Georgetown while making a film. (The exterior would be shot in Georgetown.) It was a three-story set. At street level were the living room, dining room, foyer, entrance hall, study, and a complete working kitchen. The central stairway in the main hallway led upstairs to three bedrooms and a bath. In the ceiling of the upstairs hallway was a string where one could pull down a flight of stairs that led up to the attic, where Chris was to investigate the sounds she heard in the night. It was a complete, functional three-story house. Stage II contained a replica of Regan's bedroom that was refrigerated so our breaths would vaporize during the exorcism. This was called "the cold set." There were other locations, too—hospitals, Fordham University, and so forth—but the bulk of my shooting would be on these two soundstages. Above the stages, up a metal stairway, were all the production offices, as well as the dressing rooms and Dick Smith's makeup room.

Most of the roles were cast. Linda Blair was set for Regan, Jason Miller for Father Karras, Max von Sydow was trying to work out his complicated schedule with Ingmar Bergman as well as being the lead actor in the Stockholm National Theater. Lee J. Cobb was set for Detective Kinderman and Jack MacGowran for the role of Burke Dennings, the director of the film within the film. A young actress named Kitty Winn, whom Billy and I had seen playing Ophelia to Stacy Keach's Hamlet in Central Park, was cast as Sharon, my assistant.

In the meantime, Jeff arrived with Mark from their cross-country camping adventure and I learned from Henry that Neil was in New York, staying with his cousins on 84th and Madison, just three blocks from the apartment I'd rented, so I had to be on the lookout every time I left the building.

I moved into my dressing room in the production office above the stage. I brought wall hangings, pictures, music, my tape recorder, and the tape Reshad had made for me. I planned to start each day playing Reshad's tape and doing the meditation and practices he recorded. Within a few days my dressing room was robbed. The thief didn't take much. But he did carry away my tape recorder with Reshad's tape in it. To me, it felt as if we were being put on notice. Billy hired a night watchman to stay in the production office at all times. He was a young, personable, strong African American guy. He looked like he did martial arts. He was very friendly and all of us liked him a lot. Within two weeks he was dead—shot by mistake on his doorstep in Harlem by a policeman who "thought he was reaching for a gun." He was unarmed. He was replaced by a professional security company.

As we got closer to the first day of shooting, I spent more and more time at the production office, doing fittings and rehearsing. The rehearsals were going well and I really liked Billy. Often I would stroll down the hall to his office and we would talk about his latest ideas. In California, Blatty had shown me a report by Dr. J. B. Rhine, the most famous scientist investigating paranormal events. He did his research at Duke University and had investigated the case Blatty used as the basis of his story. The first line of his report read, "At the very least we would have to say this is the most remarkable case of poltergeist activity we've ever seen." One day Billy told me about the conversation he'd had with the aunt of the actual boy who had been possessed. She described how the furniture moved across the room of its own volition. Billy was excited. He said, "I'm going to have the whole chest of drawers come at you." And he held his hands up over his head and moved at me like a monster chest of drawers. He was laughing gleefully as he did when he had a great idea.

Billy took me to museums and showed me paintings that inspired him, works by Francis Bacon and Edvard Munch. He also leafed through art books for images that could stimulate him or trigger an idea for a shot. Once he was practically dancing up and down as he said, "Look at this!" He opened a book on René Magritte to the painting, *Le Bouquet Tout Fait* (The Ready-made Bouquet). "That's Merrin's arrival at your house in Georgetown." The shot that was developed from this initial inspiration became the poster art for the film and all the subsequent ads for it. It's one of the most famous shots in film history.

We were only a few days from our start date of August 14. I was scheduled to begin on Stage I on August 18. The set was nearly finished when Billy called me into his office and told me that there would be a delay of at least two weeks. He had fired the art director and the set designer and the new guys were flying in from California.

"What happened?" I asked.

"Among other things, the goddamn walls are too short! If I shot up from a low camera angle, I'd be shooting off the set."

I sat in his office, stunned that our forward motion had to be checked. Billy spoke with me calmly. A delay like this would cost Warner Bros. plenty of money. The budget was escalating and we hadn't even begun shooting. The whole company would be getting paid while on hiatus. I asked what Warner's reaction was when he told them. He shrugged. "I haven't told them yet." But someone did. Probably David Salven, the production manager and associate producer, because a moment later our talk was interrupted by Billy's secretary over the intercom: "Mr. Friedkin, Mr. Bluhdorn is calling."

Charlie Bluhdorn was the top money man at Warner Bros. Billy, without missing a beat, leaned into the intercom and said in a steady voice, "Tell him if he's calling to fire me, I'll take the call. Otherwise, I'm busy." And he picked up our conversation where we'd left off.

I was so impressed. These were power games the likes of which I'd never seen played before. I loved Billy as a director, but I also admired him. He seemed infallible to me. He was like a king ruling his realm. I was spellbound. It wasn't a romantic attachment that was forming, it was a creative one. My diary in this period is all about Henry Madden and whether he did or did not call me; or if he was warm at dinner or cool at breakfast. This was the beginning of a love affair with Henry that would last several years. No, my relationship with Billy was something else. It was deep. It was real. And it was immensely creative and powerful.

I think Billy approached *The Exorcist* initially from a psychological perspective. It's one reason he was careful to stress the absence of Regan's father on her birthday, and have Regan overhear her mother yelling into the telephone as she tries to find him, and telling her assistant that he didn't care enough to even call Regan on her birthday. The dialogue for this phone conversation was not in the script. I improvised it. In the majority of cases where possession is assumed, the subjects are pubescent girls. Billy's understanding here was psychologically sound. From a Jungian point of view, when a father is absent, it can leave a kind of hole in the psyche that the contents of the collective unconscious can use to enter and overwhelm a weak ego. I think Billy started from that basic psychological viewpoint. Fairly quickly, though, he came to admit other interpretations.

At the very beginning of shooting, Jason Miller was on the beach with his wife and three children. A motorcycle appeared out of nowhere and smashed into the head of Jason's five-year-old son, Jordan, who had undergone cranial surgery the year before. The child was unconscious for ten days and no one knew whether he would recover. Everyone prayed for him, especially the Reverend Thomas Bermingham, who was an old friend and professor of William Blatty and had a role in the film. He stayed at the hospital daily with Jordan and prayed by his bedside. For those ten days, a pall hung over the company, and after Jordan's recovery, there was a decided change in everyone's attitude. Billy began having each new set we used blessed by Father Bermingham or the other priest in the film, Father

O'Malley. It was clear we were playing with fire. That metaphor soon became reality.

At the time, the city of New York had some distinguished visitors from Africa, on an official United Nations mission, who wanted to visit a movie set. Our sets were completely closed—no press, no visitors. But Billy agreed to have a party for these African guests on the set of Chris MacNeil's house. All cast and crew were requested to attend. A caterer was hired, the rooms were beautifully illuminated by candles, waiters circulated with trays of champagne and canapés. It looked like a real home. The visitors arrived in colorful African dashikis, caftans, and headdresses, and we were all introduced. As the party progressed, I looked around the room and became aware of how white we were. This was in the days before a conscious effort was made to integrate the film community. As I looked around, I felt embarrassed at our uniform whiteness. Then I remembered that we did have one African American person with us, a publicist. Thinking *she must be here somewhere*, I scanned the room and spotted her sitting on a coffee table, holding a glass of champagne and talking to someone on the couch. She was wearing a light yellow leather jacket. Her back was to me. On the coffee table behind her were three lit candles. As she laughed and leaned back, her jacket swayed into the flames. I darted across the room and shoved her away from the candles.

She turned to me startled and I said, "Your jacket almost caught on fire."

She thanked me, and we moved the candles and mopped up the champagne I'd spilled.

Perhaps it wasn't meaningful that the only African American person in our company had to be saved from catching on fire at a party for a delegation from Africa, but it seemed weird to me. That was just a prelude. One weekend, with no one in the building except the security guards, the "cold set" on Stage II erupted in flames and had to be rebuilt. No explanation for this fire was ever found.

By now we were all spooked.

I went to Billy and said, "Negative energy can create more negative energy. An accident happens. Everyone gets nervous and that creates more accidents. Don't let it get you. Just hold firm." I don't know if I was telling him or myself, but I felt a need to say it.

The unsettling events continued.

On his first working day in Georgetown, Max von Sydow got word his brother died.

Linda Blair's grandfather died.

The assistant cameraman's wife had a baby. It lived only three days.

The man who designed the refrigeration for the cold set died before we finished shooting.

Whatever the forces were that were called into play, they were manifesting all over the place. It continued throughout the eight months we were shooting.

During rehearsals I told Billy that I didn't agree with the conclusion Chris MacNeil reaches at the end of the script. After all she's been through, all that her daughter has been through, after two priests have died trying to save her daughter, in the final scene as she and Regan are leaving the house, Father O'Malley, playing Father Dyer, asks her, "What do you think happened in there?" Blatty had Chris say, "Well, as far as God goes, I'm still a nonbeliever. But when it comes to the devil—well, that's something else, Father. That I could buy." Then Father Dyer answers, "But if all the evil in the world tends to make you believe in the devil, how do you account for all of the good?"

It made no sense to me. We'd take this long journey with Chris MacNeil and then have her end up a believer in the devil? *Only* the devil? Not good *and* evil? Wasn't that what the whole movie was about, the tension between the two forces? A person doesn't experience the kind of overwhelming event Chris had just gone through without an opening occurring. If she's just going to end up being "a believer in the devil" without any awareness that the devil represents one side of a polarity, then frankly, I didn't know how the hell to play her.

Blatty resisted changing that scene, although he rewrote it many times.

We rehearsed a version that still had Chris believing in the devil because he "keeps doing commercials." But toward the end of the rehearsal period, Billy called him in and had him watch the scene. In *William Peter Blatty on The Exorcist*, his book about the filming of *The Exorcist*, Blatty wrote:

> Billy had been rehearsing the scene as was his custom the night before shooting. And he told me the "good in the world" scene wasn't working; would I please listen and give him my opinion. The cast ran through the scene, coming apart where Chris says "the devil keeps doing commercials." There wasn't a doubt that the scene did not work. And in my opinion no remedy was possible. For the problem, I was convinced, was Ellen Burstyn's powerful subconscious block on the subject of Satan's existence. She'd objected to the line some weeks before in New York and I'd already rewritten it for her several times. In the final script, the scene ran as follows:

> DYER
> What do you think happened? Do you think she was really possessed?

> CHRIS
> If you're asking if I believe in the devil, the answer is yes. Yeah. I do. Because the devil keeps doing commercials.

> And now in rehearsal, Ellen stiffened up on the line and made it stilted. In a word—"My hunch—my opinion"—as Detective Kinderman would say—she subconsciously took a dive and I felt that she'd do it again when we shot. So we scrapped the scene.

It wasn't subconscious at all. It was very conscious. Writers will sometimes put lines in characters' mouths because they want a certain thing said, and they use that character to say it or to set up another character's saying it. But I'm not a puppet whose words and actions are manipulated by the director and writer. I create a living character, and once she is alive in me, I can feel what she would say and what she cannot. Blatty wanted to use Chris to set up Dyer's line, "But if all the evil in the world tends to make you believe in the devil, how do you account for all of the good?" which Blatty wanted said. But my job is to create a character that is real. If she is real to me, I know she will be real to the audience. One of the reasons *The Exorcist* is considered the scariest movie of all time is because the characters have been brought to life and are utterly believable. If an audience doesn't believe in the characters, they won't take the inner journey. It's the inner journey that engages them emotionally in the story. If they are not engaged in that way, they just sit and eat their popcorn and watch a movie. They're not in the experience with their hearts pumping. The level of reality and believability that we were all able to attain was created with a ruthlessness to all concerns but the one hundred percent belief in every line we said, every move we made. Chris MacNeil was a smart woman who had just been through hell. After all the events in this story to save her daughter, she should end up saying, "I believe in the devil"? Blatty had written a better character than that. I did not take a dive because of a psychological block; I stood up for my character and refused to allow her to be used as a setup. I was deeply grateful to Friedkin for backing me up on this.

One day in early September, while we were still waiting for the sets to be rebuilt, I was strolling down Park Avenue. It was one of those crystalline days in New York when the light is clear and the trees are swaying with an autumn-tinged breeze. I passed a hotel whose plate-glass window revealed its bar behind it. I stopped and looked in, remembering a day in 1956. Blossom's beloved, Jack Goodman, vice president of Simon and Schuster, had died. After the funeral, Frank Satenstein, director of the Jackie Gleason show, and I brought Blossom here to this bar and sat at a table in the back. I could see the table and the empty chairs around it. Then suddenly, the chairs were filled with the three of us drinking and laughing in a kind of Irish wake mixture of bawdiness and tears. I remember Frank told some filthy jokes and we laughed until we cried.

As I stood on the street on this windy day looking at my young self drinking, laughing, and crying with her friend, I wanted to catch my younger eye. I wanted to send her a mental message to turn her head and see her own future calling to her from the other side of the window. She couldn't hear any wisdom I might want to impart or any warning of danger, but if she could just see me, a famous actress about to embark on this huge movie, perhaps she would take heart. She'd know she was going to make it, come through it, sadder but definitely wiser. But she would not turn. She took another drink of—what was it? A drink of Frank's. A mixture of vodka and a yellow liqueur that tasted like anise. I couldn't remember its name. But it was lethal. My efforts at being a future attractor could not get past the besotted hilarity of that moment.

And had my young self turned, would she have seen me? Or recognized me? That I'll never know. I just know that as I turned from the window of the bar and walked through the brilliant breezy day, I thought, *Oh God, I love New York. Why did I ever leave here?* And I stopped dead in my tracks as I realized I never wanted to leave New York. I had been dragged away by my husband and I didn't have a husband anymore. I didn't have to return to Los Angeles. Ellen doesn't live there anymore!

And I didn't. New York became my permanent home. Not the city, but the state. I am in that state as I write, so maybe there was a future attractor that did work and it was me, now.

My first day of shooting was a scene that took place in the office of Dr. Klein, one of the many doctors Chris MacNeil consults regarding her daughter. Because the MacNeil house set wouldn't be ready for more than a month, in the meantime we shot all the scenes off that set. After two weeks, we ran out of doctors' offices and Fordham University sets, so we went on hiatus.

During this time I learned from Henry that Neil was in a mental hospital. His father put him there after Neil gave him a black eye. When the blows landed on his parents instead of me, they were ready to admit he needed hospitalization. While in the hospital, Neil received the first of many shock treatments he would have over the years.

Finally, on October 6, the house set was ready. It was beautiful. Billy insisted it be furnished with real antiques and fine art. There was a Degas on set and other valuable pieces. There was an original watercolor by Erté that I admired. At the end of the shooting, Billy took it off the wall and handed it to me. It hangs in my dining room today.

The first scene we were to shoot was my introduction in the movie, me waking up in the morning. Joe Fretwell, the costume designer, and I had picked out some white satin pajamas at Bonwit Teller for this scene, but when we showed them to Owen Roizman, the director of photography, he thought they might be too "hot," too bright on camera, and suggested they be taken down a bit. So Joe dyed them a pale pink. But on the day we were to shoot, they didn't look good on me. The color was too close to my skin color; I looked washed out. I hemmed and hawed in my dressing room trying to figure out what to do—be a good girl, as was my habit, and not say anything, or risk making trouble. I decided it was my entrance into the movie and it needed to be right. I brought my concerns to Billy. He flipped out. He canceled shooting for the day and demanded to know who was responsible for ruining his day. I was near tears and begged Billy not to call off shooting, just solve the problem and not blame anybody. During this tearful plea, I saw Billy scrutinizing me, watching my nose and eyes turn red and blotchy and calculating that if this continued, he wouldn't be able to photograph my face. It was a many-layered exchange, and I saw Billy decide that he couldn't yell at me. I cried too easily and ruined my face. He'd have to be careful. He never yelled at me again. Everyone else, to be sure, but if he was going to blow, he would actually tell me to leave the set and go to my dressing room. We were able to get new pajamas and shoot that day.

Six days later, *The King of Marvin Gardens* was shown at the New York Film Festival. The audience gave it a very warm reception, but the critics received it like toxic waste. It would be almost twenty years before it was released on video and appreciated for the original, eccentric, and artistic work that it is. Many people, including me, consider it to be Jack Nicholson's best work. In my opinion, everything he is credited for in *About Schmidt* he did earlier and better in *The King of Marvin Gardens*.

We shot in New York for two weeks, then made the move to Georgetown to shoot the exteriors in the beautiful autumn light. The owners of the house allowed us inside to make our entrances and exits. Little did they know what they were in for. After the movie opened, their house became so famous and attracted so many tourists that they couldn't stand it and they sold it. The new owners soon learned what problems they'd purchased and, after one or two more sales, it became clear that no one could ever live there and the house had to be demolished.

On Election Day, 1972, we shot Father Karras's leap from the window and subsequent fall down the stairs. Between setups during the long wait, I watched election returns with Billy. Nixon won by a landslide. For the rest of the shooting, every day in the makeup room, we read in the newspaper about the break-in at Democratic headquarters, the revelations of Deep Throat, and the unraveling of the Nixon presidency.

Before we left New York, Billy had warned us that the problem of shooting in Washington is that it is wedged between two major airports. The longest period without the sound of an airplane overhead was one and a half minutes around three A.M. on a Sunday morning. That meant that everything we shot in D.C. would have to be looped, lip-synched, back in the studio. I had a long difficult emotional scene coming up where I walk with Father Karras and ask him to perform the exorcism. I knew I'd wobble and burble my way through it with small stops and starts and repeated syllables because that's the way we talk in life. Only when I get on the looping stage and I see the transcript of the scene do I realize what kind of sounds I make while shooting the scene. It's pretty funny to read, actually. I knew this scene was going to be a bear to loop, but I didn't want that to inhibit me. I didn't want to tidy my speech so it would be easier to loop. In the scene I'm questioning Father Karras about exorcism, but not tipping my hand about why I want to know; I have a black eye under my dark glasses because my daughter has just slugged me and her behavior makes it hard to conclude anything else but that she's possessed. All that has to be hidden from Karras, but present for the audience. When I finally break down and tell the priest who it is that needs an exorcism, I say, "Father Karras, it's my little girl."

Later Blatty would tell me that when he was preparing his book on the filming of *The Exorcist*, he discovered that the line in his script was, "Father Karras, it's my daughter." He said, "I didn't realize you changed it to 'little girl.' Then he added generously, "That's much better. I always loved that line. I didn't realize I didn't write it."

We got the scene. Billy was happy. We went out for a hamburger and beer to celebrate.

My diary tells me that during this meal I spoke to Billy about an article I'd read about Margaret Fuller in *Ms.* magazine. She was the great transcendentalist friend of Ralph Waldo Emerson who had a brilliant mind and, for a nineteenth-century woman, an amazing life. I thought her story would make a great film, but this diary entry is significant because it tells me I was beginning to examine my own attitude toward the feminine. I was reading *Ms.* magazine. Gloria Steinem, God bless her, started us on a brand-new path. My generation of women was awakened in the seventies by Steinem, Betty Friedan, Germaine Greer, and other writers who promoted the radical idea that a woman is an equal human being to a man; not equal in abilities, tendencies, talents, hormones, interests, or propensities, but simply equal in value. Different, but not less. This glimmering that was planted in my brain at this time would blossom fully for the next two years and be expressed in *Alice Doesn't Live Here Anymore* when Alice says, "I mean, it's my life. It's not some man's life I'm helping him out with." That was a true awakening for me. I thought women were assistants. You find a man. He's got the life and you help him out with it. The fact was that even though I was supporting myself and my son and I was becoming famous, I still had no sense of myself except in relation to a man. In other words, I had no self. It was at this time that I began to grow one.

We shot my exit from the picture where Regan and I leave the house in D.C. and talk to Father Dyer. This is the scene that Blatty said in his book was "scrapped." The scene wasn't scrapped at all, just those two lines. Chris and Regan are returning home to Los Angeles. Billy told me he was friends with the *Chicago Sun-Times* columnist Irv Kupcinet and his wife, who lived in Chicago. Their daughter, Karyn, had been murdered in Los Angeles. When Billy saw them after the murder, he said Mrs. Kupcinet looked as if she had aged fifteen years. So I asked Dick Smith to do an aging makeup on me. But because Chris is a movie star and returning to Los Angeles, I asked him to then put regular makeup over the aging. His work was perfect. I look in that scene as if I've been through hell and it has aged me, but I'm doing my best to hide behind a mask.

Soon after that, we returned to New York to continue shooting on the soundstage. On November 29, we shot the first scene on the rigged set. It's the scene where Regan's bed was tossing her violently up in the air and she's yelling, "Mother, make it stop," and I'm standing looking at her, horrified. Linda was strapped on a board under her nightgown and during the shot a strap came loose and was smashing the board into her back. She was being hurt and tried to yell, "Stop—stop!"—but that was in the script and she couldn't think of how to tell them she was screaming "stop" for real. Finally she yelled "Stop *really*!" I told her afterward to yell, "Cut, Billy."

Even though her back was bruised, she did the scene again for other camera angles. Throughout this whole shoot she was incredibly brave.

As we got into the more difficult material, with all the vulgarity and violence, Billy hired an actress named Eileen Dietz to do Linda's off-camera work. He wanted to spare thirteen-year-old Linda from shouting, "Fuck me. Fuck me," when the camera was on me and the other actors. I was relieved that Billy did that. He tried to protect Linda in every way he could. But it backfired. Eileen Dietz wanted credit on the film and Billy refused to give it to her. She went to the press and what they wrote made it seem as if she had done a major portion of Linda's role. She did manage to get a shoulder or her back on camera a few times, so after she'd gone to the press, Billy went through the whole film and clocked how long any part of her body was actually on film. All together, it was eight seconds. Billy tried to counteract her claims, but the damage was done. Coupled with the news that Billy had used Mercedes McCambridge's deep voice to overdub some of the demon's lines, the impression was that Linda had done far less than she actually did. Billy and others, including myself, feel that's why Linda didn't win the Oscar she deserved. She was a sweet, innocent adolescent girl who gave one of the scariest and most difficult performances in the history of motion pictures. She should have been granted the award.

December 7, 1972

I'm forty years old today. I never used to imagine what 40 was like. At least, I'm working. What more could anyone want? To be doing my first really big starring role in the biggest picture of the year. It's going well. The work is good. Better than good. I'm doing my best work. All is well with me. I'm not fat. I'm in love. My kid is doing good in school. I have money in the bank.

Oh Thou, sustainer of our bodies, hearts and souls, bless all that we receive in thankfulness. Amen.

We had time off between Christmas and New Year's. I went to the Strand Book Store and bought all the books I could find on Margaret Fuller and the transcendentalists, Emerson and Thoreau. Then I went home and got the flu. I spent New Year's Eve and Day in bed, reading about Margaret Fuller in Boston in the mid-1800s.

Coincidentally, during this period, I was also reading the work of the great futurist, mathematician, philosopher, and inventor Buckminster Fuller. During this period, Bucky was giving a talk at Carnegie Hall on the future of the world. He was the most stimulating speaker I'd ever heard. As I sat in my seat listening to him, I felt as if I were running in place at top speed just to keep up with him. And then suddenly a thought popped in my head—*Fuller! Margaret Fuller! Buckminster Fuller! Is there a connection?* During intermission, I read his bio in the program. He was from Boston, as was Margaret. And he went to Harvard. Margaret was the first woman ever admitted into the Harvard library. I thought they must be related.

At the end of Bucky's lecture, the audience stood and roared its approval. Bucky held up his hands and silenced the ovation and said, "Thank you for that. I think you'd like to know that wherever I go, people do that. It doesn't really mean anything for me, but it does for you. All over the world, people come because they really want to know. Know that you are not alone."

I went home inspired and looked through all my books on Margaret Fuller, searching to find out if they were related, and found it in one of the books that had a family tree on the inside cover. Margaret's maternal grandmother was Anne Buckminster. I decided to find a way to meet Buckminster Fuller and find out what he knew about his great-aunt Margaret Fuller.

On January 22, 1973, we began shooting the scene where I enter the room and Regan, covered in blood, plunges a crucifix into her vagina. It was a terrifying scene to shoot and the scariest one in the film. It was Linda's fourteenth birthday.

We used to do a trick as kids where we would take several deep breaths, then hold our breath as we linked our index fingers and pulled hard. It made us dizzy. I did this before each take off-camera for my close-up reaction to the horror of what Regan was doing. On the sixth take, I flipped out—maybe I was over-oxygenated. Billy was playing a recording of the real exorcism of a ten-year-old kid roaring and bellowing. I went right into the sound and, terrorized, lost contact with reality. Suddenly I heard Billy yelling, "Cue, Ellen! Where's Ellen?" That brought me back. I was afraid I'd had an acid flash. Then on the next take, I was still shaking and Billy shot a loud prop gun in my face. We had a birthday party for Linda that I could barely make it through—I went home and was in bed by eight-thirty for a long night of twitching and bad dreams.

The next day, I was still very shaky. We were continuing to shoot the masturbation scene. Linda accidentally hit me during the scene and when she realized what she'd done she gasped and covered her mouth. The little girl that she was broke right through the evil demon's makeup. It was very funny.

I wondered if there was any cosmic penalty I was incurring for making this movie. There had been so many accidents and deaths, and as we got deeper into the demonic aspects, the whole atmosphere on the set became charged with a feeling of danger, both physical and metaphysical. Before long the dark forces took aim at me.

At the end of the masturbation scene, the demon smashes me and I land on the floor. My assistant, Sharon (Kitty Winn), runs down the hall toward the room; the door slams shut, and a tall chest of drawers moves menacingly across the room toward me, as had happened in the real case. I had a rig around my midriff with a wire out the back of my shirt. When Linda slugged me, the stunt coordinator was to pull on the wire, yanking me to the ground. The camera was on me, the light in my eyes blinding me. I could see only darkness surrounding the light. We did one take and I landed on my butt.

Billy called, "Cut. We go again."

I asked why.

"Because your scarf covered your face when you landed."

I felt scared. I didn't want to do another take. But I was a girl who couldn't say no. Not to a director and certainly not to Billy, the King.

I said, "He's pulling me too hard. Could he not pull me so hard?"

"Well, it's got to look real!" Billy replied rather forcefully.

"I know it's got to look real, but I'm telling you he's pulling me too hard. I could get hurt."

The stunt man stood on my left slightly behind me, listening and waiting for instructions. Billy was on my right. There was a pause. Then Billy looked to the stunt man and said, "All right, don't pull her so hard." Then he moved away and behind me so he and the stunt man were face to face. I couldn't see them. But I felt them. I felt an exchange between them behind my back. I saw only the blinding light in my eyes and the surrounding blackness.

Billy yelled, "Action."

I got yanked to the wooden floor hard. Much harder than the first time. I didn't land on my buttocks this time, but on my sacrum. It smashed into the hard wooden floor and I screamed in pain, louder than I've ever screamed in my life. It was the worst pain I'd ever felt. I looked to Billy to yell "Cut." He did not. I saw his hand touch the cameraman's elbow. I saw the lens move closer. Billy wanted to use this real pain.

I felt fury rise through my whole being and although I couldn't stop screaming, I managed to choke out the words, "Turn the fucking camera off."

Then I heard, "Cut." Only then. He couldn't use it. People ran to me. Everyone knew I was badly hurt. There was no doubt in anyone's mind. I was carried to my dressing room. Doctors were called. Nothing was broken, but everything was bruised. I was traumatized and went home early.

The next day, Billy captured the genuine pain visible in my face in close-ups. I was exhausted and anxious. We'd been shooting for more than a hundred days. All of us were exhausted. Only Billy's dedication remained unflagging.

I had one more difficult scene with Father Karras, and then the worst would be over. But Jason blocked on one line, and every time he came to it, he froze. We did the scene over and over. At least fifty takes. I don't know how many more than that because Billy made the assistant cameraman stop calling out the number of the take because it was too humiliating for Jason. My nerves were frazzled. I started crying during the scene. Billy asked me not to cry, but as we did the scene over and over, the tears just came. I couldn't control them. Finally Billy came to me and said, "Ellen, I beg you not to cry in this scene."

I swallowed hard and tried to calm down. I did everything Billy "begged me" to do. I managed to get through it. It's the scene in the basement where I've washed and ironed Father Karras's shirt after the demon puked green bile all over it. Since then I've watched the scene and noticed I was literally choking on my tears, but I managed to hold them back. Jason finally got the damn line out and we exited that nightmare.

A few days later, Billy went on *The Barry Gray Show*, a popular talk radio show in the seventies, and discussed *The Exorcist*. The next morning Barry Gray was hit by a car. Billy and I went out to dinner that night. He was very spooked by this latest accident. It had become all too clear the kind of forces we were attracting.

The next day, a Sunday, I planned a day off to give my wounded back and psyche a rest. I stayed in bed reading the *New York Times*. In the magazine section, there was an article on the devil. Because of the popularity of Blatty's novel, the *Times* ran a story on the history of the devil; its appearance in religion, its usage in literature, the fear of it, its going out of style, and now its reemergence in the public's consciousness.

As I finished the article, I felt this lazy little thought stroll across my mind. "Wouldn't it be funny if it turns out that Satan created the world and is more powerful than God?" Suddenly a maniacal voice sounded loudly in my head laughing like a hyena. It said, "That's the crack in your mind I've been waiting to enter. Now I'm inside your head." Then a raucous, evil laugh.

Panicked, I leapt out of bed, my heart pounding, and stood barefoot in the middle of the room, hearing that awful laughter in my head. It must have been what Father Karras would have heard when he jumped out the window. After a moment of running around the room terrified, I sat on the floor cross-legged and closed my eyes. Immediately, I was back up the mountain facing Mont Blanc. I breathed deeply and slowly. Then I began intoning the Sufi practices I'd learned from Pir Vilayat. My heartbeat slowed down. The awful voice went away. I finished my praying and crawled back into bed astounded at the complexity of the human mind and the power of prayer.

The battle between good and evil is fought inside us all the time. The choice we make in each moment, whether to manifest or to sacrifice our integrity, is just one way that the battle is waged. When I didn't want Chris MacNeil to say that the devil is something I can believe in, he keeps making commercials, it wasn't because of a psychological block. It was because by the end of the film, Chris had come face to face with the awesome power of evil, but she also knew the magnificent power in words. She was an actress. She was not about to be flippant using words that might attract whatever it was that had gotten hold of her little girl. She wouldn't want to have anything to do with it and surely not declare herself a believer in the devil.

Recently I was given a definition of Satan that feels right to me. Evil lives in the shadow of each of us. It is all our repressed, disowned feelings our egos hate to see or acknowledge. When there is a group that comes together to make a movie or create a culture of any kind, their collective shadows can manifest evil or Satan. The collective shadow of Germany during World War II manifested evil itself, and Satan was embodied as Adolf Hitler. But Hitler could not have thrived in a benign atmosphere. He needed the magnitude of all the repressed feelings the Germans harbored from the conditions imposed on them after World War I. When unchallenged, the shadow is very powerful. That is why it is imperative for each of us to learn about ourselves and be courageous enough to bring our own hidden impulses into the light, see them for what they are, and integrate them for our own good.

I'm still working on this. Every day. It's a duty that comes with being a human being.

After *The Exorcist* finished filming, I began seeing an orthopedist, a chiropractor, and a massage therapist for my back. This was the beginning of a long line of doctors and practitioners who would treat my back and the arthritis that developed in the scar tissue. Although I've been angry at Billy for this, I don't blame him. If I had to shoot that scene today, I would insist on padding on me *and* the floor. I would not allow anybody to yank me so hard. I would take care of myself. I didn't know how to do that then. That was not Billy's fault. Billy would do anything to "get the shot." That was his priority. I knew that about him. I just didn't yet know how to defend myself in the face of that fact. I do now.

The scene in which the bed throws Linda and me around did not please Billy when he saw it in the dailies. We reshot it. He still didn't like it. We shot it again. It was on the schedule every day for the rest of the picture. Any time we were done early, we would reshoot that scene. Five times it was reshot. After my back was injured, I could only do one angle, then lie down until the pain went away before I could do a second angle. Finally, near the end of shooting, Billy accepted what he saw in the dailies.

Every day we got another day behind schedule. As we were about to go into the shooting of the exorcism, we were forty-seven days behind. Noel Marshall, Blatty's manager and the executive producer, told me that Billy had spent $9 million over budget. He said we would have to do about $37 million worth of business before it could be considered a commercial success. He told me it would have to be the fourth biggest moneymaker of all time before he and Blatty made a nickel. The three top commercial successes at that time were *Gone With the Wind, The Sound of Music,* and *The Godfather.* We would have to come in right behind these three to break even.

When I questioned Billy, he answered, "So what? I've never yet heard one person in the world say, 'Let's go see that movie playing on the corner. I hear it came in on time and on budget'!"

The film made $126 million in its first release. For decades it was the fourth-biggest-grossing film of all time. It made millions more when it was rereleased twenty-five years later.

Jack MacGowran, who played the director of the film Chris MacNeil was shooting in the movie, and who was pushed out the window to his death by Regan, left to do a play at Lincoln Center when he was done shooting his scenes. In *The Exorcist*, Chris finds out that he is dead when the assistant director of the film she's making comes to her house and tells her. Four weeks after Jack finished, Terry Donnelly, the assistant director of *The Exorcist*, called to tell me Jack had died of influenza. I remember saying, "Why does it have to be you that tells me?" The synchronicity was too spooky. Synchronicities are defined as meaningful coincidences. According to Jung, they happen when the inner world and the outer world line up. We were teeming with them.

The shooting of the exorcism began, and like everything else in this movie, it took longer than expected. Chris isn't in this scene. I dropped by Billy's office to see how it was going. He was beside himself. He'd had to call off shooting for the day. Max blocked on a line. The line was, "The power of Christ compels you!" Max was an atheist. The power of the unconscious is amazing.

Billy said heatedly, "On a list of a hundred things that could happen on this picture, number one hundred would be that Max would—no— number ninety-nine would be that Max von Sydow would be anything but great in this movie. One hundred would be that he'd freeze on a line." He was wild with frustration.

The next day Max came through and he was, in fact, great in this movie.

They began shooting the exorcism in mid-February. They finished on April 29. It had taken so long that I reread *The Exorcist* to get back into it before I reported back to work.

In the meantime, I found a house that I loved on the Hudson River and moved out of Manhattan. I didn't have much—a bed and some towels. During this time my mother called to tell me that my biological father was in the hospital and not expected to live. She gave me the number of the hospital in Florida. I had long been thinking that I didn't want to go on carrying my anger at my father. I believed that forgiveness was healthy for the soul. I didn't want my father to die unforgiven. I called his hospital room. After I told him who I was and asked how he was doing, he said, "You know that time you wanted to borrow money, I didn't really have it, but I'm doing better now, so if you need any . . ."

I didn't remember wanting to borrow money, but I wasn't going to tell him that. I just said, "Well, that's all in the past now. Let's just forget the past."

"I'm going to leave you my house," he answered.

"Thanks, Dad, but why don't you leave it to Jack? I don't really need it. I've been doing pretty well."

"I know you have," he said. "I hope you haven't been making any of those dirty movies."

I took a deep breath. I knew from my brother Jack that my father had never seen any of my films. Even when Jack, his wife, and daughters were all going to see *The Last Picture Show*, and they asked him to go with them, he declined, saying he wanted to "remember her the way she was."

I said as evenly as I could manage, "No, actually I've made some very good movies."

"I know you have," he answered. "I don't even know why I said that. I've never been a prude. I've always believed in free love. I have no regrets. The only regret I've ever had was that I didn't make it with you when I had the chance."

I dropped the phone away from my ear and let it hang in my open hand. I looked around the empty room. There was not even a chair. I was sitting on the floor. I didn't know how to end the conversation. I put the phone back to my ear and said, "Okay, then. Hope you feel better. Goodbye." I hung up and sat there a long time in the silence and emptiness just looking at the phone in disbelief.

We finally completed shooting in New York. Billy left with the crew for Baghdad to shoot the opening scene with Max. After 224 days of principal photography, this epic was on film.

Friends of friends contacted Buckminster Fuller and told him I was interested in his great-aunt Margaret. Bucky's schedule was filled for the rest of the year, but he had some layovers in airports and was willing to see me. His secretary gave me the choice of a one-hour layover in New York, two hours in Boston, or five hours in Chicago. I took the five hours in Chicago. I couldn't resist five hours with the smartest man in the world all to myself.

We met at his hotel in Chicago for breakfast and afterward went to the airport together. Bucky was then seventy-seven, but he looked as hairless and pink-skinned as a newborn baby. His eyes were bright, although his vision was poor. He told me he had been born cross-eyed and wasn't operated on to correct that condition until he was four years old. He said when he was a child he could see the trees, but not the veins in the leaves of the tree. I asked him what it had done to him.

In his deep voice and rapid-fire speech, he said, "It taught me to think in generalized principles."

He told me about his great-aunt Margaret, the whole history of the Fuller family, and many other things. At one point I took out a cigarette and asked, "Do you mind if I smoke?"

He looked at me with kindness and said, "Oh, I don't mind for myself, darling, only for you."

I put the cigarette back in the pack.

I said meekly, "You don't smoke, huh?"

He held up his hands and examined them almost reverently and said, "No. I, being a human being, am the most sensitive sending and receiving

ELLEN BURSTYN

mechanism ever designed. And I wouldn't want to do anything to interfere with that sensitivity."

I had stopped smoking many times before, but I had always started
again. Soon I would stop for the last time, now that I fully appreciated the
deepest possible reason to stop. Also, my mother's fourth husband, Winsor
Meals, of whom I was very fond, was a heavy smoker and had contracted
lung cancer. It was a long, painful death. These two men aided me in my
effort; at last, I quit.

Bucky and I were to remain friends until his death ten years later. I spent
time with him and his wife, Anne, at their home in Maine and got to
know his daughter, Allegra, and his granddaughter, Alexandra. He was a
great friend and teacher. Slowly, one finds unique ways to fill that father-
shaped hole in the heart.

Bucky was a world-class sailor and one day in 1981 he took me sailing
in Penobscot Bay. Afterward, we had dinner in a local restaurant. Bucky
turned over his paper placemat and on the back of it, he wrote down
this poem:

WHY "YOURS TRULY"
I'm not yours
You're not mine.
My years of life
Are seventy-nine.
Mysteries deepen.
I opine.
Curvaceous, silkaceous, sylphaceous you.
I'm neigh efficacious.
What may we do?
I can't eat you
And have you too.
Let's enjoy laughter
And wisdom too.
You're eternally lovely.
The truly you.

You can't see me
I can't see you
But we may know one another
And sometimes do.
Then learn that we both love
Only all that's true
Wherever we both love
The truly you.

I'll love you forever
The truly you.

    Bucky Fuller
Very special copy for Ellen Burstyn
    Sept. 11, 1981
    Penobscot Bay, Maine

When I first met Bucky in 1973, I certainly didn't know who the "truly" me was, but I was doing my best to find out. I listened closely to what Bucky was saying to me at our first meeting. He told me his definition of the universe was: a series of only partially overlapping simultaneous events. For instance, the first star in the handle of the Big Dipper is a live show that took place one hundred years ago. The second star in the handle is a live show that took place two hundred years ago, and on through the whole constellation, with some stars being a live show that took place as long as two hundred million years ago.

I mused on that one, trying to get a clear picture of it. I got it, but the full reality of his insight would come to me with the help of my dog.

A few years previous to this event, I'd read a book called *An Experiment with Time* by J. W. Dunne. He said that our dreams are made up of images from our daily lives, past and future. He wrote that in sleep we have the ability to move around in time and pick up images from events that will happen in the near future. He suggested that it was possible to experience this by conducting an experiment that involved keeping track of your dreams consistently every morning for three months. At the end of each week, you were to review the week's worth of dreams and see how many images appeared in your dreams from events that occurred after the dream. In the third month of the experiment, I had a very vivid dream. I was walking down the center aisle of a large cathedral with a hole in the roof like the hole in the roof of the Pantheon. Rain was streaming down through the hole in a cone shape into the aisle, and I had to pass through it. The rain was luminescent. I don't remember the other details of the dream, but that image was very intense. I had a strong feeling that that dream and specifically that image were the culmination of the experiment.

Blossom's husband, Maurice Tuchman, the curator, had mounted an exhibition of contemporary artists at the Los Angeles County Museum of Art that I very much wanted to see. It was so popular that we decided I should visit the museum on Monday, when the museum was closed, to enjoy the show without the crowds. I felt sure that on this day that I was going to see the image of "a hole in the roof like a hole in the roof of the Pantheon." I assumed it would appear in the exhibition. And sure enough, toward the end of our tour, there was a tabletop construction of a coal mine, with a cart on a track. The track retreated from the eye in perspective, just like the aisle in the church. Above the cart, as though in the ceiling, was a hole. Through that hole poured light coming down in rays made of string that formed the cone shape around the cart and on the track. I stood in front of the exhibit for a long time, thinking that here it was, the image that proved the experiment, and yet I felt not quite satisfied. It was a coal mine, not a cathedral.

Blossom and I left the museum and went back to her house. We sat on the floor around the coffee table in the living room talking about our husbands and particularly about Neil and his mental illness. Blossom got up to go into the kitchen to make more coffee. I stayed sitting on the floor. Suddenly Blossom popped out of the kitchen with an impish expression on her face, holding a book with two hands. On the cover was a beautiful painting of Jesus ascending in celestial light. The title of the book was the one word, *Light*. Years later when I asked Blossom why she'd brought out the book, she said, "Because we'd been talking about Neil's Jesus complex."

But that was not what I saw at the time. The moment I saw the book I knew the line "a hole in the roof like a hole in the roof of the Pantheon" was in that book, and I read Blossom's impish expression like she was a djinn who was delivering to me this extraordinary culmination of the experiment. I leaped up and took the book from her. "That's it!" I cried. "It's in there!" I scanned the pages for the phrase. After a while, it was time to pick up Jeff from school and I still hadn't found it, so Blossom let me borrow the book. I hurried off, picked up Jeff, stopped at the grocery store, went home, put the food away, got dinner in the oven, and settled down to continue my perusal of *Light*. Not only was the line there toward the end of the book, there was even a sketch of the hole in the roof of the Pantheon with the light streaming in, just as I'd pictured it.

When I moved to New York to shoot *The Exorcist*, my housekeeper Adela and her children came from California to live with us. After the film was shot we moved out to a house on the Hudson. One day I drove into Manhattan and stayed with my friends from Chamonix, the Friedlanders, for a few days. Jeff came with me. On the third day we drove home and when we arrived, I wondered why Bernard had not greeted us. When I asked Adela, she said, "Bernard not here. I thought he with you." He'd been gone for three days. Apparently, he tried to follow me into the city. I was in a panic. I spent the next few days calling and searching the nearby animal shelters and calling ones that were farther away. None of them had a dog matching Bernard's description. I knew dogs were only kept ten days and then they were destroyed. After a week had gone by, I was beside myself. I had to find him, but how? I didn't know where else to turn. Finally, I decided I'd tried everything I knew on the physical plane. It was time to call on the metaphysical.

That night as I lay in bed, I focused my attention on Bernard. I held him in my awareness and eventually fell asleep. I dreamt I was looking for Bernard. There was a lady with a small brown wiry dog in her arms. I asked about the breed. She asked if I wanted him. I said, "No, not yet. I still mean to find Bernard."

I woke up knowing that Bernard wasn't dead and that I must find him. Again I called the shelters near my home and added ones within a twenty-mile radius. A man who picks up strays in a neighboring town referred me to a kennel in Closter, New Jersey. When I walked in, there was the lady with the small brown dog in her arms from my dream. So was Bernard! He was so excited when I took the leash that he ran to the car, pulling me over and dragging me through the gravel.

If my inner universe is a microcosm of the macrocosm, then the first star in my constellation would be the dream experiment that I did in 1970, the second star would be my desire in July 1973 to understand who I truly was. The third would be Bernard forcing me to go inside to search for him, which, if this were all a dream, would represent my instincts. The fourth would be Bucky's handing me that poem in 1981 that speaks of what is truly me. And the fifth star would be me writing this book now, putting all of this together and seeing the story of my own development and all the "only partially overlapping simultaneous events." In this "now" moment, all those individual stars are constellated in my inner universe and the resultant understanding of the whole is this: if you want to know who you truly are, the answer won't be found in the outer world; you must go inside and see where your instincts lead you.

A few months later, I closed up my house in New York and moved Jeff, Adela, her two daughters, Pamela and Cynthia, Bernard, my three cats, Georgie Baby, Moses, and Maria, back to Hollywood where I rented a house with Bob and Lelia Rudelson. I hired a tutor for Jeff, whom I was taking with me on location for the film I was about to make.

During the filming of *The Exorcist*, Warners screened the dailies and sent a message through my agent that they would like to do another film with me. They began sending me all the scripts they owned that had any role that I could conceivably play. Reading these scripts was an education. Every woman in them was either the victim, the understanding wife of the hero who was out saving the world, or a prostitute or some other style of sex object. There was no script where the woman was the protagonist. Stories were about men, and women played a role in the man's story. But it was not what I was experiencing myself. There was a movement, an energy that was igniting the consciousness of women. I saw it all around me; I was reading about it and it was flowing through me as well. I wanted to make a movie about that.

Billy had introduced me to his agent, Tony Fantozzi, and soon Tony was representing me. It was Tony who found *Alice Doesn't Live Here Anymore* by Bob Getchell. We sent it to John Calley, the head of production at Warner Bros. He liked it, too. There was only one problem. David Susskind had an option on it. However, the option was due to run out in a few days. He had no deal set up at any studio, so there was a good chance he wouldn't renew. But on the last possible day, he picked up his option. That meant we couldn't buy it from the writer but would have to deal with David Susskind, whom I knew slightly. He had a reputation for being difficult to work with and I wasn't particularly eager to go into business with him. So Tony called him and said, "I represent Ellen Burstyn. She's interested in doing *Alice Doesn't Live Here Anymore*."

"No, I'm doing this movie with Anne Bancroft," Susskind said.

"We have a green light from Warner Brothers to make it with Ellen Burstyn," Tony said.

"That's what I said," Susskind answered. "We're making this movie with Ellen Burstyn at Warner Brothers."

John Calley asked me if I wanted to direct it myself. I wish I'd said yes, but I just didn't have the confidence to do that. Instead, I told him I wanted "someone new and exciting" to direct. I called Francis Coppola and asked him if he knew a director who fit that description. Francis told me to go see a movie called *Mean Streets*.

Calley set up a screening of it for me. Warners owned it but hadn't released it yet. It was directed by Martin Scorsese. I sat in the screening room in awe of the raw talent of the director, as well as its two unknown actors, Robert De Niro and Harvey Keitel.

The only problem was that there was only one girl in the film and she had a minor role. I asked for a meeting with Marty. I sat in John Calley's office at Warner's and in walked this short, bushy-browed, high-strung New York Italian guy. He had a nervous laugh and an air of discomfort about him. He perched on a chair. I told him how much I liked his film, then I added, "But this film I want to make I'd like told from a woman's point of view. What do you know about women?"

"Nothing," he said pleasantly, "but I'd like to learn."

His intelligence beamed through his face. We went to work together.

I told Marty that I wanted to do my own singing and piano playing. I had six months to brush up on my piano and get over my block about singing. I lined up both piano and singing teachers and began.

We started casting. I wanted as many members of the Actors Studio as we could cast; I wanted a level of reality throughout the film that I knew actors trained by Lee Strasberg would be able to achieve. I read with all the actors who auditioned. Marty agreed that we should have as many women in positions of authority as possible. Marty hired my friend Toby Rafelson as art director, a rare title for a woman in those days. Then he hired Marcia Lucas (George Lucas's wife) as editor. On January 3, 1974, we found a wonderful "Audrey." Her name was Jodie Foster.

Alice Doesn't Live Here Anymore is the story of Alice Hyatt, who lives in Socorro, New Mexico, with her surly husband and eight-year-old son, Tommy. She tries to please her husband every way she can, but he will not be pleased. He is killed in an accident while driving his truck, leaving Alice with very little money and the care of her son. Improbably, she decides to return to her home in Monterey and resume her pursuit of a singing career. She and Tommy set off for California with Alice trying to pay their way by singing in small clubs. She manages to get one job, and has an affair with a man who turns out to be married and violent. Alice and Tommy flee to the next town, where Alice can land a job only as a waitress in Mel's Diner. While working there, she meets David, the owner of a small farm, and they fall in love. Now Alice must choose between marrying David and abandoning her dream of returning to Monterey to become a singer, or leaving him and moving on toward her goal.

It was a wonderful, funny, dramatic script, but Marty is the kind of director who likes to play with the script in rehearsals and see what the actors can bring to it in improvisations. Kris Kristofferson was set to play

David. Marty also cast, as Alice's friend Flo, my old friend from Bruce Dern's acting class, his then wife Diane Ladd. Six other members of the Actors Studio, including Harvey Keitel, were cast, too. We rehearsed for two weeks, fleshing out the characters and the text, and finally encountered the one big problem—the ending. I wanted Alice to pursue her dream. In the original script, Bob Getchell had Alice marry David. That struck me as a conventional "happily ever after" ending that ought to be changed. We tried it many different ways. As the rewrites were coming in to us, they were also going to John Calley at Warner Bros. When the new ending came in, I got a call from John who said in a friendly tone, "I like all the changes in the script except one, the ending."

I explained to him my reasons for Alice not surrendering her goal to "the man." John said no. "This script can't have an unhappy ending," he said. "We already made a movie last year with an unhappy ending, *Scarecrow*, and it didn't make any money."

"Wait a minute," I said. "Are you telling me that if she ends up with a man, it's a happy ending, and if she doesn't, it's an unhappy ending?"

"What I'm telling you is that if she doesn't end up with the man, we ain't making the movie."

That was not a friendly tone.

"Oh," I said.

So Marty and I agreed that that was our big problem. How do we have her move out of her husband's house (the very meaning of the title), hit the road, encounter an even more violent masculine figure, learn something about herself—who she is, what she wants—and end up in another man's house, without compromising the integrity of our work or what we were trying to say about a woman's search for independence?

That scene got rewritten and rewritten and we just couldn't get it. Finally it was the day before it was scheduled to be shot and still we had no scene. We rehearsed the next day's shooting at the end of each day. We were doing an improv on the scene trying to find the way I could give up my dream of going to Monterey and still have it be a good thing, not a surrender to patriarchal values, when suddenly Kris Kristofferson, playing David, said, "Come on, I'll take you to Monterey."

It was like the room was suddenly filled with sunshine.

"You will?" I said, feeling a smile break out on my face.

"Sure, I don't give a damn about that ranch. Come on."

We had broken through. We'd found the change in consciousness that everything in the movie led up to. The man was willing to support the woman in her aspirations. What she wanted was important enough for him to make a sacrifice. What a concept. Notice that I hadn't come up with that solution—"the man" did. Kris had to release me/Alice from the bondage of the old way of thinking. In real life, I wasn't there yet. Thank God for Kris. He was smart and awake enough to see what Alice—and I—needed.

This was a very powerful lesson for me. I was the shepherd of this film. I use that metaphor because there wasn't a title for what I was. I should have been executive producer. That's the title I would have gotten if I asked for it, but I didn't ask. "Oh, I don't need credit," I demurred. "My acting credit is enough." If I'd been executive producer, I would have been part of the deal when it was sold as a television series and had a piece of what John Calley told me were the "mega millions" Warner Bros. made from the television series, of which I had no part. So I was an actress in a film that I had brought to Warner's, sold to them, and hired the director. That's what a producer does. Why didn't I ask for credit? I was asleep—asleep to who I was and what my value was. I did not value myself enough to see that I was the engine that was moving this machine. I was getting this movie made about a woman awakening to the process of living her life as a primary, not a secondary, person. I was in the embryonic stage of giving birth to my own self in life, but it would still not have occurred to me that a man would suggest changing his life to support the woman's desires. After all, she was only a woman.

I had asked Marty what he knew about women, and he answered, "Nothing, but I'd like to learn." Well, me too.

One of the tasks of adulthood, in my view, is to look at what has been laid down in our brains early on and decide whether we want to keep that as part of our worldview. Certainly anything that got programmed in as a limitation of our possibilities needs to be examined and consciously kept or rejected. For instance, when I was a schoolgirl, I was in the glee club and was often asked to sing solos. When I was around twelve, I decided I'd like to take singing lessons and perhaps pursue singing as a career. I told this to my mother who said, "Let me hear you sing." I went to the piano in the dining room and opened the sheet music of "If I Loved You." I played the opening chords and sang the first line. From the kitchen came my mother's voice. "Awful!"

That was it! I couldn't carry a tune after that. My ear went dead. One of the things I wanted to accomplish in *Alice* was to unlock that block and reawaken my ability to sing. It didn't have to be great. Alice wasn't a great singer. I just wanted to be able to sing on key and deliver the song as best I could. I worked for months on that. The final recordings were a patch job of different takes, but I did it. I did my own singing and piano playing in the film with a lot of help and augmentation. But I did it.

David Susskind arrived in Tucson, where we were filming, and looked at all the dailies. He asked me to have dinner with him. I no longer remember what he said to me at dinner, but whatever it was, I reported it to Marty, who banned Susskind from the set. We never saw him again. From the very beginning, Marty exhibited that kind of authority. He has incredible energy on the set and gets everyone revved up to their most activated creative energy. Marty's sets sizzle with creativity. He decided to shoot the opening scene with Alice as a child in Monterey—as a kind of homage to *The Wizard of Oz.* When the film was cut together and he showed it to the powers that be at Warners, Marty came out seething. He told me they wanted to cut the first scene. He was pacing like a madman.

"What did you say?" I asked.

He stopped pacing and this young director making his first Hollywood studio film said pleasantly, "I told them to take my name off the picture." Of course that didn't happen. Marty knew how to play hardball. That's one of the things you learn on the streets of New York.

The Exorcist opened in December 1973. Billy and I attended a sneak preview in Los Angeles before the official opening. As soon as the lights dimmed, we grabbed each other's hand and held on tight throughout the film. We knew very quickly that the film worked. The audience collectively held its breath and exhaled together at the end of a scary scene. When they had to laugh to stabilize their equilibrium, we knew we had accomplished something powerful. They were scared. But nothing prepared us for the enormous reception the film received when it was released. I remember being in the kitchen of my Hollywood house making coffee as the early news on television showed people lining up for four hours in a blizzard in Montreal waiting for the movie theater to open.

While I was shooting *Alice*, *The Exorcist* opened in Tucson. I decided to invite the crew to see it on our day off and have dinner afterward. I had heard about people fainting during the film, but I assumed it was during one of the scarier scenes. It was at this screening that I saw they were fainting at the medical procedure where Linda gets a needle in her neck and blood squirts out. At that moment a woman got up from her seat, ran up the aisle, teetered, and fell to the ground. I got up and ran to her. She was out cold. Other people came and stood around us. I was kneeling beside her, holding her hand in mine and tapping it, trying to get her to wake up. Soon I saw her eyelids flutter and I knew she was about to regain consciousness. Then I realized: This woman is going to open her eyes and the first thing she sees will be my face! She's going to think she's died and gone to hell! I quickly turned to the nearest stranger and said, "Here, take her hand!" I slipped away quickly before she could see me.

I was nominated for an Oscar for *The Exorcist* while I was shooting *Alice*, but I assumed I wouldn't go to the ceremony because of my schedule. I was in every scene but two in *Alice*, and I was working fourteen hours a day, six days a week, but John Calley insisted I go and sent the Warner Bros. jet for me.

The film garnered ten nominations, including Best Director, Best Picture, Best Supporting Actor for Jason Miller, and Best Supporting

Actress for Linda Blair. Billy told me there was an intense telephone campaign waged by the more conservative members of the Academy who were shocked by the film. I wasn't sure this rumor was true, but Billy believed it. Anyway, none of us won except Blatty for Best Screenplay, and Robert Knudson and Christopher Newman for Best Sound.

In the Golden Globes we did better—Billy won Best Director, the film got Best Picture, and Linda got Best Supporting Actress. Blatty won this one, too, for his screenplay. Max von Sydow and I were both nominated for an award, but neither of us won. We got zilch.

But the film is a classic and has lasted longer and is shown more often today than any of the films we were in competition with at that time.

There was a scene in *Alice Doesn't Live Here Anymore* in which I'm having an affair with Ben Eberhardt (played by Harvey Keitel). His young wife (Lane Bradbury) comes to see me and asks me not to continue because he's been missing work and they need the money for doctor bills for their baby. In the midst of this, Ben appears, breaks through the door, and punches and kicks his wife out the door. Then he grabs me and threatens to break my jaw. Harvey was absolutely terrifying in this scene. I didn't have to act. As a matter of fact, I had a hard time controlling myself through the scene. It was like too many scenes in my life with my mother, Lou, and then Neil. It triggered a terror that was still in me. We were working on the scene all day from different angles, so I tried to distract myself between setups.

To calm myself, I decided to read a script I'd been given that was written by the wife of a producer. It was a chronicle of what it was like to be married to a man who was constantly having affairs with young actresses. This producer was a man, very powerful in Hollywood, who several years before had propositioned me. He said if I went to bed with him, he would try to get me a role in a film. I'd turned him down, but sitting on the stage reading his wife's story, I felt the whole sexual culture come crashing down on me. I identified with her, with the young actresses, with the wife of Ben Eberhardt, with Alice, who was having an affair with a man she didn't know was married. All of Neil's affairs were present in the moment—all of the liaisons I'd had with men I knew were married, all the times I'd gone on location and seen crew guys who were married set up housekeeping with the local waitresses while they were away from their wives, and all the other forms of cheating and infidelity were rising up from that denial, and they were screaming at me, pounding me, laughing maniacally at me like the Furies. And the penalty for speaking the truth was violence. When I accused Neil of things that were simply true, he raged at me and called me oppressive. All of this was raining in on me and I couldn't suppress it. I was overwhelmed by the breakthrough of that truth. Husbands cheated on wives and women were supposed not to see it, and if we did we were smashed in the face.

These were not thoughts I had during the scene, they were feelings that were erupting out of control, against my will. We shot the master, several medium shots, and a few closeups. I was a wreck. Harvey was beyond scary. I went to the makeup trailer to get my makeup repaired as it was at the beginning of the scene for a different angle. Bob Westmoreland, the makeup artist, managed to put my face back together, but it wouldn't hold. I started crying again. Soon my mascara was off, my eyes were red and swollen. We tried again, but soon gave up. I couldn't stop. I was trembling, sobbing, then laughing—I was hysterical. A whole lifetime's worth of tears was coming out. After an hour and a half, I was nearly calm enough to try again when Toby Rafelson entered the room. Toby had lost her beloved daughter, Julie, the previous year. I knew she had come in to comfort me, but I shouted at her, "Oh no, Toby. I can't see you." As the tears started smearing what was left of my mascara, I shouted, "Go out. Go out." Toby hurried back out the door. But it was too late. I was off again. Soon we just had to call it a day. They shot what they could without me and I was sent home.

That summer of '74, I bought the rights to a book called *Silence of the North* by Olive Frederickson. It would take me five years to get it made. My agency found me a producer to be my partner named Murray Shostak.

When we had agreed on most all points, Murray said to me, holding up an admonishing finger, "But Ellen, I must have final word."

It is the same thing Neil said to me before we got married, "I must win on a bump."

I would love to write that I said, "No, Murray, this is my project. I brought it to you. I must be executive producer and have final word. If you can't live with that, we can't be in business together."

But I didn't. I nodded my head to "the man" demurely and turned my project over to him.

We learn from our mistakes. This was one of mine that I repeated over and over until I got it right. I've heard it said that when you make a mistake and don't learn from it, the next time you have to repeat that lesson, it will be even harder. How many times was I going to have to learn not to turn my power over to a man just because he was a man? How many times? Too many.

I had gone to Lee Strasberg to learn how to act and he taught me well. That's what I knew how to do. On the stage I did not surrender. I stood my ground. I functioned well. It was offstage that was the problem; in life, in relationships. There I had no such teacher. I grow impatient with myself as I write this. Why did you need a teacher, I want to shout at myself back then. Wasn't life itself your teacher? Couldn't you figure it out for yourself? But it is that inner voice, that harsh, critical, disapproving voice that still speaks in me, that was always my enemy. I still wrestle with it even though I have learned to limit its power over me. You can slay the enemy outside, but when it is within, you can't kill it without killing yourself. You must learn to master it. Hazrat Inayat Khan wrote a wonderful book about the three paths of spiritual life: the path of the prophet, the path of the martyr, and the path of the master. I had no aptitude for either martyrdom or prophecy. It seems I was going to have to learn mastery. And the spiritual warrior's greatest challenge is mastery of self.

While I shot *Alice*, I was reading Studs Terkel's book *Working*. It was a collection of interviews with different kinds of people about their jobs and their attitudes toward working. I remember one man who was a bricklayer said that he had to be careful how he laid each brick. Each one had to be perfectly aligned with the next. If he allowed even one brick slightly out of line, it would bother him to the point that he would drive his car for blocks out of his way to avoid that brick. That kind of integrity is part of us all. And when it gets lost or falls away, it bespeaks of a loss of grace that is innate in us. I see it on sets today. Young actors don't study at the same level of intensity that my generation did. Of course, there are wonderful exceptions to this, but in my experience, the attitude toward work has suffered in the last twenty years. And it's not just in acting. Most professionals I talk to are reporting the same thing: doctors, musicians, workers of all kinds. Terkel's book made me want to put in a scene where someone compliments Alice on being good at her job. When she first had to take a job as a waitress, she felt it was demeaning, but I wanted to show her having pride in her work after a while, whatever her work was. We shot the scene and it was in the first cut, but it didn't make final cut. The first cut was three hours long and many of our "favorite darlings," as Tennessee Williams said, had to go. When I look at the film, I still miss that scene because the setup remains. When Alice says she took a job as a waitress, she covers her face in shame, as though being a waitress or any job at all is demeaning in itself, when truly the only demeaning thing is to do a bad job at whatever you are doing. That's where the disgrace is, not in the job itself.

Kris Kristofferson had made only one other film and just couldn't accept the fact that he was an actor as well as a musician. After every take he would cringe. One time after one of his close-ups, he winced and said, "Oh man, that was dog shit."

"What was?" I said.

"The look I had on my face," he answered, cringing more.

"Well, what are you looking at your face for? Why aren't you looking at mine?"

Light streamed through his intelligent eyes.

"Let's do one more, Marty," he called out.

Then I saw him look at me in the scene and actually connect. He was wonderful.

Kris was a Rhodes scholar and a very popular musician. While we were in Tucson, he gave a concert. The next day I asked him how it went.

"Bad," he replied.

"What was bad?"

"Everything," he laughed and winced. "My playing, my singing."

"Wait a minute," I said. "You can't act. You can't sing and you can't play the guitar. What can you do?"

"I'm a poet," he said. No wince there. He truly was a poet and he knew it.

Kris and I had a scene together in his kitchen after Alice and David have made love for the first time and are slightly tipsy from wine and giddy from sex. Marty had us improvise the scene and I told a story about my brother Jack and me when we were kids. Kris and I were very relaxed in this scene together. For me, it's the best scene in the film; the most real and the best example of what Marty's kind of directing can do. The actors are really alive in the scene, nothing about the scene feels static, tight, or rehearsed. That's the level of reality I aim for and just once in a while, the script, the director, the actors, and the camera are all in sync and can strike just the right chord.

My son Jeff played the next-door neighbor's son, Harold. My friend Lelia Goldoni played his mother. In the film, coming home from my husband's funeral, as I got out of the backseat of the car, Jeff was in front. I touched his shoulder and ad-libbed, "Bye, Harold."

Jeff, without missing a beat, said right back, "Bye, Alice." It was so strange to hear my own son call me Alice. The Fondas, the Redgraves, the Barrymores must experience that all the time. But it was just one treasured moment for me. When I look at the film these many years later, it still touches my heart.

We finished the picture and headed home. When Jeff went back to school he found new friendships had been formed, new cliques assembled. He was an outsider. He told me that he didn't want to go on location with me anymore. He wanted to stay in school. That was sad news for me, but Jeff was old enough to make that kind of choice and I had to honor it.

Around this time, Lee Strasberg asked me to serve on the board of directors at the Actors Studio. He also asked me to begin to moderate the acting sessions. I didn't feel capable of doing that, but he insisted. I owed so much to him and the Studio, I wouldn't say no. But I was one wobbly moderator when I started. One day I said to Lee, "Sometimes when I'm talking to an actor, I think of something I want to suggest to them and then I go, Wait—is that 'Method'? I don't think it is."

Lee answered, "Always rely on your own experience, dahling, and you can't go wrong." That is the best advice I ever got from him or anyone else.

J. W. Dunne says that the brain is a machine for the education of the soul. And that our experiences are what lay down the tracks in the brain with which to teach our soul. To me, experience is both a teacher for the soul and a tool to use in teaching others.

In September, back in my home on the Hudson, Neil found me. I'm not sure how, but he did. He was ranting. He claimed he'd seen a bus with a number on it that was the first three numbers of our address in Hollywood and two of the numbers from our phone number in New York. He was sure that this was a message from me that I wanted to talk to him. I assured him that I didn't and asked him to leave. When he refused, I called the police. This was the beginning of a pattern that lasted for five more years. He would arrive any time, day or night, in an agitated state, sometimes declaring his love and wanting me back; sometimes to beg my forgiveness; and sometimes to threaten my life. It always ended with the police coming to take him away. Sometimes they put him on a bus for Manhattan. Sometimes he would be so unmanageable, they would take him to the state psychiatric hospital, where he stayed until he calmed down and then they'd release him. Soon he'd be back and we'd start all over again.

There was a bizarre contrast between the success and glamour of my public life and the terror and trauma of my private life. I needed something to help me stabilize the two extremes. A call came inviting me to visit Iran.

I'd always been drawn to the poetry and mysticism of the Middle East. I was asked to be a member of the American contingent to the Tehran Film Festival. The Shah had inaugurated the festival just a year before and my friend Fred Haines's film of *Steppenwolf* was to be in competition. I also knew there was a strong Sufi presence in Iran and I felt excited to connect with the people there. I said yes.

I had no plan for how to find a Sufi group. I suppose I might have asked Pir Vilayat or Reshad, but I'd never heard either of them mention connections in Iran, although they often spoke of groups in Turkey and India. Besides, I had faith in the saying, "When the student is ready, the teacher appears." I knew I was ready for my next step, whatever that was. I counted on the teacher appearing.

I took Henry with me. The American contingent to the festival included the director John Frankenheimer and his wife, John Forsythe and his wife, and Ron Ely, the tall blond Adonis who played Tarzan, which was the most popular show on Iranian television at the time. Everywhere masses of children followed him down the street making the Tarzan call. Police had to escort us to control the crowds, who were begging Ron to make the Tarzan call, but he just smiled at them. Finally I asked him why he didn't satisfy their wish. He shrugged his massive shoulders and said, "I can't."

"What do you mean?" I asked.

He whispered in a helpless voice, "I'm dubbed by a Swiss yodeler."

One of the film festival officials told me that *The Exorcist* had not played in Iran because each of the three times they tried to dub it, the dubbing cast got too frightened and couldn't complete it.

After a few days in Tehran, we were taken to the ruins of the ancient city of Persepolis. Parts of the city had been restored, but other parts were still an archeological dig that looked eerily like the opening scene of *The Exorcist*. Our group was led into an ancient tomb and John Frankenheimer looked at me and said, "It's just too spooky being here with you." The group laughed uncomfortably, but soon hurried out of the tomb.

Next we visited Isfahan. It was astonishing. I saw people in tribal robes with bright red hair. My guide told me they were a tribe of Jews who had migrated to Iran hundreds of years ago and managed to keep their ethnicity intact over the centuries.

Walking down the street, I stopped at a red light. Next to me stood a shepherd with his entire flock waiting for the light to change. The man was dressed in a robe as in biblical times, with a modern suit jacket over it. Two eras met in this instant as we waited for the light to change. I noticed a stick in his hands lightly touching the shoulder of one of the sheep. When the light changed, he lifted the stick an inch or two and immediately the sheep started off across the thoroughfare; the rest of the flock following like . . . well, like sheep.

In Isfahan, I stayed at the Shah Abbas, an old graceful hotel built around a central court that was a magnificent garden. Peacocks, the symbol of the Shah's lineage, walked slowly around it, lifting their feet high and unfurling their gorgeous tails. At night I heard a lone bird sing a haunting song from the silence of the garden. I recognized it immediately—it was a nightingale. You need not have heard that song ever before in order to recognize it. Even the first time, it's like an old memory rising from our long-forgotten home in paradise.

The people I met in Iran were some of the most sophisticated, cultured and gracious I've ever known. From them I learned that when the Arabs conquered that part of the world, only Iran maintained its original Persian identity. The people speak of their Persian heritage with pride, and it is this connection to the Persians, one of the most advanced peoples of the ancient world, that sustains them, no matter their ruler.

Iran is the only place I've ever visited where the poet is the most exalted being. When a revered poet dies, he is not buried in a cemetery, but his tomb is placed in a public garden where people come to visit and sit and listen to his poetry being read, softly, in Farsi. I visited Hafiz's tomb in Shiraz where the pathway to the tomb was lined on either side with every variety of rose, trimmed at nose height so that as you walked, roses gently brushed your cheeks and you inhaled their intoxicating scent, each aroma slightly different from the one before. At the end of the path I entered an open-air garden with a long rectangular reflecting pool. Sitting on a worn stone bench, I watched in the dark blue water of the pool the white clouds move across the sky, making changing patterns of reflected light in the deep shadows.

Back in Tehran the festival was nearing its close and I still hadn't connected with any Sufis, although I'd asked all the Persian people I met if they knew any. No one seemed to. I knew they were there, I just didn't know where to find them. Sufism originated as the mystical branch of Islam, the inner esoteric teaching, therefore there are no Sufi temples or mosques to happen across on the street. There is usually just a private group led by a particular teacher, most often in his home.

Finally, on December 4, the festival ended in a huge and rare snowstorm. We were scheduled to leave on December 5. Henry and I planned to fly to Jerusalem. I was so disappointed that I had failed to connect with a Sufi group. We got up on December 5, packed and went downstairs to leave. The hotel lobby was a riot. People were milling about, talking excitedly. The airport was closed. The roof had collapsed under the weight of the snow. Nobody could leave Iran until it was repaired. No one knew how long that would take. I recognized surrender time when I saw it and I asked if we could keep our rooms. We could. We cancelled our hotel in Jerusalem and unpacked our bags. That night Fred and Francey Haines asked us to join them and an American journalist at a Persian vaudeville club. We sat in the balcony and watched the acts. With our party was a Persian woman named Sharoo. One of the acts was a comic in a long white woolen robe.

The audience was laughing happily at his jokes. I asked Sharoo to translate. She said it was very difficult to translate because his jokes were inside jokes for Persians. She said, "This man is a dervish. I don't know if you know about that."

"Yes," I exclaimed. "You mean he is a Sufi?"

She was surprised to hear that an actress was initiated into a Sufi group in America. She then told me she was with a group in Tehran and would be glad to introduce me to her teacher the following day.

The next day was December 7, 1974, my forty-second birthday.

In the afternoon Sharoo took Henry and me to meet Dr. Elahi, known as Shah Bahram. He and his family lived in a beautiful, quietly elegant house. We were shown into an upstairs room, where a small group of people was gathered around a low round table. Nescafé was prepared and served in small cups. Shah Bahram was a man in his forties who had an air of sophistication, grace, and focused energy.

Henry and I were treated as honored guests, which is usual in any Persian home, and also is a Sufi tradition. Over the next few days I was to learn Dr. Elahi's story. He grew up in this house with his older brother and his younger brother. His father, Nur Ali, was Pir, or teacher, of a Sufi group known as Ahl-i Haqq. Nur Ali, now called after his death Hazrat Elahu, had died the previous October without naming a successor. Everyone waited for a sign to come, signaling who that would be. The assumption was that it would be the eldest son. Finally, months after Hazrat Elahu's death, his sister had a dream wherein Hazrat Elahu appeared and named his middle son, Dr. Elahi, who was living in Paris with his wife and children and teaching surgery at the Sorbonne. Dr. Elahi promptly left Paris, moved back to Tehran with his family, and became the spiritual leader of this dedicated group.

Dr. Elahi spoke softly to us, "I do not care if you accept me as a teacher or not, but because you are here, I would like you to leave here today with at least the knowledge of how to recognize a real teacher." He said, "First of all, a real teacher will be an example of his teaching. He will not say one thing and live another way. What he tells you that you must do, he is already doing himself. Also a real teacher's teaching will show in the lives of the people around him. As Jesus said, 'By his fruits ye shall know him.'

"A real teacher will really solve problems. For instance, if a man comes to the teacher and tells him that he is in love with a woman, but she is already married, by the time the man leaves, he will no longer love the woman."

Then Dr. Elahi said, "If you are interested in the work we do, I ask you to give up five things: smoking (anything), tea, pork, alcohol, and judging." It was a very strange list. Tea was easy; I was still drinking coffee. Pork was not difficult because I wasn't a big meat eater. Smoking was more difficult because, although I'd given up cigarettes by then, I still smoked grass. That one took real effort. So did alcohol. I'd had two vodkas at lunch, not realizing they were my last. In the coming year I was about to face the most successful year of my life, winning both the Oscar and the Tony, and other awards as well. There were countless parties and celebrations. And I attended them all without one sip of champagne or any other stimulant. I was absolutely sober; therefore I was able to avoid getting caught up in the bubbly atmosphere that enormous success splashes over your inflating ego.

But it was the fifth thing that Dr. Elahi asked me to give up that required true spiritual effort. I tried not to be judgmental, but I caught myself over and over again not only judging others, but I had a deep pattern of judging myself. If a person hits us over the head and takes our money, are we not to get angry, call the police, and call him a thief? I couldn't quite understand it. As a matter of fact, it was nearly a year later, in a conversation with Pir Vilayat, that he helped me to define the difference between judging and discernment.

You discern when a person cheats you or steals from you. You report him or her; you avoid contact with him/her. You don't put yourself in a position where that person can rob you or cheat you again, but you don't judge that person. It is not our job to judge each other because we don't have all the facts or information about the person's karma. They act out their own destiny and make their own mistakes that they will either learn from or not, but that is their path, not ours. We can't even judge ourselves. Who knows what mistakes we need to make in order to learn the lessons we came here to learn? And if we learn them, how are we to judge what we had to go through to come into the light of understanding?

The night before we left Tehran, we attended the Zikr, a Sufi spiritual practice that translates as "remembrance of God." The women were in a separate room from the men, but with the connecting doors open between us. There were around fifty women in our room and seventy-five men in the larger room. The musicians were also in the room with the men, but right next to the open door between us. They started playing softly and slowly the background rhythms for the Zikr. The people began the prayer quietly at first—*La ilaha ill' allah hu*—There is no God but God. I had been taught the Zikr by Reshad in London and had done it for my morning practice when I was on the mountain at Pir Vilayat's camp. As the chant went on, the musicians increased the tempo and the volume. The intensity of the prayer grew. It felt like the energy was rising to the breaking point; that something would erupt. The women around me were swaying and many were crying. I couldn't keep my eyes closed. It felt strangely exciting, but somehow dangerous. Then just as it reached the point that I felt the whole room could explode, the musicians decrescendoed and slowly the energy was brought back down and we reentered a more normal state. I had never taken part in a collective energy that moved to that height of intensity. I felt exhilarated, mystified, unsettled, and slightly scared. All around me women were crying, and I could see they'd had a profound experience.

Soon a barefoot servant came in dressed in a white tunic and tight white pants laced around his legs. He carried a basket of fruit and gave two oranges to each woman to bring home to her children. The women received the fruit from this man as though he were a high dignitary. He presented the fruit like an offering and they bowed their heads as he placed it in their hands. Something about this man compelled me to watch him as he moved about the room. I didn't have an opportunity to ask about him until the following year, when I returned to Iran for my second visit.

As we filed out of the prayer room, the three sons of Hazrat Elahu stood at the door saying good-bye to each of the participants. Dr. Elahi introduced me first to his older brother, a kindly and quiet-looking man. Then I met the younger brother, who was strikingly beautiful, as one could imagine Jesus looked if pictured with the black hair and dark eyes he probably had instead of the blond, blue-eyed image passed to us through the German tradition. As he held my hand and pierced me with his gaze, another man who was leaving bent to the ground and kissed the shoes of the man whose eyes I was looking into. Growing up as an American in a democracy, I was both startled and slightly uncomfortable to see this man on his knees kissing another's shoes. But the eyes I was looking into did not flinch. They continued to hold mine. I could not interpret his gaze, but I felt sure he was reading my discomfort and did nothing to assuage it. It was mine to deal with. I was the one seeking my own path far from home. Not him. He was where he belonged. Was I? I wasn't sure. But I was intrigued with these people and asked the film festival organizers to invite me back the following year.

After the Zikr, Dr. Elahi told me that his aunt would like to meet me. This was the sister of Hazrat Elahu who had the dream wherein it was announced who would be the successor. She was bedridden and few people got to see her. She was highly regarded by all of the members of the group, and it was a great honor to be invited into her bedroom. Sharoo and a few others were allowed to attend with me. We were ushered into her bedroom. She was sitting up in bed fully clothed. The group stood around her bed and she spoke in Farsi. She took my hands and spoke a few sentences. Soon we took our leave so as not to tire her. Outside her room, Dr. Elahi said to me, "She said that the Master is very pleased that you have come." "The Master" is how they affectionately referred to Hazrat Elahu. One assumes he continued to appear in her dreams.

I tried to be open to what was happening, but I also didn't want to romanticize it. I felt drawn to these people and, at the same time, unsure that I belonged there. I just knew I wanted to know more.

We prepared to leave Tehran. Henry had been with me at all of the meetings and I could see that he responded to Dr. Elahi, but after the very first meeting, he grew very moody and went into one of his withdrawals from me. We barely exchanged words, although we were together twenty-four hours a day. On December 10, we flew the eighteen hours back to New York in complete silence. At JFK Airport, Jeff was waiting for me with his tutor. Henry walked away and got a taxi. That was it. At our first meeting, Dr. Elahi had said, "If a man comes to a real teacher and says he's in love with a woman, but she's married, by the time he leaves the teacher, he won't be in love with the woman anymore." I'd been married three times. Henry was Catholic. I think he took Dr. Elahi's example to heart. Our push me/pull you, on again/off again troubled relationship was over.

After the success of *The Exorcist* and filming *Alice*, I decided it was time to return to the stage. I put out word that I was looking for a play, and Kitty

Hawks, daughter of Howard Hawks and who was an agent at that time, sent me *Same Time, Next Year* by Bernard Slade. I loved the play and agreed to do it. Upon my return from Iran, the producer, Mort Gottlieb, told me they'd selected Charles Grodin as my partner and asked that we meet to see if we liked each other, as the play was about a twenty-five-year love affair, and had only these two roles.

As I remember it, I drove into Manhattan, picked up Charles, and drove him out to my house on the Hudson River for the afternoon. Charles and I liked each other immediately and decided that we highly approved of the casting. When it was time to drive him back to his apartment, I said, "There's just one thing more you should know about me. I have an ex-husband who is schizophrenic and stalks me. He could appear at any time and the police need to be called to take him away."

Charles, who is one of the funniest people I've ever known, looked at me with a face of wonder and said, "See now, what you just said has erased everything you've said today."

My last diary entry for 1974 was on December 19:

> *Had meeting with Chuck Grodin, who is very smart, talented, funny and I think we will do just fine together.*
>
> *Went to Rudolf Steiner's to see* The Nativity. *Jeff was "the first shepherd." Once he made a mistake and said, "Whoops." Everyone laughed. It was the highlight of the night.*
>
> *I am feeling very good about not smoking or drinking. As a matter of fact, I feel like I am finally becoming me.*

Forty-two years old and it is the first time in all these notebooks and diaries that I wrote a sentence like that: *I am finally becoming me.* What I see now is that the feeling of connectedness to self only came to me when I stopped smoking and drinking. Those habits that had made me feel more at ease socially were the very things that were keeping me from being comfortable with myself.

But I had a long way to go before I understood the difference between myself and the Self.

We began rehearsals for *Same Time, Next Year* on January 20, 1975. We were upstairs in the old rehearsal hall of the New Amsterdam Theater on 42nd Street, before it was refurbished. Gene Saks was directing. From the start, Charles and I wrangled with the author, Bernard Slade. It was a very funny play, but it was about a long-term extramarital affair. Doris and George are married to others, yet they meet one weekend a year for twenty-five years. It was a lot to expect an audience of mostly married people to accept. Onstage we often talked about our spouses, Helen and Harry, who would prove to be very important offstage characters. One insensitive remark about either of our spouses and we could lose the audience's sympathy. It was very tricky. I could sense when we were headed for dangerous territory, but Charles was even more sensitive to that than I, so much of our rehearsal time was spent haggling over this issue. One day, as Charles and I were standing onstage arguing with Bernie, we were interrupted by the sudden appearance of Neil, ranting and raving.

I don't know how he found out where rehearsals were or how he found his way upstairs in this otherwise closed theater, but as crazy as he was, he could always find me. The production stage manager grabbed Neil and ushered him out. Morty Gottlieb, the producer, then took elaborate precautions to secure the space. I didn't know what they were, but I was assured "not to worry, it won't happen again."

Less than a week after we began our rehearsals, *Alice* opened to marvelous reviews. After lunch that day, as I sat quietly onstage waiting for everyone else to return, an image rose in my mind of me sitting in a little restaurant in Dallas on Thanksgiving, staring down at my hamburger. Now here I was, twenty-five years later, in rehearsal for a Broadway show, and the movie I put together on its way to being a success. I actually had some money in the bank; I felt I was gaining some stability in my life. For the moment, I did. Just for a moment.

In mid-February we left for Boston for the out-of-town run of *Same Time, Next Year*. We had only one day of rehearsal onstage with the actual furniture. In rehearsal, you usually work on a bare stage with tape on the floor to indicate walls and doors, and hard straight chairs with makeshift tables; it's always a shock to make the transition to the set. The real furniture feels totally different from what your body has adjusted to; everything feels bigger, and very awkward. We stumbled through our only rehearsal before opening, with Bernie pacing in the back of the theater. At the end, he came quickly down the aisle and blurted, "The rhythms are all off."

"It's our first time onstage!" I said. "Will you get out of here and let us work!"

He took his nervous stomach and playwright's tortured soul back up the aisle. Gene Saks calmed us down and gave us notes. We were in pretty good shape to open, except for one thing: the first-scene curtain line. The first scene takes place the morning after George and Doris have made love for the first time. They have just met the night before and are feeling guilty. During the course of the scene, as they express their guilt and talk about their marriages, they actually get to know each other and fall in love. The scene had to end with a setup for all that follows and it had to be funny. No laugh on the first-scene curtain line in a comedy is not a good thing. We opened without the laugh and spent the next two weeks looking for it. Bernie wrote a new line for each performance. No laugh. Gene Saks suggested a line. No laugh. Charles came up with several. No laugh. I suggested a line: As we say good-bye, staring into each other's eyes, we suddenly get up and head for the bed, and I say, "Okay! But this is the last time." Nobody liked it. We didn't even try it.

The reviews in Boston were fantastic. Now we were ready for New York . . . except for the first-scene curtain. Finally, when we had exhausted everybody else's lines, for the last performance in Boston they agreed to try mine. At last, we got a laugh. In New York for opening night, Bernie gave me a gift of a beautiful antique silver box. On the bottom it was engraved from Bernie to me, ELLEN BURSTYN, LINEWRIGHT. When I read it, he said, "You're not a playwright, but you are a linewright."

Charles Grodin is one of the most eccentric, talented people I've ever known. We had a great time playing together. Our first onstage kiss came in the second scene. In rehearsal we would play the scene up to the moment of the kiss, then Charles would stop and say, "And then I kiss her."

He refrained from kissing me until the first performance before a live audience in Boston. Then he kissed me and he really did it. I had the sensation of an electric charge moving from where our lips met, down my body, and landing smack in my number-two chakra! When we parted lips, I stood there stunned for a moment with my lips hanging out for more. The audience laughed at my great acting. But I wasn't acting. I'd just fallen in love and it showed. After the scene, I passed Charles behind the flats and looked at him for any sign that he felt the same thing. He looked at me frankly and said, "We'll go out after the show." I nodded. He knew. We went out afterward. I knew I was in trouble. The show felt like a hit. Charles was an extremely complex, sensitive and, as I said, *very* eccentric fellow. There was no way we could have a relationship and not have it be a stormy one. There's nothing worse than having to be in love with someone onstage that you've just had a fight with offstage. I told Charles how I was feeling and what I thought about it. I suggested we have our love affair *only* onstage. He agreed, and that's what we did.

When I had dinner with Walter Matthau and his wife, Carol, years later, they talked about *Same Time, Next Year.* Walter told me that the word around town at that time was that Charles and I were in love. Walter had gotten their tickets through his agent, who asked him the next day, "What does that look like to you?" And Walter answered, "It looks like love." His agent said, "That's what it looks like to me, too."

Well, it *was* love, but only onstage. I think it was one of the reasons people responded so well to the show. It wasn't exactly a performance. To me, emotions are an energy and if you can bring that love energy onstage, it reaches out into the theater. The audience sat watching *Same Time, Next Year* and felt like they were "in love." And they were.

When we got to New York for the first previews, I was worried about running into Neil. Even though the producer had told me not to worry, I couldn't shake the feeling that Neil could appear at any time. Our first matinee in New York, Charles and I were onstage just before the end of the first act, standing face to face in a quiet moment, when out of the silence and blackness of the house came Neil's voice shouting, "Ellen." Just once. But that was enough. Suddenly the blackness of the house was alive with menace. He could shout more. He could run up on the stage. He could have a gun. We couldn't see him, but he could see us. We were sitting ducks.

Charles and I stared at each other in terror. Our eyes widened. We continued the lines of Doris and George with our mouths, but our eyes were full of sheer panic.

Soon the scene was over and the lights went out. Shaking, we hurried offstage to the stage manager's podium. "It's okay," he said. "It's under control. We couldn't legally refuse to sell him a ticket until he made a scene. Now that he has, we can refuse to ever admit him again. We placed him in the top row of the balcony. We had him surrounded on all sides with security. As soon as he called your name, they hustled him out of there. It's okay now. He'll never get in again."

That's when I learned that since Neil's intrusion into the rehearsal hall, we'd had security at all times. Plainclothes detectives were outside the theater at every performance. Opening night, as I entered the party with Charles after the show, I was surrounded by bodyguards dressed in tuxedos.

The opening-night performance went well up until the last moment. In the last scene, George comes to say that his wife has died. He wants me to leave Harry and marry him. If I don't, he says he will marry an old friend of his named Connie. I refuse and we say good-bye for the last time. It's over, he's never coming back. When he leaves, it's important the audience really believes he's gone and they feel the loss of the relationship. Then George bursts back in the room, admitting he's lied. There is no Connie. He was just trying to get me. We laugh. The audience laughs with tears still on their faces from thinking the play ended with the love affair ending. All through Boston and the previews in New York, whenever we got to that final good-bye, I cried. I believed it in the moment and never had to prepare any kind of sense memory or other device to make me cry. Suddenly, on opening night, we got to that moment and I had no tears. Nothing. I was dry. George is standing at the door saying his final lines and I'm empty. Nothing, and I've got no acting technique prepared to prod me. So this is what I did. I thought, *Oh my God! I'm dry. I've got nothing. It's opening night. And this is the climax of the whole play and I'm ruining it. The critics are here.*

They'll give us bad reviews and we'll close. So I'm really saying good-bye. Not to George. To Charles. Our love affair in this play is over. And I've done it. I've ruined the whole thing. I started bawling like a baby. The audience believed it was over. They started crying. George popped back in the door. The audience laughed with tears still on their cheeks. Charles and I embraced. The curtain came down. The audience cheered. We took our bows together. We never took single bows. As we stood looking out at the audience, we saw our children—Jeff, and Charles's daughter, Marion—leap to their feet and applaud us as we threw them kisses. The show ran for three and a half years.

Charles and I weren't in it for the whole run. Our contracts were for six months. That's the longest I've ever done one play. And frankly, I found that by the fifth month of eight performances a week, I was having a difficult time keeping it fresh. I managed, but it took all my effort not to fall into mechanical acting. I like to keep growing in a role as long as I'm doing it. For me, opening night is just the beginning. I like to find new ideas, deeper feelings, better ways to express the character, at every performance. I don't always succeed. I have an off night sometimes, but it is the intention that matters to me. Acting is my profession and my art form, but it is also my way; my spiritual way in the world. Sufism is not a path of renunciation. It is a path of doing your spiritual work in the world. My spiritual commitment is to do my best effort at all times, whether I am acting onstage or serving in a soup kitchen. I give everything I can possibly give. For me, giving is the vehicle of expressing the spirit within and to give a gift that is anything but your best is to disdain the divine.

So it was in this play that I had the longest opportunity to test my spiritual courage and commitment, not just to my work, but in "the work."

The trappings of success are in fact a trap. All the rave reviews for *Alice* meant that the press wanted to interview me to the point of distraction from my work in the play. I didn't read the reviews, but years later (much to my surprise) I saw a scrapbook my mother had put together of my press for this period. One said, "Ellen Burstyn is the hottest thing since aluminum siding."

I don't think they were referring solely to my performance. It was because *Alice* was the first picture to give voice to the emerging liberation of the modern American woman. We were awakening from centuries of sleep-walking to the dictates of the patriarchy, and *Alice* was the first film that showed just how it happened to one woman. Also the fact that I'd introduced the project to Warner Bros., then brought in the unknown director Martin Scorsese, who was soon to become a major force in American cinema, added to the fact that Marty liked to improvise and that certain events in my life were integrated into Bob Getchell's brilliant script—put it all together and the press gave me credit for everything but hanging the lights.

Time magazine even managed to hear about my breakdown in tears after the scene with Harvey Keitel, when we had to stop shooting due to my hysteria. They wrote about it in their review as though that incident was from my life. Bob Getchell called the theater in Boston to complain. He said, "Ellen, you know that scene was exactly as I wrote it." And it was. But it was too late. A woman getting a film made from a woman's point of view was such a big story in 1975 that it was a watershed that opened up possibilities for other women filmmakers. That was great, but it was also embarrassing that everybody else's contribution got short-changed.

When we learned that I'd been nominated for an Oscar for *Alice*, Mort Gottlieb thought I should fly to Los Angeles for the ceremony and take a day off to fly back. That would mean that people who'd waited for weeks to see the show would see the understudy. The people were expecting to see Charles and me, and I hated to disappoint them. I thought about it carefully and decided that it wasn't right for me to go. I must confess that this moral high ground was not so difficult for me to take because I have very ambivalent feelings about awards and award shows. Part of my character loves to put on a pretty dress and go out on the red carpet and shine my false smile for the cameras. But I don't consider that the best part of me or the deepest or most real. So when there's a choice, I have to go with my better self. There were probably other factors, too, like guilt regarding my success and the ongoing tragedy of Neil's mental illness.

After the performance that night, Jeff and I went over to Barbara and Ira Friedlander's apartment and watched the Academy Awards on television. I'd asked Marty Scorsese to accept should I win, and when my name was called, everyone in the room started screaming and hugging me and slapping me on the back, so I never heard what he said.

I was very pleased with the awards that year. My friend Francis Coppola won many awards for *The Godfather Part II,* and though Lee Strasberg didn't win for his performance in that film, he lost to his student, Bob De Niro. But best of all, Art Carney won for Best Actor in *Harry and Tonto,* in which I played Art's daughter. After *The Exorcist,* Paul Mazursky had called me and said, "I wrote a part for you in my next film. It's called *Harry and Tonto,* but it's not a huge role. Maybe now you're too big and might not want to play it."

I said, "Not at all. I think everyone should do whatever role interests them, no matter the size. Send it to me." When he told me it was to play Art Carney's daughter, I knew I wanted to do it. Now on the same night I won my Oscar, my old friend from the Jackie Gleason show won his for *Harry and Tonto.*

Was I surprised that I won? Not really. This was my third nomination. The picture was a huge success. I was getting tons of publicity for being on Broadway at the same time. As I remember it now, I expected to win that year. But once I did win, I got very quiet inside. When the awards were over, I went into Barbara and Ira's small dark meditation room, lit a candle, and sat for half an hour with closed eyes. I looked back at the long journey from Detroit. I saw Edna sitting on the floor at the window in the bedroom, dreaming of one day becoming a famous actress, and I gave thanks for all the blessings in my life. Some of the blessings came as gifts and good fortune. And some came as painful events that I called upon in my work and transformed into creative energy.

When Jeff and I got back home to our house on the Hudson, I tucked him into bed and read him to sleep, needing to soothe him of all the night's excitement. Then I went downstairs, sat in my kitchen, and called my mother, Aunt Vi and Uncle Chuck, and Blossom, who typically "didn't know it was today" and therefore hadn't watched the Oscars.

When I called my mother, she had been watching the show on television with some friends. She told me, "I said to my friends, if she wins this damn thing, I'm going to turn cartwheels, and I did! When they said your name, I got right down on the floor and turned a cartwheel! My friends were laughing so hard."

I waited to see if she had anything at all to say about me. Finally she did. After a quiet pause, she said, "Oh, honey, I'm so proud of you."

When I hung up the phone, I looked around my empty kitchen and said out loud to the silence, "There, now, that didn't take much, did it?"

The next day when I arrived at the theater, the paparazzi were waiting at the stage door. I always arrived at the theater barefaced, so I asked them if they would wait for me to put on some makeup. They kindly said they'd wait. When I went inside, the backstage doorman said, "There's a call for you, Ms. Burstyn." I stepped into his little cubicle and took the receiver of the wall phone.

"Hello?"

"Well, the alumni did pretty good last night." It had been eighteen years since I'd spoken to Jackie Gleason, but that voice was unmistakable. It seemed strange and wonderful that Art Carney and I should win in the same year. I was very pleased to receive Jackie's congratulations.

When I got to my dressing room, it was filled with flowers and there were stacks of telegrams. In my diary I wrote:

> *The press was very kind about letting me get into my makeup . . . but I kept them waiting a few minutes longer while I ripped open a stack of telegrams. I wasn't reading them, just scanning the names. I was looking for one name only—Bill Friedkin. It was like the moment in* Rosemary's Baby *when she pops the liver in her mouth without thinking, and then realizes what she has done. I suddenly saw myself keeping all these people waiting while I ravaged through a crowd of well wishers. There was only one smile I cared to have shine on me—one face—one name—Bill Friedkin. I stopped with the blood fresh on my lips, and said loud in my head, "He's the most important person in the world to me!" It was a lightning flash. "I have only him in my heart that I want to share this with!"*

On April 10, I received the letter from Billy that I'd been waiting for. He told me how proud he was of me, and pleased for me, and called me the finest actress in America. He told me he'd be in New York in two weeks and wanted to see me.

In my diary I wrote:

When the letter came from Billy, I knew why I had not gotten a telegram. Nothing fast. Something special. I was so glad. The letter was beautiful. I treasure it. I called him to thank him and I told him about my moment opening the telegrams. He said, "I love you, Ellen." I said, "I love you too, Billy." Then he added—"and I mean that in every conceivable way!"

I wondered what he meant by that. He was still involved with his girlfriend. Was he indicating a change in our relationship? I wasn't sure. I only knew that we'd been through a very profound and difficult creative experience together and my feelings for him were deep and real. Did I want a change in our relationship? Probably. Although I don't remember ever admitting this to myself. I had a gay friend named Bill Smith who lived with me. He escorted me to all the festivities and most of the award shows that year. I was in love with Charles onstage, but romantically I was alone. It seemed that the more successful I grew, the less I was pursued.

Jack Lemmon had presented the Best Actress Award to Marty Scorsese on my behalf and he was coming to see the show on April 10, along with his wife, the Walter Matthaus, Neil Simon and Marsha Mason, Paula Prentiss and Dick Benjamin, and Maureen Stapleton. They asked me to join them for dinner after the show. I called Jack Lemmon in California and requested that he bring the statuette to the theater so we could have a private presentation ceremony. Jack and Walter came back to my dressing room after the performance and we had a photographer take a picture of Jack handing me the Oscar—a picture, by the way, that causes me to cringe when I see it, because I was still wearing my stage wig from the show and the lace of the wig looks like a weird headband.

Then we went out to dinner. I was so impressed with this amazing collection of talented people as I approached the table and was introduced to all of them. I said, slightly awed, "How wonderful to see you all here." Maureen Stapleton took my hand and looked straight at me with her piercing eyes. "Don't worry, honey," she said. "You'll see all the same faces on your way down as you did on your way up!"

At dinner I sat next to Walter with the Oscar in a dark blue velvet bag on the floor between us. I was aware of it throughout the dinner. As our espresso was served, I turned to Walter and asked, "Walter, what is that down there?"

Walter answered, "Let me put it to you this way, Burstyn. When you die, they are going to say, 'Ellen Burstyn, the Academy Award–winning actress, died today.' "

My goodness, that was succinct.

Warner Bros. entered *Alice Doesn't Live Here Anymore* in the Cannes Film Festival. One night before the show, I got a call from Marty Scorsese in Cannes. He told me that the judges would give me the award for Best Actress if I would come there to receive it. I told Marty that I didn't leave the show for the Oscars and I wouldn't for the Cannes Film Festival. I held firm to my conviction that it was the work that should be honored, not the honors I got for doing the work. Besides, I'd already gotten what I really wanted. The film was a hit around the world and at last audiences were viewing a story through the eyes of a woman instead of the perpetual masculine point of view. That was my reward.

In June I was asked by the Professional Children's School in New York to pass out diplomas with Jerome Robbins to the high school graduating class. A few days before the commencement ceremony, the high school principal, Joyce McCray, called me and said, "Ms. Burstyn, I wonder if you'd do us a favor. We've just found out that Mr. Robbins didn't graduate from high school. We'd like to surprise him and start the program with you presenting him with an honorary diploma. Would you do that?"

"I'd be glad to," I replied, "but I don't have a high school diploma either."

"Oh, you want one, too?" She sounded just a mite peevish.

"Yes, please," I answered politely, feeling like a schoolgirl. I almost added, "ma'am."

So the ceremony began with me presenting Jerome Robbins, America's greatest choreographer, and an Oscar winner for his codirection of *West Side Story*, with an honorary high school diploma, and then Jerome presenting the Academy Award–winning Best Actress with hers. Come to think of it, we were hardly an argument to the students for the importance of a formal education.

That spring I won the Outer Critics Circle Award and the Drama Desk Award for *Same Time, Next Year*. Charles also won the Outer Critics. But when it came time for the Tonys, we all waited for word. The announcements were hand-delivered to all of the nominees backstage. As soon as I got mine, I ran to Mort Gottlieb to find out who else had been nominated. The play, the director, and the writer were all nominated, but Charles wasn't. I couldn't believe it. He was so essential to the success of the play, more than anyone, not just for his performance, but for his good taste and sensitivity to the script. It was just awful that we *all* were nominated except for him. I said to Morty, "Let me tell him."

I went upstairs to his dressing room and knocked. He opened the door, took one look at me, and said, "What's the matter?"

"The nominations were delivered."

"And you got nominated and I didn't."

"It's worse than that."

"Everybody got nominated and I didn't."

I could just nod my head. Charles was so amazing in this role. He didn't just get a laugh on every line; he got a laugh *before* the line and *after* the line. I'd never seen anyone do that before. The audience actually laughed in anticipation of his reaction and then again at his reaction to his reaction.

Nineteen seventy-five was a great year on Broadway, and there were many fine performances from which the nominees were selected. The voters had chosen Peter Firth for *Equus*, Henry Fonda for *Clarence Darrow*, Jim Dale for *Scapino*, Ben Gazzara for *Hughie* and *Duet*, John Wood for *Sherlock*

Holmes, and the eventual winners John Kani and Winston Ntshona for the Athol Fugard plays *Sizwe Banzi Is Dead* and *The Island.* There were many more choices than usual and our show had received so many nominations, Charles was sacrificed. That's why I hate awards.

For the Academy Awards, the members of each profession nominate their peers, but for the Tony Awards, the Producers Association does the nominating—in other words, the businessmen of Broadway control the nominations. That's why so few shows or performances that have closed by Tony time get nominated. If an actor wins Best Actor of the year in a show that may have run for months but is now closed, what good would that do the business? When Dustin Hoffman refused to do eight performances a week as Willy Loman in *Death of a Salesman* because he didn't think he was able to do the exacting, excruciating work of the role twice in one day, the producers withheld the nomination from him. Nobody ever deserved a Tony more.

Charles escorted me to the Tony Awards that year. When I was called to the stage, having already won the Oscar just a month earlier, I said, "I guess this is what is meant by being twice blessed." Then I thanked everyone connected with the show, but added that "there were only two people onstage and I couldn't possibly do what I did without the aid and inspiration of my magnificent partner, Charles Grodin. So I accept this in his name as well as mine."

But he deserved far more.

When Billy came to see the show, I was happy and excited. I could feel him in the audience all night. We went out for supper that night. We didn't discuss his letter and I didn't ask him what he meant by it. He was still with his girlfriend and our relationship, as intense as it was, was always separate and apart from anything else in our personal lives.

I told him the story about opening night when I suddenly dried up and had to talk myself into believing I was really saying good-bye, not to George, but to Charles. "You mean you can think about other things when you are acting?" Billy asked, incredulously.

I didn't know what to say. I was flabbergasted. I'd said in print that Billy was my favorite director and if *he* didn't know what actors put themselves through to achieve their results, then that says to me that directors (with a few rare exceptions) don't have a clue about the actor's creative process.

My last performance of *Same Time, Next Year* was October 18, 1975. By then I was glad it was over. As soon as the play closed I was back to the Actors Studio moderating the sessions every week.

It had been an amazing year. I was one of a handful of actresses to ever win an Oscar and a Tony in the same year. I also won the British Academy Award and many others. I'd been feted, celebrated, toasted, photographed, and written about over and over again. And yet I moved through all of it with a strange discontent.

I remember very clearly entering the opening-night party for *Same Time, Next Year.* The word was already out on the street that we were going to be a hit. From the reviews in Boston and the sold-out houses, we came into town smelling like success. The party was huge; there was an air of celebration that hovered around us. The paparazzi swarmed us, as Aubrey Beardsley said, "like bees about a bright bouquet." And what did I wear for this triumphal march through the throngs of applauding well-wishers? A long plain black dress, no jewelry. A bare face. I looked like a nun. I tried as best I could to hide under the table, as I had when the family sang "Happy Birthday" to me at my seventh birthday party, mortified that everyone was looking at me. Was I really that shy? Still? At age forty-two and an accomplished actress? At the party, I sat in a corner with Charles, sipping my soda water as the merriment swirled in front of us, flash bulbs popping, people smiling down at us while pumping our hands. Why couldn't I take part in it? Wasn't there reason to celebrate? Why this sadness behind the accommodating smile?

There is a beautiful poem by the Sufi poet Hafiz that expresses it. This translation of "Damn Thirsty" is by David Ladinsky.

First
The fish needs to say,
"Something ain't right about this

Camel ride—
And I'm
Feeling so damn
Thirsty."

That's what I felt like—a fish on a camel's back, knowing something wasn't right, and I was thirsting to find what I was missing. Not only wasn't I enjoying all the parties I was required to attend, I actually felt there was something dangerous about all the attention I was getting. If Dr. Elahi hadn't suggested I give up alcohol, I would probably have gotten sloshed to ease my discomfort and actually believed that I was something special, better in some way than everyone else. My ego would have identified with all the hoopla directed at me, and underneath the glare shining brightly on my false smile, my soul would wither and that which was most genuine in me would fade. I wanted to hold on to what was real and not feast on the empty calories of fame.

I was right. I was in danger. I was walking through a minefield. Each mine was another opportunity for an explosion of hubris.

Within a month of the play's closing, I returned to Iran.

I'd requested that the film festival officials invite me back and they did. But I spent most of my time there with Dr. Elahi. I asked him why, in this period of extreme success, I could feel no joy.

He told me that it was my "nafs" that made me think I should feel joy from the achievements in the material world. The word is short for *nafs-i-ammara*, an expression used in the Koran meaning "self-commanding evil." He went on to explain that there are two opposing forces that are in each of us: one is a spiritual force through which our soul expresses itself, the other is the force of our animal nature. They are the positive and negative poles of our being, and each needs the other. Our soul needs a body as a material garment and the body without the soul can't rise above its animal nature. It is balancing these two forces that is the spiritual path. The *nafs* is our mortal enemy on this path. It is like a dangerous animal whose mission it is to turn us away from God. Its two main tools are pride and doubt. My *nafs* had been whispering to me that I must take pride in my achievements, but my soul had the inkling I was in danger of falling under the spell of my *nafs*, or "my domineering self." In Western psychological terms, I was in danger of identifying with my ego.

Dr. Elahi also told me that he got a message from the Master that said I must not worry. I am the Master's daughter. He loves me and will protect me and my son.

I wanted so to believe that. I wanted to feel that I was the Master's daughter. Was it my *nafs* that couldn't quite connect with the feeling? Was this the doubt Dr. Elahi referred to? I liked these people so much. I loved their spiritual sincerity. I wanted to be part of this group. But was I? I wasn't sure.

I went with the group to visit Hazrat Elahu's tomb. One of the young women in the group threw her body on the tomb and cried hysterically, clawing wildly at the cold marble covering the grave. Something about the intensity of the grief made me uncomfortable. It felt foreign to me, strange, as if there were something excessive about it. But I tried not to judge it.

Then, at the Zikr, as the tempo and volume of the chanting intensified, a woman next to me erupted, burst through the chant into ecstatic and/or agonized cries, her whole body trembling violently. Dr. Elahi's wife moved swiftly to the woman and expertly laid her body on top of the woman's jolting, crying form. She stayed like that until the woman quieted down, her face streaming with tears. Again, I had an unsettling feeling that I was a foreigner in this world.

The deciding factor for me was a call from Jefferson in tears. He was distressed and having trouble in school. I decided to return home and get him back on track.

That night, Dr. Elahi announced that the following week there would be a special ceremony at the tomb of Hazrat Elahu. He thought I should extend my visit to attend this ceremony. I told him of Jeff's phone call, and my decision to leave a day sooner than planned.

Dr. Elahi then told me that one's commitment to one's spiritual training has to take priority over everything else. After all, our children are our responsibility in this life, but perhaps in another life the soul that is my son could be in another relationship to me—my mother, my father, or my enemy. He said that some souls really are our children and some children are really strangers to our souls. He urged me to honor my commitment to my spiritual work and extend my visit. I refused.

"All right, you have failed your first spiritual test," Dr. Elahi said.

I disagreed. To me, I had passed it. I said no to this man whose approval I very much coveted; I said no to my own spiritual training in favor of my son. This was the moment when I discovered how deeply I was both American (where we honor the child over the parent) and Christian (where we consider it a spiritual virtue to sacrifice our own concerns for others).

I cried during this conversation with Dr. Elahi. I suspect because I knew this was good-bye—to this group, to my ever-hopeful wish of finding a place where I felt I truly belonged.

While I was meeting with Dr. Elahi, the closing night ceremony of the film festival was taking place. I had not attended many of the festivities and my absence was noted. The next day as I was packing to leave, I got a message that an emissary from Her Imperial Majesty, Shahbanu Farah, was coming to see me and I must wait for him. I explained that that would not allow me time to get to the airport. I was told, "Don't worry."

My bags were packed when my doorbell rang. I admitted the royal emissary. He wore a dark blue double-breasted suit and black shoes and had small, intense black eyes. He asked me why I wanted to return to Iran; why I hadn't been attending the festivities; what had I been doing? When I told him I'd been spending time with the Ahl-i Haqq group, his interest intensified and his eyes narrowed suspiciously. I saw that he didn't trust them or me; that this interview was merely preliminary and suddenly I feared that I might actually be in danger of imprisonment, although I couldn't imagine for what. My Iranian friends had told me that the previous year the Shah's police had rounded up all the known dissenters and put them in jail while the world's press was in Tehran for the film festival. A year had passed and their families still had not seen them, didn't know if they were alive or dead.

After a few more questions, I saw him decide that I was not dangerous. I was free to leave, but was now late for my plane. The emissary provided a limo from the royal fleet to take me to the airport, sirens wailing the whole way.

Three years later, in 1978, the Shah was deposed in an Islamic revolution. A Hollywood star as an Islamic revolutionary? Sounds like a movie to me. But for a moment it must have sounded like real life to Her Imperial Majesty, Shahbanu Farah Pahlavi, empress of Iran.

My last few months at the house on the Hudson I'd been renting for a year had been a time of turmoil. Neil's visits were so frequent and so frightful, I really couldn't be alone.

One day I was walking Bernard along a quiet road when I saw a big old Victorian mansion. Beside it was the most beautiful giant tree I'd ever seen. It was far larger than the house. I gazed at this idyllic view and pictured the life that was lived there. I imagined multiple generations happily living and peacefully dying inside the gracious rooms. One generation passing on this lovely family home to the next. As usual, the truth turned out to be very different from my fantasies. The house was in terrible disrepair and the most recent owner couldn't afford to take care of it. Soon it was on the market and, after many complications, I ended up buying the Stone House. It had twenty-six rooms, which I restored back to its original, elegant twenty-two. There were twelve bedrooms and soon I filled them with friends and writers working on scripts. Also in the house were my secretary and our housekeeper. I'd advertised for a live-in maid and no one responded. I looked for a live-in housekeeper—again, no response. Then I advertised for a household engineer and four men answered the ad. I chose one of them. Also, a young man named Michael, who had been working on the house as a painter before it was ready for me, had no place of his own, so I told him he could live in one of the upstairs bedrooms. That turned out to be a very fortunate decision. By the sheer number of bodies living together, I felt there would always be someone at home with me. And Michael had an uncanny way of being there every time Neil showed up.

When I moved from the rented house, I hoped Neil wouldn't find me, but he did. One day, the county sheriff pulled up and Neil got out of the passenger seat. The sheriff stood beside his car and said, "I picked him up on the road. He said he was looking for his mother."

Neil took off his hat. Underneath, his dark hair had turned gray, almost white. He said in that strange artificially deep voice he'd been using since he became ill, and pointing to his hair, "Look what they've done to me, babe. Shock treatments."

All the muscles of my chest clutched at my heart. I said to the sheriff, "I'm not his mother. I'm his ex-wife. He's mentally ill and I don't want him here." The sheriff took him away, but now Neil knew where I was and would stalk me and haunt me at every opportunity. He also wrote innumerable letters full of wild ravings.

He would plead pathetically for me to help him by allowing him to come back, but by then I had learned that he was beyond help and he was so violent, I was terrified of him.

One night, everyone went out except me. Michael was in the city having dinner with his mother, when in the middle of the meal he suddenly leapt up and announced that he had to leave. I was alone in bed when Neil burst through the door and right behind him was Michael, who had sped the hour's drive back to the house without even knowing why he was rushing back. He hustled Neil out of the house while I called the police. Neil stood outside ranting loudly until the police arrived and took him away. Michael sat with me until my shaking and crying stopped and I asked him how he came to be there.

"I don't know," he said. "It was weird. We were eating and I just had the feeling that I had to get back here fast." Michael was tuned in to me to an unusual degree. He was like a guardian angel. He was twenty years younger than I was, but we had a very intense relationship for the next few years until my nightmare with Neil was finally over. Then Michael's mission was accomplished and our relationship faded. But for the next few years, he was my protector and more than once saved my life.

While I was still doing *Same Time, Next Year,* I was approached by the Brazilian playwright Roberto Athayde to do his brilliant play, *Miss*

Margarida's Way. I loved the play and wanted to do it, but the concept was a classroom with Miss Margarida addressing the audience as the class and speaking directly to them as though they were pupils and inviting them to take part. It would be too perfect a setup for Neil. I didn't dare risk it. The play was finally done in New York very successfully by Estelle Parsons.

I turned my attention to *Silence of the North*. It was an incredible story of bravery and courage and fed my desire to portray a feminine hero. I'd given the book to Billy to read. He liked it and wanted to direct it. He brought in Wally Green to write the screenplay. Wally was writing the script in California. When I went out there and read the first draft, I was dismayed to discover he started the film with thirty pages of Olive's childhood. In other words, in this story that I brought to Billy, I was not in the first quarter of the movie. I went to Billy's office and told him of my disappointment. There was so much of Olive's story that I wouldn't be able to tell if we spent so much time on her childhood.

Billy answered with a bit of heat, "I'm not going to begin the film with a middle-aged woman!"

I sat in the chair across from him, huge chunks of glamour clunking to the floor like crumbling plaster, lines creeping up my face like woman-eating vines, my shoulders drooping and hunching over with the weight of the burden of my many years. I said nothing. A movie star had entered the room, but a middle-aged woman exited.

Such is the fragility of the ego.

In 1977, Billy wrote a letter and told me that he felt great sorrow about the failure of Wally and himself, that when he first read the book, he believed there was a film there—and there still is. But he came to the conclusion he wasn't the one to find it.

I was deeply disappointed, but this doesn't seem to have affected my feelings for Billy.

Pat King later wrote a beautiful script about Olive from the book. Billy had brought *Silence* to Universal and I ended up making it with them, but there were all kinds of decisions made about the film by the studio that I wasn't savvy enough to appreciate, the most destructive being to use a Canadian director of their choice who wasn't ideal for the material. I still wish Billy had directed it, but in that period, I wanted Billy to direct everything I did.

In the spring of 1976, I went to Paris to shoot *Providence* for Alain Resnais with John Gielgud, Dirk Bogarde, Elaine Stritch, and David Warner. I have a treasured memory from this picture. We were in Limoges, France, shooting on an empty estate that had once belonged to the Haviland family. It was a gorgeous old seventeenth-century house with amazing architectural details and no furniture at all. We were shooting the exteriors here, using the beautiful grounds and gardens. The inside of the house was set up with makeshift furnishings for us to use as dressing rooms, wardrobe, makeup rooms, and production offices. I had selected a lovely spacious salon on the second floor overlooking the garden as my dressing room. They'd brought in some tables and big old chairs, and did their best to make it habitable, but there was no heat and although it was springtime, the skies were dark with low-moving clouds and there was a blustery wind. We were playing like it was summer out on the grass, but we were freezing in our light clothes. The clouds kept moving across the sun and we'd stand shivering waiting for them to clear so the light would match the previous shot.

We came to a sequence that I was not in, so I ran inside while John and Dirk stayed out in the cold. But inside was nearly as cold as outdoors. I had a large old fireplace in my room, so I went out to the woods and collected fallen branches. Soon I had a nice fire going in my hearth. It didn't heat the large salon, but if I sat close to it, I could feel its welcome warmth. I spent hours there reading, feeling sympathy for my confrères out in the cold. After a while, the dark clouds settled in for a long stay and the director of photography announced that shooting was done for the day. I heard John and Dirk coming up the wide central stairway. I invited them into my room to warm themselves by my fire. They collapsed into the chairs and held out their hands to get warm. I got blankets from wardrobe and covered each of them. Dirk said between his chattering teeth, "I've got some brandy in my room. Could you get it?"

I fetched the brandy on Dirk's small round tray with two snifters, and poured them each a drink. Then I sat on the floor next to John, close by the crackling fire as I listened to these divine men tell stories about their lives in the theater. John stroked my hair as I laid my head on his blanketed lap. At treasured moments like these, one doesn't need to have had a father. And yet I wonder what it was in me that so loved serving these two fine men? Was it something innately feminine? Do we women have some kind of gender-specific "serving" gene? Did the fact that they were both gay and great actors influence me? Would I be so happy serving and warming them by my fire if they were two chilled roustabouts? It was the nature of "the feminine" I was trying to understand in that period.

As I was exploring this issue in myself as well as historically, I came across the startling information that in our early history, before the written word, God was conceived of, multiculturally, as female. The world was spawned by a Goddess. That imagery prevailed into early Greek times and was widespread. I had only heard of God as the Father. The acceptance of this imagery presupposes a limited role in the world for everything feminine. If we are made in God's image, and God is a man, then man is the image of the divine and woman is something lesser. But when I pictured "the divine" in feminine form, something in me was soothed. And strangely stirred.

The years 1976 through 1979 were the most active years of my life on the outer plane. On the inner plane, I was taking part in the worldwide reawakening of the long slumbering Goddess.

I began 1977 with a trip to India for the film festival in Delhi. I brought Michael along with me. I met the prime minister, Indira Gandhi, at a breakfast in her palace. She had eyes like an eagle and an intensity to match. "I've not seen your films, but I know who you are and what you are doing for women," she said to me.

I told her that I'd seen a film the night before by Satyajit Ray about a middle-class Indian family that is so strapped for money that the wife decides that she must go to work. She is a very sympathetic character, but when her husband slapped her face, the whole audience applauded, including the women. I asked the prime minister why.

"Because they're stupid!" she said. I was shocked she was willing to be so blunt about her own people. Then she softened and added, "The trouble with women in this country is they'll believe anything a man has to say. Our first job is to educate them."

Michael and I flew from India to Katmandu, Nepal. We were taken to see the Living Goddess. From the street, the temple looked like a building made of intricately carved wood. Once we'd passed through the low door, we were in an inner courtyard without a roof. The courtyard was filled with large bronze statues of the gods and goddesses Shakti, Shiva, and Ganesha. Children were playing on the statues as our children would play on swings and slides. One of the little boys pointed to our shoes and instructed us sternly to remove them. It was then explained to me that children are the guardians of the temples. They play here and learn all the tales of their religion. Here they are safe and at home.

A barefoot child of six or seven, carrying a baby of no more than eight months, asked me if I'd like to see the Living Goddess. I said that we would. She collected my money, the equivalent of about twenty-five cents, and disappeared into the temple while we waited in the courtyard. Soon the wooden shutters of a window on the second floor of the temple opened. There appeared a pretty child with an elaborately painted face and wearing a colorful costume. She sat at the window for a few minutes, unsmiling, allowing us to gaze at her goddessness. After twenty-five cents' worth of gazing, hands reached from the darkness within and closed the shutters.

I asked our guide how the goddess was chosen. He said the priests from the temple went to the villages and selected the most beautiful two-year-old girl they could find. She was then brought to the temple and trained to be the Living Goddess. When the present goddess attained puberty, the new goddess took her place. She never left the temple once she was inside until her term was over.

"What happens to her then?" I asked with some trepidation.

"Oh, she's taken to the outskirts of the city and given a little bowl to beg for food."

"Doesn't anyone take her in?"

"Oh, no! The people give her rice, but they cannot touch her."

"Why not?"

"She is untouchable. A goddess. Nobody can touch a goddess."

"How long does she live like that, as a beggar?"

"Oh, the rest of her life."

I thought of our many screen goddesses that we are allowed to gaze on as long as they are young, and then the shutters begin to close on them. Perhaps it is not a cruel fate when, like Marilyn Monroe or Jean Harlow, they die young. Perhaps it is the kindest fate for a living goddess.

Varanasi is the holy city of India. There Michael and I walked down to the Ganges River before dawn and watched the sky flame red. The Ganges reflected the burning light. Sacred wild monkeys were all around and we were part of a sea of people chanting, praying, meditating, lighting incense and candles. We got on a small boat and drifted among thousands of candles floating on the water. It was an atmosphere unlike any I'd ever witnessed; fervent and heady, intoxicating with its lush colors, pungent smells, and hypnotic rhythms of the chanting all around us. Our guide escorted us to a temple whose doorway was carved with Shiva and his feminine consort, Shakti, locked in every conceivable sexual position. I'd never before known of a religion that incorporated the sexual act in its religious iconography.

The next day our guide took us to witness the sacrifice to Kali. As we slowly drove up the road to the temple, we saw people leading by rope protesting domestic animals—sheep, goats, or lambs. One boy pulled a lamb who was bleating pitifully, her eyes wide and frightened as if she knew where she was going and why. When we arrived, crowds of people were there meditating, talking, eating, and chanting. The air was thick with incense and the sounds of the chants reverberated off the rocks. In front of the altar stood two priests wearing brown rubber slaughtering aprons, splashed thickly with blood. The people stood in a line in front of each priest with their animals straining against their ropes. The smell of fresh blood and the cries of the animals filled the air. As each person stepped forward and offered an animal, the cries intensified into loud shrieks.

When I realized what I was about to see, my knees grew weak and I felt as if I were about to faint. My eyes snapped shut, but I said to myself, *No, Ellen, you are here. Don't turn from it. Witness it.* I took a deep breath and made myself open my eyes. The little boy I'd seen on the road approached the altar and offered his terrified lamb as sacrifice.

The priests chatted with each other, smiling casually as they took the shrieking sacrifice, expertly stretched its neck and slit its throat. At their feet there were piles of rice studded with brightly colored flowers. As the priests severed the animals' heads, blood poured on the rice. A woman in a bright green and orange sari scooped up a few grains of blood-spattered rice and reverently stuck it to her forehead. The priest then took the severed head to the altar and made the sacrificial offering to Kali by placing the head on the altar with the other heads. The rest of the lamb or kid was given to the family who carried it to an old oil drum filled with cooking oil that sat on a blazing fire nearby. The headless corpse sizzled as it entered the drum. Other families were already eating, pulling the meat off the bones and tossing the bones to the waiting hungry dogs that hung around the edges of the feast.

I learned that sacrifice for the Hindus is not merely to placate the gods, but actually to nourish them. The gods rely on humans for food; without the sacrifice the gods would not live and could no longer protect human beings. This is a deep and profound concept—that the relationship between humanity and the divine is one of mutual dependency. The gods created the world, but humans keep the gods alive by their willingness to sacrifice for them. In many Hindu texts it is revealed that animals were created for the good of the whole world. The animals represent the lower qualities and it is their purpose to be the means by which those qualities are exchanged through the transformation of their energy into the higher qualities in humans—the qualities of goodness and compassion. We sacrifice our lower nature to ascend into our higher consciousness. The gods always represent the highest qualities that are latent in our souls. As we sacrifice our desires and lusts for corporeal pleasures, we call forth these higher qualities and they manifest in our soul's evolution.

In Christianity, the soul's evolution is the gradual building up of the Christ in us. And, of course, it is Christ, the lamb of God, the ultimate sacrifice, who taketh away the sins of the world. It's another manifestation of the same idea.

The religious philosopher Emanuel Swedenborg says, "The sacrifices and burnt offerings signify the regeneration of man by the truths of faith and the goods of love."

One of the reasons that I am a Sufi is the Sufi's search for truth everywhere, in all the traditions of the great religions. Over and over it is revealed that, although the form is different in each religion, the truth is always the same.

Billy had introduced me to Alain Resnais and encouraged me to work with him. In the months that preceded the opening of *Providence,* Billy and I saw each other every time he came to New York or I went to California. We seemed to be getting closer than ever and our deep friendship was finally blossoming into a romance. One day, while he was in France and I was awaiting his return, I was at the hairdresser's and leafing through an issue of *Time.* His name caught my eye in a column and I read that he had gotten engaged to Jeanne Moreau.

I was stunned. Could this possibly be true? I waited to hear from him. He didn't call. The next time I saw him was at the premiere of *Providence.* He attended with his new fiancée and introduced us to each other as the paparazzi photographed my grim smile. In their effort to capture the glamorous international couple, they were stepping all over my toes, both literally and metaphorically.

Providence opened in New York on January 24, 1977, to mostly uncomprehending reviews. It was a very complex and intellectually intricate film that probably required several viewings before an opinion could be formed. Alain Resnais said to me, "I think I've made a film you must see twice to understand." Well, the American critics didn't bother. The film came and went without much notice. In France, it was a different story. It was hailed as a masterpiece and won almost every award a film could possibly win.

Since I'd given up smoking, I'd been battling my weight. A friend recommended a psychic nutritionist in Los Angeles named Eileen Poole, who was a delightfully eccentric British character. She used her arm as a pendulum, while her other hand went down a list of food on her desk. Her pendulum hand indicated which foods were good for you. She also treated with something called Bieler's Broth, a disgustingly bland combination of green beans and zucchini. I was meant to eat it every day. I lost weight, but I couldn't stomach Bieler's Broth for long. Jeff, who was now fifteen years old, had gained a lot of weight, so I decided to take him to see Eileen as well. As I sat at her desk and she did her pendulum thing, talking to me in her airy British voice, Jeff slouched on her couch, humming. When it was his turn, he approached her desk and said, "I'm not eating any Bieler's soup."

Eileen said, "As for you, dear . . . You don't need a diet. No! Not at all. You're perfect just the way you are. The only thing is, dear, you're drinking too much milk. You have milk poisoning. You're drinking milk as though it were water, and of course it's not. Learn to drink water and you'll be fine."

When Jeff came to Paris while I was shooting *Providence,* he'd been just awful; hostile and resistant. I worked with him for a while and he finally broke down and said that he hated the way he looked. He was so fat, he couldn't stand to look in the mirror. That's what made me bring him to Eileen. And she told him he was perfect! He didn't need a diet. He started drinking water instead of milk and within a remarkably short time, he lost twenty pounds.

Eileen was a true healer. It wasn't the arm-as-pendulum or the Bieler's Broth. It was finding the way into the person. Eileen addressed Jeff's real problem, his shame about being fat. She told him he was perfect just the way he was. Those were magic words. Within a few months he was a long-haired, skinny, cool musician. The fat boy was gone. I find myself on occasion missing that little fat boy. But as his therapist had predicted, that was a wall he'd built around himself for protection. When he was ready to give it up, he did.

After my very first visit to Eileen, I wrote this in my diary:

Sylvia Wolf took me to see Eileen Poole, a psychic nutritionist. My mother was along and it was an amazing experience. I felt that she was the first one I've ever met who really could understand what it was like for me to be mothered by my mother. She saw it. Saw my mother's fear—emptiness—and hollowness—her cover story—the lies she tells—her lack of identity—her absence of a sense of self. Eileen saw it all and the effect it had on me—the good and the bad—for there was good—I cannot deny that—not just the good when she tried to be good, but the good character that I was able to develop in reaction to her. Eileen went right to my tubes—said all of my energy is blocked there. It's the seat of my sadness. She's right, of course. I have the strangest feeling that with her diet I could unblock them and perhaps might even get pregnant—now that I've given that up and probably it would not be too wise to have a baby at my age. If I did, I'd do it at home with a midwife and Blossom.

I just never really gave up that yearning to conceive until it was physically impossible.

I remember Eileen said to me regarding my mother, "It was like being mothered by General Patton. And, oh dear, you were so sensitive!" It does seem an accurate image of the situation. But then I must ask, "What did that serve?" Assuming, as Plato and other philosophers thought, that the soul chooses its parents and life circumstances in order to best learn the lessons it came to learn, what did my soul have in mind, choosing the parents that I did? I've been working on that one for years now.

In the summer of 1977, Jules Dassin brought me to Athens to make a film with his wife, Melina Mercouri. It was a modern-day *Medea* story called *A Dream of Passion.*

Toward the end of shooting, I got a call from my agent telling me about a script called *Resurrection.* "The story is: Jesus Christ comes back to earth as a woman," he said.

"Oh, I like that!" I said.

I was very excited about the idea, but when I read the script, I didn't like it. An American schoolteacher visits Jerusalem and while there, gets the stigmata. But it really wasn't a spiritual story. As I saw it, the mystery of the stigmata was exploited to make an "ooga booga" story—semimystical, not that scary, not very exciting. So it was Jesus Christ comes back to earth as a woman, and she's got nothing to say.

I turned it down.

But the producers and director still wanted to fly to Greece, meet me, and talk about it.

When we met, I told the producers, Renée Missel and Howard Rosenman, and the director at the time, whose name I don't remember, that I'd recently read Raymond Moody's *Life After Life,* a book of interviews with people who had been clinically dead, some for as long as fifteen minutes, and then resuscitated. All these people reported going through a tunnel, meeting a being of light, reviewing their lives, and then, when they were brought back to life, being permanently altered by the experience. I suggested to the producers that if the character went through some kind of near-death experience and afterward found she had some of the abilities that Jesus had, such as the power to heal, that would be more plausible and more interesting to me. I told them of my other studies about the feminine in early spiritual traditions, about the combining of the spiritual and sexual energies. Only later were those two realms divided, when the Church fathers decided that the spiritual had to be separate from the sexual. I talked to them about the early Church killing off the natural healing powers of the feminine when they tortured and burned at the stake any woman who clung to the old religion by using her intuition, or healed with the old herbal wisdom that had been codified for centuries and then later demonized.

After a while, the director said, "Well, that's a very interesting movie, but we have a green light from Universal to make this movie," and he tapped the script on his lap. "Do you want to make this movie or not?"

I told him no.

They left and within an hour, I got a phone call from the producers.

"We like your movie better than our movie," they said. "With your permission, we'd like to go back to Universal and start over with a new director and a new writer and make your movie."

I was thrilled.

Later Howard and Renee hired Lewis John Carlino to write the script based on my ideas, as well as other incidents from my life that Lewis learned and transmogrified through his own creative genius into the script that would become one of the most meaningful films of my career.

In the meantime, I still had *Silence of the North* in development with Universal. When Billy withdrew from the project, I found Pat King and together we worked to translate the life of Olive Fredrickson into a script. Olive's story fit perfectly with my concept of the feminine hero. Her heroism didn't involve leading an army, like Joan of Arc. She was a simple woman who was married and had two daughters. She and her husband carved out of the wilderness of northern Canada a life for themselves. When her husband was killed, Olive transcended society's conditioning of what a woman can do and braved the wilderness by herself with her children. From her book I knew she was an animal lover who would take in a wild animal or bird that was wounded and nurse it back to health. Yet she hunted, killed, and flayed deer and moose to feed her children. When I went to meet her in her little suburban house in Canada where she retired, I asked about her time in the wilderness. Did she ever have trouble eating the animal she had killed? "No," she said in a quiet voice, looking directly at me. "I could eat the meat with the blood still on my hands."

I sat silently a moment, picturing myself buying lamb chops wrapped in cellophane at the supermarket, neatly protected from the reality of the death and gore of the animal who I would be "too sensitive" to kill. Then Olive added, "Oh, sometimes at night the deer would appear in my bedroom and gaze at me."

We were sitting in her living room. "I'd offer you dinner," she said, "but I don't know what movie stars eat—if it would be good enough." I'd been traveling all day and was very hungry.

"Whatever you eat," I said.

I sat at the kitchen table covered with an oilcloth and watched this woman who had defended her children against wild bear, braved a life while starving in forty-below-zero temperatures, and planted and harvested her own farm in the Far North. To the ticking of her wall clock, she moved around her kitchen with the same quiet confidence she must have had in the wild woods, making me a meal of mashed potatoes and a fried egg.

When Billy dropped out of the project, he told me it was because he "couldn't find a classic myth to hang it on." But that was the point—classic myths, with few exceptions, were stories about male heroes.

I was exploring the nature of the feminine hero and how she was different from a heroine. I'd read somewhere that a hero goes out into the world, meets his enemy, prevails, and founds a new order, while a heroine simply endures. I felt that a feminine hero goes out into the world, meets her enemy, which in one form or another is the limitations imposed on her by her culture, and she not only endures, she also prevails and founds a new order.

Perhaps Olive didn't found a new order, but I wanted to tell her story because not only did she triumph over terrible adversity, the death of her son, and other challenges, she broke through the limitations that society imposes on women. Her life was very hard, there was much distress, but she never acted like a damsel and never was rescued. She was illiterate until she learned to read while helping her daughter with her school lessons. Later she wrote her life story. She became her own person and met her fate as a complete and independent woman.

I guess I was trying to create a new myth for women. I didn't succeed, but success isn't the only gauge of the value of an effort.

I was in California that September for meetings on *Silence* and *Resurrection*. One night, Eileen Poole invited me to dinner to meet Carlos Castaneda. I've always been surprised that journalists and writers claimed that Castaneda was not a real person, and that all his stories of sorcery in the Mexican desert were fiction. Carlos Castaneda was very real, as were his experiences. He was dark-skinned with black hair. He told me that sometimes a reporter would catch him working in his garden and he would pretend to be the Mexican gardener who did not know the man who lived in the house. "He always away," he would explain with a thick accent. At one point during dinner, Carlos turned to me and said, "You are the true sorcerer! Because when I see your work, I believe more in your reality than my own!"

Carlos told me that "Carlos Castaneda" is a nom de plume. He was born with another name to a Spanish aristocrat who wed a woman from a wealthy Turkish family in an arranged marriage. The other children were light-skinned like their father, but Carlos inherited the dark skin of his mother. His father favored the light-skinned children and Carlos was kept hidden from view. He left home at an early age and had no contact with his father for many years. After he'd become a philosopher, a professor at UCLA, a sorcerer, and a world-famous author, he returned to his father's house in Spain. His father invited him into his library and they sat on either side of his father's desk and had a nice long conversation. However, Carlos's father did not know that his son had changed his name and, even though Carlos could see all of his own books lined up on the shelves just over his father's shoulder, he never revealed to his father that he was Carlos Castaneda. What freedom he must have felt!

He asked me what I was doing next. I told him I'd just read the first draft of *Silence of the North* and, if Universal approved it, we would be looking for a director and going into production. Early the next morning, the doorbell rang and there was Carlos at the door holding a large manuscript. He put it in my hands and said, "This is my next book. It's not published yet. It's called *The Second Ring of Power*. If there is anything in there that you can use for your movie, take it!"

Holding the thick manuscript, I said in awe, "Carlos, that is the single most generous thing I've ever seen anyone do."

"Oh, no," he said lightly. "Don Juan said I must always be of service to an impeccable warrior. And he told me not to worry, that I wouldn't meet too many."

Reading Carlos's brilliant and profound manuscript, I was captivated by his stories, but there was nothing that I wanted to lift whole for the film. But that he was willing to have me do that was a great teaching in how to walk one's path. Knowledge, understanding, and wisdom should be shared, not hoarded. To be called an impeccable warrior by Carlos Castaneda was for me equal to being dubbed a knight by the queen of England.

By mid-September, I'd returned to New York and the challenge of dealing with the dark forces manifesting in my life. In that period I was probably the only actress in Hollywood who was initiating her own projects. Yet with all the heady success, when I went home to my beautiful house and three-acre garden, I lived in fear for my life. So far, every time Neil appeared there was someone there to protect me. But I lived in terror that someday he would find me alone and kill me.

My explorations into the feminine hero had led me directly to the work of Carl Jung. He writes about the shadow, the parts of ourselves that we do not want to own, which then manifest outside of us for us to look at and deal with. I wondered if in some shadowy way there was something about myself that I was denying that I had to bring into the light. I read *Ego and Archetype* by Edward Edinger, a Jungian analyst, and saw that he had a private practice in New York City. I began to see him.

On September 18, 1977, my journal entry reads:

Neil appeared before 6:00 a.m. shouting outside. Jeff and I were alone. I called the police. Neil broke through the front doors and came up the stairs. Jeff greeted him with a lead pipe in his hands, roaring at him to leave. After ten minutes, Neil asked "to see the kid." He hadn't recognized Jeff. When he asked Jeff what his name was, Jeff answered, "Tom." The police came and took Neil away in handcuffs. I signed the complaint at the police station. Jeff was sick to his stomach and I kept him home from school.

Jeff went with me to Edinger's, then we had lunch and we went to Henry's. Edinger said that I am not going to be free of Neil until I understand on a deep unconscious level what he means to me. He said, "I can tell from your dreams and other events in your life that it is your destiny to have a deeper understanding of the unconscious than most people. It is not fortuitous that you were in The Exorcist.*"*

I said, "How do I do that?"
He said, "We're doing it."

Now I would question exactly what he meant by that, but at the time, I hadn't learned to question men in what seemed like positions of power. I always held my tongue, as I did with Billy. Edinger made that cryptic statement as though I should understand what he meant, and I did understand the last part. Therapy is the process by which we come to have a deeper understanding of the unconscious. But what does it mean that it was not fortuitous that I was in *The Exorcist*? I wish I'd asked.

Alan Alda was cast opposite me in the film version of *Same Time, Next Year*. I had hoped they would use Charles Grodin in the film, but nothing I said could convince them. The guys at Universal had the false idea in their heads that Charles had no "box office" and once they get that thought about an actor, no amount of my pleading about how great he was in the role could shake their closed minds.

That said, Alan Alda is a wonderful actor and we had a great time working together. We went to Mendocino for two weeks of shooting outdoors. The plan was to "open up the film" and shoot many scenes outside in the breathtakingly beautiful natural vistas around the inn that we were using. But Mother Nature had other plans for us. I have memories of standing outdoors in makeup, wig, and costume under an umbrella waiting endlessly for a break in the weather that never came. We managed a shot here and there, but we ended up moving many of the exterior scenes to interiors, which were then shot at Universal Studios back in Los Angeles.

The weekend that we arrived in Mendocino, Alan and I discussed how we were going to get to know each other before we began this onscreen love affair. We didn't have much time. "The fastest way I know to get to know someone is to get drunk together," I said.

After my year of sobriety with Dr. Elahi, I had resumed my old habits. I wasn't smoking cigarettes, but I did smoke grass again and drink alcohol until the day finally came when I'd really had enough of that self-destructive behavior, but that would take a few more years.

So Alan and I went out on a tear and, I have to say, it was fun. I don't remember too much of it, except at one point we went into a supermarket that was still open, though the bars had closed. There was a big wire bin of beach balls and my memory is of Alan and me running up and down the aisles playing catch. There were no other people in the store except one cashier who was about to close up for the night. He watched our hilarity warily. He had an expression that said: *I'd like to throw those drunks out of here, but am I crazy or is that Alan Alda and Ellen Burstyn?*

We went back to the lodge where we were staying and stayed up all night in Alan's cabin drinking a bottle of brandy (what were we thinking?) and eating a box of Triscuits.

The next morning, my hangover was so bad, I thought I was going to die. I considered crawling to the glass doors of my cabin and out onto the deck and rolling off into the grass. Perhaps that would catch someone's attention and they'd take me to the hospital. But I couldn't get the sliding doors open from a supine position, so after crawling to the bathroom, where I banged my head on the tile floor so hard I thought I'd cracked my skull, I crawled back to bed and lay there in misery all day hoping help would come. Sometime in the afternoon, I heard a tapping on my glass door. I looked up to see a stranger I didn't know peering into my room. Whoever he was, he was welcome. I dragged myself to the door, on my feet at last, and admitted Lewis Carlino, the screenwriter whom we had selected to write *Resurrection*. (You know, the one where I was to play this spiritual woman with the healing powers of Jesus.) I fell back into my bed and told Lewis I had the world's worst hangover and he should pull up a chair to the bed and we'd have our meeting. I don't remember a thing that was said, but this was our introduction, and we'd get to know each other better when Lewis came to the Stone House for a week's visit.

I stayed in bed for the rest of the day and the following day, on the set, Alan and I took one look at each other and started groaning, moaning, and laughing, each of us knowing what the other had been through the day before. We did become close friends quickly, in time for the shooting, but there are healthier ways to achieve the same thing using acting techniques.

By late summer of 1978, I'd completed filming *Same Time, Next Year*. *A Dream of Passion* was due to be released in the fall. *Silence of the North* was written and would be shot the following year, and *Resurrection* was written and ready to go into production. I felt my career was riding high.

Watch out for that "riding high" feeling. There's always a plunge waiting for you around the next turn in the road.

When Lewis Carlino had visited me in the Stone House, I shared with him my thoughts about the return of the goddess, the feminine hero, as well as feminine spirituality. I also told him about Raymond Moody's book *Life After Life*. Lewis asked me many questions about my personal life and, among other things, I told him about Neil. I had to. Nobody could be a guest in my house without being warned of a possible unexpected visit. When Lewis left, he went to a place on the beach in California and wrote the story of *Resurrection* in eighteen days. When I read his script, I was surprised to see that Neil had gotten into the story in the form of Cal, the character played by Sam Shepard, who goes a bit nuts and fixates on Edna and tries to kill her. (Lewis adapted my original name, Edna Rae, to Edna Mae.)

I loved what Lewis had done with all of the ideas we'd discussed. I felt at last I was working on a film that said what I had to say. I'd seen Jefferson's face be miraculously healed by Rosemary Russell's radionics box with its healing vibrations. I saw Eileen Poole transform Jeff's whole body and attitude with her intuitive penetration into his problem. I'd felt Reshad and Kenny on the Isle of Wight "remove the neggies" I'd picked up at the healing ceremony, and I'd watched Reshad teach healing techniques to a group of Sufis high up in the Alps. Why couldn't I actually learn to heal and do it on film?

I decided to find people who were authentic healers and see if I could train myself to do whatever it was that they did. I met a few so-called healers in California who didn't impress me. Eventually someone recommended I meet a woman in New York named Hilda Brown.

Our first appointment was in October 1978. She was a pleasant-looking woman around my age, with chestnut-colored hair. She lived in a modern condominium on East 79th Street. Her apartment had a small terrace with a lovely view of New York City. I told her why I'd come and she answered that the best way for me to understand what she did was for her to heal some situation in my life. That way, I could experience her method first-hand. I told her that the only situation in my life that needed healing was my ex-husband.

We talked for about an hour and I told her my history. We made an appointment to begin work a few days later. She said that we would not go directly to Neil, but would first begin looking at my "mother energy" and my "father energy" and clearing that. I wasn't sure what she meant. In our first session she did a psychic reading of me in which she reported that I was already a healer, that I too could "see" and heal people through my work. The danger of this was that when I met a person, I went right to the essence and saw their soul, often missing what was going on in their personalities and therefore accepting them somewhat naively. On the next visit three days later, she said that we would begin the clearing.

On the morning of our session, I left the Stone House to keep my appointment with Hilda. When I got up the hill and slowed for the traffic light, there was Neil. He looked awful: bloated, unshaven, wearing a blue shirt that was half out of his rumpled pants, his bare belly bulging out. He saw me and made a lunge for my car. I was terrified. My heart began pounding. I knew I couldn't wait for the light. I pressed my foot on the gas pedal, praying there was no oncoming traffic, when mercifully, the light changed. I pulled out fast, making the left onto the main road, but Neil managed to throw himself at my car. If I sped up, I might kill him; if I slowed he could reach me through my open window. He was on the hood of my car. I managed to swerve to the right and he slid off to the left. He shouted my name. I could see him through the rearview mirror, screaming, "Won't you even give me a lift?"

I was trembling and couldn't catch my breath. I made myself concentrate, relax my body, focus my attention, and calm down enough to get on the highway.

I arrived at Hilda's a wreck. As soon as I began telling her about Neil, I started shaking again. She decided that because of what happened, we would not work on mother and father energy as planned, but go right to Neil.

We sat on two chairs facing each other before the opened glass doors leading out to her terrace. Hilda said, "All right. Close your eyes and bring Neil into the room."

I felt reluctant to do this because I was so afraid of him, but after a moment I was able to get a clear image of him. She asked me to describe him and I said that he didn't look the way he looked that morning. He was wearing a white shirt and his hair wasn't gray. He appeared the way he looked before his mental illness descended on him.

Hilda asked me to describe his energy and I said, "It's gray and dripping. It's like graveyard energy."

Hilda asked me to ask Neil what he would like to do about this gray, dripping energy. After a pause, I said, "When I asked him, he smiled and said, 'I don't know, babe. I think I look kinda good like this.'"

After a few more questions, Hilda asked me to describe where Neil and I are connected. "Our foreheads," I told her. "There is a beam of blue light from his forehead to mine."

"A third-eye connection," Hilda said. Then she asked what I would like to use to cut this connection. I struggled with this for a while, then she prompted me and suggested it could be, for instance, a sword of truth. I agreed to that. In my mind's eye, I lifted the sword of truth and severed this laser beam of light between our third eyes. Each beam hung limply from our foreheads like two umbilical cords. I reached over with my right hand and tied a knot in the end of Neil's cord and it retracted into his head. At that very moment, an explosion rang out from the street so loud that Hilda and I jumped and gasped. After I resettled, I reached up again with my right hand, tied a knot, and the umbilical cord of light disappeared into my third eye. At that precise moment, there came another explosion, like cannon fire. Again we jumped. "That was for me," I said.

Hilda then asked me to repeat after her and speak the following words to Neil: "Neil, I forgive you for any harm you've done me throughout time anywhere in the universe. And I ask you to forgive me for any harm I've done you throughout time anywhere in the universe."

I was sobbing as I spoke these words. Then Hilda asked me to dance with Neil. He took me in his arms and we waltzed in wide circles around the room. When the dance was over, at Hilda's prompting, we said good-bye. And it was over.

But not really. When I returned home, Neil was still in the street. He'd been in the neighborhood all day. A neighbor had called the police. They came, gave him a good talking to, put him on a bus for Manhattan, and left. But he'd gotten off the bus and was waiting for my return. I got to my house and in the door before he could reach me. I called the police. They came immediately and took him away, this time putting him in jail.

I called the sergeant and, feeling brave from my healing with Hilda, I told him that I had tried everything I could think of to keep Neil from harassing me, but the only thing I'd never tried was sitting down with him face to face and calmly asking him to end this nightmare. I hadn't been able to do that because I was afraid he would kill me. I asked the sergeant if he would stay with me so that I could. He agreed.

I went to the station and the sergeant showed me to an office chair. He assigned two officers to stay with me. I sat and waited. In a few minutes, two more policemen entered the room with Neil between them. As soon as Neil saw me, he came at me with his hands raised and curled like he was going to choke me. He looked wild and growled, "Oh, this woman." A police officer quickly stepped between us, threw Neil down into a chair, and snapped, "Act like a man."

Neil and I talked with a policeman on either side of us. I can't remember all that he said. I do remember that he was crying. He told me that he loved me. We were sitting facing each other, knee to knee, as Hilda and I had sat earlier in the day. Neil's face was streaming with tears as he looked tenderly at me and said, "I know that I've hurt you. Oh God, how I've hurt you."

And I said, "I forgive you, Neil."

Then the rest just came out, unplanned. I said, "I forgive you for any harm you've done me throughout time anywhere in the universe. And I ask you to forgive me for any harm that I've done you throughout time anywhere in the universe."

Neil was looking at me intently and began blinking his eyes hard as though he were seeing something that he was trying to blink away. I said to him, "And now it is time to release me from your obsession. I am asking this of you."

Neil nodded. I rose and the policemen held Neil by his arms, restraining him until I was out of the room.

Two days later, on Wednesday, November 8, 1978, the police came to my home and told me that Neil's father had called the station and asked them to tell me that Neil was dead. He'd jumped from the window of the ninth-floor apartment where he lived in Manhattan.

I did not know what to think. I held on to my head with both fists, trying to stay steady so the harpies of guilt and blame did not grab at my sanity and run off with it. I tried to collect myself as a rider controls a horse by pulling a gallop into a collected canter. I stayed focused on what needed to be done.

I told Jeff. He did not cry; neither of us did. I knew I was in serious psychological danger. I had tried to heal an intolerable situation and this was the result. Was this the only possible way he could do what I asked, to release me from his obsession? How would I ever know? I knew I needed help with this. It was too big, too overwhelming. I had no idea what to do.

A telegram arrived from Neil's parents. It read: "CONGRATULATIONS! YOU'VE WON ANOTHER OSCAR. NEIL KILLED HIMSELF."

I called Reshad in England. He said, "Light a candle of remembrance for Neil and keep it lit for three days. Don't let it go out. Light the new one from the flame of the old one. Keep him in your consciousness and prayers. Stay with him while he makes the journey over to the other side." I lit the candle and set it on the mantle over the fireplace in my bedroom.

I called Lee Strasberg and asked to see him. He received me in his living room that evening. I told him what happened. As usual Lee's reaction was surprising and unique. He said, "I must say, I'm very impressed. I didn't think he had the courage to do that."

I hadn't thought of it that way. It must have taken enormous courage for him to let go of his grip on me, on life.

Back home I sat in my darkened bedroom looking at the flickering light of the candle, and wondered where Neil was right then. Was his soul crossing over to the other side, as Reshad said, making his passage through the Bardo, as *The Tibetan Book of the Dead* teaches? Could he hear my prayers for him? Or was this candle-lighting and praying an exercise in denial? An empty gesture to soothe my troubled conscience? I felt my faith rise to the possibility of his soul's journey. And I felt my cynic braying like a donkey at my feeble attempts to justify my complicity in his death.

Throughout the night I slept in short shifts. Each time I turned or opened my eyes, the single light of the candle danced on my wall, reminding me of Neil.

By this time I'd already decided to go to the funeral. I wanted it to register that the nightmare was over. I'd been so terrified of him and now I was afraid that, even in death, he could haunt me. I wanted Jeff to see him, too.

We drove to the funeral home on Long Island. As we walked in the room filled with Neil's relatives, the low murmur in the room rose to a loud rumble. We approached the coffin. It was open. I forced myself to look at him. Jeff didn't. He closed his eyes tightly. Whatever of Neil's body was injured in the fall was not apparent as he lay at rest on his white satin pillow.

Someone led us to a side room for the immediate family. His mother looked like a zombie. I assumed she'd been sedated. His father cried and said something like, "If he could know that you came today, he'd consider his death worth it."

"Will you come to the house after?" his mother asked through an immobile face.

"No," I said, "I can't do that, Flo."

I could forgive them their unconsciousness and cruelty in sending me that telegram, but I sure wasn't going to let myself in for a free-for-all at their house.

The day after the funeral, I went to my third appointment with Hilda.

When she answered the doorbell I saw her take one look at me and know something had happened. As I walked into her apartment, my whole body was shaking. "He's dead," I said. "He killed himself." I sat down and told her everything that had happened since our last session.

We began our work. Hilda asked me to bring Neil back into the room. I told her that he was there in two aspects. The bloated gray Neil that I last saw was there against the wall, wearing that blue shirt and crying. Then there was the Neil in the white shirt who sat near me and was radiant. Hilda asked me if there was anything else I wanted to say to him. Through tears I said, "I feel I want to thank him."

I guess I had received his death as a gift from him to me. I thanked him and we said goodbye. Was this a healing? In a way it was. I no longer had to be afraid he would jump out from dark places. I didn't need body-guards anymore. I could be alone. All of the outer situation was healed. But I would spend the rest of my life trying to heal the inner situation that was created because of that resolution. Neil haunted me in my dreams for years. Sometimes he had never died; other times he was back from the dead. Often I'd gone back to him and wondered how I was ever going to explain it to my friends. Time would reveal to me the other ways that the repercussions of his death would manifest in my life. It would take all of the effort I was capable of to descend into the shadows of my own psyche and be able to find what was hidden in the darkness and say, *This is mine. It may not be me, but it is mine. Mine to own, to deal with, come to terms with in whatever way I can.*

A few years ago I ran into Hilda Brown. I had not seen her since the events of November 1978. We chatted for a few minutes, then she mentioned she had just written a book about her experiences as a healer. "Did you write about Neil?" I asked.

"Oh, no," she said quickly, holding out both hands in front of her as though to ward off any responsibility that might want to come toward her. "That's yours," she said. "Not mine. That's yours," she repeated firmly.

I almost chuckled at her determination to own no part of it. I couldn't blame her. I wish I didn't have to own it either. But I do. This is my life, my journey. To be whole, which is my goal, I must pull my demons from their lair and embrace them, even love them. After much work for many years, I was able to remember how much I loved Neil. The fear finally left. The nightmares stopped.

I only dream of him occasionally now and the dreams are no longer terrifying.

A few years back, I did a retreat at the Ashram, a wonderful spa in California. One night a medium who channeled people who have "crossed over" came to speak. I gave this man Neil's first name. He gave me a message from Neil. "I understand now that I was not your teacher. You were my teacher. I am just now learning about all the things I thought I knew but didn't."

If the mystery of channeling has any validity, I'm glad for Neil that he is learning what he needs to learn. But it is not quite accurate to say he was not my teacher. Because of Neil and all that occurred, for me there's been no alternative but to spend my life committed to trying to understand the forces at work in me and, therefore, the world around me. I know that we are each a microcosm of the macrocosm, and if I can just work my way to clarity and consciousness, I will be able, as Kazantzakis says in *The Saviors of God,* to report to God as a soldier reports to his general at the end of each day, and say, "This is what I did today, this is how I fought to save the entire battle in my own sector, these are the obstacles I found, this is how I plan to fight tomorrow."

I know that I am the soldier.

I also know that I am the battlefield.

At this point in my life, it became my mission to realize that, just like everybody else, I am also the general.

Three weeks after Neil's death, I drove to the Abode, the Sufi compound in New York state where Pir Vilayat stayed and taught when he was in this part of the country. At that time, Pir had a beautiful partner named Taj. She was also a very respected teacher. I asked her to assign a retreat for me. I wanted to do a retreat in my bedroom at home for six days before I left for California to shoot *Resurrection.* I wanted two things: to fast and lose some weight, and to spend six days alone, in silence, meditation, and prayer. I hoped to achieve a transformation in that time that would help me to truly heal as I shot the film. It was a naive presumption on my part, but I barreled ahead as though grace could be summoned at will with nothing more than a lack of food, a few good prayers, and a whole lot of good intentions.

Taj warned me that this was not the way a retreat was done. She assigned me the Alchemical Retreat and said that it was normally done in a retreat house with your food brought to you and a guide checking on your progress. But I needed to lose some weight (as I always did before a film), and I thought the fast would take me to a high level, and frankly I was boldly (and blindly) using Jesus' model in the desert. If he could fast and pray for forty days and nights, surely I could for six. No? Actually, no. But I wasn't there yet.

When I left Taj, I was equipped with some tapes of beautiful angelic music to listen to at specific times of day, along with the prayers, most of them by Pir's father, Hazrat Inayat Khan, and instructions for eighteen hours per day of Zikr, meditations, and Wazifas. In the Sufi tradition, the Wazifas are the ninety-nine names of God. Each name is a different quality of the divine, such as forgiveness, majesty, or compassion. In Arabic each word carries that quality in the tone. As you chant the word in a particular way, you are actually intoning that quality of the divine into the vibration of your own being. It brings each specific aspect of God into you by the use of sacred sound. I went into my room on December 1 and was to reemerge on my birthday, December 7, transformed, healed, and ready to become a healer. I'd arranged with my friend Bill Smith to check my door every day. If I had any needs, I'd slip a note under it.

There were three flaws in my plan. First of all, Taj was right. It was too demanding a process to complete on a fast. By the third day I was too weak to keep to the eighteen-hour schedule and I began to falter.

Second, Reshad used to teach that "everything manifests in reverse." Meaning that what is happening on the inner plane reverses itself as it comes into manifestation on the outer plane. It's actually not unlike the Jungian concept of everything having a shadow. There's the stated phenomenon, and on the other side of it lurks its opposite. A good example of that is in Somerset Maugham's play *Rain,* where the minister is obsessed with saving the prostitute from sin and ends up falling prey to his own sexually repressed feelings for her.

Third, and most important, my intention with *Resurrection* was to bring into the public's consciousness the image of the feminine, the sacred feminine, complete with her sexuality, her healing powers, and her message that God/Goddess manifests in human beings as love.

So why would I choose a retreat that comes from the Islamic tradition? Judaism and Christianity are patriarchal enough, but Islam is the most patriarchal of all religions. I love the Wazifas, Pir Vilayat's teaching, and the ancient Zikr. But for this project, what I was trying to do was resurrect the lost sacred feminine. I needed to go to another source for that. I should have turned to Mary, Quan Yin, or even one of the spiritual feminine archetypes embodied in the Greek or Roman goddesses. But I didn't.

I managed to stay in my room until my birthday, and I did complete the fast and lose seven pounds, but by the fourth day, the "everything manifests in reverse" law was taking hold of me. I had some Bieler's Broth and realized I couldn't listen to any more angel song. I wrote: *I couldn't listen to the meditation tape of Pir Vilayat. I didn't want to pray anymore. I didn't want to retreat from the world. In fact, I loved the world, more than ever. I missed my friends, their jokes, their foibles, their humanness. I started to crave beer hall songs and lusty laughter, a juicy steak. The world of the flesh never seemed sweeter.*

I went through such anguish about what I perceived as my failure for not completing the Alchemical Retreat; I vacillated between guilt and justification. Finally, I reached an understanding about the character of Edna in the film: She really loved people in all their humanness, without judgment. My task for this role was to learn to really love people deeply.

The day after my retreat ended, I flew to California to take part in a healing seminar at Sky Hi Ranch to be conducted by the doctor/healer Brugh Joy. Sky Hi was a retreat house in the desert country about an hour and a half's drive from Los Angeles. There were about thirty people gathered for the seminar. Brugh is a doctor who happened upon a personal discovery of the energetic field of the body. He could feel the subtle energies of his patients with his hands. He didn't even know that other people could feel them and was relieved to discover that in the East, they had understood about these energy centers for centuries and even had a name for them. They were the chakras. Brugh wrote about the development of his healing techniques in his book, *Joy's Way.*

Brugh is tall, Nordic-looking, with impossibly high cheekbones. His hair now is like white silver, but in 1978 he was still very blond with ice-blue eyes and pale skin. He looked like a being of light that had floated down from the north and landed in this hot desert country, dazzling us all with his deep reflections.

We started each day with an early-morning meditation, then breakfast, followed by the morning session with Brugh. At the first session we sat on the floor in a circle and joined hands. Brugh had a contraption that looked like the body of a flashlight without the light. It emitted a sound when a current was established. As we held hands, the current that traveled through us caused the object to sing its electronic sound. Then Brugh asked two people on the far side of the circle from him to drop their hands. When they let go of each other, the object in Brugh's hands fell silent. There it was, proof that energy (electrical or otherwise) was running through us and when we held hands we connected the current and it ran through us all. We literally attuned to each other then, according to Brugh. We brought all our energy into the same vibration. That's what caused the particular pitch of that tube. It's why we hold hands when we pray. We are actually coming together in attunement.

On our second day, Brugh suggested we design a ritual. He talked about how ritual has always been a part of the human experience. Today we have only a few rituals left—like weddings, funerals, christenings, or naming ceremonies—but we have allowed the Church and the merchants to dictate how these are conducted. So Brugh didn't give any instruction about how to design a ritual. He told us that it was an innate capacity in all humans and we just had to tap into it and we would know what to do.

I decided to drum up the moon. I'd seen the full moon rise over the desert the night before just as the sun set, so I decided to go out into the desert about an hour before sunset and create a moon-rising ceremony. I got some pots and wooden spoons from the kitchen and set out away from the ranch toward where I'd seen the moon rise. Once I found my spot, I collected rocks and formed a circle with them and cleaned all the debris out of the circle. It took about an hour to do this and then I sat on the large flat rock in the center of the circle and, facing the setting sun, I meditated. I could feel the sun's hot pink light on my eyelids and when it was gone I opened my eyes to a sunset-streaked sky. The temperature dropped quickly and I put on the Irish poncho I'd worn up to Mont Blanc. I turned around on the rock facing the sky opposite where the sun had disappeared. Now I picked up my pots and wooden spoons and began drumming. I drummed for a long time, but the moon did not rise. Funny! Last night the moon came up just as the sun set. What could be wrong? This was when I learned that the moon rises about fifty minutes later every night. I drummed and drummed on the kitchen pots as the temperature dropped and the moon did not rise. Darkness fell and still no moon. I drummed on. Surely the moon must rise sometime. Perhaps I was in the wrong place. What was that? Something moved. Something alive was just over that rock there. Was it coming closer? Should I run? No, I kept drumming. I could sense it behind me. Then over my left shoulder. It was moving away. Then circling me. Something alive was just outside of my circle. It heard me, was interested in me, but didn't enter my circle. It was as if the circle was protecting me. As though nothing could enter my space. My arms were getting tired, my legs felt stiff. My back was aching. Where was the moon? I wondered if I'd concocted a dud ritual. What was I doing? Sitting in the desert on a hard rock beating on a kitchen pot and being circled in the dark by who knows what shuffling beast. Was I mad? Give it up, fool. But wait! What is that on the horizon? The darkness was lifting, just there directly in front, a lightening, a brightening. My drumming grew stronger. It was no longer a kitchen pot and I was no longer a fool. I was an ancient woman, appointed by her tribe to drum up the light into the night sky. At first a sliver of light, then a rising bright arc, and finally there it was huge, round, and bright, beaming over the horizon for one brief instant and then sailing on higher, losing size as she rose. Once Luna was safely in the sky, my drumming subsided and I felt the wind blow me back into my body, the one that ached and was cold. I scattered the rocks, deconstructed the circle, went back to the ranch, returned the pots, prepared for dinner. But I was secretly smiling. I'd entered mythical time, archetypal storyland, and those drums beat in me, in my bones. Some psychotectonic plates shifted deep in the inner core of me. I was Moon Woman.

People were quiet at dinner—eyes downcast, talking low. At the evening session after dinner, Brugh asked if anyone wanted to share anything about their ritual. Silence. No one did. Years later, I mentioned this to Brugh. He answered, "No one ever does. It's deeply personal."

Next morning, Brugh taught us how to turn on our hands so that we could feel the subtle energetic field of the body. It's hard to describe the process of doing this, but the best I can come up with has to do with intention. You hold your hands two or three inches above the body on which you are working. At first you feel nothing, but then as you focus more on the palm of your hand, you do notice something. It might be a temperature change or a tickling or prickling. However it begins, you say, *Oh yes! I do feel something.* Then you stay with that feeling, "intending" to feel more and soon you do. It intensifies. Soon your hand gets warm and the energy field feels like a gossamer wing brushed against your palm. Then you find you can channel energy through your hand into that energy center and you do this simply through intention.

On the third day, Sunday, we were to work on an actual patient. In the morning session, we sat in the circle facing Brugh and he introduced us to a young woman with cancer. She told us about her life and described herself as a very happily married mother of two children whose serene life was interrupted by this terrible disease. Brugh sat quietly beside her, listening attentively as she painted this ideal picture of her life that was now so sadly destroyed. When she was finished, Brugh asked a few quiet, but very direct, questions. In just a few moments, the whole story was transformed and we learned another version of her life which was not the image she had first presented. She had told us the truth as she held it, but then out came this story:

She was very close to her mother and sister. They had lived in the same neighborhood and their lives were intertwined daily. In the previous year, her husband got transferred to a place where they didn't know anybody and when she moved away from her mother and sister, she felt lost. To top it off, right after they moved, there was a season of unusually bad weather. The children were confined in the house. They had no friends and being only two and three years old, were very demanding of their mother's attention and relied on her for entertainment. Her husband was involved with his new job. She felt alone and trapped with her children in an unfamiliar environment. She made the astonishing statement that just before she got cancer, she was actually afraid she was going to "stick their heads in the toilet and drown them."

Then Brugh asked one final question. "What happened after your diagnosis? Who took care of the children?" She answered, "My mother and sister. My husband was able to get his old job back and we had to move back home so I could get treatment."

Certainly not in every case, but in this case, it did seem that the illness served a purpose. It provided an escape hatch.

I couldn't tell from her reaction if she was aware of this and Brugh didn't say it explicitly, but it was so evident that her body had provided her with a way out that the idea hovered in the room, patiently waiting to be grasped by whoever was willing to look at illness in this new light. After a moment, Brugh asked her to lie down on the massage table and for us all to gather round her. Neither Brugh nor the patient told us what kind of cancer she had or where it was located in her body, so at a word from Brugh, we all held our hands over her to feel her energy field and then to channel energy to her. My hands went to the area of her lower abdomen. I immediately felt raging heat pouring from the area where her fallopian tubes would be. It was much stronger than anything I'd felt the whole weekend from anyone else's field. I stayed with that area. Other people moved around. Some stayed with her heart, others her head. Some ran energy up from the soles of her feet. But I was so struck by the enormous heat I was sensing, I just stayed there and gave her whatever energy I was capable of channeling to her. Later when Brugh and I had a few minutes alone, he said to me, "You know, she had both of her tubes removed and your hands went right there like a homing pigeon. You really are a healer." Then he smiled and said, "If you ever want to give up acting, just let me know. I know another profession for you."

I have no idea what happened to this woman, whether the work that we did on her helped her or if her cancer had reached the point of no return. But this is what I do know from that weekend with Brugh: There is a field around the physical body that can be felt with another person's hands. Some say that this field emanates from the body and is what is called the "subtle body." Others, including Reshad, say that the physical body emanates from the subtle body. That physical manifestation is the last plane of existence, each plane manifesting from a more refined and less dense plane, and all of it beginning on the plane of spirit. This sounds right to me, but I can't say that I *know* that from experience. What I do know is what I have experienced personally. There is a discernible field coming from, or manifesting as, the physical body. It can be felt and energy can be given to it. I do not believe that anyone can be healed without their wanting to, both consciously and unconsciously. I know that when I've been in situations where I'm overworked or overtired but feel I can't stop and rest, my body will step in and give me a good bout of flu that sends me to bed. Is that my body doing that? My mind? Or my mind in my body? Pianists will tell you that the mind of a pianist is not just in the brain, but also in the hands. Our minds in our bodies have a wisdom of their own. When we can't make up our minds how to get out of a situation that we want out of, our minds in our bodies take over and create an exit strategy.

When we made *Resurrection*, healing was not a well-known practice in America, as it was in other parts of the world. In the last twenty-five years, healing has permeated conventional medicine to the point that many hospitals now have healers as part of the surgical team in the operating room. When I had bilateral knee replacement in 2003, I asked friends who know how to channel energy to work on me. When I went back to the doctor for a checkup two months later, he said I was at the stage of healing usually achieved after four months.

Brugh told me that the healer who was most like Edna Mae in our script was a woman named Rosalyn Bruyere at the Healing Light Center in Glendale, California. I contacted Rosalyn, sent her the script, and in January 1979, I drove to Glendale and met her at her healing center. Rosalyn was a big woman with a pretty face and magnificent healing powers. Her reaction when she read the script was, "My God! They've written my story." I worked with Rosalyn for the next few weeks. When I was with her my hands were always easily ignited as they were with Brugh. Rosalyn taught me how to turn on my hands by myself. I spent the next few weeks making all my friends hold still while I felt their energy fields. I found Rosalyn's guidance so helpful that I was able to convince Howard and Renée to hire her as technical adviser and have her on the set every day. She proved to be an invaluable asset, not only to the film itself, but to the day-to-day making of the film.

Most of the crew considered the story and the subject of healing to be somewhere close to science fiction, until one of the crew guys dropped a lamp on his hand and smashed it. The fleshy part of his thumb and fingers turned purple. He was bleeding profusely. Arrangements were being made to drive him to the nearest hospital, many miles from where we were shooting out in rural Texas. Rosalyn pushed through the crowd hovering anxiously around him. He looked seriously frightened. "Let me see that hand," she said.

After a quick examination, she pressed her fingertips over the wound in his swollen hand and in a few moments, the swelling subsided, the color eased back to normal and before long, the gash began closing. The rest of the day he would say to anyone he happened to pass or stand next to, "Look at this! Unbelievable! She's something. Look at this!"

Another time, Rosalyn and I entered the makeup trailer and, as I approached William Tuttle's makeup chair to sit down, Bill said to me with a terribly pained expression, "Ellen, my assistant will have to cover for me for a few hours today. I have to go to the dentist." It was an hour and a half to the nearest town, so I knew this must be an emergency.

"What's the matter, Bill?" I asked.

"I've got a toothache and it's killing me. It must be abscessed or something."

Rosalyn, standing nearby, said, "It's not your tooth. It's your ear. Sit down. I'll take care of it for you."

I stood up and Bill sat in the makeup chair. Rosalyn stood behind him and placed her fingertips behind Bill's ear. After a few moments, Bill said with a startled expression and tone of voice, "Oh! I just felt it drop!"

"Yeah, that should do it," Rosalyn said. The infection or whatever it was had dropped from his ear to a part of the body where it could be carried away.

I asked Rosalyn how she knew it was his ear and not his tooth. She said simply, "I could see it."

I really didn't know what she meant by that. See it how? How did it appear? On him? Physically? Or in the air between them? In her mind's eye?

I got the answer later that year. I was in Canada making *Silence of the North* and taking violin lessons because my character in the film played violin. My teacher came to my hotel room for my lessons. One day he was feeling some tension in his back so he stretched it out in a peculiar method he had developed. He stood in a doorway, his back against the doorjamb, his hands braced in front of him, and he pushed into his spine going down one vertebra at a time. With each push there was a slight pop as his spine released the tension. I was impressed with his technique and watched him as he worked his spine loose. But when he stopped, I immediately said, "No, there's one more." He resumed his position and curved his back to the place where he had stopped, then curved it further so that the next vertebra down was the contact point and pushed. There was a loud pop.

He looked at me curiously and asked, "How did you know that?"

Without thinking I said, "I could see it."

Only later did I reflect on that remark and realize that I had just experienced Rosalyn's "seeing." Yes, it was in my mind's eye. It was a seeing, a feeling, and a knowing all at once. I did not actually see the vertebra inside his body. I saw him stop before he was finished, as though I'd expected that final pop and he stopped before he got there. These kinds of insights are so hard to describe because our language is designed to communicate what we perceive with our five senses. When we get into the sixth, seventh, eighth, and even more senses (I think more than twenty have been identified so far), then language falters. It's like trying to use Aramaic to delineate the processes of quantum physics. That's why so many people doubt the experience when they hear about it. If they haven't had it themselves, language is a clumsy tool with which to communicate it.

Every morning in the makeup trailer, Rosalyn would put her hands on my head for a few minutes. She called it "fluffing my aura." There was much good-natured joking about this. But one day Rosalyn phoned and said she had to take care of some personal business and would be a few hours late. I got my usual makeup from Bill Tuttle, had my hair done, got into my wardrobe, and proceeded to the soundstage. After rehearsal and waiting for the lights to be hung, I was called to the set and stood on my marks. There seemed to be much murmuring behind the camera and the camera operator squinted first at me and then the lights. Finally, he called over the director of photography and they murmured some more. The operator approached me and said, sotto voce, "Ellen, did Rosalyn fluff your aura today?"

"No," I said. "Why?"

"Because it shows," he answered sheepishly.

I asked, "What does it look like?"

"I don't know," he answered. "You just don't look right. Not as radiant as usual."

I hurried off the set to where Rosalyn was just arriving and asked for a dose of her magic . . . for that is what it is, isn't it? All of these techniques were once part of what women did naturally in the old times before the Church decided, as they institutionalized their new religion, that it was necessary to call the way of the Great Mother evil. For at least two hundred years, any woman who was caught practicing "the old way" of natural healing was cursed as a heretic and tortured until she confessed that she was a witch. Promises that if she confessed, her children would not be tortured, were not kept, and whole families were tortured, burned at the stake, and their homes and farmland were then confiscated by the Church.

It took all of the fourteenth and fifteenth centuries for the Church to completely suppress in European women the healing techniques and the herbology that had been practiced since pre-Christian times and are still practiced in Eastern medicine. Midwives were the most victimized, but women all over Europe were subjected to torture that is so horrendous, it's almost impossible to believe that it was done in the name of the gentle and loving Jesus.

This is not to say that Western medicine isn't a wondrous miracle of civilization—my new knees can attest to that—but the transfer of energy from one human to another is an amazing adjunct to modern medicine and, at last, it is being utilized.

In the story of *Resurrection,* Edna Mae MacCauley is almost killed in the car accident that kills her husband. In the emergency room, she has a near-death experience. After Edna recovers enough, she is brought home to Kansas by her cold, remote father to live in a small cabin on his farm. Also living on the farm is Edna's grandmother and it is she Edna tells about going through the tunnel of light while she was technically dead and out of her body. Her grandma then tells her about a woman she knew who had the same experience and how, when she returned, she had "the gift" of healing. Edna decides to see if she has "the gift" too and sets out to heal her crippled legs, and succeeds. For the rest of the film, Edna is a healer.

The role of the grandmother was extremely important because she's the one who lays out the premise from which the rest of the film unfurls. If the audience doesn't believe her, they won't believe the rest of the film.

In New York, I met with the great stage actress Eva LeGallienne, who was then eighty years old and had never appeared in a film. We had tea together at a lovely old hotel in Manhattan. She wore a purple plush slouch hat and held her Yorkshire terrier on her lap. She was beautiful, articulate, and dazzling. I had long ago read her amazing biography of the great Italian actress Eleanora Duse, and had even brought it backstage to be autographed when I saw her in *The Royal Family.* I was utterly enchanted with her. Our director, Dan Petrie, agreed and this most elegant actress of the American stage was hired as my Kansas farmer grandmother. Not only was she spellbinding in the role, I had the honor of giving the world the gift of seeing the work of this great artist in the only film in which she ever appeared. She is gone now and all of her artistry is buried with her except this one role.

Her entrance in the film is when I return home, my legs in braces, and must be lifted from my father's truck by my cousin, Buck, played by my dear friend and fantastic masseur Ralph Roberts.

As we shot the scene, LeG (as she preferred to be called) was looking on horrified at my crippled legs. The only thing was, she was a little too horrified. Her expression could be read in the balcony of any theater. At lunchtime, I invited Dan Petrie into my trailer and said to him, "Miss LeG is playing too big. You've got to tell her that she doesn't have to do so much." Then quoting Peter Bogdanovich, I said, "Tell her to just think the thoughts of the character and the camera will read her mind."

Dan suddenly looked about ten years old as he said, "You want *me* to tell one of the greatest actresses in American theater how to act?"

"Yes!" I said. "You're the director. Now, go do it."

I never asked Dan how he told her, but after lunch, her work was transformed. No longer aimed at the top balcony, her emotions were life-sized, simple, and real. At the end of the day, I said to her, "You catch on fast, LeG."

She was sitting next to me and she thumped my knee with the back of her hand and said rather gruffly, "Well, I've been watching you, dear."

In her last scene in the movie, Edna Mae is leaving and says good-bye to her grandmother. It's one of the most beautiful scenes I've ever worked in. LeG was magnificent. At one point she says, "That's it, isn't it? If we could just *love* each other the same way we say we love Him, I expect there wouldn't be so much bother in the world."

Every time she said that sentence, she dropped her voice right into her heart when she said the word "love." She did it all day. Every take of the master shot, the two shots and the close-ups. Every time she said the word "love" from that place in her heart, it brought tears to my eyes and I could never figure out how she did it. Did she technically lower her voice? When I watch the film I see that her voice does not really drop into a lower register, but something drops. Something falls into her heart and is spoken from there. She did it every time. It's like a miracle of acting. We don't get to meet many masters in life. She was one.

Then, a moment later, she says that she thinks this is the last time she's ever going to see me. Edna Mae says, "Will you save me a good seat on the other side?"

"I'll save it," she answers. It was her last scene in the only film she ever did. It was a real good-bye to the world, and we both knew it. It's there on the screen for all to see.

We had other miracles during the filming of *Resurrection*. There is a scene where Edna Mae's healing abilities are being tested at UCLA as Rosalyn's had been. The testing culminates in an attempt to straighten the body of a patient who was distorted by a rare disease. I stood next to the bed as they did the finishing touches on the lighting. The actress playing the patient was lying in bed, the covers up to her armpits. We'd introduced ourselves and chatted lightly as the final work was being done. When rehearsal was called, the actress assumed the position she would play. Her hands curled under and were pulled up around her shoulders. Her face contorted and her whole body twitched. We began the scene. At one point, I pulled her blankets and sheet down to reveal the length of her body. This actress was very believable in what she was doing, but I was amazed to see what she was able to do with her feet. They were bent inward at the ankle, but the toes were bent also. They curled on top of each other in the most awkward and disjointed manner. Could she be a contortionist? I looked more carefully. No, she wasn't doing this. That's how her feet grew. I looked up at her. She had been watching me look at her feet. A soft smile spread across her lips and tears came to her eyes. She said, "I've been ashamed of my feet all my life. At last, they're going to be of use to somebody."

She wept softly as I put my hand on her hand and my other hand on her disfigured feet. On talking to her further, I discovered that nobody in the production knew about her feet until I uncovered them. It was by chance that she was cast. Her feet, which she had been so ashamed of, became a great gift to us. There is a close-up of them in the scene and they make the scene so beautiful. This woman left the set that day looking cleansed of an old burden.

In another scene, Edna has been trying to heal herself and, after weeks of effort, she is about to give up. She's sitting in bed with her legs outstretched and she surrenders all attempts to heal herself. She's failed. She can't do it. She just doesn't have the juice, she says. A fly lands on her toe and she wiggles it off before she realizes what she's done. Suddenly, she understands what's just happened. She's moved her toe! And that is the beginning of her learning to walk again.

So how do you get a fly to land on your toe at the right moment and fly off when the toe wiggles it away? Well, just as you hire a horse wrangler for a Western, you hire a fly wrangler! The fly wrangler arrived with his trailer, which he parked outside the soundstage. He had with him forty flies that had been frozen alive. He was to put a frozen fly on my toe at the last second, and just as the director called action, the lights would melt the ice and I would wiggle my toes. The fly flies away and I proceed to play the scene. That was the plan. But it turns out that it's not quite so simple. Of the forty flies that were frozen alive, more than half of them died inside their icy shrouds. By the time we got to shooting the scene, another ten had perished from God knows what. We began shooting with only ten flies. We quickly worked our way through that group. One melted too fast and flew away before the camera was running. Another melted and plopped off my toes, belly up. Soon we were down to the last fly and we hadn't gotten one print. If we didn't get this last fly, we'd blown a whole day and all that money on this one scene, and have nothing to show for it. Just as we were about to shoot, Dan, the director, was about to call "Action!" I said, "Wait. Stop! God/Goddess, we need help with this one. This is our last chance! I'm asking you to help us now. Please make it work. Okay, we can go."

The set was silent. Nobody moved. Sound was rolling. Camera rolling. Nobody breathed. In the stillness, Dan said very quietly, "Action." With his tweezers, the fly wrangler picked up this last frozen fly from his portable cooler and delicately placed it on my toe. He ducked out of the set. The lights melted the ice, I wiggled my toe. The fly flew away. I played the rest of the scene.

"Cut! Print. We got it." One print. That's all we had. That's what's in the film. I gave thanks for the help we received. Ask and ye shall receive.

There were several things I wanted to accomplish with this film. The original idea was "Jesus Christ comes back to earth as a woman." Well, I didn't feel any of us were capable of writing a new Sermon on the Mount, but if some of the qualities of Jesus could manifest on earth again through an ordinary woman, I felt it could give us an opportunity to explore several things that were interesting me at the time.

First of all, in other older religions female sexuality was a source of power in goddesses. Christianity had stripped the spiritual feminine of her sexuality. Through the years Christian religious women would be celibate nuns like Teresa of Avila, Hildegard von Bingen, and Mother Teresa. I wanted to reunite spirit and body in a modern spiritual woman. That's why, soon after the film begins, we see Edna in bed with her husband. Second, I wanted to present the ancient art of energy transference as an available modality of healing—effective, repeatable, and something to be explored by science, not scoffed at in ignorance. Third, I wanted to show death not as an end, but as a release into the light. The undertakers' lobby of America has actually succeeded in making it illegal in this country to handle your own dead as all humans have done throughout time. We can't prepare a body for burial or bury on our own land. Consequently, we have become unfamiliar with the physical reality of death. There was a healing quality in the loving preparation for burial, of making a coffin, digging a hole, and laying to rest someone we loved. It was a worldwide ritual that has been taken from us by the professionals. Preparation for death has become something secretive, frightening, and to be kept out of sight.

I wanted to show Edna with her father as he died and entered the light. That scene was also an act of forgiveness for Edna. She confronted her father about making her have an abortion, a nasty illegal one so that she could never conceive again. That spoke to the patriarchal attitude of our culture that forces girls into dire acts when they are ashamed of themselves, as I was when I got pregnant and had an illegal abortion.

I wanted the sexuality to be real, so I asked for Sam Shepard to be cast as Cal because, to me, he was the sexiest man around. I was very attracted to him. Then in the film as Edna develops her power and grows famous, he becomes frightened and finally psychotic. I hadn't known that Lewis

Carlino was going to put that in the film, but I'm glad he did. Why is it so frightening for a woman to have power? Why should that elicit a psychotic reaction in a man?

After Cal tries to kill Edna, she goes away. At the end of the film we see her running the Last Chance gas station in the desert. She's taken it over from Esco, played by Richard Farnsworth. He's gone to Machu Picchu, as he always dreamed of doing. She still has her healing power, but she's relinquished the fame and is healing anonymously those who find her out in the desert, where hangs the sign, "God is love and versa vice."

That is really the message of the movie and that's what I wanted to say. Edna heals by loving. We tend to limit our definitions of that word to sexual love or familial love, but there are so many kinds of love. Why could Jesus heal? Because he truly loved unconditionally the person before him. Seen in this way, love is total acceptance of the person. Accepting him or her without judgment. When people are accepted as they are, with all their flaws and frailties, they bloom. They blossom. They are healed.

It's what Lee Strasberg did for me. He saw me. He accepted me and in that, he healed me of the vacuum left by my absent father, healed me of the feeling of being wrong, valueless, mistaken, in need of punishment and correction. He looked at me and said, Yes, you have something to offer—yourself, which is a true and worthy offering. No one had said that to me before. I had always tried to hide whatever it was that I was, but Lee said, no, don't hide. Come out. Just as you are. That's what we want to see. Offer us your most hidden, tender part. We receive it gladly. That's healing. That's what I wanted Edna to do. I wanted people to see that the only power on earth that truly heals is the power of love. As the Bible says, "Love bears all things, believes all things, hopes all things, endures all things."

Scientists tell us that everything is energy. That energy can be attuned, made to vibrate at a higher or lower frequency. Different frequencies of the electromagnetic field have different effects on humans, as has been demonstrated by testing the effects of meditation on the body. Rosemary Russell's radionics box attuned a portion of Jeff's hair to a healing vibration, and that attuned the rest of him. How is that possible? One time, I was forced to have a tree on my property cut down. As the trunk lay on the ground, the energy field could still be felt, standing where the tree had stood. It was a definite, palpable, vibrating force field in the shape of the tree. And I wasn't the only one who could feel it. My friend Candy was there. I said, "Feel that?" She said in wonder, "Yes! What is that?" I said, "It's the tree's living energy. It hasn't dissipated yet." In Kirlian photography, which photographs the energy field of living objects, when they cut away half of a leaf, the photo shows the energy field of the whole leaf. We are all energy fields walking around bumping into each other, and those fields can be affected by changing the rate at which they are vibrating. An old Sufi saying (according to Reshad) is, "If you want to change your life, change your being." You do that by changing your vibration. Loving energy changes your rate of vibration.

"God is love and versa vice." I wanted as best I could to manifest love on film for all to see. And people do. Not everyone. But those with eyes to see, do.

Finally, I wanted the film to present a spiritual woman who loved and appreciated the work and teaching of Jesus, but not within the confines of any one religion. Jesus' teaching is available to all. He was not a Christian. He was a Jew. He did not start the Church. The Church fathers created the Church based on the work of Jesus. I wanted Jesus to be seen in his own light, not through the eyes of the Church fathers. Throughout the film I referred to Jesus in a reverential way, but not in a "churchy" way. I was very disappointed when the producers made the decision to remove every mention of Jesus but one. I think it was a mistake. But an even greater mistake was mine. I never claimed the power that would have prohibited their doing that. Just as with *Alice Doesn't Live Here Anymore,* I didn't ask for executive producer credit.

Grandma says to Edna, "The power is a gift, child, to use and to share." But any power must be owned before it can be used and shared. That was my failing. It was like a curse. I could not own my own power. Why not? It would be a decade before I could even ask the question.

As I waited for *Resurrection* to go through post-production, I went to work on *Silence of the North*. We began shooting in searing heat, bitten by black flies. By the end, we were three thousand miles north of the United States on a frozen lake. With only seven hours of light per day, we had to take advantage of every moment. No lunch break. Between shots, Tom Skerritt and I could get out of the wind in an army tank that came with us, loaded with equipment. The physical demands of the film were beyond anything I'd ever experienced. It was also funny. At one point I was sent out on a road with an assistant director who was receiving messages through her walkie-talkie from the other assistants and the director. I was waiting for my cue. It was a scene where I was to confront a wild bear. This is the conversation I heard over her walkie-talkie:

"Cue the bear!"

Silence.

"I said, cue the bear!"

Silence.

"Cue the bear! Cue the bear!"

"I can't, sir!"

"Why the hell not?"

"Sir, I'm afraid the bear shit has frozen shut the door of the cage. We can't get it open!"

I laughed so hard I almost cried, but I dared not or my tears would have frozen.

We were visited once by an executive from Universal. He got out of the car about eight feet from where I was standing. His hair was black. In the few steps he took to reach me, I saw his hair turn white and icicles hang from his nose hairs.

There were icicles hanging from the windows *inside* my trailer. One morning, the temperature made the crankshaft explode into flames. A teamster reached for the fire extinguisher. I yelled, "Don't put it out yet! Let me get into my wardrobe by the fire."

He turned his back and let the crankshaft burn while I changed by the only heat I'd felt in days.

When we flew to this location I saw from the plane that there were no buildings, no roads, just trees. It was truly the wilderness. When we arrived at Fort MacMurray, Alberta, there was a landing strip, a lake, and a few houses peopled by a handful of Eskimos. We were so isolated that the crew went primitive and became a pack. The wardrobe mistress told me that if you connected each name on a chart with a ribbon to each name the person had slept with on the crew, every name would be attached to every other name.

The *Silence* crew became an entity that would keep its coherence over the years. Whenever a crew member would start a new picture, they'd check the set to see how many other *Silence* crew members there were. Twenty-five years later, sometimes I walk on a set in Toronto, Montreal, or Vancouver, and someone will walk up to me and say, "Ellen, I was part of the *Silence* crew." Many have retired or gone on to other things, but those of us who are still working remember it as one of the wildest highlights of our lives.

We made many mistakes, some major ones, but it was a heroic effort for all involved. Not as heroic as the real life of Olive Fredrickson. Despite all our hardships, we didn't do her justice. But it was a worthy attempt.

Resurrection was shown at the Toronto Film Festival and was well received. The Oscar buzz started and, sure enough, I was nominated. I had great hopes of winning another Oscar.

Just before *Resurrection* was due to be released, I called Brugh and asked, "Will it be a success?"

There was a pause in which I could picture Brugh switching from outer vision to insight. Then he said slowly, "No, not in the way you are hoping for. But it will be later in another way."

That was not what I was hoping to hear, but it did turn out to be the truth. The film was released by Universal. As I understand it, at that time the studio had a set release pattern for seven different categories of films—comedy, love story, Western, et cetera. *Resurrection* was a metaphysical film. There was no such category at that time. So the studio dropped it into what it considered to be the closest category . . . science fiction! It was released as a science fiction film in a test market for three days somewhere in New Mexico. The people who came to see a science fiction film were disappointed and said so on the cards they filled out afterward. The studio's reaction, as it was quoted to me, was, "Nobody wants to see this film. Kill it."

The first review that came out said, "Just when it looked like Sissy Spacek, in *Coal Miner's Daughter,* had a clear shot at the Oscars, along comes Ellen Burstyn in *Resurrection.*" *Coal Miner's Daughter* was also a Universal film and had been deservedly very successful. The studio made what it called a "straight business decision" and when Sissy was nominated for her beautiful work in *Coal Miner's Daughter* and I was nominated for *Resurrection,* the studio backed the film that had already proven itself a moneymaker. They pulled *Resurrection* out of theaters in Los Angeles where it had just been released, and rereleased *Coal Miner's Daughter.* In New York, *Resurrection* was running in only one theater and it was not advertised in newspapers. I called Universal and said (or maybe "shouted" would be a better description), "I've got a nomination for Best Actress in a movie that's running with no ad in the newspaper!" The next day, an ad the size of a postage stamp appeared. Soon the picture was yanked from the theaters. Universal would be able to declare it a loss.

The first part of Brugh's prediction came true. Later, the other part also proved to be true. The picture didn't quite die. It would appear on television now and then. People began writing to me about it. I found out that there was a kind of cult growing around it. People would tape it off their television and make tapes for friends. It was being used at healing seminars. Health care professionals were interested in getting copies. After seven years, I'd received so many letters from people asking me if I could help them obtain a copy to use in their workshops or classes, that I finally wrote to Universal. I sent them copies of a few of the letters I'd been getting. I asked that if they had no plans to release the film on videotape, would they give me the right to release it myself so I could make it available to all the people who had requested it. That did it! I got an immediate response that they would be releasing the film on videotape right away. I thought, at last this film that was so important to me, that had more in it of what I wanted to say, would finally be available to people.

I still have people approach me on the street to tell me how important the film was in their lives. Some will say that because of *Resurrection,* they were at their parents' side when they died. That it changed the way they viewed death. Some people have told me that they stopped denying their psychic abilities after seeing the film and actually developed them instead of hiding them for fear they'd be thought weird. Some people, many in fact, told me they went into the healing profession because of the film. And others told me about feeling healed by the film. One woman asked how it was possible. She said, "I walked into the movie theater with a throbbing headache I'd had for days. When I came out, it was gone. How did the film carry the healing power? In the celluloid or what?"

I said, "It's not physical. It's metaphysical." It's a simple explanation and she accepted it, but really what does it mean? Metaphysical is that which is beyond the body, beyond the material.

That woman's headache was surely located in her head, but the cure, the healing, happened somewhere beyond that and whatever it was that was healed by seeing that film, no longer was present to manifest a headache. That's how I understand it, at any rate.

Then of course, we have to ask, "What *is* beyond the physical?" Ah, that's the big question. I'm sure the answer is, "the spirit," but what exactly does that mean? To many people it means God. But then, God is love and vice versa.

After the disappointment of *Resurrection,* I hoped *Silence of the North* would fare better. But it didn't. First, Universal decided it was a "woman's picture," and there was no market for it, so they planned to retell the story. Olive Fredrickson had written about bringing her children up alone in the Far North. Universal's idea was to rewrite the narration and have the story told by the husband she later married! I was apoplectic. It felt like creative rape. I prevailed in that battle, but I lost the war. Universal didn't release it theatrically; instead they sold it to pay TV. I was devastated.

When I was in New York I moderated the sessions at the Actors Studio every Tuesday. Lee always did the Friday sessions. I was considering doing a play about Sarah Bernhardt called *Memoir.* I signed up to do an acting exercise for Lee, based on Sarah. I just needed to expose my work to his penetrating eye to see where I was going wrong. Something was going very wrong. I wrote in my diary that I was crying all the time. I felt that there had been a reversal of fortune in my life and I didn't know why, but that I couldn't help feeling I'd brought it on myself.

I did a television special on the trial of Jean Harris, who had killed her longtime lover, Dr. Herman Tarnower. I was nominated for an Emmy for it, but it wasn't my best work. Jean Harris was asked to comment on the show, which she watched in prison. She said, "She was too nice. If I'd been that nice, I would have gotten off." She was right.

I was asked to direct a play called *Judgment* off-Broadway, which I did, and it received excellent reviews, but I was paid very little for it. I was running out of money with no offers in sight.

And I finally broke off my long-term relationship with young Michael, so there was no warmth in that aspect of my life.

But there were some good things. There was a big ball held in honor of Lee's upcoming eightieth birthday and I was asked to speak. In my speech I said, "Other acting teachers teach you how to create illusion on-stage. Lee teaches us how to explore the nature of reality." Lee's wife, Anna, later told me that when I said that, Lee leaned toward her and said, "Gee, I never thought I'd hear anyone say it in public." I was pleased I'd been able to acknowledge him publicly for the depth of his teaching.

It began to dawn on me the implications of Lee's turning eighty. He wasn't going to live forever. How much longer would we have him in our lives? I thought I had better prepare myself for that eventuality. One of these days I was going to have to get along without him. But how does one go about preparing for that? I wasn't sure.

The producer Manny Azenberg sent me a script called *Duet for One* by Tom Kempenski, which was currently playing in the West End in London. He asked me to read it and if I liked it, he wanted to fly me to London to see it, starring Francis de la Tour, who was the wife of the playwright. I loved the play and soon flew to London. It is the story of a great violinist named Stephanie Anderson who is diagnosed with multiple sclerosis and can no longer play. She goes from denial of the emotional pain to deep depression. It takes place entirely in her psychiatrist's office, and the only characters are the violinist and her doctor, Dr. Alfred Feldman. It was a funny, deep, profoundly moving play, and I immediately wired my agent that I wanted to do it.

As I watched the performance, I kept picturing Lee Strasberg as the psychiatrist. I felt that the relationship between the two characters was very similar to mine and Lee's. The doctor leads her out of her depression and squarely into feeling the pain of her loss so that she can stop denying it and begin to heal. He gets her to feel how truly important her talent and artistry are to her so that she can honestly mourn their loss. Lee had introduced me to my own artistry. Through his recognition of me, I began to see myself through his eyes instead of my own tainted lenses. Lee had just had great success in *The Godfather Part II* and seemed to enjoy his return to acting. I was very excited about the idea of doing this beautiful play with him.

I took the script to him to see if there was any chance in the world that he might consider doing it with me on Broadway.

After a few days, Lee called and asked me to come by his apartment on Central Park West. Anna greeted me and showed me into their beautiful living room with its lovely view of Central Park. Lee held the script in his hands. He said, "I was very moved by this script, dahling. You know the music world has recently been mourning the loss of the great cellist Jacqueline du Pre. She also has multiple sclerosis and there hasn't been a cellist of her virtuosity since Casals. And she was young yet! The cello is an instrument, unlike some instruments, where the musician only gets better with age. We can only imagine how far she might have gone. It's a great loss. So, yes! I found this play, I must say, very moving." He nodded his head as he stared out the window.

I could feel my heart thumping in my chest. In the quiet of the room I asked him, my voice shaking, "Does this mean you'll do it?"

Still staring out the window, he said, "You know, I'm given scripts all the time. I read them, some are good, very good. Some not so good, and I always thank the people, but I say no. But this time . . ."

That's when he turned and looked at me, his usual eagle expression softened.

"I'm going to say yes. Frankly, just for the opportunity to work with you."

I cried, murmured, "Thank you," burbled my good-byes, and ran out of there, embarrassed, excited, stunned. I got on the elevator and flattened myself against the wall. I couldn't believe what I'd just heard. I took a cab to Manny Azenberg's office. I ran in without an appointment. I leaned over his desk and said breathlessly, "I gave the play to Lee Strasberg to read and he liked it! He said he'll do it."

I expected Manny to jump up with joy. Instead he said in a mild voice, "You really think he could play that part?"

"Play it? My God, he's perfect for it!"

"Hmm, well let's get a director first and then we'll decide."

We started talking about directors. I couldn't believe any director in their right mind wouldn't want Lee Strasberg to play my psychiatrist. He practically *was* my psychiatrist. We started looking for a director, but I had to leave for France, since I was serving on the jury of the Cannes Film Festival. In the meantime, Anna Strasberg called and said, "We haven't heard from anybody and Lee has to set his schedule."

I faltered, "I'm having trouble convincing the producer that Lee's right for it. But as soon as we get a director, I'm sure he'll agree with me."

Anna said softly, "Oh well, then, if they don't want him . . . I didn't realize that."

I interrupted her. "I want him and I'm sure it will work out."

While I was in France, I read something about Bill Friedkin in the newspapers. It may have been that he was ill or that his marriage had ended, but whatever it was, it impelled me to call him. I'd never spoken to him about my disappointment regarding his marriage or the way he handled it with me. I wouldn't. I'd always looked up to Billy, and the last thing I'd ever do is criticize his behavior.

As I was talking to him on the phone in my hotel room looking out at

the Mediterranean, Bill asked me, "What about you? What are you doing?"
I told him about *Duet for One,* how good it was and how frustrated I was
that I couldn't get Manny to agree that Lee should play the psychiatrist.

Billy answered, "He's crazy. Lee would be wonderful in that role." The
sun was sparkling on the blue Mediterranean waters.

"Really? You think so?" I got excited.

Billy said, "Of course. He's perfect."

I gulped. "Do you want to direct this play, Billy?"

"Well, I'd like to read it."

I called Manny who sent him a copy. Billy liked it! He agreed to direct
it. I was ecstatic. Billy met Manny. They liked each other a lot and went
into negotiation. By the time I got home from Cannes, Billy's deal was set.
Then he called me and asked, "What do you think of Max von Sydow in
the role?"

A chasm opened.

"What happened to Lee Strasberg?" I asked.

"Oh, he's not right for this," Bill said.

"But Billy, you said he was perfect for it. That's why I asked you if you
wanted to direct it."

I was teetering on the edge of the chasm, shale slipping away beneath
my feet.

"I didn't take this play under the condition I cast Lee Strasberg,"
Billy said.

I fell over the edge, stones falling around me as I tumbled into the crazy
abyss of betrayal. I felt sick at heart.

I read the play again and loved it even more. I wanted to do it so badly.
I called Manny and asked for a meeting with Billy. The three of us went
out to a restaurant. After pleasantries, I said, "I've read the play again. I really love it. I very much want to do it . . ."

Manny interjected, "I hear a 'but' coming."

"But," I said, "I feel like I've been stabbed in the back. So I will do the
play if Lee is cast. Otherwise, I won't do it."

There was a moment's silence, then Manny said, "I'm really sorry you
feel that way."

"Well, I do."

More silence.

"Okay," I said. The play was on the seat beside me. I handed it to Manny, and then I left.

I called Anna and told her what happened.

I felt rotten. Truly rotten. I wrote Manny a letter.

Dear Manny,

I had a conversation with Kazan today and told him what happened. He was very disappointed—thought the idea of Strasberg playing my psychiatrist was a brilliant one and was very much looking forward to seeing it. He couldn't imagine anybody not seeing what a fantastic event that would be . . . agreeing with Coppola and Penn, who felt the same way.

You once said to me, "We've only got one mistake to make." It is my opinion that you've made it.

At any rate, I feel lousy and I'm sure you do, too, but you have my very best wishes. It's a wonderful play and deserves a big success.

Billy did cast Max von Sydow, who is a brilliant actor and whom I admire very much. Despite half-informed newspaper reports that I had left the play when Max was cast, he had nothing to do with my decision.

Anne Bancroft was cast as the violinist. Billy had almost cast her in *The Exorcist* and she had almost played *Alice*. Anne and I had a career-long history of getting parts away from each other. She was a fine actress, a student of Lee's, and I had only admiration for her work, despite the fact that we competed for so many of the same roles. To round out this circle of our overlapping careers, I went on to work with Arthur Penn in a play at the Actors Studio called *Monday After the Miracle,* playing Annie Sullivan, the role Anne had created on Broadway in *The Miracle Worker,* and for which she won an Academy Award for the film. I wasn't very good in this play. Annie should have done it, but she was busy doing the role I should have done.

Duet for One opened and quickly closed.

On November 17, 1981, Lee Strasberg turned eighty years old. I was asked to join Lee and Anna on a morning talk show. It was on that show, as I remember it, that Lee made the statement comparing the actor's work to everyone else's involved in a film or play. "As hard as it is to push those heavy lights around the stage, that is nothing compared to what it takes to move the human soul."

Three months later I was asked to run for president of Actors Equity. No woman had ever held that position before, and I thought it would be good to change that. My career was in a shambles. I needed a new sphere to explore, a new place to invest my energy. I decided to accept.

Alexander Cohen produced an extravaganza to raise funds for the Actors Fund. It was called *Night of 100 Stars*. One of the many highlights of the show was a chorus line of male stars. Lee appeared in the routine positioned between two of his students, Al Pacino and Bob De Niro. Many of the other men in that line were also students of Lee's.

It was a long, tiring day. The show was being taped and many numbers had to be retaped. When we weren't working, we hung out in the dressing rooms or the greenroom and talked or just gawked at each other. Late in the evening, I wandered into the greenroom and saw Lee sitting next to Anna, watching the taping on the monitor. I sat next to him and we chatted a little. Lee wasn't one for small talk, so I didn't stay long. But before I got up, I said, "Lee, I've been asked to run for president of Actors Equity."

He reached over and patted me on the back, "That's wonderful, dahling. Congratulations." He so seldom touched anyone that his pat felt special and warm. I took my leave.

Those were the last words he ever said to me.

Two days later, early in the morning, I was still asleep when the door to my bedroom opened. I woke up and saw my friend Katherine Cortez, who was working as my assistant and living in the Stone House, enter the room and walk toward me. She always called me by my spiritual name. "Hadiya," she said. "We just got a call. Lee Strasberg died."

"No, no, no," I wailed, over and over. "I'm not ready," and pulled the covers over my head. I had told myself that I must be prepared for this, but I was not prepared. What was I to do now? Who would I work for when I was preparing a role? Who would I go to when I was in trouble?

I called the Strasberg number and learned that Anna was at Roosevelt Hospital. I threw on some clothes and drove to Manhattan. The hospital personnel took me into the cubicle where Lee was lying. His son, Adam, was with him. Anna was on the phone making funeral arrangements. I sat with Adam beside Lee and put my hand on Lee's arm. I took his hand and held it as the remaining warmth left his body. Adam and I talked and joked about his father through our tears, wondering if Lee could see and hear us.

We could hear Anna on the phone across the corridor having an argument with a synagogue. It seemed that they were not accepting Lee's funeral because the Strasbergs had had Adam's bar mitzvah somewhere else. Anna was outraged. She was a tigress through all of the arrangements. She didn't allow Lee's body out of her sight until he was laid out. She wouldn't turn him over to anyone else. After the argument with the synagogue, she chose to have him laid out at Frank Campbell's Funeral Home. I went with her to select a casket. I stayed with her all day, and that night I slept in bed with her so that she wouldn't be alone.

Later, our closeness would be ruptured by a dispute regarding the tapes of Lee's sessions at the Studio. Anna declared the tapes her property. The Actors Studio board felt that they belonged to us. A judge agreed with Anna. At one point, the judge said, "Why can't you separate the voices on the tapes? Mrs. Strasberg take Lee's voice and you take the actors'." I said, "That won't do us any good!" What we wanted was to be able to listen to Lee speaking to us. That's what we had lost when he died, and we wanted to hold on to that experience. Even if it was what he'd said in the past. Maybe there was something we missed. Something we'd understand better or deeper now. Just to hear what he saw in us. That was our loss and what we were trying to keep alive. The judge awarded the physical tapes and the rights to use them to Anna, but with copies to us to listen to. We never got them. Anna was estranged from us for years. Only recently have we started speaking again. She has invited me to take part in two ceremonies honoring Lee and I have been grateful to her for doing so.

Lee Strasberg began his career in the chorus line. His last public appearance was in a chorus line at Radio City Music Hall. It was ironic that his memorial service was held at the Shubert Theater where *A Chorus Line* was playing. Lee's coffin was brought down the aisle and placed center stage. Everybody in the theater world came—actors, writers, directors, producers, and most, if not all, his students. He was a giant of the theater and was deeply mourned. Those of us who had the great good fortune to be fertilized and quickened by his genius would feel the loss of him for the rest of our lives.

I spoke at the memorial service and told the story that I had once referred to Lee as a master, like a Zen master. Lee had responded, "Just call me a human being." I added, "He was the best human being he could possibly be." Then I read the Twenty-third Psalm.

When all is said and done, is there really a better aspiration anyone can have than to be the best human being one can possibly be?

Soon after Lee's death, we called a meeting of the Actors Studio board. In attendance were Elia Kazan and Cheryl Crawford, two of the original founders of the Studio. Also Arthur Penn, Al Pacino, Shelley Winters, Estelle Parsons, Lee Grant, Martin Balsam, Frank Perry, Carl Schaeffer, Liska March, and Anna Strasberg.

We asked Kazan to take over, but he declined, saying it was time for the next generation to step forward. Lee always had been both president of the board and artistic director. Anna nominated Paul Newman as president. We quickly elected him—much to Paul's surprise when I called to tell him. But he did accept. Artistic director was more difficult. There were several of us present who moderated the sessions, but there didn't seem to be a consensus on who could even attempt to fill Lee's vacant chair. Kazan suggested a troika until we could settle on one person.

Kazan agreed to serve on the troika for the time being. Arthur Penn and Al Pacino were voted the other two. When the votes were announced, I remember someone spoke up. "Hmmm, all men." I had gotten the next most votes, so Kazan said, "I know! Let Ellen be an alternate." Everyone agreed to that.

Around this time I was elected president of Equity and moved into my new office just a few blocks from the Studio. After a few months, the Actors Studio board voted Al Pacino and myself co–artistic directors, and a few months after that, Al said he was confident that I could handle it alone, and resigned.

Although I served in both capacities gratis for three years, they took an enormous amount of time and attention. I was always running between my office at the union on 46th Street and Broadway to the sessions at the Studio on 44th Street. One day, as I was preparing to dash from a meeting at the Studio to one at the union, Paul Newman said to me, "My God, you are a Type A." I didn't think of myself that way, but I could see I was behaving like one.

I immersed myself in the affairs of the union and teaching at the Studio. I thought of them as two different aspects of the profession. Actors Equity was concerned with the quantity of jobs for actors and stage managers, and conditions in the workplace. The Studio's concern was for the quality of the artistry.

I had wondered how I was going to stand on my own without Lee's guidance. Now I had no choice and no time to think about it. I was completely involved with these two positions. Soon after I was elected, *The Hollywood Reporter* asked me for a comment on the failure of *Silence of the North.* I said, "Hollywood has had all of my heart I'm going to give it. I'm just going to concentrate on my job at the union and work on Broadway." I meant I wasn't going to develop pictures and make the kind of investment I made in *Silence* for seven years. I did not mean that I would turn down a good role if it were offered to me, but that's how it was interpreted; that I did not want to work in films anymore. I had, effectively, put myself out of the film business.

I hardly noticed that I made no films for the next three years, something unheard of in my career. I did do a Broadway play, *84 Charing Cross Road,* but it wasn't a success. The director, James Roose-Evans, said to me during rehearsals that I seemed distracted, and I was. But I was too distracted even to know that I was distracted.

In a newspaper interview from this period, I was quoted as saying that I'd trained my mind to compartmentalize, and I could drop other considerations when I focused my attention on the job at hand. But I was fooling myself. True, I could drop the union while at the Studio, and vice versa, but when it comes to creativity, the unconscious needs to be engaged, and the unconscious is not so easily controlled or manipulated. My work was flat in this play. And I knew it. I just couldn't connect with the character. While we were doing two weeks of previews, I began having horrific attacks. One was so bad that I called my former therapist, Bluma, whom I'd not spoken to in years. I couldn't catch my breath and I had terrible stomach cramps. She identified my symptoms as an anxiety attack. I'd never experienced that before going onstage. I had always been excited to open in a play. Suddenly I was dreading every performance. I didn't know what I was doing out there. It was like I'd forgotten how to act. I could teach others how to do it at the Studio, but it was slipping away from me. It was like a nightmare where you try to run, but can't. I struggled through the previews. The audience enjoyed the show, but mostly they enjoyed what was happening on the other side of the split stage, where Joe Maher and the rest of the company were happily playing with each other in the London bookshop. I was alone in my apartment on my half of the stage, no other face to relate to, reading my letters out loud to the dark. During the curtain calls there was warm and enthusiastic applause for each cast member as they entered. Then I came out last, being the so-called star, and there was a dip in their fervor, a diminishment of warmth, a chilling confirmation of what my stomach pains were telling me already. I was no good in this play!

Alex Cohen thought we should open on December 7, 1982, my fiftieth birthday. He wanted to have a big birthday bash on opening night. I pleaded with him not to heap on any additional pressure, but he said he was too much of a showman not to take advantage of this opportunity. We opened on my fiftieth birthday. My mother and brother, Steve, came. Brugh was my escort. It was a big splashy event, but my stomach was in knots. I felt frail and vulnerable. When I entered the party, the flashbulbs popping felt like an attack. I was afraid of what the critics were going to say. I didn't think I could handle another failure, and yet I didn't feel strong in the play. Where had my creative energy gone? It was like it was deserting me and I had to go onstage without the support of any talent whatsoever. Just sheer will. And there was no Lee to turn to. I was on the high wire with no net, my legs were trembling, and I was afraid.

I didn't read the reviews. We managed to run for three months. I did improve during that time, but only after all the critics were gone, the party was over, and I could settle down to work. I found my way to an acceptable level of performance, but I never soared.

After we closed, Mel Brooks bought the rights to *84 Charing Cross Road* for his wife, Anne Bancroft, to do the film. I was getting great lessons in how to roll with the punches.

When I bought the Stone House in 1975, my career was at its peak and the house was in terrible shape. When I sold it in 1986, my career was at its nadir and the house had been restored to its original elegance and beauty. I saved the house and, in the end, the house saved me.

The Stone House was built in 1876, designed by J. Cleveland Cady, who designed the old Metropolitan Opera House. The original owner, a man named Tonetti, was a lover of trees and a world traveler. Even before the house was built, Mr. Tonetti planted a tree he'd bought in Paris when it was a twenty-year-old sapling. The tree, indigenous to Japan, was a fern leaf beech. It had a branching habit of reaching out, touching the ground, and taking root. New trees sprung up from these branches so that the tree grew a wall around itself. By the time I bought the house, the tree was at least as high as a five-story building with the foliage growing right to the ground so that in summer you could not see the massive double trunks in the center. There was an opening in the outer circle of branches like a doorway and when you entered there, you were inside the cathedral that the tree had built, standing in the magic of dappled light that on a breezy day, when the leaves quivered, shimmered with quickly alternating patterns of light, dark, and light again. It was the most enchanting atmosphere I've ever experienced. The approach to the house was down the driveway toward the tree and then the driveway made a complete circle around the tree to the main entrance of the house. The house had always stood on five acres of property, but the previous owner, desperate for money, had sold off two acres, cutting into the circle on the far side of the tree. The driveway would have to be reconfigured.

Reshad came for a visit before I moved in and we walked around the property. When he saw the tree and I told him about the driveway, he said, "That circle has been protecting the tree all these years."

I knew that Reshad knew about these things, having been the dowser that acupunctured the gravelly land that became Findhorn in Scotland, one of the richest, most productive gardens in the world. It produced giant-size, prize-winning vegetables from its fertile soil.

I asked, "What do I do?"

He answered simply, "You must redefine the circle."

It was two years later before we found the way to redefine the circle, but first we went to work on the house. My partner in this enterprise was my friend and roommate, Bill Smith. Although Bill wasn't a licensed architect, he was an extremely talented artist, designer, and carpenter. We restored the gracious proportions of the original house, tearing down cheap room dividers and jarring contemporary additions. We built a room upstairs with an incredible view of the Hudson River, added a raised hearth and my prized Buddha lamp, and called it "the chapel." The room had windows on three sides, so it was the perfect room in which to meditate and watch the sunrise over the Hudson. In the evening, the reflection of the sunset in the west turned the river into a living Monet.

We were to continue work on the house for eleven years, but we had it in pretty good shape after two years. I got the idea to do a production of *Midsummer's Night Dream* outdoors on the property. It was to be an actors' production; no director, no stage managers, and the actors were to make their own costumes. Rehearsals were whole weekends at the house, every room filled and many sleeping bags on the floor. Most, if not all, of the actors were from the Actors Studio and we invited our friends as audience. The price of admission was enough food for ten people. At the end of the play, the faeries led the audience to form a circle around the tree and send loving energy to the stately giant. Afterward, actors and audience plowed into an Elizabethan-style feast.

People ate, cavorted, turned cartwheels, strolled barefoot in the grass, and lay down on their backs with their arms flung wide, having sloughed off their city restrictions and reveled in the wide-open freedom of a midsummer's day. The event was such a success, people left saying it was the most beautiful day of their lives. I still meet people in New York who tell me that they were there and they'll always treasure that day. We did it two years in a row. The second year, the audience doubled to over two hundred.

The production was photographed by Steven Arnold, whom Bill Smith brought to the event. Steven was to become one of my closest friends for the next thirteen years until he died of AIDS in 1994.

My early years in the Stone House were a particularly happy period of my life and I enjoyed all the days I spent there. Even after my career took a dive, I was busier than ever teaching. I'd become a Sheraga, which in the Sufi order is like a minister. I performed two weddings at the Stone House, one under the giant fern leaf beech tree and one facing the river. I was giving seminars in "Acting as a Spiritual Path." I was trying to share what I'd learned from my teachers and from my own experience. But I wasn't getting paid for anything I was doing.

By 1985, I'd run out of money.

My accountant took out a loan and put up the Stone House as collateral. The following year I had to come up with a million dollars or lose the house. I'd never yet made a million dollars in one year, so how was I going to do it when my career was in the doldrums?

There was only one way: a television series. My agent, Todd Smith, had been trying to get me to agree to a series for a long time. Although I'd made a few movies for television, I'd managed to avoid a series. Now I relented. I probably should have done a drama, but somehow we settled on a sitcom. It was a mistake. There are people who are good at this. I'm not one of them.

But I did earn the million dollars and paid off the loan. But by mid-

1986, my finances were tight again. My accountant told me that the house was draining my resources. I was finally convinced that I had to give up my beloved Stone House, so I sold it to my neighbors across the street.

I rented a six-room house up the road. I decided that whatever didn't fit couldn't come with me. I went around the house putting green stickers on everything that I truly cherished; blue stickers on the things that would be boxed and put in the storage room; and red stickers on everything else to be sold. A great lesson in "letting go."

I was asked to deliver a prayer for peace at the Cathedral of St. John the Divine on New Year's Eve. I accepted, even though that day was moving day. I had signed a contract that the house would be delivered "broom clean." I called the new owners and told them I would be out on the last day of the year, but the house would not be "broom clean" until the following day.

On the morning of January 1, 1987, I walked down the road carrying my broom and dustpan. As I approached the house, I stood on the spot where I had first seen the magnificent tree and the stately mansion. I'd had eleven glorious years there, and I'd left the house restored and sparkling with new life. I was turning it over to people who could take care of the house and its land. I felt pleased as I walked down the driveway to the house.

It was a beautiful, bright day and the sun streamed through all the many windows. I started on the first floor and swept out each of the rooms. Then I went up to the second floor and did the same. On the third floor, I saved the chapel for last. With the whole house empty and "broom clean," I entered the chapel.

The Buddha lamp was gone from the central place I'd designed for it. The hearth was cold. I sat down on the cushions of the window seat and stared around the room. The whole atmosphere had changed. The sense of awe and holiness was gone. It wasn't a chapel anymore. It was just a room with a pretty view of the river. I sat still for a moment feeling this astounding difference. I always thought it was the room itself that caused everyone to hush their voices when they entered. Now I saw that it wasn't the room at all; it was the use of the room, the intention invested in the room that had infused it with its sense of sacred space. When that intention was withdrawn, it was just a room. I had projected my own inner sacred space into this room, and when I sold the house, I had withdrawn the projection and I could see it for what it was: an empty room with a pretty view. When I closed the door of the Stone House for the last time, I walked away with a sense of carrying my own chapel within me.

Pir Vilayat had come to visit me in late 1986, just before I moved out of the Stone House. He told me that my career as an actress had developed certain of my qualities, those of my persona, while other qualities of my soul went undeveloped, so that I had not yet found out who I really was. He suggested that I was in a transitional period and that my next work would be in the spiritual realm. My need to create beauty around me was a way of asserting myself, he said, but the time would come when I wouldn't have to do that; that I would become what it is that I had been asserting.

Early the following year I went on retreat with him. He spoke of mastery. Pir's father had written a book on the subject and said that mastery involves having control of all the details—and no addictions. I still had so many addictions: wine, grass, judging, gossip, negative thinking, the material world, and on and on. And so I began my efforts to develop mastery on the inner and outer planes. Of course it is difficult to develop mastery in your outer life when, in your chosen profession, you are not at the top of your form.

There are never many good film roles for women, but what there were, I was not being offered. I did do *Pack of Lies* for Hallmark on television and was nominated for an Emmy. I did a movie with Gene Hackman and Ann-Margret called *Twice in a Lifetime,* which was very well received by the critics but not popular with audiences. I continued to work enough to keep myself afloat, but I just wasn't satisfied with the quality of my work. I always tried to do my best, and sometimes I did, but it wasn't at the level

I'd been able to achieve in the past. I looked around at other actresses my age, among them other Academy Award winners, and felt the same about their work. I wondered if menopause was to blame—do creative juices ebb with age? Elia Kazan, in his autobiography, wrote the chilling line, "Talent, like beauty, fades!" Was that what was happening to me? Or perhaps my inner demons were holding me back.

I investigated these questions in every way I could. I went to Elisabeth Kübler-Ross's seminar, "Death and Dying," thinking it could be a way to explore any hidden guilt I might be carrying about Neil's death. As I went through the profoundly painful and cathartic exercises, however, I found that the death that came up for me to work on was not Neil's, but the baby's—my abortion. I was shaken to my core to discover how deep that pain was and how much shame, regret, and guilt were there. But with the help of the guides, who had been trained by Kübler-Ross, I was able to bring it to the surface and let it scream its full, horrible intensity. I believe I finally integrated that painful event into my wholeness.

After completing *Pack of Lies* in London, the producer Bob Halmi invited me to his home in Kenya. I took my brother Steve with me on safari, and I developed my passion for photography. My work began to be shown in galleries and to appear in photography magazines.

Still, I knew I was not the person I wanted to be. And I didn't even know who that was.

I felt an urgency to know myself and a yearning to know God.

I had to find out why I was here, and what on earth was the purpose of my life.

I began attending the Asilomar Conference at the close of 1992, conducted by Brugh Joy and David Spangler, the philosopher. The conference usually began on December 27, with four days of stimulating speakers and workshops by people like David Whyte, the poet, or Jean Shimoda Bolen, the Jungian analyst who'd written the wonderful book *Goddesses in Everywoman*. Each year, all of the leaders addressed a theme, usually an archetype. I ended each year at this conference until the series was completed in 2000.

Brugh Joy's work included dream interpretation. I told him about two big dreams I'd had recently. One was a dream about a cow in a hotel lobby that I tried to move and couldn't. She was too heavy with milk and I had to milk her. The other dream was about tracking the Wild Man, a great prehistoric man dressed in animal skins, long dead, but fully preserved. He was extremely tall and when I found him, I crawled up on him, put my arms around his neck, and nestled in his arms like a baby.

Brugh helped me to identify the cow as a symbol of the Great Mother, the archetype of nurturance and abundance. The Wild Man was the long-buried image of the archetypal father. Though he was not appearing in the form of a living man, still he was there in me for comfort. These two dreams were telling me that there was rich activity in my psyche that was portending change and growth.

Then I began dreaming night after night huge, strange, sometimes frightening dreams. It was as if Psyche were opening the cellar doors and all the figures that had been imprisoned in the shadowy dungeons down there were erupting and fleeing into the light of day.

By then I'd made friends with the Jungian analyst and author Marion Woodman. I called her at her home in Canada and read the dreams to her.

"Ellen," she said, "You need help with those."

I said, "I know. Who should I go to?"

She asked, "Do you want a man or a woman?"

Something told me the work I needed to do now should be with a man.

"A man," I answered. "Know anyone?"

Marion said, "The best one I know in New York is named Nathan Schwartz-Salant."

On my first visit with Nathan, I walked in the door and said, "What do you make of this dream?" I read him a long dream that ended with being tripped up by an entity made of green protoplasm. Although it was only the size of a half dollar, it was powerful enough to move all the furniture in the room into a straight line. Then it ran up the wall and hid behind a picture.

Nathan said, "Have you ever been the object of envy?"

Those were the first words he ever said to me, and they would prove to be my introduction to a whole realm of fear of which I was completely unconscious. At the end of the session he handed me a book by Helmut Schoeck called *Envy*.

The book was a study of envy around the world, how it functions in different societies. There are many theories on the assumption that the normal person's drive is to acquire the greatest amount of property and power. But these theories overlook the fact that in many situations the object of human activity is a diminution, a lessening of assets. Primitive people who are more successful and prosperous than their neighbors often try to disguise their good fortune by hiding it. A farmer will buy several small fields instead of a large one and wear old clothes in order not to attract the envy of his neighbors. For a person who excites envy may become the victim of the evil eye, causing his crops to fail, his family to fall ill, and other misfortunes to befall him.

It took years of work with Nathan to understand how, step by step, I had come to fear the evil eye directed at me, and how I seemed to have attracted envy, first from my mother and then from Neil. I had good reason to fear it—it had cost me the love of my mother and the life of my husband.

Saying that sounds so pat, but understanding didn't come easily. After all, it was not conscious thinking; it was feeling that accumulated in hidden corners where the younger and more primitive aspects of the psyche live. Understanding this didn't come right away, but it helped when I remembered when I was president of Actors Equity and artistic director of the Actors Studio and gave a newspaper interview to one of the New York tabloids. When it came out, there was a full-page picture of me on the cover of the arts section with a banner that read, "The Most Powerful Woman on Broadway." I remember thinking, "Oh, no!" I felt utterly dismayed. Soon after, I declined to run for a second term as president of the union.

It's an odd reaction that I just accepted at the time, but looking at it in light of the work I was doing with Nathan, it seemed symptomatic of what I was grappling with. I told Nathan that I felt I was carrying an inner saboteur that was undermining all my efforts. I wanted to be free of him. He'd been operating since Neil's death and I could only assume it was because of guilt. Nathan pointed out that I'd allowed myself to work, to function, even to have some success, but I'd kept a lid on it.

So that's what we had to work on. I understood it intellectually, but it took years of effort to completely give up the habit of self-sabotage.

Within a year of my work with Nathan, I ended my drinking days without any effort. They just came to an end. When I reread my diaries of the 1960s, I was appalled to see how much denial I was in about Neil's sickness and how I refused to face reality.

Nathan asked, "How much were you drinking at the time?"

"A lot," I said.

"Yes," he said quietly. "Alcohol is poison for you."

And that was that. I stopped. I think it was the trust I felt for Nathan that allowed this to happen. I'd already stopped smoking grass a few years before. So that was cigarettes, marijuana, and alcohol gone. But there were other, subtler habits left to work on.

Nathan spoke to me about money and my disdainful attitude toward it, which I had developed in reaction to my mother's overemphasis on material possessions. She always seemed money-hungry and I made a point of saying that money wasn't important to me.

"You've got to want money," Nathan said. I was shocked.

He encouraged me to strengthen my "phallic side." My inner masculine figure was undeveloped, not assertive.

Two years after I started this process, I was making more money than in any year since Neil's death and bought a beautiful old house on the Hudson River that I loved. It was smaller than the Stone House, but the view and the two-acre garden were even more beautiful.

In one of the first sessions with Nathan, I told him I wanted to take hold of the process of becoming myself—my authentic self. Not my persona, not my ego, which is something I created, but the "I" who created my ego.

One image of the self is called by Jung the "temenos." It is the image of an inner courtyard, a sacred ground wherein rituals, meditation, and prayers can take place. It is a place of inner safety. Over and over, during the next ten years, I was to dream of that image.

With Nathan's help, I came to see how, as a child, when I should have been looking at my mother and saying, "I want to be just like you when I grow up," I was saying, "I don't know who I'm going to be, but I know I don't want to be like that." (The clinical term for it is a "negative mother complex.") It works, to a certain extent, but there's one big problem with it: When you consciously form your structure in a negative way, you unconsciously take in your mother in ways you don't realize. In other words, your mother becomes your shadow. I had an urge to slap Nathan's face every time he said that to me. Just as my mother used to slap me. It was my shadow flaring up when confronted with what I refused to see in myself.

For a long time I thought of the shadow as the container of the dark impulses in humankind, but eventually I came to understand that the shadow can be made up of any aspect of our personality that we do not want to see and are turning away from.

Much of my time with Nathan has been spent grappling with my wounds regarding Neil. I couldn't stop wondering if my success caused his illness. The conditioning starts early, at least as early as that letter in *Seventeen* magazine that I read as a young girl, which asked if a girl plays tennis on a date, should she let the boy win? How quickly and deeply such cultural attitudes sink in and do their cunning work in young minds.

I never did find in me the wish that Neil was dead, or that he would kill himself. Had I wished it and then it happened, I probably would have felt somehow that magically I'd caused it. I did want the situation to end. I did ask Neil to let go of me. But I never found anywhere in me, either consciously or unconsciously, a desire for him to die. What I did find was a consistent refusal to own my own power. And that went all the way back to early severe punishments for asserting myself. That's where it began; Neil's death was the confirmation of what happens when a woman is powerful. Neil killed himself at the height of my career. Nathan showed me all the ways, dating from immediately after his death, that I gave away my own power.

I've since found this to be a big issue with many women. That cultural conditioning is widespread. Men are lauded for asserting power and handling it well. It is a rare woman whose ego is strong enough and healthy enough to let loose all her energy and thrive. I know a few, and there are more now than in the past.

Nonetheless, my efforts to reestablish equilibrium were beginning to pay off. An opportunity presented itself to do some real work on my artistry.

The scientist Joseph Children Pearce, in his book *The Biology of Transcendence*, says that our brains are hardwired to reach for transcendence. And if we ignore that urge, very often the result is its opposite: violence. Some people experience this feeling of transcendence through meditation, prayer, or yoga. Some artists experience it while creating. Mozart spoke of it when he said that music just came through him and that all he had to do was write it down.

It's difficult for an actor to have this experience while making a film because of the interrupted process of filmmaking. It is more likely to happen onstage.

I was offered the chance to be in Horton Foote's great play *The Trip to Bountiful* at Theaterfest in Montclair, New Jersey. Even though it wasn't Broadway, I leapt at it because I was ready to test in my work the liberation I was experiencing. I loved working on this role. Horton Foote came to the rehearsals and cried and cried. This was the beginning of our friendship. When we moved the play to the Phoenix Theater Company on the SUNY Purchase campus, Horton brought a director named Michael Wilson to the performance. Soon Michael and I worked together on another of Horton's plays, *The Death of Papa*. We had such a good time that we did a production of *Long Day's Journey Into Night* at the Alley Theater in Houston and a year later at the Hartford Stage in Connecticut, where Michael had become the artistic director.

It was during *The Trip to Bountiful* that my creative energies returned to me in a flood and I had my first experience of transcendence through the creative process. By then I'd answered my own question of why, as Kazan said, "talent, like beauty, fades." It came to me in a quote from Ouspensky: "Art is the search for beauty, as religion is the search for truth." The operative word here is *search*. It is not the finding; it is the search. That's why, after an artist has won awards and received the world's acclaim, she can make the mistake of believing that she "knows." It is in the "not knowing" that the search occurs. It is a living process where creativity thrives. It is standing in the space of "I don't know" with dissatisfaction with what has already been achieved, and eagerness to open up to the unknown.

One day, some of the other cast members from *Bountiful* picked me up at my house to take me to the theater. In the car, on the way to the theater, I felt wild. I couldn't stand being in the car. I wanted to get out and run. Finally I opened the window and hung my head out like a dog. I couldn't wait to get onstage. That night, the play just poured through me in a great torrent. Bram Lewis, the company's artistic director, came backstage at intermission, his face streaming with tears, and asked, "What is going on?"

"Good show, huh?" I said.

"It's more than that—something beyond that."

He was right. It was creative energy blasting me wide open. It had come roaring back to me with full force, beyond anything I'd ever experienced.

It was not to be the last time I experienced this feeling of transcendence. Once an actor has that experience onstage, it keeps us going, hoping for it to come again. But we can only prepare the ground for it and receive it if it comes. We can't make it happen. It's like grace. It's happened in every play I've done since, but only once or twice in each run.

A few years ago, I went to visit a friend with Alzheimer's who was in the Actors Fund Home. Vivian Nathan had had a long, distinguished career as an actress in the theater, as well as being a beloved teacher at the Actors Studio. Her long-term memory was intact, but she had no short-term memory. Soon after I arrived, she referred to this experience of transcendence onstage. She said, "Sometimes you are onstage and something happens. It's like you are no longer acting. The play just comes through you and you just get out of the way and let it come. When that happens, it's like a door opens to another dimension and you get a glimpse that there is something beyond this plane that we usually experience as our everyday reality. Once the actor experiences that, he's never the same. It's what keeps us going."

Then she looked at me directly and said, "You must know that. You've experienced it, haven't you?"

I told her that I had. We went on chatting for a few minutes and then she said, "Sometimes you are onstage and something happens . . ." And she repeated the same thing again. She told it to me over and over, always as if she had not already said it. I was there for over an hour, and in that time, she must have related that experience fifteen or twenty times, always with a feeling of reverence. It was both sad and profoundly spiritual. I thought, "So this is it, then. At the end, there is nothing left but the transcendence."

Central to my education in the self was learning to take responsibility for my own character. I didn't want to go through life blaming my misdeeds and shortcomings on my mother's violence or my absent father. I was determined to develop the inner stability of becoming my own loving mother and guiding father. Jung says that we don't have a neurosis; we have the memory of a neurosis. We recreate it anew every day like a habit. I had practice in giving up habits. Now I wanted to give up the habit of feeling intimidated by the Mother, longing for the Father, and drifting in a state of uncertainty as to where I belonged.

One day, needing a particular feeling for a role I was doing, a feeling of safety and being loved, I did the following exercise. Jung called it active imagination. I closed my eyes and visualized my childhood home in Detroit on Hazelwood. I entered the house and walked through the rooms until I came to my own bedroom. I saw seven-year-old Edna sitting on the bed. I told her I'd come to take her out of that house, that I would take care of her and she would one day be a famous actress.

"Really?" she said.

I held her hands. "I guarantee it."

We walked out of the house together. Everyone who lived there—her mother, brothers, and stepfather—was on the porch. She said good-bye to all of them. On the sidewalk, she turned and waved and called, "Thank you." And together we walked away.

Next, I needed to find an image of the Father that was alive in me. I'd had that one dream of the Wild Man, but he was a fossil. I wanted a more active image I could relate to, so on a night in July 1994, as I went to sleep, I requested Psyche to give me an image of the Father.

I dreamed I was in Ireland with a priest and a teacher. What could that mean? My biological father was Irish. Could there be something there for me? Some ancestors with whom I could relate? I wondered if I should go to Ireland.

In 1991 Robert Halmi had asked me to make a film for television with Walter Matthau called *Mrs. Lambert Remembers Love.* I hadn't worked with Walter since *Goodbye Charlie* in 1964 and I wanted to work with him again. Mrs. Lambert has Alzheimer's in the story and I thought (or maybe hoped) I looked too young for that. I made a fateful decision to don a gray wig and play older than I was. That was it! For the next ten years, those were the only parts I was offered.

However, there is something wonderful about playing older than you are. For ten years I moved forward in time, donning gray or white wigs, adding lines to my face, and a widow's hump to my back. I could look in the mirror and see myself as an old lady. At the end of the day I had the great pleasure of removing my age and stepping lightly back into my younger vigor. I was not less for being older. And defining creatively where age would take up residence in my body, I have been able to deter it somewhat. Now as I actually age, the biggest change I've noticed is that the light at the end of the tunnel is so much closer. I don't have that long left, probably twenty years as a rough estimate. *The Last Picture Show* was twenty-six years ago, and that was the day before yesterday. As Lee Strasberg once said, "Go for it! You have about ten seconds before you're just a whisper in the dark."

Anyway, Paul Huntley, my wigmaker since *Same Time, Next Year,* said I kept him in business with all those gray wigs. I think people actually thought I looked like that. I got a call in 1993 that the Oscars would be celebrating their sixty-fifth anniversary and wanted all the past acting winners to appear onstage. I think everyone was shocked to see what I looked like without aging makeup and a gray wig.

Nineteen ninety-five was a very busy year for me. I made a couple of movies for television and then I made a wonderful independent film, *The Spitfire Grill,* another one of my old lady parts in a gray wig. While I was on location in Vermont shooting it, I continued my sessions with Nathan by phone.

I had been living a solitary life since Neil's death. I'd allowed my passion to go dormant. Part of my healing process was to reawaken Eros in me, my relatedness. Nathan allowed me, even encouraged me, to dare to feel again. He accepted the transference of all my repressed feelings and love ignited in me for him—while all the time understanding that this was our process together. At first I was afraid of my feelings for him, especially when I returned to New York and saw him face-to-face, but he convinced me that he would protect our boundaries and I didn't have to be concerned about either of us stepping over any invisible therapeutic lines. I had it in the back of my mind that, in some way I had not consciously intended, my love for Neil proved destructive. After his death I was afraid to love. And I didn't. Seventeen years had passed. I loved my son, my brothers, my dogs, and my friends, but I dared not love a man again. Nathan understood this. And he allowed me to love him. And he did not die. He didn't even go crazy.

While working on *The Spitfire Grill* I told Nathan how much I liked my costar, Marcia Gay Harden. Nathan asked me to write a description of her as an exercise. This is what I wrote:

Marcia Gay Harden is first of all beautiful in an unusual way. Her face isn't perfect; it is arresting. The thing that strikes me the most about her is her sensitivity and talent. Also her intelligence and humor. She is very funny. She really makes me laugh. She has very keen perception and insight. Also she is artistic and expresses her artistry in many different ways. She has self-awareness and seems to be striving to act consciously.

I feel her moral base is authentic and her spirituality connected in true awareness of soul. She is a real actress in the ancient sense, an enactor of the sacred rites of Dionysius, the god of theater. She walks with a sense of the beauty and sacredness of life. I see her compassion and empathy in her eyes; her ability to feel others. She is a kind person. At the same time she is strong and keenly honest. I like her sense of play and fun. She enjoys life and enjoys her gifts. She is very gifted. She has the ability to love and receive love. There is some disturbance in her man/woman relating, but I feel she is working on that and will some day achieve her deep desire for true union, not just merging.

All in all, I would say that she is a rare, deep, talented, intelligent, sensitive, beautiful human being. I feel that God is pleased with her. The Potter loves that particular pot He threw into creation.

After I read this to him, Nathan asked me to read the whole thing again, but in the first person, saying "I" instead of "she." It felt so strange: All of my conditioning rose up telling me I must not brag; I must be modest and not conceited. When I tried to read it that way," I felt very uncomfortable and told Nathan I couldn't see myself like that.

"I can," he said. "I can love you in ways that you can't love yourself. You know why you have all those feelings for me? It's because you know that I see you."

At the Oscars when I was nominated
for *Requiem for a Dream,* 2000.

PART V

The Road Home

Of all the creatures of Earth, only human beings can change their pattern. Man alone is the architect of his destiny. The greatest revolution in our generation is that human beings, by changing the inner attitudes of their minds, can change the outer aspects of their lives.

WILLIAM JAMES

week after I finished shooting *The Spitfire Grill*, I traveled to Ireland with a group led by David Whyte, the poet. We were to hike all over Ireland while learning about Irish poets and musicians. David is a bard who carries about 250 poems in his head and recites them in his beautiful voice.

On the first night we gathered together, David announced that the theme for our time together would be "belonging." He told us to ask ourselves, where do we belong? It was the very question I had been asking myself. As soon as David posed the question, I knew this was the precise reason I'd come to Ireland. When I thought about my parentage, it was as though I had been spawned by my mother and the other side was a vague blur. I felt that perhaps I could skip over my actual father and make a paternal connection to the land of his forebears. Could it be that this was where I belonged?

David introduced us to his friend John O'Donohue, who was a Catholic priest, a poet, writer, spinner of tales, wit, and fine companion. So this was the answer to the dream about being in Ireland with a teacher and a priest. We spent the day tromping through the peat bogs, stopping every now and then for John to give a "blast" (as he called his spontaneous sermons), or for David to induct us into a deeper layer of Ireland with a poem. It was a beautiful, stimulating journey, and yet I still felt like an outsider.

After we'd been there close to a week, John invited all of us to the sheep farm where his ancestors had lived for hundreds of years. John's mother showed us around their simple thatched cottage and we climbed the hills to see the sheep herded home as his father and forefathers had done for generations. We hiked for a long time along the top of the rise. The land was rocky and the sky brooding behind the clouds. Suddenly, the land fell away and we were standing on the edge of a huge sinkhole or crater. John said the locals speculated that it was caused by a meteorite in prehistoric times. There were some boulders scattered about in the crater. John pointed to a large one in the center and said, "That's my rock. I used to come here as a boy and spend hours in prayer and staring at the sky."

We descended the steep slope of the crater and spread out, each of us selecting a rock to sit on or lean against. I sat on the lush green grass, leaning my back against a huge boulder. There was hardly a sound, save for a bird now and then calling down from the sky. Some people closed their eyes and meditated or prayed. Some just sat quietly in the soft clean air. No one spoke. John was right in front of me leaning against his rock. He was tall with curly black hair and bright eyes. He wore a dark green sweater, woolen pants, and big muddy boots. He looked so quiet, so calm, so at home there. I felt tears rush to my eyes as I thought, "He looks like he belongs here. This is what belonging looks like."

And suddenly I could no longer stand to feel so unconnected. Inside I cried out, "Oh, God, please tell me, where on earth do I belong?"

And the answer came in a thunderous roar inside me. It was like a poem attached to a golden arrow that pierced my heart and impaled me against the rock. It said:

You belong
Everywhere
I am.
And
I am
Everywhere
You find me.

So the responsibility is mine. I must remember to see the Creator in all of the creation—including in myself. When I do that, I am where I belong.

In June 1996 I had a dream that I was with a group of people in a room and we were working to make the room and everything in it disappear. We succeeded, and when everything—the room, its contents, and the people—had completely dematerialized, there was nothing left except an awareness of the pattern that had been there. Then the awareness spoke: "Ah, consciousness remains, and that consciousness fills the inner screen with light." In the dream I thought, "You need ego to do this."

When I told Nathan this dream, he said, "Yes, if you can get to the dimension of patterning, that's where you can make real changes."

The dream says that when the material body is gone, consciousness remains. Is that the soul? I have a feeling of having a soul, but it's a difficult concept to translate into words. To me, soul is that organ of perception that experiences consciousness. It's the container of my awareness, the holder of the template.

Three months after that dream, I was attending a lecture by Bob Thurman, a professor of Indo-Tibetan Studies at Columbia University and the first American to be ordained a Buddhist monk by His Holiness the Dalai Lama. At the lecture, he spoke of psychonauts who travel to inner space, and about the dimension between incarnations where one has no body, no form, and yet is still an entity. It is here where some determination can be made about your next form. He seemed to be talking about the same thing I'd dreamed. After the lecture, I introduced myself to him and his gorgeous daughter, Uma. He told me he was taking a group to Bhutan. I signed on.

Our plan was to leave from San Francisco on November 14, 1996, so I flew there a few days early to celebrate my mother's eighty-ninth birthday. By this time my mother had many ailments, but she insisted on living at home, so we hired a full-time caregiver for her. We gave her a small birthday party, and Steve and I crossed our fingers that the caregiver would stay on the job. My mother wasn't an easy person to work for. Before I left I wrote in my journal: *Who knows what will happen or who I'll be by the time I arrive back at my mother's house on January 1, 1997? I'll have gone from here to Bangkok, Bhutan, Cambodia, Bali, Los Angeles, the Asilomar conference, and then stop back at my mother's before leaving for home. Just writing the names of those places conjures up such possibilities. I am going to throw myself, fling myself, into each moment of this trip. I don't want to miss any of it. I am prepared.*

Bhutan is a small Buddhist kingdom high in the Himalayas surrounded by Tibet, China, and Thailand. Scattered throughout the mountains and villages are ancient temples. We visited many of these. Bob Thurman gave us the history of each one, and the stories of the gods, goddesses, and demons depicted in the many tangkas, wall paintings, and murals.

The first day, Bob led us in a meditation on the appreciation of being human—celebrating the magnificence of our human achievement evolving up through scorpions and crocodiles to the glories of being just a milliminute from full Buddhahood. It is a new way to look at our fellow humans, to know that we are all alive in one moment of life's long evolution toward full enlightenment. Looking at life with that in mind, how can we ever not respect the amazing development we've accomplished?

Each day Bob developed his themes. The second day's theme was death—the certainty that we will die, the uncertainty of when, and the realization that nothing will help us in that moment except what we have come to understand of the dharma. I think of dharma as the understanding we've come to about the nature of reality, the reality that lives behind the veils of our projections, fears, and misconceptions.

I remember reading somewhere that how we handle our greatest wounding is how we will handle our death. To me this means that learning to overcome or transform our suffering transforms ourselves into the being who greets our death. If we resent our wounding, we will resent our death. If we are afraid of being wounded, we will be afraid of our death. If we have done the work that helps us to see our wounding as the vehicle of our growth and be grateful to it, we will be able to see the approach of death as the ultimate transformer. That is my belief—so far, personally untested.

The theme of the third day was karma and how all that we are in this life is the result of our actions in previous lives, and whether or not we enacted the positive or negative aspects of "right action." Bob listed the right actions. They are similar to the ten commandments in many ways—not to kill, not to steal—but there are some differences. Two of them that attracted me were freedom from dogma and nonattachment.

Dogma is one of the things that drove me away from the Church. All of the various versions of, "This is the answer, the only answer; all else is sin and will send you to hell, and we're willing to sacrifice our children to kill your children to prove it."

My experience has been that to study the teachings of Jesus, Buddha, or Muhammad aids you in understanding your own path. The Buddha said many times, "My teaching is like a finger pointing to the moon. Do not mistake the finger for the moon."

Over and over I find in the teachings of all the great teachers this admonition to find the truth in one's own experience, not to take in dogma as though it is our own experience when, in fact, it has been swallowed whole and not really digested. As a Sufi, I learn from all the wisdom traditions without being restricted to just one way. That gives me the opportunity to see truth shining through many different forms. The Vietnamese monk Thich Nhat Hanh has written that most of the boundaries between traditions are artificial. Truth has no boundaries. The differences are mostly in emphasis.

The other right action that Bob talked about was nonattachment. When I first started thinking about it, it seemed that not to be attached to something would lead to not caring or a lack of passion. But now I see that it is deeper than that. It is to be nonattached to your deepest passion. In other words, to do your work as though your very life depended on doing a good job, and it is the fullest expression of who you are at your most profound level of commitment, and then not to be attached to the *results* of that. I'd already learned that discipline onstage. It's what Lee taught—to be in the present moment of time, neither savoring the moment that just passed, nor anticipating the moment to come. But practicing it in life requires constant reminding. It is so easy to fall asleep and get lost in your own mind.

The fifth day's meditation was on mothering. Bob spoke about being grateful to our mother for her love and nurturance, cuddling into her arm and breast as a place of safety, and knowing that throughout all incarnations we have been our mother's mother, father, sister, brother, child, enemy. So whoever is our enemy in this life, we can embrace as having once been our loving mother.

I wrote in my journal, "This is a tough one for me." I meditated on this for a few weeks, trying to feel my way into it, not just accept it because Bob said so, but I had trouble focusing on it. I found my mind going hazy when I tried to grasp it. Soon, in a temple in Bali, I was to have a fuller realization of the meaning of this meditation for me.

From the beginning of the trip, each time we sat down and closed our eyes as Bob began to talk, an inner image of Jesus walked toward me and sat in a lotus position, facing me. Throughout the meditation, he sat there radiating light. On the fourth day, as Bob talked, I realized that although I loved the beauty of the temples, the tangkas, the stories, and the teaching of the Buddha, I was a tourist here. This was not my path. That's when I understood deeply that with all my studies of other religions, basically I really am devoted to Jesus. I am not a church-going Christian, not a conventional one by most standards, but in my heart, Jesus is my guru.

After the strenuous Bhutan trip was over, I flew to Thailand for a two-day rest at a hotel. I wanted to see the ruins of the ancient city of Angkor Wat in neighboring Cambodia, and I asked Brent, our guide, if his company could arrange a trip there for me. Brent told me that he would take me there himself if his company could get clearance that it was safe. Cambodia was still studded with land mines. Pol Pot and the Khmer Rouge had retreated to the jungle, but the political situation was extremely un-stable and everyone feared an imminent coup or revolution. Brent's office also warned us of snakes, vipers, and poisonous insects. In the safety of my plush hotel in Thailand, I felt fear and caution rise in me and I tried to un-derstand whether my emotions were reasonable and I should heed them, or whether they were unnecessary and keeping me from a big experience.

In the end, I decided to face my fear and I went. Brent met me in Phnom Penh with two members from the Bhutan trip. We had one day be-fore we left for Siem Reap, the closest town to the ruins of Angkor Wat. We spent the day seeing the sights of Phnom Penh with a guide named Khan. In the car she told us stories of the suffering of the people of Cambodia that were almost unbearable to hear.

She said that when the Khmer Rouge entered Phnom Penh, the people welcomed them as liberators after years of conflict with the Vietnamese, followed by American bombing. They were told by the Khmer Rouge that they were all to get on trucks and be taken to the countryside for three days, where they were to be processed and assigned jobs in the democratic Kampuchea, their new name for Cambodia.

Once in the country, they were interviewed about what kind of work they did. They willingly answered the questions under the assumption that they would be given jobs where their abilities would be employed to re-build their country. But this was not the intention of the Khmer Rouge. Pol Pot and his partner, Khieu Samphan, envisioned a utopia that was an agrarian labor society. Consequently, all those who admitted that they were doctors, lawyers, teachers, actors, musicians, artists, or any profession at all, were executed. Anyone who even wore glasses was murdered. In one blow the Khmer Rouge eliminated all the professions of Cambodia. Everyone educated was killed. The rest were put to work in the fields as slave laborers.

In the meantime, their deserted homes in Phnom Penh and other cities were ransacked. The Khmer Rouge stole the money from banks and the sil-ver off dining-room tables. Art and treasures of the country became their booty. They claimed all the land as their own; all the farms, all the live-stock, everybody's life savings were now theirs. They forced children to shoot their parents, and parents to kill their own children, while they laughed at the spectacle of their suffering cries.

I felt as we rode in the car through the streets of Phnom Penh that Khan had this job specifically so that she could tell these stories to Westerners. She wanted the world to know. If we hadn't witnessed the events, then at least let us witness the telling of the stories.

We stopped at a sprawling market to shop for gifts, but it was a sad day. Not even in India had I seen so many beggars missing an arm or a leg or a hand. When I asked Khan about it, "Land mines," she explained. "There are so many left over from the war and nobody knows where they all are. Twenty percent of our male population that has survived is missing at least one body part."

The following day was our first visit to Angkor Wat, one of the most astonishing places in the world. It was built in the twelfth century at the same time as the magnificent cathedrals of Europe. It is a temple complex as large as a small city. Originally dedicated to the Hindu god Vishnu, it later was used by Buddhist monks and then fell to ruins and became completely overgrown and hidden for centuries by giant trees. In 1863, a French naturalist named Henri Moubot revealed to the world the existence of the ruins, which have been in a state of nearly constant excavation ever since.

Each day we chose another section of the complex to walk through and examine. The carvings on the walls are intricate and depict battles in great detail, along with the myths, stories, and the history of these ancient people. There are many ways to interpret these carvings, but I think it is safe to say that the underlying theme of most of them is the endless battle between the forces of good and evil.

On December 7, my sixty-fourth birthday, our third day in Angkor Wat, we visited a very tall pyramid in one of the most beautiful and intact temple areas. The stairway up was long. My knees wobbled and I had to stop many times to catch my breath. Finally we reached close to the top where there were giant stone heads that could be seen for miles around. We stumbled and climbed over the partially ruined rocks until we came to what surely must be the very top. Through a crumbling archway, I caught a glimpse of a child in a brightly colored costume, then another, then another. I said to Brent, "There is something going on. A performance or something."

I felt excited as I climbed through the archway that opened onto an area being used as a stage. A few chairs had been set up facing the stage. Brent pointed me toward one of the empty chairs.

"Oh, no!" I said.

Brent smiled. "It's for you."

"What?" I was confused. What did he mean?

"Happy birthday," Brent said.

I looked around me. I was standing on top of one of the oldest monuments in the world, from which I could see for miles in all directions. The sky was blue and immense. The children were huddled together in green and pink theatrical costumes, makeup on their young faces, waiting to begin the program as a present to me. I couldn't believe it. Then Brent told me that when the Khmer Rouge murdered all the actors, dancers, musicians, and other artists of the Cambodian National Theater, they wiped out the carriers of the theatrical tradition that went back over a thousand years. But there was one woman, a dancer, who was out of the country at the time. She was in Paris. After the Khmer Rouge finally deserted the devastated country, she returned home. The streets were filled with homeless orphans who had escaped when their parents were murdered. It was these orphans that this dancer took under her wing and taught the history of Cambodian culture through the dance. Now they were the carriers of their country's entire history. They were presenting it to me. I was profoundly honored to receive it.

We had only a short time back in Phnom Penh before we left, but I wanted to see Tuol Sleng prison, which Khan had urged us to visit. By this time I had the sense that the least we could do for these people was to bear witness to their suffering, so we drove the twelve miles out to the notorious torture center that is now a memorial to the victims who were murdered, as well as those executed in the Killing Fields.

Hannah Arendt spoke of the "banality of evil." That was certainly true of this building, which had been an ordinary high school. The Khmer Rouge took it over as their headquarters for processing what they considered enemies of the state. They called the prison S-21. Walking into the quiet corridors of this simple building, I was shocked to see the faces of every person who had been executed there. Case after case lined the wall with photographs of the victims the Khmer Rouge had meticulously photographed moments before their deaths. Each face was looking directly into the camera, some showing signs of torture, some looking terrified, some profoundly calm, but all having the certain knowledge of death in their eyes. I looked into the eyes of each one. I received their woe. I acknowledged their suffering. I moved on to the next one. My heart grew heavier with each face until my chest felt like I was being sucked into the earth.

After viewing all the pictures, we went into a cell with an iron bed, no mattress, just chains. On the wall was a large photograph of the mutilated body that was found chained to the cot when the prison was liberated.

Only nine people who were held in the prison lived to tell their stories. One of them was an artist. The last large room was hung with his paintings. One large painting that filled the far wall was set in the Killing Fields. The ground was strewn with dead and bloody infants. The soldiers were throwing babies high into the air and then catching them on their bayonets as they fell; the hysterical mothers screaming and clawing the air.

Another painting showed a woman, naked and tied down. One soldier had heated iron tongs over a fire and having already seared off one of her nipples, was applying the burning tongs to her second nipple. The second soldier had removed from a box teeming with scorpions one large scorpion that he held in a pair of pincers. He was about to apply the poisonous insect to the woman's already mutilated breast.

I stood before the painting for a very long time remembering Bob Thurman's statement that human beings had made the long evolutionary journey from scorpions to being just a milliminute away from full Buddhahood. Was this a snapshot of that horrible milliminute? Did this scorpion and this human being come together in that blazing moment of time?

I knew I was looking at unspeakable evil. I tried not to dissociate and deny its existence, as William Blatty had accused me of doing. There was a glimmer of truth in what he said, but I don't deny evil's existence—I just don't focus on it for fear of attracting it. But here I was staring right into its terrifying face. I had volunteered to witness this suffering, so I stood there and let the paintings come alive for me. I entered the scenes of horror, smelled the blood, and heard the screams.

Just as Pol Pot's evil vision was foiled by one dancer who carried the spirit of her people in her heart and was able to seed it into the orphans who lived in the bloodied streets of Cambodia, so too had one artist survived to paint the picture of that evil vision so that no one could forget all that transpired in this moment of evolution's struggle. It is the artist that carries the message of a culture. That is the way the generations communicate to each other. We learn from the stories that our ancestors speak to us in song, dance, and all the arts. To be an artist is both a gift and a responsibility. As I stood sadly witnessing the suffering of these people, I deepened my resolve to shine my mirror brighter so as to reflect back to the people of my culture their own deeper stories.

I proceeded to Bali. I stayed with my friend Nadya, an American designer who employs the native craftspeople and uses their sophisticated textile work in the clothes she designs. I'd been wearing her designs for years. Also visiting Nadya was a woman named Anna Ivara whom I knew from the Asilomar conference.

One day Nadya and Anna invited me to join them in a special retreat at Tonah Lot, a temple on a rock in the sea. At low tide you can walk out to the temple, but when the tide comes in, you can't get down from the temple as the water fills in and the tides are treacherous. Westerners are usually not allowed in the temple, but Anna and Nadya had made special arrangements with a priest who was going to stay there with them for the night, meditating until the tide went out in the morning and they could once again access the mainland. Anna said the sunset from the temple was one of the most beautiful sights in the world. I thought it sounded like a perfect setting for a deep spiritual experience. I've never meditated through a whole night and the idea of doing so in an ancient temple built on a rock at sea sounded like a wonderful and rare opportunity. I quickly said yes to the offer. Then Anna said, "I must warn you, there are rats."

"Rats?!" I exclaimed. "Wait a minute. What do you mean, rats?"

"They don't bother you," Anna explained.

"Oh! They'd bother me, all right," I added nervously.

Nadya said, "Well, let's just drive there. It takes about an hour. We'll enjoy the sunset, visit the temple, and if you don't want to stay, we'll come back."

Late that afternoon we drove to the ocean. The temple looked beautiful perched on the huge rock facing the setting sun on the ocean. We stepped off the sandy beach onto the rocks that were our path to the temple. The tide was out, the waves were crashing in the distance, and the sun was a huge orange ball lowering itself into the bright blue ocean. I felt exhilarated as I climbed the stairs to the temple carved in the rock. But as I reached the top stair and could look into the open walls of the temple, my heart jumped in my chest. The place was teeming with scurrying rats. Thousands of them, even hundreds of thousands. I nearly turned and ran down the stairs. They were everywhere and moving fast. I gasped and froze. Anna grabbed my arm.

"They won't bother you!" she said quickly.

"They're already bothering me," I choked. Anna moved me forward.

I could feel the fear in my whole body. Why didn't she? Why was she moving me into the temple, the rats scurrying away from us as we advanced. Nadya took my other arm. She didn't seem afraid, either. Why not? My reaction seemed perfectly normal to me. Theirs seemed inexplicable. We were greeted by the priest who was going to lead the retreat. We bowed to him as he bowed to us. I just wanted to go. I was not having a good time. I said as much.

Nadya tried to help me. Her dark eyes widened with a comforting thought. "There's no bubonic plague on the island," she offered.

I was not comforted. There were a whole bunch of things this side of bubonic plague that I didn't want to happen. Perhaps I was being irrational, but a rat bite or even a rat skittering across my toe or hand or any other part of me was not something I cared to experience. I wanted to go back to the shore before the tide came in and compelled me to stay in rat paradise for the night. Anna assured me that I had a whole hour before that happened and that it would be good for me to stay at least that long and face my fear. Nadya also encouraged me to stay and said she would leave with me in an hour. I urged her to spend the night if she wanted to, that I could go back alone, but she insisted—one hour and then we'd go . . . if I still wanted to. Hah! I had no doubt about that.

Anna suggested we circumambulate the temple. Was she mad? She wanted me to walk *toward* the rats. No! Not my kind of thing! But once again, Anna coaxed me to "face my fear" and pulled me forward. As we walked, the rats parted and moved in waves in front of and away from us. The floor was thick with rats, but always they made an open path a few feet ahead of us. Anna had a tight hold on my arm. My body was consumed with fear. My hands were clutched close to my face, my elbows into my body. I may have been whimpering. I was my fear and nothing but my fear.

The priest explained to me that in Bali people don't consider rats vermin, but fellow inhabitants of the world that was no more ours than theirs, as well as all of the other life forms that lived in harmony on the island. It was a beautiful thought. I liked the idea, but my body was pumping with fear. The sun had set. The light was fading and the tide was rising.

The priest began the ceremony, making offerings of rice, flowers, and incense on the little altar on the floor. He sat in a lotus position facing the altar; Nadya and Anna sat on their heels behind him. There was a table behind them on which I sat, with my legs dangling. Anna turned around and suggested I sit on the floor. I told her I preferred to sit up there. I didn't say out loud, "above rat level."

Anna tugged at my leg and whispered, "No! You can't be higher than the priest."

I sat on the floor behind them. The priest prayed on in Hindi. Then a rat found the rice on the altar and helped itself to the offering. This was not my idea of a spiritual experience.

When the sky darkened to deep dusk and the tide was swirling menacingly around the rocks, the initial blessing was finally over and the silent retreat about to begin. Anna asked me one last time if I was sure that I wanted to leave.

I was *so* sure.

Nadya and I said good-bye to Anna and the priest, and we descended the steps into the surf that was now up to the top of our thighs. We held our skirts up and made for shore. I was later informed that the water at that point was full of poisonous snakes. I'm glad I didn't know that.

I spent the next few days exploring Bali, but the experience of being flooded by all that fear stayed with me for days, simmering on the back burner of my mind. I kept wondering at the contrast between my behavior and that of the other three people. Mine seemed normal; theirs was inexplicable. Yet I'd just decided to visit Cambodia to face my fear, and as soon as some authentic terror presented itself to me, I ran from it as fast as I could.

I visited a complex called the Water Palace in Tirtagangga. Suddenly Bob Thurman's face appeared in my mind and I recalled his talking about the safety of our mother's arms. I sat down on the stone steps of the temple and started crying like a baby. At first I didn't know why I was crying. As I examined the images that presented themselves to me, I realized I had never had the experience of feeling safe in my mother's arms. I didn't know what that felt like. In fact, I could only remember being afraid of my mother's hands.

Images rose up of running from her as her hands landed blows. I saw her face saying to me when Jefferson was about a year old and still in diapers, "Well, my children were all toilet-trained by the time they were eight months old. You've got to let them know right away what you expect from them." I'd had years of experiencing just how she'd go about letting us know.

Then I heard my mother's voice telling me to go down to the basement and hang up the laundry. The basement of our house was dark, below ground, and had rats! They were caught in the traps put out for them with their necks broken and their bloody insides spilling out. I was terrified of them, of the basement, of the dark underbelly of the house of my childhood, where the rats lived and my fear had to be choked down, where my brother Jack hid in dark corners and leapt out at me. When I screamed, he would laugh and laugh like the scary clown in those tunnel rides at the carnival.

I was sitting beside a long reflecting pool near an ancient king's palace.

I looked down into the water at my streaked face and asked myself the question I always ask: Why did I come in this time and choose to live the life that I've led? The answer seemed to be that my soul needed to experience a life without safety. Otherwise, I would have had it. Now, why would a soul need to experience that? Perhaps because previously I'd been too dependent on love and protection. If that were true, my lessons for this life would be to learn to live without the protective wings of a loving mother and the guidance of a wise father. I had come in to learn to find my own way, and if I needed help, to find that, too.

That night I couldn't sleep. I was throwing up all night. I was alone in Nadya's living room and repeatedly running to the bathroom. I knew I was purging something from myself. Something terribly toxic was being thrown up and out of me. No doubt it was all that fear I'd been carrying inside my whole life.

The next morning, Nadya and Anna said they'd experienced no discomfort during the night, and we'd all eaten the same food. So it wasn't food poisoning. It was something else. Something that I was ready to release. You might even say I exorcised it. And I slept all day. I'd wake up and talk to Nadya for half an hour in a semi-dreamy state, then drift off again.

Nadya said, "Bali is a magical place. People have many kinds of reactions to the energy here. But I'll tell you this—it is a healing place."

When I left Bali, I flew to Los Angeles and arrived just days before Christmas. We drove through Beverly Hills. The Christmas decorations looked garish to me. My eyes were still filled with the bright natural colors of Bali. The people were rushing about anxiously, loaded down with huge shopping bags. The lights blinked their advertisements and a mechanical Santa Claus shouted ho-ho-ho through a loudspeaker. I searched for some presence of spirit in all this bustling activity in preparation for the holiest day in the Christian tradition. I couldn't find it.

You belong everywhere I am and I am everywhere you find me.

It was up to me to see through the eyes of spirit. To see with compassion my fellow humans scurrying about in the throes of our consumer culture, all happening in the milliminute before total enlightenment. But I was having a hard time. The contrast was shocking. I felt as if I needed a debriefing or decompression. I felt as if I was returning to Earth from another planet.

I was glad to be in the city of my friends whom I consider an alternate family. Katherine Cortez, who had been my assistant in New York, was now in a committed relationship with another member of the Actors Studio, Catlin Adams. Both girls have been to me like the daughters I never had. They have two sons, Gabriel and Joe Joe. I am a surrogate grandmother for the boys and was happy to spend Christmas in their warm and loving home after all the jolting events of my trip.

I felt changed, deepened; both saddened by all that I'd seen and, at the same time, joyous, appreciative of the many ways that the divine expresses itself in our world, and moved by the efforts of people everywhere to make some sense of their lives and find the deeper meaning to the fact of our existence. Also, I was excited to get back to work. I couldn't wait to immerse myself in my creativity.

The day after Christmas I headed north to end the year at the Asilomar conference with Brugh Joy, David Spangler, David Whyte, and Father John O'Donohue. On New Year's Day I made my usual trek up to my mother's home. As feared, her caregiver had quit after being repeatedly accused of being a thief, not only stealing my mother's cookies, but also taking a Santa Claus from a present. No amount of reasoning by Steve or me could convince my mother that her accusations were unfounded. I stood listening to her angry accounts and I wished, just once, we could have one real conversation, one exchange where we could truly relate to each other.

My mother asked if I was making any new movies. I was planning to go to Chapel Hill, North Carolina, to work on a play that I loved of Horton Foote's called *The Death of Papa*. I told her about it and she said, "Well, do they pay you anything for that?"

I said, "No, it isn't really a large-paying job."

"What are you doing it for then?" she said. "You're just in it for the money, aren't ya?"

I didn't know what to say. I knew that my mother liked to brag about me to her friends, and this play in a North Carolina theater wasn't bragging material compared to a movie, but it always amazed me how little she really knew me. I tried to explain that I'd had several cameo roles in films that year for which I'd been very generously paid, and that allowed me to do this play, which truly interested me.

"Aren't you going to retire soon?" she then asked. "You're getting up there, you know. You'll be sixty-five next birthday. You can't go traipsin' around forever like you're a teenager."

I left the room.

I intended to study my lines for the play, but I remembered something John O'Donohue had said during his talk at Asilomar a few days before. "The moment you accept that this is the way it is, the transformation has begun."

Standing in the spare room of my mother's house, I said, "Okay, this is the way it is. Can I accept it?" I decided that I could. This is my mother. This is our relationship. It probably won't change. I accept it. Let the transformation begin. I reached into my suitcase for my script and my eyes fell on a book of poetry that I'd brought with me, by the great Sufi poet Rumi. I opened it at random, and this is what he said to me:

You personify God's message
You reflect the King's face
There is nothing in the Universe
That you are not
Everything you want, look for it
Within yourself. You are that.
If you are in search of the place of the soul
You are the soul.
If you are in search of a morsel of bread,
You are the bread.
If you know this secret, then you know
That whatever you seek, you are that.

I heard that.

I knew it to be true.

Now all I had to do was . . .

Remember it.

⊘

I was home for only three days before I left for Chapel Hill. I was resolved to do three things in the Horton Foote play. First, I wanted to mar-
shal all my forces, to see how deep I could go, to move into the
unconscious of my character, Mary Vaughn, and share with the audience
what I had come to understand about the unperceived forces that operate
in us. I wanted to make the audience understand what Mary did not understand about herself. And I wanted to reveal it in her behavior without
demonstrating it in a didactic way. It was my goal to make the invisible visible, to consciously manifest the unconscious.

Second, I wanted to be alive creatively in every performance, tuned in
to every new impulse, and give expression to them authentically, sponta-
neously, and consistently for the whole run of the show. I wanted to surprise myself to the very end.

And finally, I wanted to address my inner saboteur. I wanted to end his
reign of tyranny over me. One of his favorite ways to discredit me was to
make sure the critics only saw me at my worst. He had an uncanny knack
for knowing when they would come.

For example, when I replaced Pauline Collins in *Shirley Valentine* on
Broadway, the *New York Times* critic came on a Tuesday night. No one told
me he was there. I had no conscious thought about his being there. I
thought he was coming at the end of the week. I have an excellent memory and never forget a line, but on that Tuesday night onstage, alone in a
one-person play, I went sky high. I forgot a line, had to ad-lib my way back
into the text, and as I stumbled about trying to get back on track, I dropped
my accent. I was in shock. Backstage after the show, my friend Candy was
there and I was in agony that I did that. I said, "But I've got three more
days to get solid."

Candy said, "What?"

"I mean, till the *Times* comes."

Candy shook her head. "They were there tonight."

Immediately, I knew. My inner saboteur was at work. I could feel it. Was I ever going to have my best work reviewed? Or was I condemned always to do my best work *after* the reviews? Sure enough, the review mentioned that I "dropped my accent."

With *Death of Papa*, I accomplished all my goals.

Michael Wilson was a wonderful director. He let me soar. The audience was right with me and told me, both by their laughter and their tears, that they got it. I could feel how strong I'd grown creatively. My power was back, and now I wasn't afraid of it. I'd silenced the saboteur and opening night was relaxed, alive; I really "played." At last my instrument (Lee Strasberg's word) was in tune and I could play on it the music of my soul.

Michael suggested we do something else together. He directed often at the Alley Theater in Houston, and he asked what I'd like to do. I said, "Let's do the hardest thing we can think of. How about *Long Day's Journey Into Night*?"

I'd worked on Mary Tyrone a few times at the Actors Studio and I knew how challenging a role it was. Michael agreed and made the arrangements for us to do a production at the Alley.

A few months earlier, I'd had a dream that Neil no longer loved me and had moved out of my house. Even in the dream I was ecstatic that he was gone. Then, right after I got home from Chapel Hill, I had this dream.

A young man appeared. He was in his early thirties and was so beautiful, he was dazzling. His hair was blond. His teeth extraordinarily white and pearly. They glistened when he smiled. His eyes were as blue as a clear sky on a summer's day. His skin had a radiance like an apricot ripening in the sunshine. I was so drawn to him, I felt dizzy and helpless to do anything but love him totally. He was like a god. I wondered if he was Adonis.

He said to me, "I am appearing like this so that you will have this feeling that you are feeling right now, whenever you think of me."

At that point in the dream I wondered if perhaps he was not Adonis, but Jesus himself. I decided that he was.

This is the moment that I knew that my psychic structure was healing. Despite the gifts that I was born with and that supported me all the way to international success, I still had to do the work on my inner house, tearing it down to the very foundation, until I reached the root of the problem and could begin real restoration. The root of the problem was in me, not in Neil or my other two husbands. This was my inner dynamic that had manifested over and over again. After Neil died and I ended my relationship with Michael, I didn't enter into any new alliances with men. I was never going to change that patterning if I continued in my habitual way. I was alone for twenty-five years altogether; not even a date, but I did it. The positive animus finally appeared in my dream, and I knew Eros was coming alive in me again.

There is such a difference between working on most of the roles that come your way during a long career and working on a great role in a great play, something like the difference between playing "Chopsticks" and a Beethoven concerto. There is just so much more there to discover, reveal, and express. Working on Mary Tyrone was one of the most sublime creative experiences of my life.

On the surface she would seem to be a very different person from me. She lived at the beginning of the last century within the confines of her family and was addicted to morphine. But once the surface is penetrated, the psychological terrain starts to feel familiar. Mary's addiction was her way to hold down all the pain she says she felt in her hands. But the hands are the extension of the heart, and that's where Mary's real pain was—the guilt she felt about the death of her child. She blamed herself and couldn't forgive herself. I was able to bring to Mary all my feelings of remorse— my baby became her baby; my grief and regret, hers. All of my past addictions were brought forth and called morphine. I could embody all the ways that I used marijuana, alcohol, food, and sex as ways to kill the pain.

We completed the run at the Alley Theater in Houston, then Michael Wilson, who had become the artistic director of the Hartford Stage, booked us to do *Long Day's Journey* there the following year. In the meantime, I did a few movies, including *The Yards* with Mark Wahlberg, James Caan, Faye Dunaway, Joaquin Phoenix, and Charlize Theron. It was directed by James Gray, who looked like a red-haired, fourteen-year-old computer whiz loaded with talent.

At the Asilomar Conference in December 1998, the theme was on being an elder. David Spangler talked about the need to bust the myth of aging. The myth says that we lose power as we age. That's not true! We grow conservative. I liked that. I took a vow then to move into the next period of my life boldly, to take risks, challenge myself more, to look at what I was afraid of and move toward it, not away from it.

All that year, Mary Tyrone was cooking in me, and when I let her out again in Hartford she'd grown wilder, more complex, and difficult to control. Although the *New York Times* quibbled about some aspects of the production, I understand they were very enthusiastic about my interpretation of Mary, calling it "a girlish domestic terrorist." I must confess I liked that. I'd hoped we'd be able to bring the production to Broadway, but it didn't happen. I feel that it was my best work, but it was fated to stay "out of town." I felt a bit like Edna Mae in *Resurrection,* doing her healing at the Last Chance gas station. But so be it. The forces had other plans for me.

While we were still in rehearsal my agent sent me a script with a modest offer to do a small independent movie called *Requiem for a Dream.* I confess I did not immediately recognize the value of this script. It seemed so depressing to me. Who would want to sit through the dreary lives of these people? Besides, it was about addiction. Did I really want to continue this theme? The character was a woman named Sara Goldfarb who is a compulsive eater. When she tries to lose weight, she becomes addicted to diet pills. Also her son, his girlfriend, and his friends are heroin users.

Requiem was based on a book of the same name by Hubert Selby, Jr., written and to be directed by Darren Aronofsky. I thought it was too dreary, too hard. Why should I put myself through all I'd have to do for hardly any money? I turned it down.

My agent, Courtney Kivowitz, said, "Before you turn it down, let me send you Darren's first film."

Home from Hartford for the weekend, I slipped the DVD in my player and sat back to watch *Pi*. After the first few images, I sat up straight. Less than four minutes into the film, I said out loud, "Okay I get it. The guy's an artist." Darren came to Hartford to see my Mary Tyrone. I agreed to do his film.

After *Long Day's Journey* closed, I threw myself into the role of Sara Goldfarb, which turned out to be as challenging as any role I'd ever played. My friend Paul LeBlanc, who had done my hair for many films since we first worked together in *Silence of the North*, was hired by Darren to design the many wigs I wore as Sara. Paul moved into my house, set up a wig shop in my basement, and began the process of creating the wildest, most imaginative wigs I've ever seen. Darren tested them all on film, along with the fat suits and prostheses I wore.

On September 18, 1994, Jefferson married the lovely Patricia Pieroni, and in 1999, during this exciting creative period, I became a grandmother. Emily Lucca was born and became the light of my life.

Darren and I spent time together in Brooklyn, where he introduced me to his mother and her friends. Darren has beautiful, devoted parents who were on the set every day. When I complimented them on their support of Darren, his mother said, "We're not here to support him. It's just the most interesting thing in our lives." Of course I knew that not only had they helped Darren raise money for *Pi*, his mother had also cooked delicious meals for the whole cast and crew every day. I had always wondered what kind of a person would be the result of a mother and a father who were loving, intelligent, and supportive. Now I knew.

Darren was only twenty-nine years old when we met; I was sixty-seven, but I felt that we were true partners in creativity. As Sara developed, I felt that Darren knew her as well as I did. He gladly accepted what I offered when it was right on, and he had an unerring sense of when I needed a nudge in this direction or that.

The most difficult scene was one in which my son realizes I'm on speed. It was a nine-page scene, but the last three pages were my soliloquy. I told

Darren I wanted to do all the coverage of the entire scene, except those three pages that would be shot in close-up. I wanted that close-up to be last. That was not the economical way to shoot the scene. Normally, the director shoots everything in one direction and then turns the camera around and shoots everything in the other direction. I was asking for walls to be put up, taken down, and then put up again. That takes time, and in movies, time costs money. But this was a pivotal scene that was beautifully written, and I knew what I needed to do it right. I had never before asked for my creative needs to take precedence over economic considerations. But I had learned to stand up for what I truly needed in order to do my best. I had been testing myself for the last couple of years; testing both my talent and my technique. I knew what I was working with and what I could deliver. Darren and I trusted each other. He told the producer, his friend and partner, Eric Watson, that he wanted to do it my way. They scheduled a whole day for those three pages. I could feel what was there waiting to be expressed. It was my own feeling about aging that I hadn't been aware of, but which surprised me one day in rehearsal. As soon as I felt that little rise in emotion when I said, "I'm old," I knew where the reality of the scene was for me. I had to bank that fire, then wait for the right moment. I had to ask for the right conditions to let that slender shoot of truth expose itself at just the precise moment. All my training and effort I'd put in over the years blossomed in that moment of truth. We got it on the first take. We were finished with our day's work by lunchtime. It ended up costing less time and less money by doing it right creatively. There's a big lesson here.

On May 5, 1999, Darren showed me some footage. When I told him how much I liked the film, he returned the compliment and repeated something the producer said as he watched my dailies: that I was one of the greatest living actors. I could feel the inflation rise in me and knew I was getting all puffed up, so I went and sat in my trailer and meditated on the image of polishing the mirror and then leaving so that God's face can shine through. That's the charge in all of this: to remember that when it comes through, it is God who is shining through, not one's personal ego.

It's such a paradox. We must put in all the effort to shine the mirror and then walk away. But isn't that the same as one's work in life—to learn how to die consciously? To build the entire structure of one's life, then breathe—let go—breathe—let go—breathe and then finally, let it all go.

It takes practice.

I shot for two weeks in my fat suits. One added fifty pounds and then, after Sara begins her addiction to diet pills, the second fat suit added only twenty-five pounds. Then I was off for two weeks. While Darren shot other stuff, I went on the cabbage soup diet and managed to lose ten more pounds.

When we finished shooting, I wrote Darren a letter and thanked him for the opportunity "to mobilize my entire army, and for wanting what I got and letting me give it."

I'd completed three films that hadn't yet been released, *The Yards*, *Requiem for a Dream*, and *Walking Across Egypt*, a wonderful little film that I loved, but the novice producers got cold feet and sold it directly to video. I had a Hallmark made-for-TV movie coming out and a movie of the week, which didn't stop my mother from continuing to urge me to retire.

I'd been working so much that I decided it was time for a retreat. Often between acting jobs I'd just retreat to the sanctuary of my home. But this time I was ready for something different. I remembered the vow I'd made not to grow conservative with aging, but to be bold and challenge myself. My friend Bernie Glassman, a Zen priest, takes small groups of people on retreat in the streets of New York and other cities around the world. The idea appealed to me to leave behind all of my habitual props—my bed, my televison, my radio, my beautiful garden, my pets, money in my pocket, and all the other accoutrements of my very comfortable life—and choose to live on the streets of Manhattan for just a weekend, to experience life without any comfort except what is available to people who live on the street. I understood that their experience is different from what mine would be. They are homeless; I am not. I was not trying to duplicate their experience. I simply wanted to have my own, living under those conditions for three days.

Each member of the retreat made a contribution of $1,080, a sacred number in Buddhism, with the money to be donated to the shelters where we would eat. But we could not use our own money. We had to ask our friends to support our effort. I hadn't asked anyone for money since my uncle Dave helped me escape from Texas. Since then I had been financially independent. I could feel how proud my ego was of that. For me, the purpose of a spiritual retreat is to isolate my ego so that I can feel the essence that lives behind it, the mystery that longs to be known.

The retreat was scheduled for Easter weekend. On the morning of Good Friday, I dressed in my most ragged clothes, not to pretend to be a homeless person, but simply to blend in with the people who lived on the street. I packed one small bag of toiletries. That's all: no money, no identification, no food.

We met on the steps of the Cathedral of St. John the Divine. There were about fourteen of us, many clerics, monks, and other religious practitioners. One was a rabbi, David Cooper, who wrote a book called *God Is a Verb*. There was a young man who was studying to be a Tibetan Buddhist monk, and a wonderful Zen teacher, Paco, a Latino who taught in a barrio of the Bronx, and two other local Zen teachers.

Sally Kealy, one of the Zen teachers, was the only other woman in the group. I was the oldest person there. As we sat in a circle on the steps of the cathedral, Bernie laid out the guidelines for us. We would sleep on the street the first night. The second night we were to sleep on the floor in a mosque headed by a Sufi sheik who was one of the few women ordained as a sheik in the faith of Islam. The third night we were to spend on the Staten Island Ferry. In the parks of Manhattan, one is not allowed to sleep lying down. You can sleep, but only sitting up. On the ferry you can lie down, but you have to get up every twenty minutes, get off the ferry, then reboard and lie back down. We would eat at different soup kitchens around the city and meet at those designated places. Getting to and from each place was up to us. We'd either walk or hitch a ride. If we took a subway, we would have to beg for the fare or collect bottles and turn them in for the coins. There seemed to be an awful lot of walking involved and my knees by this time had degenerated to the point that they started to give out after a while. I was only good for about ten or twelve blocks. I confessed this at the first meeting. Bernie said, "Okay, that will be part of this retreat. We'll incorporate your knee problem into our effort and do what we need to do to handle that."

Our first meal was to be from a truck that arrived each day around six o'clock in front of the cathedral. We waited and waited. So did a few other street people, but the truck never arrived. We waited an hour. The truck was from one of the churches and made stops around the city. We never knew what happened that night, but it didn't come. Bernie said, "Okay, we'll have to fall back on our own devices and see what we can find."

We started walking down the street. After a few blocks, I saw a truck parked on a street that I recognized to be a movie truck. I said to Bernie, "They're shooting a movie around here. That means there is a craft service truck somewhere. They always have lots of food. Maybe we can beg from them."

We located the movie set and the craft service table. I approached the man running it. He immediately said, "Oh, hello, Miss Burstyn." So much for my blending in. I then explained about our retreat and pointed to the scraggly group across the street. He answered, "Oh, perfect! We have a bunch of sushi we used as props and I was just wondering how I was going to get rid of it. I hate to throw so much good food away."

I waved the group over. Our motley crew stood on the sidewalks of New York eating delicious sushi. So our first meal was a bit of a cheat. There was a lesson here—you can leave your identification behind, but your identity travels with you.

Soon we began our preparations for our sleep on the streets. We scoured Broadway for boxes large enough to crowd inside and newspapers to cover ourselves inside the boxes. We were to sleep in our clothes and shoes, and the newspaper, if we had enough, would act as insulation. The temperature dropped to 43 degrees that night. Sleeping with only cardboard between our bodies and the cold ground would be very uncomfortable. So we were ecstatic when we found reams of discarded but unused paper in a trash can on Broadway. Bernie suggested we sleep on West End Avenue, where there was some scaffolding over the sidewalk at a construction site. But I suggested that we were only a block from the Hudson River, so why didn't we walk through Riverside Park, enjoy the sunset, and sleep along the river? I live on the Hudson and enjoy the beauty of the sunrise on the water every morning from the other side. I thought it would be lovely to watch the sunset from this side of the river.

We hiked through the park in our vagabond clothes and found a stack of discarded branches that had been trimmed from the trees. We helped ourselves to them and for the rest of the weekend, we each had a walking stick for our tramping uptown and down. We reached the river just before sunset. It was both Good Friday and Passover. Rabbi Cooper had brought a special kind of matzoh for the seder. We gathered in a circle by the side of the Hudson and Rabbi Cooper conducted the service. All through the service, I was keeping in mind that it was this same service that Jesus was conducting that evening at Mark's house when he instructed his disciples, "Before the cock crows, one of you will betray me." I was both experiencing the Jewish ceremony with the special matzoh and having communion as I ate it, hearing Jesus' voice say, "Take this. This is my body."

As the seder ended, a few streaks of red hovered low in the sky and then twilight descended on us. The temperature dropped a few degrees; a chill breeze blew toward us off the river. As I looked at these people sitting quietly in a circle around the candles, I was filled with such love for them and for all people who light candles, who bow down, who try in whatever way they can to contact the spirit within or to appeal to God out there, to propitiate the gods, to please their creator, to come to terms in one way or another with the magnificence and source of all creation. As I gazed at these people sitting quietly in their earnestness and feeling utterly and completely benign and at peace, there appeared . . . a rat. He came over the seawall, climbing up from the river to find his bed for the night. I prayed he did not find his bed near mine.

As we continued to sit in the circle, we took turns sharing whatever thoughts we wanted to offer about the ceremony. I told them about my experience in Bali at the temple with the rats and how frightened I'd been and had rejected that as not my idea of a spiritual experience. And now here I was on a spiritual retreat and what should appear but the source of all that fear. As we sat there, another rat appeared over the seawall. Now I was worried. How many more would come? How many rats were down there that were coming up for the night? Was this just an advance scouting party and, once it was dark, would there be hordes of rats scaling the ramparts? I could feel my fear rising.

We found space near the fence of some tennis courts that was obscured from the walkway by bushes. There we could set up our boxes and not be seen by patrolling police. We hid our boxes and papers there and then sat on the benches and stood around talking, trying to keep warm until around eleven P.M., when we decided to turn in. We were to get up at four A.M. and vacate the park before light came and the police could see us.

I lined the bottom of my box and crawled in, then covered myself with the additional paper. It took a long time to get all parts of me covered and then, resting my head on my arm, I tried to sleep. Every time I heard a noise outside, I jumped and peeked out my top flaps to see if it was a rat or some other terrifying intruder. Then, once again, I would resettle my papers around my body. This went on for a few hours. Every time I laid my head down, all I could think about was what I would do if a rat entered my box. Each time I jumped up, I'd try a new position, but there was no comfort to be found on that hard ground. And always my mind was alive with scurrying rats, just as many as there had been in the temple in Bali. Somewhere around two A.M. I realized I had only another two hours before we had to get up and I said to myself, "Look, Ellen, you are not being kept awake by rats. You are being kept awake by fear of rats. Give it up and go to sleep." And I did. The next thing I knew, I heard stirring next to me. I opened my flaps and looked out. Bernie was standing there. I said, "Good morning."

"Did you get some sleep?" Bernie asked.

"Yeah, I did."

"Then you are the only one who did," Bernie said.

We disassembled our makeshift beds and returned them to the garbage cans on Broadway. We were going a few blocks down Broadway to an all-night restaurant Bernie knew about where we could use the facilities.

As we walked, Paco came up and fell in step beside me. He said, "Ellen, I want to tell you how much I admire you. After confessing your fear of rats, you still were able to sleep with all those rats there."

I said with a gasp, "There were rats?"

Paco said, "Oh, you didn't know? There was a highway of rats running right by your head all night."

"Oh my God," I said in awe, realizing that if one had entered my box, I probably would have died of heart failure.

"Yeah, one of them got on Sally's box," Paco told me. "I knocked it off, but that was it. We decided not to sleep for the rest of the night."

Soon we arrived at the restaurant and stood outside looking in through the window. Bernie pointed to the back of the room. He said, "There's the restrooms. Men on the right. Women on the left. Just walk straight to it like you know where you're going. Don't ask. Just go there."

I followed his instructions and, once inside the small bathroom, I got out my toothbrush and set to work performing my morning toilette. I looked in the gray-streaked mirror over the sink. A yellowish bare lightbulb over the mirror was the only light in the dim room. I looked to myself too healthy to be a street person. My teeth too white and my skin too cared for, but other than that, I was pretty scuzzy-looking. I thought about the night's lessons. The rats in my mind had kept me awake. When I let go of the idea, the real rats running past my head didn't bother me at all. The idea of separating the fearful images my mind was creating from the actual objects of fear would stand me in good stead in the awful days following the attacks of 9/11.

When we'd all taken turns using the restrooms, we set off down Broadway. We were in the upper 90s and the church that served breakfast to the people of the streets was on 33rd Street. We had about sixty blocks to walk and I knew my knees couldn't make it. A couple of the guys collected big plastic bags full of tin cans and we took them into the grocery store to redeem them. The people in the store treated us with the rudeness and disdain that homeless people usually receive, but they gave us the money. Soon we had enough to ride the subway downtown.

At the church, we got in the long line on the street. Some priests came out with a coffee cart and, when it was our turn, we each got a cup of hot coffee and a cold bun. Then we set off for a park some blocks away where we spent the day hanging out with the park regulars.

At lunchtime we went into the building bordering the park where a meal was served. We sat at the long tables with the street people who all seemed to know each other and there was a sense of community here. A ragtag community, but friendly nevertheless.

I met an African American woman named Shirley who was wearing a bright red dress. Her eyes were bloodshot and she spoke with the unmistakable slur of an alcoholic. Back in the park after lunch on this gray Good Friday with rain hovering above in the clouds, Shirley announced to us that it was her birthday. Everyone around us joined in singing "Happy Birthday." She swayed a bit as she stood, listening like a little girl and smiling. Shirley couldn't be having a very comfortable life. She had slipped down to the lowest rung of the ladder. Actually, she had slipped off the ladder completely, but on this day, when she had so few choices she was capable of making, she did choose to have this one happy moment. All eyes were directed at her. The gray day was filled with a heartfelt song and Shirley had her one moment in the sun.

We were to spend the night at the mosque. It was too far for my disabled knees to take me, so I was going to have to ride the subway again. I told the group that I didn't feel right about taking the money they had found or collected from bottles. I said that I would get my own money.

I would beg.

Across the street from the park was a restaurant with tables outside on the sidewalk. Bernie said that this restaurant used to be a favorite hangout of the poet Allen Ginsberg. He suggested it might be a good place. I wouldn't have to go inside. I could ask someone for money who was eating outside. I spotted two women in their thirties and decided to approach them. I felt scared as I crossed the street. Frightened. Of what? Scorn? Rejection? I was crossing over some line in the sand that I never consciously knew was there. I asked myself, "Who begs?" I was surprised at the answer that came: Losers. People who are lazy or who can't take care of themselves. Oh, I see. It was my scorn that I was projecting onto them. My ego was involved here. And I was purposely stepping through my ego to experience what was on the other side.

I approached the women who were in conversation. I decided not to lie, but simply to state the truth. I said, "Excuse me. I need a dollar for the subway. Could either of you spare a dollar?"

The woman closest to me reached in her pocket and pulled out a dollar and handed it to me without taking her eyes off the face of her luncheon companion. I took the dollar and said thank you, turned and walked away. I looked at the dollar in my hands and felt a strange pride, almost the same pride I felt about the first money I ever earned when I was a teenager in Detroit. The light changed and I stepped off the curb feeling I'd really accomplished something. I felt happy for a few steps and then I felt tears rise up in me. What's this, I thought. Why am I crying? Then the realization: Because they didn't look at me.

I continued walking across the street, but inside I was at a dead stop. I got the dollar. They gave me what I asked for, but I was disregarded. I wasn't seen.

In the months that followed as I reflected on this retreat, I would come to understand that this was the moment at the heart of this experience.

It doesn't mean that I always give money to the people who live on the street when they ask. It does mean that whether or not I do, I still try to look them in the eye and acknowledge their presence, their humanity.

At the mosque Sheik Fariha greeted us and, after some Sufi dancing and chanting, we were given sheepskin rugs that we laid on the floor and fell into a deep sleep despite a room full of loud snoring.

In the morning it was raining hard. At the mosque we were given plastic bags that we wrapped our feet in and tied closed with tape and rubber bands. We also got large garbage bags, slit a hole in the bottom, and pulled them over our heads. Then we stepped out into the teeming rain. The group was going to hike twenty or thirty blocks uptown. I knew my knees wouldn't make the hike and, besides that, I couldn't afford to catch cold. I had to leave on Monday to appear at a film festival that was showing *Walking Across Egypt* and then fly the next day to visit my ailing mother, who was now ninety-three years old, in a convalescent home, and, I knew, nearing the end. I told the group I would wait for them at a nearby church. They had to come back downtown because our dinner that night was to be compliments of the Bowery Mission.

The front door of the church was locked, so I went to the back door. I explained that I had no place to get out of the rain and asked permission to sit in the church for a few hours. The priest looked at me disapprovingly, but, perhaps remembering what Christ said about "the least of them," nodded his head without a smile and admitted me to the church. My plan was to just sit alone in the church and meditate for a few hours. But I wasn't alone. There were two women cleaning and scrubbing the nave and chatting happily in Italian. I thought surely they'd be gone soon and leave me to my meditation, but they were there the whole time. When their work was finished they sat in the front row and continued their lively and loud conversation. So, no meditation, and no quiet. Now, what was I to do for four hours? I thought and I prayed. Mostly about my mother.

In the past few years, I'd increased my visits to her. Steve had been carrying the burden by himself and now had developed prostate cancer. I wanted to relieve him as often as I could, so I visited her many times in those years. She'd suffered a stroke and, for at least a decade, had complained about "noises in her head," dizziness, lack of balance, headaches, and myriad other complaints. She had no spiritual practice to help her separate from her discomfort, so she lived every day inside her fears, anxieties, and complaints. It was difficult for her to talk about anything else. It was very hard on my brother.

My mother said to me once when she was in her eighties, "If I ever get to the point where I can't take care of myself, don't put me in one of those homes. Just leave me here to starve to death." She held Steve to the same promise.

But then she fell in the night and broke her arm and we convinced her to move into an assisted-care facility. My nieces and I got her two rooms instead of the usual one, and by the time she was ready to leave the hospital, we had moved in her furniture and decorated her apartment, which had a sliding glass window looking onto her patio. It was very cheerful and looked as much like her own home as possible. She liked it and resigned herself to living there.

But soon we worried that she couldn't stay there for long. The place was threatening to throw her out if she didn't stop her demanding behavior. She'd summon the nursing staff early in the morning and tell them to wash the fingerprints off her glass doors. Her complaints mounted. She was entering into a state bordering on paranoia. During one of my visits the previous year, she complained that there was something wrong with her eyes and wanted them examined. When the doctor reported he could find nothing wrong with her eyes, I got an intuitive flash that she was having delusions, that she was seeing things. I questioned her and, sure enough, she confessed that she saw children out of the corner of her eyes. They came and sat at her table at lunchtime with their elbows on the table. When she turned to look at them, they were gone. I remember Reshad talking about other realms of being, like elves, fairies, and gnomes that could only be seen with peripheral vision. They disappeared if you turn your head. My mother said the children came in the night and opened her packages and used her makeup. She taped all her packages closed so they couldn't take things from her. She called Steve repeatedly asking for more tape, until he lost patience with her.

I sat in the cold church listening to the pelting downpour outside and the chattering Italian of the cleaning ladies inside, and thought how sad it was that when my brothers and I were children, we were punished so often for breaking her things, or finding her hidden candy, or not taking care of her things properly; we used to feel that her things were more important to her than we were. And now, in the last years of her life, that early hell of ours had become her living hell. She had her things, but she was tormented by imaginary children who were taking them from her. And she couldn't use enough tape to keep all her things safe. Perhaps it was a metaphor for what was really being taken: her life force.

She stayed in assisted care for less than a year. Then she fell again and the facility insisted she be moved to a convalescent home. She'd been there for a few months. I'd flown across the country to visit her several times during that time. She was going downhill fast. I knew the end couldn't be too far off. When I went this time, I was going to stay with her as long as she held on. I planned to be with her until the end.

The rain didn't let up all day. It was coming down in sheets, pounding hard against the stained-glass windows as Bernie and the group came in, drenched from head to foot. We set out for the Bowery in the rain and arrived like a bunch of drowned rats.

The Bowery Mission is one of the oldest shelters in New York City, but we discovered that it is a last resort for many homeless people because "ya have to listen to the sermon before they feed ya." When we came in the door, dripping wet, the people greeted us and took us back to "the store," a large room containing racks of clean, neatly hung secondhand clothes. We helped ourselves to dry clothes, and then boxes of donated boots were brought out, and everyone got dry socks and brand-new boots. They even fit. I asked how they came to have this huge assortment of new boots and was told that they had been discontinued by a factory and donated to the mission. Once we were dry and newly outfitted, we were escorted to the beautiful little chapel to sit and wait for the arrival of the minister. After a very long wait, it was decided that the minister wasn't going to come, and a makeshift service was organized by the guys who worked there, all of whom had once been jobless and homeless before they were rescued by the mission. A group of them gave testimonials and then we picked up the songbooks and sang hymns together as the rain continued to beat down on the roof of the chapel. When the service ended, we ate a delicious meal in the cafeteria. Bernie used their phone to call Sheik Fariha and reported back to us that we were welcome to sleep on the floor of the mosque again, out of the rain.

In the morning, the rain slowed to a drizzle. We had breakfast at Dorothy Day's soup kitchen. I sat across from a man who was a homeless Vietnam vet. He told me a long saga of what he went through to get a place to live that was provided by the state. After months of red tape, he was finally given an apartment, but it was on Staten Island, so he turned it down.

"Why?" I asked him.

He said, "I don't want to have to take a ferry to go home. Besides, I don't know anyone there. All my friends are here."

Even at that level, there is a choice. As Shirley had chosen to receive a birthday song from the people of the park, this man chose to live near his friends, even though he had to live on the street instead of in an apartment.

Again, that lesson: we can't always choose our circumstances, but we can choose our response to them.

We got back up to the Cathedral of St. John the Divine in time for Easter mass. The celebration of the resurrection. New life! I felt I was making a new beginning somehow. The retreat had acted upon me in some way that I couldn't articulate. I needed time to process it.

A few weeks later I realized the full impact of the shift that had taken place in me. I was in New York City one day and suddenly realized I'd forgotten my wallet. I had one moment of panic and then I said: "Wait a minute. This is just like the street retreat." Suddenly I felt completely safe and at home, not just here, but anywhere. The people hurrying by were no longer strangers, just people whose names I didn't know that I could approach for help if I needed to.

On the way home from the retreat, my thoughts drifted again to my mother. I knew my brother was there and my niece Maureen was being a very dutiful granddaughter, but still I was anxious to get to my mother's side. I hoped I could be of some comfort to her.

Nathan had told me, "If you can see God in your mother, you will be able to see God in anyone. It will build compassion. You just have to remember that your mother has a soul and her soul is suffering."

The next morning, as I dressed to catch my plane for California, the phone rang. My assistant Susan answered in the next room. I heard her say, "Oh, Steve, I'm so sorry." I knew that was it. I'd missed my mother's exit. I took the phone. Steve was at her bedside. He'd arrived ten minutes too late. However, Maureen had arrived in time, after the nursing home called her and told her my mother had lapsed into a coma.

So my mother was not alone when she died. Her granddaughter was with her.

I flew to Walnut Creek, where she lived. All three of her children and most of her grandchildren were present at her funeral, and many of her wide circle of devoted friends. There were not many tears until her favorite song was played, "Fascination Waltz." Then the whole lot of us hit the deck.

After the service, the family went back to Maureen's house. It was a rare occasion for all of us to be together at the same time. We had learned over the years that my mother's wish "to have her whole family together" just never worked. There was always too much tension, and before many hours passed, there would be an explosion, doors slammed, dinner ruined. So we visited her in small groups and never stayed too long.

But at Maureen's house after the funeral, Jack's oldest daughter, Diane, walked by me and said sotto voce, "Have you noticed what's happening?"

I looked around the room and saw the whole family talking noisily, laughing, enjoying themselves together for the first time. It's what my mother always wanted, but could never have, as long as she was there.

The adult we become is already growing in the child we were—like the oak tree in the acorn. I always knew, if not consciously then certainly unconsciously, what kind of person I wanted to grow into. The stress between my mother and me was that we had two different ideas about who I should be.

When I became successful, my mother could finally see that my vision for myself was a valid one, and it suited her. Then she tried to take credit for my accomplishments. I resented that. I felt I had achieved what I did in spite of her harsh mothering. I tried not to harbor resentment, but I did. From this perspective now, I must ask myself, wasn't I really doing the same thing? She had grown my face and body out of her genes, and yet I didn't want her to take credit for that. I kept shouting at her, "I'm not you. I'm me!"

But wasn't I also her? Not only genetically. She is my shadow. All the things I resent that she did, I continued to do to myself. The critic that lives in me, always nattering in my ear that I'm not good enough, the punishments I've inflicted on myself for my sins, the ways I've held myself down at times—that's my shadow, and it will not go away. I don't have to act it out, but I do have to be conscious of it and then integrate it.

On the other hand, aren't we all simply the divine life force manifesting itself in this body or that? Is that divinity any more me than my mother? Of course not. I resisted her all of my life. Finally it's only in collapsing the resistance that the mirror is polished so God's face can shine through.

Writing the truth (as I see it) about my mother has been the most difficult part of this book. Always the commandment to honor thy father and thy mother hangs over my head. When I'd finished writing this section of the book, I thought I'd said what I had to say, but I was uneasy. The next day a letter arrived from my mother's only living sister. My aunt Florence is eighty-nine years old and lives in Idaho. It was very unusual to get a letter from her. We exchange Christmas cards every year, but we don't generally correspond. She is a very devoted Christian. She wrote:

> *I don't know why you have been brought to my mind so strongly this evening—when the Lord brings someone to my mind that I haven't really thought of in quite some time I figure He wants me to pray for them. So—I have been praying for you—I don't know what your need is, but God knows. He will take care of that need. You may not even know you have a need for prayer, but God is watching over you and your loved ones.*

I sat holding her letter in my hands, once again humbled by the great mystery of the forces at work in the universe. I knew this was a message to me and I must meditate on it. Go deeper. This is what came:

The mother archetype has a wide range, from Kali the Terrible Mother in the Vedantic tradition all the way to the Blessed Virgin Mary, Mother of God. Most of us would choose the good mother of folklore who is all-loving and endlessly sacrificing and nourishing. Although I carry that fantasy in me as a wish, it is not the mother my soul chose to impel me along my particular path. I chose a mother with an iron will so I could develop one myself in order to survive her, and I did. I did not have a storybook mother/daughter relationship, but what I did have, painful though it was, has served me well. I was driven to leave home early, strike out on my own, learn independence, and find what was truly meaningful to me this time around. I am grateful to her for all that I learned from being her daughter.

Two weeks after the death of my mother, I saw *Requiem for a Dream* at a private screening. It was apparent to all of us that this was going to be a very important film. It was invited to be shown at the Cannes Film Festival, although the producers chose to show it out of competition, which I'll never understand.

The Yards was in competition there, however. I was appearing in two films at the same festival! That had never happened to me before. I decided to attend. Both films were received with long and enthusiastic standing ovations.

The next few months were like a merry-go-round on fast forward.

I was executive producing and starring in a movie for Showtime called *Within These Walls*, this time with credit for both. The television series I agreed to do, *That's Life*, was going into production. I began doing publicity for *Requiem*, and everywhere I went, the words "Oscar nomination" came up. And indeed I was nominated for my sixth Oscar.

I hadn't been to the Academy Awards ceremony for over twenty years. It had changed in that time. The red carpet was like walking the gauntlet. More of everything—lights, cameras, microphones, people. Bleachers were set up for the huge crowds. I'd never really enjoyed the glittery dazzle of Hollywood, and I was truly shocked to what extent it had grown, but I guess I had changed, too. Darren was my escort, and I brought Jefferson and his wife, Tricia, with us. I even had a good time. My favorite designer in San Francisco, Catherine Bacon, made a dress for me that I loved and I got to wear a Christian Dior diamond-and-gold necklace that was like a sunburst around my neck. I must say I looked just as I felt. It was as though in the twenty years since I'd attended this strange rite, I'd been cleansed, swept clean of my psychic demons, the cobwebs of guilt and shame had been vacuumed away, and the walls of my inner room were flooded with light. I could walk down the red carpet knowing it was a return into the spotlight from the recesses of my travels in psychic spiritual darkness, and I felt like light was able to shine through me. I had polished my mirror.

I didn't win the Oscar that year. It was Julia Roberts's year. Everyone said so from the time *Erin Brockovich* was released. Julia won every award there was to win. But as Emerson said, "Everything that is ours comes to us." That one was Julia's. But I know what I did in *Requiem*.

Does that mean that once I'd allowed myself to achieve that level of work and success that I'd never again experience failure? Not at all. In fact I suffered a monumental failure in 2003 when a play I loved, called *Oldest Living Confederate Widow Tells All*, closed the day after opening. But by then I'd truly learned not to identify with either success or failure. Too often I'd seen what looked like a disaster turn out to be a blessing, and what seemed like a boon, harbor a hidden bomb.

On September 10, 2001, I was in Los Angeles shooting the television series *That's Life*. We were working fourteen- and fifteen-hour days and I arrived home exhausted at the house I rented in Malibu. I had the next day off and planned to sleep as late as possible. When my phone rang before seven A.M., I groped for it, still asleep. I heard Candy say, "Ellen, I know you're sleeping, but two planes just crashed into the World Trade Center." I stumbled to the television, thinking, "Two planes? How could two planes crash? What does this mean?"

I sat transfixed in agony in front of the television and heard that two more planes crashed. It was unthinkable. I watched horrified as the networks showed, over and over, footage of people leaping from the burning top floors of the World Trade Center. Their flailing arms and legs reminded me of the babies that were tossed into the air to come down on the bayonets of Pol Pot's soldiers in those paintings in Cambodia. But this was America. How could this happen? Again, I asked myself, "What does it mean?"

As the day wore on, I learned just what it meant. That in a single morning, the whole world changed. Now we live in a terrified and terrorized world.

In the years that have passed since the attacks, we've seen the terror grow. Now there is more hate, more death, and more destruction.

What can we do to change this? No one seems to know. I certainly don't. I know only what Jesus taught, and Gandhi repeated, and Dr. King, Nelson Mandela, and the Buddha said, too: "Hate is not conquered by hate. Hate is conquered by love. This is a law eternal."

But how are we to live that law in the face of all this horror? I have learned that whenever there is a problem, I need to turn to the spiritual dimension for an answer. There, I can see complex forces at work—all the experiences, the traumas, the fears that are causing me to react unconsciously. Waking up and responding *consciously* always requires an effort of will. I must be as honest as possible, put all blame aside, and have a good, clear look at all of the various energies that are involved.

I believe we live in an intelligent universe, an interactive one. It speaks to us if we "have ears to hear." It speaks to me in my dreams and in the synchronicities that occur so frequently in my life. My dreams have told me when I was in danger, and they have shown me when I have some real changes to make and have to descend into deep Psyche to do some necessary rewiring.

What is the dream of our culture? I think that one way to understand this is through our art. And not just what some have called "high art," but also in popular entertainment, like movies, television, video games, and contemporary music. If we took a random sampling of those media and interpreted them as though they were our collective dreams, I think they would offer us a vision of the work we need to do on ourselves to transform our world. Humans don't seem to be able to really change someone else, but I have learned that if I do the work I need to do on the inside, the transformation manifests not only there, but outside as well.

Sometimes I allow my consciousness to float out into space, as I learned to do lying on the ground of an Alpine peak. From out in space, I look back at our planet. I can't see the flags of any countries or the uniforms of their armies; all I see are the explosions. The human race is committing suicide. The planet is so excruciatingly beautiful from out here. Why on earth are we destroying it?

As I said earlier, I like to believe—I choose to believe—that we incarnate having chosen our life circumstances in order to learn the lessons we came in to learn. I choose that belief because it helps me to view life and all that happens in it as part of my process of unfolding, and not to fall into the debilitating habit of blame. I take full responsibility for my life and all that happened to me. I know I came in loaded with gifts, and it was up to me to develop those gifts to the fullest and use them to overcome any obstacles in my path, especially the obstacles in my own conditioning.

I read somewhere that all we can know of God is what we grow to be. I like that. I think of myself now as a vehicle for the divine radiance to shine through. And I look at others as vehicles for the same thing. Not just other people, but sunsets, flowers, mountains, oceans. The spirit of life shines out everywhere. And not just from that which pleases me. The radiance is shining also through the darkness, the things I don't like and are terrifying. All of the difficulties in life are opportunities for transformation. Our lessons are always embedded in our suffering. "I am everywhere you find me." God is in the longing, the searching, the seeing. It is up to me to see the radiance everywhere. That is my practice.

I feel the life force pounding in my heart. I feel the desire to know, to understand, to evolve, alive in me, alive in everyone and everything around me. As I turn over a trowel full of dirt in my garden and see it oozing and crawling with life, I know that an unseen force could turn over a trowel full of the surface of Gaia and we would all tumble out with the tigers and the redwood trees. We live on the surface of her skin. We are embedded in the derma of the Goddess and we are as eager to build our castles on her body as the ant was to transport that orange rind that I observed as a child. And we are as unthinking, as unconscious.

I know that becoming conscious is a never-ending process. My prayer is that by the actual end of this life, I will exit wearing my own true face and be completely unmasked. Authenticity has been my aspiration. Whatever is in the shadow, own it, pull it into the light, and let it shine.

At the Temple of Poseidon in Sounion, Greece, 2005.

Epilogue

K
ierkegaard said that we understand our lives backward, but must live them forward. Writing this book has been the most extraordinary vehicle for understanding my life. I have marveled at the intricacy of the pattern that has emerged from reading back over my diaries, notebooks, and interviews.

I was startled to read in the first interview I ever gave, right after *Fair Game* opened in 1957: "I couldn't make up my mind if I wanted to be an actress or a writer. So I decided I'll act now and write later." I have no memory of saying that. As a matter of fact, I so thoroughly repressed that thought that over the years whenever I was asked to write something, I would agonize over it and say that I couldn't write, that I had writer's block.

Then in 1980 there was a big change. Several things happened whose significance I did not understand until now.

For one thing, in April of that year a young actor from Greece began attending the Actors Studio. He always observed the sessions from the balcony. Twenty-four years later he would give me a great gift.

Also in 1980 I had a dream that informed me that my writer's block had been lifted, and I was flooded with poetry. As I awoke I could remember only the last poem:

Mama Moon
Teach me to see like a poet
And speak like a wild songbird
Carrying words like grain in tight fists
Food for a hungry wind.

This was right after the disappointment of *Resurrection*, when my acting career was beginning to take a dip. It seems that Psyche was telling me it was time to start writing. So I began what eventually became this book. But first I wrote a letter to myself. I came across it the other day quite by accident. It's from Hadiya to Edna in 1980.

Dear Edna,

I know there are many things you want to do. You can do them. Perhaps not all at once, but you can achieve what's in your heart if you make room there for the love that is necessary to write from. When you feel that love, you can use your blood for ink and it will be a valentine to God. And it will be the truth.

Love,

Hadiya

When I completed the first draft of the manuscript in 2004 I realized that I'd mentioned the wounded Eros in me, but never got back to it and resolved that issue. I thought, *This book should end with a healthy, beautiful love affair, but unfortunately that healing took too long. Now that I know I am ready at last to love well, I fear it is too late.* It didn't seem possible at this late date to find someone I could truly love, even though I fervently wished that I could.

Then, in that miraculous way that has happened so often in my life when I am clear about what I want and I'm ready, that actor who always sat in the balcony at the Actors Studio came downstairs, now a mature, attractive man and a successful teacher. He confessed to me that he had been in love with me for twenty-three years.

At first I resisted him, not quite believing it could be true. Then he said, "Ellen, this is Eros knocking at your door."

Those were his words! I almost fainted.

He added, "I don't know. Maybe Eros knocks at your door every day."

"No," I murmured, barely able to speak.

"I have a gift for you with your name on it. Won't you accept it from me?"

Who could resist that?

Not me.

And because of all the lessons I'd learned in my twenty-five years of being alone, I was able to give him a gift I'd never truly had before to give to anyone.

I gave him my self.

ACKNOWLEDGMENTS

I would like to thank David Vigliano, the literary agent who called me after reading an interview I gave to the *New York Times* during the Oscar campaign for *Requiem for a Dream* and said, "You should write a book." He introduced me to Susan Petersen Kennedy, who believed I could write a book and that Riverhead should publish it. I thank her for that and for assigning to me Julie Grau, who was an inspired and brilliant editor of the first two drafts of this book. I also thank the discerning and wise Jake Morrissey, who guided me through the last drafts.

Being unskilled at the computer or even the typewriter, I wrote this entire book longhand. For five years every word I wrote and rewrote was translated from my scribbles to neatly typed pages by my assistant, Susan McTigue. The first draft was 743 pages, but Susan must have typed ten times that. She shared in this effort since it began and I have relied on her not only for her typing skills, but also for her enormous heart, as she handed me pages with tears in her eyes or a quizzical tilt to her head that told me that I hadn't been clear enough. I shower her with loving gratitude.

There isn't room in one book to tell the whole story, so many people who are important to me didn't make the final cut. I would particularly like to acknowledge some of the many powerful women in my life who aided in my healing, like the therapist and Sufi Elaine Resnick. Although I have mentioned Candy Trabucco, Katherine Cortez, and Catlin Adams, those mentions do not express how important these women have been to me. I thank all three of them for their love, insight, and steadfastness of friendship.

I would like to acknowledge the contribution to my development of all the women in the Solstice Circle who have met once a year for the last sixteen years, especially Saphira Linden, Jean Houston, Marion Woodman, Emily Devine, Nancy Roof, and Davine DelValle.

And last, my family. My beloved son, Jefferson, who shared much of this journey with me, and sometimes was left behind as I set out for my next adventure. He never complained and even encouraged me by saying, "You go, Mom," and sometimes even, "You go, Mommy Swami." I thank him for his constant support and everlasting forbearance. Also I thank his wife, Patricia, who has had to cope with an unconventional mother-in-law and has done so with grace and patience. Finally, I give loving gratitude to my adorable granddaughter, Emily Lucca Burstyn, who, when I find it necessary, will allow Edna to play dolls with her.

CREDITS AND PERMISSIONS

The author gratefully acknowledges permission to quote from the following:

"Why 'Yours Truly'" (on page 282) by R. Buckminster Fuller © 1974 The Estate of Buckminster Fuller.

"Damn Thirsty" (on page 319) by Hafiz, from *The Gift*, translated by Daniel Ladinsky (Penguin, 1999). Used by permission of the translator.

Poem by Rumi (on page 415) translated by Shahram Shiva, from the book *Hush, Don't Say Anything to God: Passionate Poems of Rumi* (Hohm Press, 1999).

PHOTO INSERT

Me at around four or five years old. *From the author's personal collection.*
Me and my mother. I'm about fourteen here. *From the author's personal collection.*
My mother's friend Mary Amperin, Jack with our dog Rusty, my mother, Steve

449

(kneeling), and a very glum me. I can tell from my expression that my stepfather was taking the picture. *From the author's personal collection.*

My cousin Carmen, me, my brother Jack, and my brother "Butch" in our Easter outfits. My mother made mine—brown tweed with Kelly green trim. *From the author's personal collection.*

The cheerleading team of Cass Tech High in Detroit, around 1950. The star on my arm meant I was the captain. *From the author's personal collection.*

I used to pose for camera clubs. I'm around fifteen or sixteen here, and still in Detroit. *Photo by George Booth.*

At a Ford Motor Company display at the Michigan State Fair; I'm third from the left. We long-skirts had lines to speak; the short-skirts handed out brochures. *From the author's personal collection.*

My first composite for modeling, around 1954. *From the author's personal collection.*

At age nineteen, soon after I arrived in New York. *From the author's personal collection.*

A modeling photo, New York, about 1955. *From the author's personal collection.*

A modeling photo. I'm about twenty-three and living in New York. *From the author's personal collection.*

My first TV appearance, with Betty Hutton in *Satins and Spurs,* at the opening of New York's first color TV studio in 1954; Mayor Robert Wagner is at center. *From the author's personal collection.*

Neil and me on the set of *Goodbye Charlie* in 1964. We don't look much like a couple, do we? *From the author's personal collection.*

With Jefferson wearing the elf outfit I made for him one Halloween. *From the author's personal collection.*

With my beloved Dalmatian, Daisy Mae. *From the author's personal collection.*

At the premiere of *The Last Picture Show* with Peter Bogdanovich and Cybill Shepherd in 1971. *Copyright © 1971 Columbia Pictures Industries, Inc. All rights reserved.*

From *The Last Picture Show. Copyright © 1971 Columbia Pictures Industries, Inc. All rights reserved.*

With Cloris Leachman. *Photo courtesy of Bill Eppridge/Time Life Pictures/ Getty Images. All rights reserved.*

In *Tropic of Cancer,* 1970. *Copyright © 1970 Paramount Pictures, Inc. All rights reserved.*

From *The King of Marvin Gardens,* 1972. *Copyright © 1972 Columbia Pictures Industries, Inc. All rights reserved.*

With Linda Blair in a scene from *The Exorcist,* 1973. *Copyright © 1973 by Warner Bros., Inc., and Hoya Productions, Inc. All rights reserved. Photo courtesy of Warner Bros. Pictures.*

On Broadway with Charles Grodin in *Same Time, Next Year,* 1974. *Photo © by Martha Swope. All rights reserved.*

With Jefferson backstage on the opening night of *Same Time, Next Year. Photo by Gene Spatz.*

With Lee Strasberg at his eightieth birthday party. *Photo © by Ken Regan.*

On the set of *Alice Doesn't Live Here Anymore* with director Martin Scorsese, 1974. *Copyright © 1974 by Warner Bros., Inc. All rights reserved. Photo courtesy of Warner Bros. Pictures.*

With Sir John Gielgud and Dirk Bogarde in *Providence,* 1977. *From the author's personal collection.*

With Buckminster Fuller, sailing off the coast of Maine. *From the author's personal collection.*

With Alan Alda in the film version of *Same Time, Next Year,* 1978. *Copyright © 1978 Universal City Studios, Inc. All rights reserved.*

My mother was an extra in *Resurrection. Copyright © 1980 Universal Pictures Company. All rights reserved.*

In *Resurrection,* 1980. *Copyright © 1980 Universal Pictures Company. All rights reserved.*

With Eva Le Gallienne in *Resurrection. Copyright © 1980 Universal Pictures Company. All rights reserved.*

On the set of *Silence of the North,* 1980. (The baby next to me is a doll.) *Copyright © 1981 Universal Pictures. All rights reserved.*

My mother, Steve, me, and Jack at Jack's daughter's wedding. I think we were all pretty high. *From the author's personal collection.*

One of our productions of *A Midsummer Night's Dream* at the Stone House, with me as Titania and Bill Smith as Bottom, in the early 1980s. *From the author's personal collection.*

With Steve at my sixtieth birthday party, 1992. *Photo by Susan McTigue.*

In the one-woman play *Shirley Valentine,* 1989. *Photo from the Wellington Theater, Chicago.*

As Carrie in *The Trip to Bountiful,* 1993. *Photo courtesy of TheaterFest, Montclair, New Jersey.*

As Mary Tyrone in *Long Day's Journey Into Night* at Houston's Alley Theater, 1998. *From the author's personal collection.*

Vagabonding on a street in New York with Sensei Bernie Glassman. *Photo by Peter Cunningham.*

A Christmas card for 1999. That's me with the big mouth, holding Emily and dog Molly. Tricia is on Jeff's lap. *Photo by Paul Undersinger.*

As Sara Goldfarb in *Requiem for a Dream,* 2000 (three photographs). *Copyright © 2000 Artisan Entertainment, Lions Gate Films. All rights reserved.*

Other Photos

Frontispiece: *Photo © by Martha Swope. All rights reserved.*

PART I

In my uniform, St. Mary's Academy. I was six or seven. *From the author's personal collection.*

CREDITS AND PERMISSIONS

PART II

Posing for a camera club, around 1948. *Photo by George Booth.*

PART III

Me as Sally in *The King of Marvin Gardens.* She was one of my favorite
characters. *Copyright © 1972 Columbia Pictures Industries, Inc. All rights reserved.*

PART IV

As Chris MacNeil in *The Exorcist. Copyright © 1973 Warner Bros., Inc., and Hoya
Productions, Inc. All rights reserved. Photo courtesy of Warner Bros. Pictures.*

PART V

At the Oscars when I was nominated for *Requiem for a Dream,* 2000.
From the author's personal collection.

EPILOGUE

At the Temple of Poseidon in Sounion, Greece, 2005.
Photo by Andreas Manolikakis.

ELLEN BURSTYN's career has encompassed more than forty years on-stage, in film, and on television. She has been nominated six times for an Academy Award, and won the Best Actress Oscar in 1974 for *Alice Doesn't Live Here Anymore*, as well as a Tony for her performance in *Same Time, Next Year*. She is co-president of the Actors Studio.